Lecture Notes in Artificial Intelligence   1834
Subseries of Lecture Notes in Computer Science
Edited by J. G. Carbonell and J. Siekmann

Lecture Notes in Computer Science
Edited by G. Goos, J. Hartmanis and J. van Leeuwen

Springer

Berlin
Heidelberg
New York
Barcelona
Hong Kong
London
Milan
Paris
Singapore
Tokyo

Jean-Claude Heudin (Ed.)

Virtual Worlds

Second International Conference, VW 2000
Paris, France, July 5-7, 2000
Proceedings

 Springer

Series Editors

Jaime G. Carbonell, Carnegie Mellon University, Pittsburgh, PA, USA
Jörg Siekmann, University of Saarland, Saarbrücken, Germany

Volume Editor

Jean-Claude Heudin
International Institute of Multimedia
Pôle Universitaire Léonard de Vinci
92916 Paris La Défense Cedex, France
E-mail: Jean-Claude.Heudin@devinci.fr

Cataloging-in-Publication Data applied for

Die Deutsche Bibliothek - CIP-Einheitsaufnahme

Virtual worlds : second international conference ; proceedings / VW
2000, Paris, France, July 5 - 7, 2000. Jean-Claude Heudin (ed.). -
Berlin ; Heidelberg ; New York ; Barcelona ; Hong Kong ; London ;
Milan ; Paris ; Singapore ; Tokyo : Springer, 2000
  (Lecture notes in computer science ; Vol. 1834 : Lecture notes in
  artificial intelligence)
  ISBN 3-540-67707-0

CR Subject Classification (1998): I.2, I.3, H.5.4-5, H.4.3

ISBN 3-540-67707-0 Springer-Verlag Berlin Heidelberg New York

Springer-Verlag is a company in the BertelsmannSpringer publishing group.
© Springer-Verlag Berlin Heidelberg 2000

Typesetting: Camera-ready by author, data conversion by Boller Mediendesign
Printed on acid-free paper   SPIN: 10721983   06/3142   5 4 3 2 1 0

Preface

Virtual Worlds 2000 is the second in a series of international scientific conferences on virtual worlds held at the International Institute of Multimedia in Paris - La Défense (Pôle Universitaire Léonard de Vinci).

The term "virtual worlds" generally refers to virtual reality applications or experiences. We extend the use of these terms to describe experiments that deal with the idea of synthesizing digital worlds on computers. Thus, virtual worlds could be defined as the study of computer programs that implement digital worlds. Constructing such complex artificial worlds seems to be extremely difficult to do in any sort of complete and realistic manner. Such a new discipline must benefit from a large amount of work in various fields: virtual reality and advanced computer graphics, artificial life and evolutionary computation, simulation of physical systems, and more. Whereas virtual reality has largely concerned itself with the design of 3D immersive graphical spaces, and artificial life with the simulation of living organisms, the field of virtual worlds, is concerned with the synthesis of digital universes considered as wholes, with their own "physical" and "biological" laws.

Besides its applications in simulation, computer games, on-line business, etc, this approach is something broader and more fundamental. Throughout the natural world, at any scale, from particles to galaxies, one can observe phenomena of great complexity. Research done in traditional sciences such as biology and physics has shown that components of complex systems are quite simple. It is now a crucial problem to elucidate the universal principles by which large numbers of simple components, acting together, can self-organize and produce the complexity observed in our universe. Therefore, virtual worlds is also concerned with the formal basis of synthetic universes. In this framework, it offers a new and promising approach for studying complexity.

This, the second Virtual Worlds conference, has confirmed the interest of the scientific community in this new trend of research and applications. Unlike the first one, this conference was organized as a single thread of presentations. This was decided in order to catalyze discussions and information exchanges between speakers and other participants during the conference. As a consequence, the selection level was higher than two years ago and only a reduced set of the submitted papers were finally accepted. The approaches and works covered by the resulting program is rich and diverse. It reflects the impact that this new trend of research has on the scientific community.

As expected, the production of these proceedings was a major task, involving all the authors and reviewers. As the editor, I have managed the proceedings in a classical way. Every contribution that was accepted for presentation at the conference is in the proceedings. The program committee felt that these papers represented mature work of a level suitable for being recorded, some of them requiring modifications to be definitively accepted.

Besides the classical goal of a proceedings volume, the idea was to recapture in print the stimulating mix of ideas and works that were presented. Therefore, the papers are organized to reflect their presentation at the conference. The material covered is diverse and falls naturally into a number of categories: virtual worlds communities and applications, virtual worlds technologies and tools, virtual humans and avatars, art and virtual worlds, artificial life and complex systems, virtual reality and interfaces. This collection of papers constitutes a good sample of works that appear necessary to achieve the goal of synthesizing virtual worlds. My wish is that the reader will find in this volume many motivating and enlightening ideas that will help him to contribute to the new and fascinating field of virtual worlds.

Acknowledgments

Many people and groups contributed to the success of the conference. My sincere thanks go out to all of them. I would first like to thank all the distinguished authors that contributed to this volume. The committee which selected the papers included the editor along with :

Bar-Yam, Y. (NECSI, USA),
Best, A. (MeetFactory, FI),
Best, M. (MIT Media Lab., USA),
Bonabeau, E. (EuroBios, FR),
Bossomaier, T. (Charles Sturt University, AU),
Coiffet, P. (Versailles & St. Quentin University, FR),
Damer, B. (Contact Consortium, USA),
Estève, P. (Shooting Star, FR),
Frank, I. (Complex Games Lab., JP),
Grand, S. (Cyberlife, UK),
Holman, T. (TMH Labs., USA),
Ijspeert, A. (UCS, USA),
Kanade, T. (Carnegie Mellon University
Kisseleva, O. (Artist, FR),
Komosinski, M. (Poznan University of Technology, PL),
Lattaud, C. (Paris V University, FR),
Louchet, J. (ENSTA, FR),
Magnenat-Thalmann, N. (Geneva University, CH),
Mange, D. (EPFL, CH),
Pagliarini, L. (CNR, IT),
Paniaras, Y. (University of Art and Design Helsinki, FI),
Puustinen, M. (MeetFactory, FI),
Ray, T. (University of Oklahoma, USA),
Refsland, S. (Gifu University, JP),
Semwal, S. (University of Colorado, USA),
Stone, L. (Microsoft, USA),
Thalmann, D. (EPFL, CH),
Ventrella, J. (There Studio, USA),
Vogel, C. (Semio, USA),
Wilcox, S. (Writer, USA),
Winter, C. (Cyberlife, UK).

I am also grateful to IBM and CanalNumedia (official partners of the conference), Perfect Video, and Alias Wavefront for their support. Special thanks are due to Pierre Estève and Shooting Star for their active participation. Thanks to the New England Complex System Institute, the EvoNet Network of Excellence in Evolutionary Computation, the Contact Consortium, and the International Society on Virtual Systems and Multimedia for their support. Also many thanks to Pixel Magazine and Create for promoting the conference.

I received significant help in the organization and running this conference. Most of the staff of the International Institute of Multimedia fall under this category. First and foremost, I have to thank Monika Siejka and Claude Vogel who encouraged and supported me at every step of the project. Thanks are also due to Sylvie Perret, Sandra Sourbe, and Jerome Levitsky. A very special acknowledgment to the team of students which designed the conference web site and helped me in organizing the conference: especially Christelle Berte, Philippe Bourcier, Guy Coelho, Barbara Laurent, Virgile Ollivier, Agnès Peyrot, and Philippe Da Silva.

Finally, all the staff of the Pôle Universitaire Léonard de Vinci were once again a pleasure to work with.

May 2000   Jean-Claude Heudin

Table of Contents

Virtual Humans and Avatars

Art and Virtual Worlds

Artificial Life and Complex Systems

Virtual Reality and Interfaces

Author Index

Conferences and Trade Shows in Inhabited Virtual Worlds: A Case Study of Avatars98 & 99

Bruce Damer[1], Stuart Gold[1], Jan de Bruin[2], and Dirk-Jan de Bruin[3]

[1] Contact Consortium, P.O. Box 66866, Scotts Valley, CA 95067-6866, USA
Bdamer@ccon.org
[2] Tilburg University, P.O. Box 50913, 5000 LE Tilburg, The Netherlands
J.A.W.deBruin@Kub.nl
[3] Multi-User Virtual Worlds Consortium, Houtzaagmolensingel 47, 1611 XK Bovenkarspel,
The Netherlands
DdeBruin@VirtualWorlds.org

Abstract. Contact Consortium (CCON) is exploring the possibilities of organizing large-scale events in Inhabited Virtual Worlds (IVW)-Cyberspace. CCON held two such events, called Avatars98 (AV98) and Avatars99 (AV99), completely in Cyberspace. These events consisted each time of a conference and trade show. This paper starts with a quick look at the origins of IVWs. The focus is then on the manifold types of social activities that are already possible in IVW and its rapid expansion. One new social phenomenon is the trade show, which was a part of AV98 and AV99. The organization of large-scale commercial events in IVW-Cyberspace is a sign that IVWs are increasingly emancipating themselves from their origins in the realms of pastime and chatting. We applaud this development because social technologies from all social realms should be incorporated in IVWs in order to make them more real 'worlds' in the philosophical (cosmological) sense.

View of attendees standing at 'Ground Zero' at the Avatars98 conference and trade show

J.-C. Heudin (Ed.): VW 2000, LNAI 1834, pp. 1-11, 2000.
© Springer-Verlag Berlin Heidelberg 2000

1   Imaginary Organizations and the IVW Movement

The landscape of organizational life is rapidly changing. Our information society gives virtual or imaginary organizations (Hedberg et al., 1997: 14) a tremendous opportunity for growth. Imaginary organizations utilize an inspiring vision, information technology, alliances, and other types of networks to initiate and sustain a boundary-transcending activity. They are mainly based on integrative forces such as trust, synergy, and information technology.

Contact Consortium (CCON) is such an imaginary organization that is one of the spearheads in the movement to colonize Cyberspace and transform it into a galaxy of interconnected Inhabited Virtual Worlds (IVW). Virtual organizations need large-scale events to reinforce and maintain the inspiring vision, necessary for its boundary-transcending activities. Inhabited Virtual Worlds (IVW) on the Internet are a new medium for launching such events.

It is important to take the meaning of the concept of 'world' to heart. This concept, so much discussed in philosophy, implies an all-encompassing context in which the totality of human activities and experiences is possible (Düsing, 1986). Sociologists use the concept of 'society' more or less in the same way.

CCON works toward the ideal of transforming IVW into real worlds or societies. It works in that direction by organizing several types of large-scale social events in IVW. In 1998 and 1999, CCON organized a conference and a trade show entirely in a universe of interconnected Virtual Worlds.

This growing galaxy of interconnected IVWs is a new social reality. In point 2, we give a short overview of the history of IVWs as a new medium. We pay attention to the different social contexts that were important in shaping them and could become even more important in the future. In our opinion, one of the central developmental influences that will move virtual spaces as such toward really Inhabited Virtual Worlds is the convergence and merging of the various forms of ICT in different social contexts.

In point 3, we give a general decription of the central elements of a well-structured, large-scale social event in IVWs, using as our point of reference CCON's experience with AV98. The organization of large-scale events, difficult as it is, is a necessary stepping stone toward the situation in which IVW function on a permanent basis with all the institutions associated with it. Large-scale events in IVW are the laboratory for new institutions in IVWs.

Point 4 focus more in depth on the way IVW can be used for marketing purposes. The 'developmental construct' of going from traditional trade shows to trade shows in IVW is tentatively sketched. We consider the organization of conferences (conventions) and trade shows in IVW to be the logical conclusion of a series of steps.

In point 5, we summarize our experiences derived from AV98 on this particular type of virtual (mass) meeting in IVW and enumerate the lessons we learned.

In point 6, we speculate on the future of IVWs.

2   A Short History of Inhabited Virtual Worlds

The technological roots of IVW lie in the text-based multi-user environments of the 1970s and '80s. In the '90s this continued on the World Wide Web. The next development was the merging of text-based chat channels with a visual interface in which users were represented as 'Avatars'. By using Avatars, one can feel the emotion of being 'in world' without having to bother about complicated – and expensive – VRequipment. For its graphics, the development of 3D-rendering engines, originally used for gaming application, was important. Online IVWs could spread over the Internet because they could run effectively on a large range of consumer computing platforms at modem speeds. There is now a growing literature on IVWs (Damer, 1998, 1999; Powers, 1997, Wilcox, 1998).

At this moment, all kinds of IVWs can be observed on the Internet. There are, for instance, the multimillion, multi-user worlds built for gaming by companies. Many IVWs are built for research purposes. Universities and other knowledge centers were quick to observe the possibilities of IVWs for educational purposes. And we should not forget the home brew IVWs, erected by dedicated private persons from all over the world. Having a lot of these IVWs is important because new uses for IVWs can be invented. If we see a new social invention spread from one IVW to others by imitation, the process of spontaneous institutionalization, as sociologists would call it, manifests itself.

The rise of e-commerce and digital marketing techniques, such as virtual trade shows, is another new opportunity that can serve as a testing ground for IVWs. In a world in which globalization is supposedly a major trend, organizations will increasingly be adopting the characteristics of virtual or imaginary organizations. Its boundary–transcending activities can be of different kinds.

First of all, there is the growing use of computer-moderated collaborative work, done by Virtual Teams recruited from a network of organizations. In the second place, there is the category of boundary-transcending activities of a virtual organization with its (potential) customers and clients. Both types of activities can be done using various technologies. Electronic mail and chat room technologies are still the most frequently used.

The trend is towards rich multimedia digital conferencing on the Internet. Various prototypes are being produced at this very moment. The intention is to 'marry the user-friendliness and pervasiveness of Web-based multimedia browser interfaces with on-line interaction and collaboration, using text, graphics, and voice communications.' (Bisdikian et al., 1998: 282).

However, this approach is still about interfaces; users don't feel like they're in a place. This feeling is of paramount importance in IVW. But we must also stress that the (architectural) attention given the graphical component which creates a 'place' must not obscure the important fact that, in the end, IVWs are all about social interactions and the bandwidth of human experience.

The medium IVW is, however, still in its infancy. At the July 1998 Avatar conference, consensus emerged that it was too early to know how the medium would ultimately be used and that Avatar-Cyberspace should therefore continue to evolve for its own sake and not to serve possibly inappropriate applications. Each of the aforementioned realms created a different 'context of discovery' for the further development of IVW.

It is our belief that putting IVW to the test of applying them to different types of social events will speed up developments. The focus of attention in relation to IVWs will gradually shift away from the technological problems of the interface to the study of social technologies we need to serve up in IVWs different types of social events and - in the end - really full-fledged societies.

3   Avatars98: The First Large-Scale Event inside IVW

3.1   Event and Technology Platform

CCON (www.ccon.org) hosted AV98, the worlds' first large-scale social event totally online inside Cyberspace, on November 21 1998. DigitalSpace Corporation (www.digitalspace.com) produced AV98 for CC.

A number of Virtual World platforms, such as Active Worlds, Blaxxun, Traveler, WorldsAway and Roomancer, and several webcast technologies were used. In the Active Worlds platform the AV98 world, a one-kilometer square space in which a conference hall was constructed, was built as the main focus. This world was designed to be usable by attendees on low-end computers on minimal net connections. The world was populated by specially designed Avatars, animated 3D models of users. It can still be visited by using the browser from www.activeworlds.com and selecting the AV98 world.

In relation to the concept of 'world', it is important to stress that AV98 was certainly a large-scale event with over 4000 attendees represented as 'Avatars'. It also encompassed a broad range of types of virtual meetings.

3.2   The Diversity of IVWs

The famous sociologist Durkheim called 'social reality' a 'reality in its own'. Cyberspace should also be granted a distinct ontological status If we are speaking about IVWs, the obvious approach is to start by designing IVWs as a kind of simulation - and imitation - of social life. In later - and more complex - points of view, we should more and more give meaning to its own and distinct status.

Even though still in infancy, they can support several types of social interaction: collaborative work, learning processes, gaming and so on. IVWs can have small meeting spaces, but can also handle mass and large-scale social events and meetings with thousands of attendees from all over the Earth.

The diversity of AV98 can be demonstrated by enumerating the types of meeting spaces that the conference hall featured:
- a) a landing zone for new attendees;
- b) an awards area;

- c) forty participating locations all over the world, some of which were connected by using streaming webcasts;
- d) a conference with six 'speaker pods' for parallel tracks in virtual 'breakout rooms';
- e) an art gallery;
- f) a trade show of forty-eight exhibits for participating companies and organizations.

In point 4, we shall go into more detail about the phenomenon of exhibits, particularly trade shows.

3.3   The Typical Elements of an IVW Suited for Large-Scale Virtual Meetings

Let us briefly go over some characteristic elements of IVWs, such as the use of Avatars, the diversity of types of meeting spaces, public spaces and crowd management, the importance of having extra events to create the feeling of a total experience in IVWs, and finally, the all important role of a facilitating and coordinating team for the event. We touch lightly on the types of ICTtechnologies that were used at AV98 to guarantee an adequate functional performance in all those areas. We also, but only tentatively, glance at the differences between IVWs and other types of virtual and real-life meetings.

Central to the concept of IVW are Avatars, the visual embodiment of people in Cyberspace. By using Avatars, you can go beyond simple virtual meetings in which only (spoken) text and documents are exchanged. Avatars can, increasingly so, also embody such important aspects of human social interaction as gestures, proximity to the group, and emotion. This enables the building and maintenance of the trust we spoke about before. A conversation between people as Avatars in an IVW comes closer to the feeling of a face-to-face conversation than a conversation which is only the exchange of text by e-mail.

A second important characteristic of IVWs is the possibility to construct various types of virtual meeting spaces. For the design of these types of meeting spaces, we can use different generative metaphors. The meeting space can be small, being functionally equivalent with 'rooms' in physical space. Electronic meeting rooms (EMR) are also not one of a kind. IVWs can be the meeting space for the private auditorium, where 'one-to-many' presentations are given to usually closed audiences with the assistance of bot-driven slide shows or audio. IVW can also cope with EMRs, where 'a two-way interaction' exists with one or more speakers and responding audiences in a distributed environment. This can be done by web links, live video and audio streaming and backchannel chat for questions and answers. Communication in the conference tracks that was carried by text out during AV98 was instantly logged for the conference proceeding.

The third element is the use of public spaces and the management of crowd flow and the keeping of social order in them, particularly if we design large-scale events in IVW. That IVWs have meeting spaces that are functionally equivalent to 'public spaces', as social scientists would call them, makes us realize once more that the concept of 'world' goes far beyond the concept of 'room'. Therefore we should also use generative metaphors other than that of a room. One of the functions such public spaces render is to give a crowd the possibility to find its way to more specific events. Crowd management in public spaces is very important in all large event spaces, such as conferences with multiple tracks, exhibitions, and theme parks. An eye-catching difference with physical reality is that, in IVWs, visitors can instantaneously 'teleport' or 'warp' themselves from one location to another. Central in AV98 was a tall 3D billboard of events with times and meetings. We return to this topic in point 4.

A fourth element of events in IVWs that promotes the feeling of total immersion in a world is achieved by adding extra elements (side events) to large-scale events. For instance, AV98 included an art gallery permitting the public to submit 2D artworks or photographic images for display. There was also a 'webcasting wall' to display live camera views of a number of participating real-world locations or news broadcasts. In general, mediacasts can provide streams of video and audio from real-world locations directly onto surfaces in the virtual world or onto parallel web pages and generate an encompassing context for the (large-scale) event.

And last but not least, every virtual meeting will have some physical team locations coordinating the action in that world. The proper definition of roles, clearly posted information about schedule, group dynamics, and a culture of respect and quality hosting, handling fatigue after hours at the keyboard, and providing interesting visuals by webcasting from the 'operations center' are all activities which bring a virtual event to life.

4   Exhibitions and Trade Shows in IVW

4.1   Exhibitions as Broad-Ranging and Multi-level Marketing Instruments

Various kinds of exhibitions can be organized in IVWs, e.g., science, art, and trade shows. An art gallery was operational in AV98, but this was nothing more than a side event in order to increase the total experience of really being in a world. AV98 was mainly a conference and a trade show. The trade show was in AV98 only a modest experiment and not really a commercial endeavour, but more a fund-raising instrument for CCON.

With this in mind, we pay attention to the possibility of organizing trade shows in IVW. One of our main points is that the general characteristics of IVWs can also be applied to trade shows in IVW on the Internet. In addition, we try to give these characteristics a more specific meaning while speaking about trade shows.

In relation to the development of multimedia ICT, organizing trade shows in IVWs is, as we see it, a logical step in a developmental process. First traditional trade shows in physical space started using more and more advanced multimedia applications and ICT. For instance, the tracking of attendees can be done be adding bar-codes to their badges and scanning them at the booth for a statistical analysis of attendance. The next step is to create virtual trade shows on the Internet where customers, by using more or less sophisticated search engines, can choose from a certain stock of products put into some kind of electronic catalogue. This type of broker application is made more visually attractive by designing 3D-graphics. An example is the virtual 3-D 'Millennium Christmas Trade show' with 3D booths, operational on the Internet from October 29 till Christmas 1999. Of course, this is not an Inhabited Virtual World: customers do not interact with one another. In an Inhabited or Avatar Virtual World, clients and customers are aware of each other and can interact socially. Trade shows in IVW on the Internet fulfill their broker function by being a place where complicated social interaction is possible.

In the arsenal of non-direct selling marketing instruments, trade shows in physical space stand out as instruments with a large bandwidth of consumer contacts. Trade shows fulfil a lot of selling, but also non-selling performances. Attendees can see the products, experience hands-on demonstrations, ask questions and receive direct answers, hear and read complex messages about the products, and compare them with other products. Other marketing instruments like direct mail, advertisements in print, sales calls, and radio messages do not match this performance. All this is about products and selling. Interaction mediated by Avatars and - eventually - complemented by video and audio streams in IVWs can come close to face-to-face selling interactions in physical spaces. Trade shows can also have important non-selling functions.

In general, we believe that trade shows in IVW can in the future increasingly perform a broad range of social functions in relation to clients and customers, which can be arranged as a hierarchy. In one of the few articles in which a conceptual framework for the study of trade shows is presented, the activities at a booth during a trade show are categorized as information-gathering, motivational, relation-building, and image-building activities (Hansen, 1999).

This type of action analysis brings the AGILscheme of the sociologist Talcott Parsons to mind. He theorized about four distinct functional aspects of action, which could be ordered in a hierarchy. At the lowest level, he placed the adaptive function of action, followed by the goal-attainment, the integrative, and the latency function.

The action criteria that can be deduced from the AGIL-scheme are flexibility of the means, attainment of specific goals, social cohesion, and trust centered on a certain set of values, a concept, or an image.

In the research on trade shows, attention is mostly paid to the lower functions. In our opinion, the networking society and its virtual or imaginary organizations, cohesion-building, and the creation and maintenance of trust are also very important problems.

In the (near) future, trade shows in IVWs will have the possibility of combining the traditional booth activities, focused on the product and - eventually - selling, with lectures and talks in some kind of conference room (important for image-building) and with the prospect of in-depth discussions, the performance of collaborative work, and complicated negotiating being done in electronic rooms powered with the tools of groupware. (group decision support systems). In that way, the higher function receives more attention. In section 4.2, we limit ourselves to the lowest level, the functional themes of flexibility and effectiveness.

4.2   Trade Shows in IVWs: Flexibility and Effectiveness

First of all, in the social sciences, the theme of flexibility is related to the amount of information and the elimination of various kinds of constraints (time, space, and cost constraints).

As we suggested before, all kinds of registration techniques are used to gather information about the flow of attendees through the trade show in physical space. An advantage of virtual trade shows on the Internet is that tracking and 'click through' path tracing can be done quite easily. It is also an important aspect of trade shows in IVWs that bots, acting as automated conversational agents, can be employed. Such bots can perform simple tasks in the process of information exchange. They can also drive the visitor's web-browser to retrieve their conference pass information and perform a 'card swipe' operation in exchange for sending information or delivering free gifts. Of course, the booth as such can also perform information broker functions. It can serve as a portal into either the organization's website or to custom-built virtual worlds where special talks or events might be sponsored during the period of the trade show.

An obvious advantage of virtual trade shows is that the trade show can be set up quite quickly. For instance, the Active Worlds technology provides streaming and reuse of 3D objects in a Lego-like manner. Therefore, trade show and booth designers can put together and duplicate a lot of prefabricated objects and design booths of all sizes. The arsenal of 3D objects will grow quickly.

Exhibits for companies and participating organizations such as Boing

In the literature on trade, a great deal of attention is paid to staffing the booths. In trade shows in IVW, this can be done by persons from the sponsoring organization, but in future, bots can play a larger part in the booth activities. This implies a better division of labor between bots and persons. People can then handle the more complicated questions from clients and customers.

One other thing that trade shows in IVW can handle quite efficiently is the allocation and transportation of people to their chosen location. The technique of a 'big board' conference and trade show schedule, borrowed from Neal Stephenson's novel *Snow Crash*, brings people to the desired location (booth) with a click of their mouse.

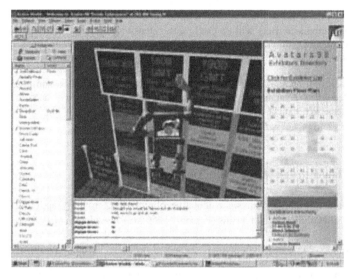

Active Worlds browser showing the 3D view with conference chair Bruce Damer waving in his custom Avatar floating by the schedule board, chat window below, webpage showing the exhibit hall to the right and a list of active users on the left

5 What Was Learned about Virtual Meetings in IVWs

If we look at AV98, the following positive claims for the hosting of large-scale events,, such as conferences and trade shows, in IVWs can be made:

- *More attendance*: The attendance, calculated at over 4,000 visitors, was ten times that of the previous 'physically located' conferences.
- *Cost-effectiveness*: The budgetary outlay, excluding the extensive volunteer time costs, was 10% of the previous years.
- *Mobilization of groups*: By moving the conference inside Cyberspace, we empowered local groups and organizations to host their own events. Art museums had public openings with the Virtual Worlds displayed on the walls, Cybercafes created evening parties and discussion, school and university classes convened and connected in, and people hosted gatherings in their own homes.
- *Satisfied customers*: Attendees reported to us that they had enjoyed the presentations and discussions. Order was kept by a volunteer organization that disciplined unruly attendees by ejecting them from the world for periods of time. No attendee reported undue disappointment with the event other than reflecting the sometimes slow performance of their browser in heavily populated areas.
- *Fundraising*: The sale of booth space in the exhibit hall raised funds for the Consortium (although much of this space was donated, as the exercise was still very experimental).

- *Laborsaving automation*: 'Bots', or automated agents, helped answer questions and direct attendees. Bots will be used more extensively in the future to man exhibits and interact with attendees, offering them web tours, video promotions, capturing visitor data in 'card swipe' fashion and awarding prizes.

In conclusion, while quite labor intensive, virtual conferences and trade shows modeled after Avatars98 will produce wide coverage and easy access for large audiences. We expect events like this to be increasingly part of the online time of ordinary and business net users alike in Cyberspace.

6   The Future of the Medium IVW

We close this paper with some tentative observations, roughly applying Parsons' theory of evolutionary universals (Parsons, 1966) to the evolution of IVWs.

In the early stages of colonizing Cyberspace, it is natural that a lot of attention is paid to architectural work on the layout of the world, its buildings, and Avatars. Many IVWs are in this 'spadework phase' and are only creating the preconditions for becoming a society.

The second phase starts when the basic social institutions are erected to regulate social life within an IVW. These are the 'basic anthropological institutions' with the function of streamlining human activities around basic human needs, such as sex (the institution of marriage), the institutions of communication (language), and of giving meaning to life (religion) and so on. Such IVWs can be labeled 'primitive societies'.

In the modern phase of IVWs, we typically observe a functional differentiation of societies and the formation of specific institutions. Institutions such as a strict division of labor (for instance, in the form of bureaucratic organizations), money and market systems, universalistic systems of law (basic human rights and so on), a system to guide society and develop policy (a political system).

CCON is facilitating the breakthrough of IVWs from the primitive to the modern phase of societies. The content of all the major institutions in the modern phase is discussed in CCON's Special Interest Groups. In our opinion, IVWs need the social technologies associated with various functional subsystems of society.

The realm of pastime, personal chat, and gaming must remain important for the further growth and development of IVWs. However, there is also the growing use of IVWs within the economic system and government. From that realm we may expect the inclusion of Groupware to facilitate (virtual) meetings. The development of e-commerce and the use of virtual trade shows in the economic system is another impulse for a whole new array of ICT- and social technologies that can be used in IVWs.

To include these technologies in the VW browsers would make IVWs an even more exciting place to be, but would also make them more suitable as an exercise ground for the policy, organizational, and commercial tasks of real life.

References

1. Almeida, V., et al.: Efficiency Analysis of Brokers in the Electronic Marketplace. Computer Networks (1999) 1079-1090
2. Bisdikian, C., et al.: MultiMedia Digital Conferencing: A Web-enabled Multimedia Teleconferencing System. IBM Journal of Research and Development (1998) 281-298
3. Benedikt, M. (ed.): Cyberspace: First Step. MIT Press, Cambridge (1991)
4. Damer, B.: Avatars!: Exploring and Building Virtual Worlds on the Internet. Peachpit Press, Berkeley (1998)
5. Damer, B., S. Gold, J. de Bruin, D-J. de Bruin: Steps toward Learning in Virtual World Cyberspace: TheU Virtual University and BOWorld, In: A. Nijholt, O.A. Donk, E.M.A.G. van Dijk (eds.): Interactions in Virtual Worlds. University Twente, Enschede (1999) 31-43.
6. Düsing, K.: Die Teleologie in Kants Weltbegriff. Kantstudien. Ergänzungshefte. Bouvier Verlag Herbert Grundmann, Bonn (1986).
7. Hansen, K.: Trade Show Performance: A Conceptual Framework and Its Implications for Future Research. Academy of Marketing Science Review (1999) 1-18
8. Herberg, B., G. Dahlgren, J. Hansson, and N-G. Olve: Virtual Organizations and Beyond:Discover Imaginary Systems. John Wiley & Sons, Chichester (1997)
9. Parsons, T.: Societies: Evolutionary and Comparative Perspectives. Prentice-Hall, Inglewood Cliffs (1966)
10. Powers, M.: How to Program Virtual Communities, Attract New Web Visitors and Get Them to Stay. Ziff-Davis Press, New York. (1997)
11. Wilcox, S.: Creating 3D Avatars. Wiley, New York (1998)

Biographical Information

Bruce Damer and Stuart Gold are members of the Contact Consortium. Damer co-founded the organization in 1995 and Gold has headed up TheU Virtual University projects since 1996. Dr. Jan de Bruin is a policy scientist at Tilburg University, trained as an economist, sociologist, and political scientist. Dirk-Jan de Bruin is a member of Contact Consortium and founder of Multi-User Virtual Worlds Consortium.

HutchWorld: Lessons Learned
A Collaborative Project: Fred Hutchsinson Cancer
Research Center & Microsoft Research

Lili Cheng[1], Linda Stone[1], Shelly Farnham[1], Ann Marie Clark[2] ,and Melora Zaner[1]

[1] Microsoft Research, Microsoft Corporation, Redmond,WA,
98052 USA 1-425-882 8080
{lilich, lindas, shellyf, meloraz}@Microsoft.com
[2] Fred Hutchinson Cancer Research Center, 1100 Fairview Ave. N., B1-010,
Seattle, WA 98109-1024 USA 1-206-667-2992
{aclark}@fhcrc.com

Abstract. The Virtual World Group (VWG) in Microsoft Research and the Fred Hutchinson Cancer Research Center (the Hutch) are collaborating to develop and study online social support systems for patients at the Hutch. Medical research has shown that social support contributes positively toward psychological and physical well-being. However, in the real world, it is difficult for immune-compromised patients, their families, and their caregivers to interact with others facing similar challenges. In order to address the needs of Hutch patients and their caregivers, Microsoft and the Hutch developed HutchWorld, a Virtual Worlds application, to provide online, computer-mediated social and informational support. The present paper describes the approach of each design phase of the project, and lessons learned about a) developing an interactive online support system for a specific audience, b) the deployment of the online social support system to its target audience, c) the rigorous study of both its use and its impact on user well-being, and d) issues affecting collaboration among technology, medical, and research groups.

1. Introduction

Medical research shows that social support contributes positively toward healing. The Virtual Worlds Group (VWG) in Microsoft Research and the Fred Hutchinson Cancer Research Center (the Hutch) are collaborating to study how online social support networks affect online identity and social interaction. In the real world, it is difficult for immune-compromised patients and their families and caregivers to meet with others with similar problems. HutchWorld is a Virtual Worlds application designed to provide online, computer-mediated social and information support of the Hutch patients and their caregivers. This software application will be deployed to patients and their support network. The effect of the application on social support will be studied using methods accepted by both the computer science and medical research communities.

J.-C. Heudin (Ed.): VW 2000, LNAI 1834, pp. 12–23, 2000.
© Springer-Verlag Berlin Heidelberg 2000

1.1 Project Goals

It is hoped that medical patients and their support networks will experience improved social support when provided with HutchWorld. We predict that a graphical, integrated virtual world (HutchWorld) that includes social support services, information services, and diversionary activities will further increase users' quality and quantity of social interaction. Based on our own experiences and other research, we predict that using HutchWorld will improve the social support of patients and their caregivers.

Microsoft Research, the Hutch, and users will benefit from this collaboration. For Microsoft, HutchWorld provides a way to conduct important social/technical research by demonstrating how cutting edge technologies can be applied. For the Hutch, this project will enhance services for its patient community and help the Hutch better understand how to plan for future technology integration. Finally, this project serves a population that can greatly benefit from online social support.

1.2 Background

The Fred Hutchinson Cancer Research Center (the Hutch) [6], located in Seattle, Washington is one of the top five comprehensive cancer research centers in the world. It is recognized internationally for pioneering work in bone marrow transplantation through work done by researchers such as Nobel prize winner E. Donald Thomas [15]. The Hutch is known for its interdisciplinary research and ability to quickly incorporate bench-to-bedside transition of new technologies. The Hutch, together with the Cancer Care Alliance (Hutch patient services), has over 400 patients that annually participate in patient services. The progress of over 3000 bone marrow transplant recipients is currently being tracked using clinical treatment protocols.

The Virtual Worlds Group (VWG) in Microsoft Research [18] designs and develops tools and technologies that contribute to effective online communication between individuals and among groups. As part of the process of developing the Virtual Worlds research platform [19], Linda Stone, director of the VWG, looked at existing Internet service offerings (bulletin boards, discussion lists, chatrooms, etc.) for health-challenged individuals. In the spring of 1997, she then approached the Hutch with an idea for a research collaboration to work together to design and deploy a software application that would offer social support and information exchange opportunities for a population within the Hutch. The Hutch reviewed and approved the collaboration, and the Director of the Arnold Library, Ann Marie Clark (also responsible for the Hutch Internet sites), ultimately became the Hutch liaison with Microsoft and the project manager for Hutch. Funding for the project was primarily provided through a charitable donation from Microsoft to the Hutch. This type of donation is unusual for Microsoft in that healthcare is outside of the corporation's charitable giving guidelines. Due to a pre-existing relationship between the Hutch and Microsoft and the potential research opportunities an exception was made to fund the project.

1.3 Related Research

The primary research area we draw upon is the area of social support in medical environments. Past research has shown that social support enhances both the psychological adjustment and physical well-being of people with cancer [2, 11, 14, 16]. For example, in one striking study, Spiegel and Bloom [14] provided social support to women with breast cancer through group therapy. They found that those who received the group therapy lived on average twice as long as those who did not receive group therapy.

Cancer patients receive several forms of support through their social interactions. First of all, cancer patient receive direct, instrumental support, such as assistance getting in and out of bed every day, or assistance in dealing with doctors and nurses. Second of all, patients receive informational support. Cancer patients may learn from each other what to expect from their illness, and how to cope with their illness. Finally, patients receive emotional support. They experience reductions in anxiety and loneliness through the mere presence and affection of others. In sum, social interactions allow people with cancer to cope more effectively with their illness through the help, knowledge, and affection they share with others [11].

Given the benefits of social support, it is not surprising that a growing number of support groups may be found online, in the form of bulletin boards, discussion lists, and chat rooms [2, 5, 9, 13, 21]. Computer-mediated forms of social interactions afford people a means for overcoming barriers to social support systems such as geographical isolation, physical debilitation [21], and fear of self-disclosure [9]. People subscribe to such online groups for both informational and emotional support [3, 5, 13]. However, few studies have examined use patterns of online support systems, and whether the support provided by such online support systems have a meaningful impact on people's psychological and physical well-being.

One notable exception is provided by studies of the Comprehensive Health Enhancement Support System (CHESS) [4], a program developed by a group of scientists to provide online information and discussion groups for people with health problems. Researchers studied the use of CHESS by acquiring both log data on patterns of use and responses to questionnaires. People tended to actively use the CHESS program. In a study of 116 people with HIV/AIDS infection, CHESS researchers [2] found that over three months people accessed the program on average more than once per day. People tended to use the social aspects of the program more than the informational aspects of the program. [7, 10]. Gustafson et al. [7] also examined how the use of the CHESS program affected people's well-being. In comparing a group of CHESS users to a group of non-CHESS users, they found that those who used CHESS reported a higher quality of life and lower utilization levels of health care services.

In sum, the research described above indicates that online social support systems have a lot of promise: online support systems can provide social support; people can get social support through asynchronous interactions such as found on bulletin boards;

both social and informational support are used; and both beginning and experienced users will use online support systems. The advantage of online support systems is the opportunity for increased self-disclosure, access to support any time of day or night, and access despite geographical or physical limitations.

More research that examines the impact of online social support systems on psychological and physical well-being is needed. With the exception of the CHESS research, most studies done by computer science researchers provide conclusions based on anecdotal information, without quantitative data to support these findings. The unique contribution of the Microsoft/Hutch project will be our quantitative study of the effects of online interaction within a known medical community. The Hutch/Microsoft team has approached this research with the goal of meeting the standards of both the medical research community and the technology community. The research measures the effectiveness of the project using traditional academic research procedures and measures developed by medical researchers. However, in addition to the use of standard procedures and measures, we incorporate measures and procedures that accommodate issues specific to measuring online interactions. The research described below will benefit people in both the field of computer-mediated interactions and the field of medical support services, as well as the users of the system.

2. Defining the Design Process

The following section reviews the design objectives and the lessons learned via the HutchWorld project between early 1997 and the present. Building HutchWorld required us to gather input from content experts at the Hutch and former patients, to review research in the related medical and computer science fields, to build prototypes, to run user studies, and to conduct limited deployments. We have completed three of the four design phases described below.

2.1 Phase 1: Preliminary Design

Our goals during Phase 1 were to develop an effective collaborative structure between the Hutch and Microsoft, select an audience, establish design guidelines, and design and develop a prototype using the Virtual Worlds software developed by Microsoft Research.

Core team: Initially the Hutch hired a team of three outside contractors to execute the preliminary design and Hutch-Microsoft project managers served as mentors. However, the outside team created an ineffective communication layer. There were too many people involved for effective decision-making, and there was too much technical responsibility placed on the Hutch. Both parties determined that it would be more effective to work together directly without the contractors, with Microsoft driving design and development of the prototype. The smaller, interdisciplinary, cross group core team was able to define a decision making process, set a design direction, build the technical infrastructure, and create a prototype of a 3-D virtual world for the Hutch patients.

Audience: During Phase 1, the Hutch-Microsoft project team invited various members of the Hutch staff to help identify potential audiences. Hutch researchers, doctors, volunteers, patients, patients' support network (caregivers and friends and families) were all identified as potential audiences. The Hutch team felt strongly that the Hutch patients and the patient support network would benefit most from social support services. The target audience for the preliminary design was patients and their support network. In later phases of design, the audience was further focused on patients and their support network undergoing the treatment phase at the Hutch facility in Seattle. The audience was also limited to post-transplant bone marrow transplant, adult residents at the Pete Gross House patient housing facility. The team intentionally focused on the support of friends and families in addition to the patients themselves as it was expected that often the patients may be "too sick" to socialize. Also, the patient caregivers and support network have fewer existing support systems (than patients) while at the Hutch.

Design Guidelines
To better understand the patients' social interaction in the physical environment, the Hutch-Microsoft project team toured the Hutch/Swedish hospital facilities, the Hutch school, and the Hutch research facilities. The Microsoft team also met with the volunteer services team, reviewed the Hutch Web pages and all reference material sent to patients prior to their arrival in Seattle, and interviewed Hutch volunteers.

The initial design theme was an abstract Zen garden. This design was confusing and did not relate well with the necessary patient information, yet the concept of a peaceful and diversionary garden was a good idea. After reviewing the existing content, both the Hutch and Microsoft teams agreed that a realistic design based on a public place where patients gather in the real world would provide a logical, familiar entry place for the virtual world. The team chose the outpatient lobby portion of the medical building where Hutch patients received treatment.

In the Phase 1 prototype, the graphical virtual world was divided into four different areas. Users entered the virtual world in the lobby. From the lobby, users could visit a variety of places including an auditorium (modeled after the lecture room at the Hutch), a school, and an abstract garden. Private rooms were also planned, but not implemented in the prototype.

The teams also decided that the content would not to supply personal medical information to cancer patients or medical advice/counseling, but rather social support information. HutchWorld contained a subset of the information given to patients by the Hutch. The purpose was not meant to replaces existing services provided by the Hutch staff, but provide additional social support services. The Hutch provided content and Microsoft helped to create digital versions of the key items. The Hutch felt strongly that access should be restricted to maintain patient trust and security. The Hutch determined patients, approved family/friends of patients, all Hutch staff, the Microsoft team, and qualified volunteers could have access to HutchWorld.

Design Description:
The Phase 1 prototype was designed and built by the Microsoft team with input from the Hutch team. The application design was based on research on virtual worlds and social interaction, influenced by software products such as the Palace [12] and Worlds Inc [20], and text MUDS such as LamdaMOO [8] and MediaMOO [3]. The application design focused on real time, synchronous communication (text chat) over asynchronous communication (email, bulletin board, discussion list) and full-focus attention (3D graphical view with avatars) over partial attention or multi-tasking type applications.

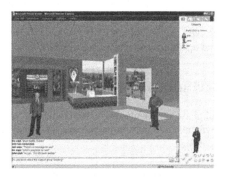

Fig. 1. Phase 1: Preliminary Design, view of the HutchWorld entry

In the Phase 1 prototype, users could move a photographic avatar through the 3D representation of the outpatient lobby, the auditorium, the virtual garden, and the school. Users could click on objects in the 3D space to interact with the object, or move through the space to trigger actions. By moving the mouse, or clicking on the arrow keys, users moved their avatar in the space, dynamically changing their position in the room. They could look at the space in first person point of view (through the user's eyes) or from another camera point in the room. Users could see other users logged on from a remote location in the 3D space, and communicate with one another via text chat. The text controls were located at the bottom of the screen. A list of other users was located on the right side of the screen, with a self-view and avatar gesture controls in the lower right. This application was technically fully-integrated to the Web, but the design of the page had the "look and feel" of a more traditional software application. Most textures for the 3D space were designed by taking photographs of the actual rooms and modifying for use in the Virtual World.

In the lobby, a volunteer sat behind the volunteer desk, greeted users, and handed them a note welcoming them to the space. In the lobby space, just like in the real world, Seattle information was located around the volunteer desk. A Hutch desk was also located in the space. Patients received general information about the Hutch by clicking on links to the site on the desk. Unlike the real space, in the lobby, users could write their own inspirational saying on the wall, they could go to the mailroom to send and receive gifts and notes, they could get free virtual gifts (images of roses, candy, etc.) from the giftshop, and they could access the auditorium, the virtual garden, and the school. The auditorium design was based on the auditorium at the Hutch research facility. In the auditorium an actual presentation given to patients was shown onstage, and users could click on various documents to view other presentations. Users could also drag and drop files to and from their computer desktop. Users entered the virtual garden by "walking into" a painting. In this abstract diversionary space, various animals (including butterflies, bugs, etc.) inhabited this space, providing amusement.

At the end of Phase 1, we determined that we needed to get user feedback before continuing on the development of the prototype. Also, without running a limited deployment of the prototype, we would not have enough experience or data to make decisions on many of the operation and maintenance issues.

2.2   Phase 2: V-Chat Prototype and Deployment

The value of the second phase was twofold—understanding logistical and operational issues for future deployments, and getting participant (Hutch patient, staff, and volunteer) feedback on the design.

Phase 2 overview: The goal of Phase 2 was to test deploy a simplified version of the technology prototyped in Phase 1 in the Hutch hospital setting. An existing Microsoft product, Microsoft V-Chat, was used for the test. V-Chat is a 3D, multi-user graphical chat environment with custom graphics for avatars. [17] The Virtual Worlds Group initially developed V-Chat in 1995, and the VWG team had experience running live chats with many users. The Microsoft role was to build the Hutch V-Chat prototype and the Hutch role was to manage the operations and hosting. Both groups agreed to evaluate usage and gather data on logistical and operational issues that would be relevant for the HutchWorld deployment. Initially, we expected that this trial would last as long as six months. Parallel to the Phase 2 V-Chat deployment, the Hutch was in the process of creating a program to provide project-provided computers and Internet access to patients. Participants in the Phase 2 trial used these computers.

Design description: Hutch V-Chat provided a subset of the features shown in the Phase 1 prototype. For the content in the 3D space, we decided to only test the main lobby space, and we did not build the auditorium or the school. Like in the Phase 1 prototype, the users could move a photographic avatar through the 3D representation of the outpatient lobby and could click on "hot objects" in the space to access Web pages. Again, users communicated with one another via synchronous text chat using the text chat windows, and a list of users currently in the room appeared on the right side of the application with a self-view image of the user below it.

The V-Chat application provided a few additional features not fully developed in the prototype. Users could create their own rooms and could decide if the room was public or private, and a directory was provided to give access to the various end user-generated rooms. There was also additional information including codes of conduct, patient surveys, and emergency contact information. We also created a hosting schedule, and we took turns hosting activities in the space. These activities primarily focused on diversionary activities.

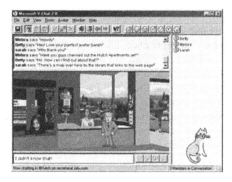

Fig. 2. Phase 2: Hutch V-Chat, view of the Hutch V-Chat entry

Logistics and operations: As mentioned earlier, the Hutch had never before supported computers for patients in the hospital setting, and was just then defining a patient computer program. Before the Hutch team could begin to plan for the V-Chat operations, the six computers needed to be networked and set up at the Hutch, and Hutch staff and volunteers needed to be identified and trained to host the Hutch V-Chat space. The Hutch Volunteer Services Group needed to address many issues before the Hutch V-Chat could be deployed, including: the need to provide technical support and training support for patient machines; the need for a process for deciding where to place machines in the hospital; the need for a process for determining which patients could use the machines; the need for a process for determining what software in addition to Hutch V-Chat would be installed on the machines; and the need for a process for managing security, network, and hospital hygiene requirements.

For operations and maintenance, we learned that training and hosting events in the 3D chat room required trained and dedicated staff on the Hutch side. Without this staffing, maintaining a project like HutchWorld long-term was not possible. The formal support (hosting, training, etc.) of Hutch V-Chat was ended after only 3 months due to support issues. The V-Chat space did remain on the patient computers, but it was not used due to its limitations (see user feedback in this section).

On both sides, we learned that we had been too optimistic in setting the schedule and the expectations for technical support and operations at the Hutch. At Microsoft, like most technology companies, projects are developed and deployed at an extremely high rate. At a medical institution, even the Hutch, which is known for its ability to quickly transition technology into the hospital, studies typically take years to complete. In this phase we learned to set realistic expectations for technical support in the hospital setting, and to set realistic schedules.

User feedback. The design and deployment of the V-Chat space was primarily based on the preliminary design. Our users showed us that the Phase 1 prototype had many shortcomings. We never achieved critical mass in the chatroom, required for the synchronous communication to be successful. The small patient community, staff and volunteers were not interested in stand-alone synchronous, 3-D text chat communication. The immersive chat experience did not support "lurking"—users felt compelled to talk with one another. Patients did not always desire this. In addition the community was small, and often the 3D chatroom was empty. Users did not return if their first experience was not interesting, and usage was very low. In contrast, we found that the patients constantly used the computers. The patients used the computers for asynchronous communication (email, discussion list, bulletin board), information retrieval, and diversionary activities (games). Usage was extremely high despite little patient training and no packaging or integration of the online tools and information.

This turned out to be a crucial lesson for us in understanding how to evolve the technology. We had conceived our approach to designing a virtual world (primarily synchronous communication, with full attention on an immersive 3D space) based on our experience with existing virtual world software applications. With this deployment we began to understand that when technology is used for communication, a strong base of asynchronous communication is crucial. Also, communication appears to require a partial attention component. Like a telephone, while waiting for a call, users need to be able to perform other tasks.

2.3 Phase 3: Re-design—HutchWorld "Portal"

In Phase 3, we redesigned the HutchWorld to solve the design and operations problems discovered by running the Phase 2 V-Chat deployment.

Design description: The current HutchWorld application acts as a Hutch "portal," integrating information retrieval, communication tools, and diversionary activities. This re-design put all key Hutch information in one "portal" for patients, and it is purposefully designed for a small user population. To support the partial attention mode and asynchronous communication, we incorporated email, a bulletin board, text chat, and a Web page creation tool into the virtual world. While surfing for information, playing a game, or reading email, users can "glance up" and see others currently present in the 3D view window. The user interface increases the likelihood that patients will be online together doing other tasks, letting them interact in real-time with others in the 3D view if desired.

In addition, rather than base the user interface design on tradition software applications, we designed the user interface after a Web page because people are primarily using Web-based applications for online communication and information retrieval. Here we tied all of the content navigation to a place in the 3D world. Clicking in the navigation bar to a content area updates the Web pane and moves the user to the appropriate area in the 3D view.

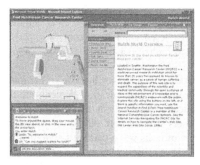

Fig. 3. Phase 3: HutchWorld Portal, view of the HutchWorld entry

User studies: To quickly test the design of HutchWorld, we ran formal user tests at Microsoft. We invited users with a range of computer skills (from beginners to experts) to try using HutchWorld. The response was extremely positive; however, there were some usability issues. Some specific aspects of the various features were confusing (for example, the whisper dialog). We went back and redesigned all of the key items to address these usability problems.

2.4 Phase 4: Future Work: Study of HutchWorld Deployment

The HutchWorld deployment research is scheduled to begin during the spring of 2000, beginning with a pilot study and then a full experiment. HutchWorld will be deployed to patients and their caregivers in a Hutch patient housing facility (Pete Gross House) wired for Internet access. In this controlled environment, we hope to be able to manage the medical and operational aspects of running the study. Depending on the study results, we will look at releasing this software to a wider audience and to other institutions.

The study design is currently being developed through an examination of the research literature, a review of other operation models for delivering technology in a hospital setting, and consultation with research scientists at the Hutch. Researchers at the Hutch and Microsoft are working closely together to develop a research plan that is acceptable to the medical research communities as well as the computer science research communities. Using a research model similar to that in the Gustafson study of CHESS [7], quantitative data will be collected across three conditions: no use of computers, use of computers with Internet access but without HutchWorld, and use of computers with Internet access and HutchWorld. We will measure the usage patterns of HutchWorld and test for the impact of HutchWorld on patients' experiences of social support by measuring social support levels across the three conditions.

3. Conclusion

The design objectives of the project between early 1997 and the present have changed significantly as we have gathered input from content experts, built prototypes, run users studies and conducted limited deployments. Some of the key lessons we have learned include:
1. Design the virtual world application for the size of the intended audience. If the audience is small, asynchronous communication elements are especially critical.
2. Synchronous communication applications should be able to be monitored with the user's partial attention. Users familiar with online communication are accustomed to being involved in a variety of tasks while waiting to communicate or communicating with others. An exception here is users playing immersive games.
3. Web navigation as a model for the user interface rather than a traditional software application is easier to use because of the high usage of the Web for online information retrieval. We have closely tied locations in the 3D space to content in the Web page as a means to organize information spatially.
4. In a medical environment, going through the formal review process is time consuming. Quick and dirty prototyping, user testing and trial deployments of the system prior to review are strongly advised.
5. When beginning the design process, keep the interdisciplinary team small and work together directly to define the goals, the audience, and the design direction. This helps to build cooperation in the core team, and provide a clear vision for the design.
6. Project timeframes for medical institutions and technology companies differ greatly. It is important to understand the schedule and staffing limitations in order to properly set expectations and plan schedules.
7. Deploying online technologies to patients is a relatively new research area. The ethical, legal, and access policies need to be determined by the hospital treatment staff. Typically there are no formal channels for decision making, so this process may differ significantly between health organizations.
8. It may be too early and costly for many hospitals to maintain and operate shared computers for patients. It is important to be able to prove quantitatively the value of the systems to justify the staffing and cost for these machines by the hospital.

As we continue to work on this project, we hope the methodology we develop in our research plan will influence traditional medical research to further study computer-mediated support. We also hope to adapt this to study to a wider audience and other institutions and applications.

References

1. Blanchard, C.G., Albrecht, T.L., Ruckdeschel, J. C., Grant, C. H., & Hemmick, R. M. The role of social support in adaptation to cancer and to survival. *Journal of Psychosocial Oncology*, 13 (1995) 75-95
2. Boberg, E. W., Gustafson, D. H., Hawkins, R. P., Chan, C., Bricker, E., Pingree, S., Berhe, H. & Peressini, A. Development, acceptance, and use patterns of a computer-based education and social support system for people living with AIDS/HIV infection. *Computers in Human Behavior*, 11(1995) 289-311
3. Bruckman, A., Resnick, M. The MediaMoo Project: Constructivism and Professional Community. *Convergence*, 1:1, pp 92-109, Spring 1995
4. Comprensive Health Enhancement Support System CHESS Web site (1999). http://chess.chsra.wisc.edu/Chess/
5. Culver, J. D., Gerr, F., & Frumkin, H. Medical information on the Internet. *Journal of General Internal Medicine*, 12 (1997) 466-470
6. Fred Hutchinson Cancer Research Web site (1999) http://www.fhcrc.org/
7. Gustafson, D. H., Hawkins, R. P., Boberg, E. W., Bricker, E., Pingree, S., & Chan, C. The use and impact of a computer based support system for people with AIDS and HIV infection. In *American Medical Informatics Association, JAMIA symposium supplement, SCAMC proceedings*. PA: Hanley & Belfus, Inc. (1994)
8. LambdaMOO Web site (1999) http://www.c3i.gmu.edu/~uzeno/cs499_Webpage/moo/
9. Lamberg, L. Online support group helps patients live with, learn more about the rare skin cancer CTCL-MF. *JAMA*, 277 (1997) 1422-1423
10. McTavish, F. M., Gustafson, D. H., Owens, B. H., Hawkins, R. P., Pingree, S., Wise, M., Taylor, J., & Apantaku, F. M. CHESS: An interactive computer system for women with breast cancer piloted with an undeserved population. *Journal of Ambulatory Care Management*, 18 (1995) 35-41
11. Nelles, W. B., McCaffrey, R. J., Blanchard, C. G., Ruckdeschel, J. C. Social support and breast cancer: A review. *Journal of Psychological Oncology*, 9 (1991) 21-34
12. Palace Web cite (2000) http://www.thepalace.com/welcome/index.html
13. Sharf, B. F. Communicating breast cancer on-line: Support and empowerment on the Internet. *Women & Health*, 26 (1997) 65-84
14. Spiegel, D., Bloom, J., R., Kraemer, H. C. & Gottheil, E. Effect of psychosocial treatment on survival of patients with metastatic breast cancer. *The Lancet*, Oct. 14 (1989) 888-891
15. Thomas, D. E. (1990). http://nobel.sdsc.edu/laureates/medicine-1990.html
16. Uchino, B. N., Cacioppo, J. T. & Kiecolt-Glaser, J. K. The relationship between social support and physiological processes: A review with emphasis on underlying mechanisms and implications for health. *Psychological Bulletin*, 119(1996) 488-531
17. V-Chat (1996) http://research.microsoft.com/vwg/
18. Virtual Worlds, Microsoft Research Web site (1999) http://research.microsoft.com/vwg/
19. Virtual Worlds Plaform (2000) http://www.vworlds.org/
20. Worlds Inc., Web site (2000) http://www.worlds.net/
21. Weinberg, N., Schmale, J., Uken, J., & Wessel, K. Online help: Cancer patients participate in computer-mediated support group. *Health & Social Work*, 21, 24-29 (1996)

Organisation and Visualisation of Tacit Knowledge in Virtual Communities

Koen Bruynseels and Johan Vos

Sesuad'ra, H. Consciencestraat 17, 3000 Leuven, BE.
koen@sesuadra.org

Abstract. Tacit knowledge is unstructured knowledge that is implicitly present in a community, but is not readily organized or available for its members. Virtual communities can be instrumental in the organization and presentation of such tacit knowledge. In this document we present a platform for the implementation of tailor-made virtual communities, which can be designed and optimized according to the task or the problem involved. Tree examples of multi-user worlds based on this scheme are presented.

1. Introduction

1.1. Tacit Knowledge and Virtual Communities

Lots of information in an organization is often distributed and unorganized. Conventional means of gathering and presenting this kind of information are often laborious and inefficient. Usual steps include the organization of meetings, the gathering of the information, selection of the relevant information, processing and presentation (for instance as a manual). These solutions produce static results and will have to be repeated each time the situation changes.

Virtual communities offer promising ways of organizing tacit knowledge. Newsgroups and mailing list already prove to be a good tool for problem solving (users can ask a question to the group) and for the organization of knowledge (e.g. the production of a FAQ based on previous discussion threads). The main advantages of these virtual communities are that they can be asynchronous (no simultaneous presence is required), their availability on a network (no physical presence required) [1], and – if designed properly – they can profit from the self-emergent dynamics to select and structure the information [2].

1.2. General Approach

Multiple parameters in the design of the virtual community determine the efficiency with which information is gathered and structured. We present a software platform for the implementation of tailor-made virtual communities. This platform is based on a model composed of adjustable objects and methods. The model is used to clarify the structure of the community, and thereby give the software platform a solid ground, on

J.-C. Heudin (Ed.): VW 2000, LNAI 1834, pp. 24-31, 2000.

which different communities can be build with a minimal programming effort. The model also clarifies the actions needed to improve the efficiency of the virtual community. Three virtual communities based on this model are shortly discussed.

2. World Model and General Implementation

The model we use to construct the platform is depicted in Fig. 1. The central elements in this system are: 1.) users, 2.) data, 3.) containers, and 4.) rules. The software platform we wrote enables a flexible redefinition of these elements. Users can enter their data in the containers (rooms, topic trees, ...) that constitute the world. A set of rules governs the (re)distribution of this information over the different containers during the process.

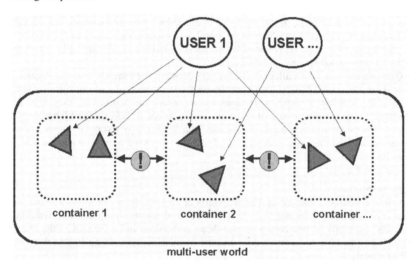

Fig. 1. General model for structuring tacit-knowledge oriented virtual communities. Users (top of the scheme) can put their data (triangles) in the different containers that constitute the world. The containers are in relation to each other, a set of rules dictates the relationship between the content in the containers (indicated by the exclamation mark).

Users have to give a password on logging in to the system. This is necessary for keeping track of user preferences and actions. These preferences and actions are stored in a main user database. Groups of users can be granted different permissions (for instance containers that can be written only by a specified subclass of users).

Data that are entered by the users are stored as serialized objects in java. Depending on the application, these data can be texts, URLs, drawings, pictures, avatars, etc., or a combination of these (e.g. a text associated with a shape).

Containers are logical structures in which the data can be stored in the world. They can be organized hierarchically, or in a cartesian way (all containers of equal value).

The amount of data in a container can be restricted to only one, or to a limited amount of entries, or it can be unrestricted.

A set of rules is used to govern the reorganization of the data over the containers. Application of the rules can be periodically (e.g. each night the data are re-organized), or can be triggered by entry of new data. The rules can take into account the content of the data, their lifetime, the status of the other containers, and so on.

3. Examples of Different Implementations

3.1 The Matrix

Inspiration
The 'Matrix' is a concept described by William Gibson in his visionary S.F.-novel "Neuromancer" [3]. Gibson's 'Matrix' is a full 3-D experience: one can fly through the data-space. Data are represented by crystal-like structures, dynamically growing in the infinite virtual space.

Gibson's story is a nice allegory for the mix between the Platonic and the Organic. Platonic in the sense of 'ideal': not attached tot the body or to any physical limitation. Organic in the sense of complex. Data are not any more 'on themselves': they exist in an increasingly complex tissue of relations. In the words of Gibson the Matrix is "A graphic representation of the data abstracted from the banks of every computer in the human system. Unthinkable complexity." For this reasons we found it a good starting point for our first experiment.

Implementation
Data in the matrix is entered as a combination of an URL (or a text), and a shape. A 'data-crystal creator' window (fig. 2.b.) can be used for this purpose. The window contains two cards: in one card a crystal shape and color can be created, in the other an URL or a text has to be entered. The shape (crystal) will serve as a link to the data (URL or text).

The containers in the matrix are points in a cartesian lattice (fig. 2.a.), capable of having one data entry. Attaching a new data-crystal to the matrix can be done by clicking on an empty place (container). Visitors can zoom in on parts of the matrix, and move by use of the arrow keys. If a visitor clicks on a crystal in the matrix, the content of that crystal will be shown in the main browser window. One thus can browse through the web-pages in the Matrix by clicking on the 2-dimensional representation in the corner window, while in the main window the pages will be shown.

A set of rules is periodically applied to the matrix, aimed at favoring the clustering of crystals. Visitors are encouraged to pin their own crystals near crystals with similar content. If one appreciates a web-site linked to a certain crystal, one can decide to put a link to the own web site next to this crystal. Since the server calculates which crystals are too long 'alone' (get no neighbors) this enlarges the chance for your own crystal to remain in the matrix. The server thus eliminates the crystals without neighbors, or crystals that remain too long without new neighbors. This makes that there appear growing and shrinking clusters of crystals in the matrix, surrounded by a noise of rapidly disappearing solitary crystals. The size of a crystal will depend on its neighboring crystals: the new crystal will always be somewhat smaller than the smallest neighbor. By doing so, it is easy to see which crystals were first (the biggest ones), and which came later in the neighborhood.

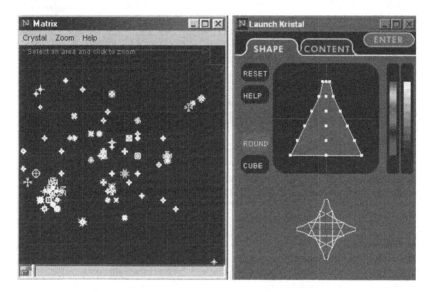

Fig. 2. Two-dimensional representation of the Matrix (left panel, a) showing clustering of information. An example of a data-crystal in the crystal construction interface. Text or an URL can be attached by clicking on the 'content'-tab (right panel, b).

We used java-enhanced VRML2.0 to translate the 2D-version to a 3D-space on the Internet. The space is black and filled with platonic-like crystals (Fig. 3.). Visitors can fly through the space freely. On approaching a crystal, the shape will fragment and its content (the website or the text to which the crystal links) will be shown in the browser window. The semi-transparent spheres around the crystals are used to facilitate the rendering of the world on low-end computers: only crystals that are close enough will be shown.

3.2 The TextTree

Inspiration
This virtual community is constructed to write different scenarios interactively, by many users. Its inspiration is biological: tree-structures with growing and decaying branches. One user starts with entering the start of a story. Other users then can link

their own sequel to this text, and so forth, giving rise to a growing cluster of narratives.

Fig. 3. Screenshot of the VRML-representation of the Matrix. Only crystals that are close enough will appear in their soap-bubble. Crystals will explode when touched, and subsequently their content (a website or a text) is presented in a separate window.

Implementation

Data in the texttree consist of a text (a short paragraph) entered by the user. A fixed shape (instead of the user-modifiable crystals in 3.1.) represents this data-entry.

The organization of the containers is comparable to that in the matrix described under 3.1: a cartesian field of containers that are able to capture one data-entry.

The main difference with the matrix are the rules. In this case, the universe starts with one single text-entry in its center. Users are strictly forced to link their own text-entry in the immediate neighborhood of an already filled container. Texts thus have to be linked to already existing texts, giving rise to a text-tree. Branches of the tree that do not grow further within a given time will be eliminated gradually by the server.

3.3 The Noösphere

Inspiration

Noösphere in designed as a tool to investigate ideas that live in a community. This virtual community is inspired by the visionary view of De Chardin on the growing world of ideas [4].

Implementation

Noösphere is a 3-D virtual community with avatars. An early implementation was reported previously [5] In this case, the data entered by the users are avatars, to which a text string (a slogan, one-liner, …) can be attached. The avatar should represent the idea; therefore the avatars cover a broad spectrum of shapes. This is accomplished by letting the visitor create his/her own avatar from a set of organic-shaped feelers, bodies and tentacles. The different body parts can be decorated with 'alien skin', ranging from dark to bright patterns.

The containers in this world can only contain six avatars. The containers are organized hierarchically towards the center of the Noosphere. The aim is to get your avatar in this center. Authors can do this by forming alliances with similar avatars, or by showing aversion for opposing avatars.

This voting behavior is used to calculate the most 'successful' in each container. These avatars are promoted, the less successful will descend. Other strategies to promote your avatar are: mutation (changing the appearance), and to comment on other avatars via the attached discussion-threads. Recalculation rules are triggered each time new data is entered. The main focus of this system is not the creation of a virtual ecology, but the organization of the ideas attached to the avatars. Moreover, cooperation rather than 'struggle for life' is promoted by the rules, making this system very different from virtual ecologies like Technosphere [6].

All elements and avatars can be viewed in 3D (VRML2.0 worlds). A 2D image representation is also available, and ensures participants of non-power users.

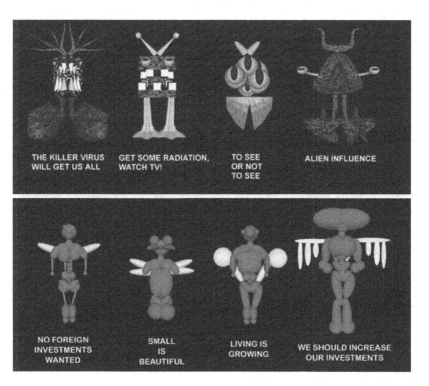

Fig. 4. Different sets of avatars used in the Noösphere. The oldest version (on top) allowed the choice of different skin colors. To the newer avatars (shown below) sounds can be linked. Each avatar is accompanied by an "idea".

4. Discussion

The double goal of the described system is enabling both the presentation and the organization of tacit knowledge. As other attempts in the field of collaborative virtual environments show [7] [8], these two aspects are closely intertwined. The way in which the data are visualized and positioned in the virtual space is instrumental for users to develop optimal strategies for entering their own data.

The representation of the data (2D or 3D, colors, sounds, text, etc.) strongly depends on their nature, and the need for a coherent navigation [9]. For instance, linking the size of crystals in the matrix to their success gives a simple visual clue on what is relevant. Visualization in 3D-spaces can be interesting for more complex data-visualization [10] but is often difficult to navigate.

In developing the tacit-knowledge system, we started from the viewpoint that information is constructed by humans acting in larger contexts, rather than just being a property of data [2]. Users and data are therefore intimately linked in our system. In this view, the 'rules' and 'container' give structure to the community and can aid in developing systems with 'self-emergent' properties - this means: giving a spontaneous organization of data in clusters relevant to the users. Experience with the Noösphere and the matrix-system indicate that such self emergence can occur, but that it largely depends on the fine-tuning of the applied rules.

5. Conclusions

We established a software platform that can be used in the creation of very different virtual communities, aimed at both the presentation and the organization of tacit knowledge. The model we used proved to be general enough to cover a broad range of virtual environments. Further elaboration of this model will be focused on direct user-user interaction.

The software platform could be tailored to meet vastly different questions. Illustrations include the design of virtual worlds, used to explore ideas living in a community, virtual worlds to interactively write manuals or reports, and worlds to flock related information. These implementations illustrated the use of virtual worlds in the handling of tacit knowledge. Optimization of the rules and interfaces is now the main challenge.

References

[1] Rheingold, H. "The virtual community, home steading om the electric frontier" Addison-Wesley (1993)
[2] Crowe, M., Beeby, R., Gammack, J. "Constructing systems and information"; McGraw-Hill (1996)
[3] Gibson, W. : "Neuromancer", ACE paperback (1984)
[4] De Chardin, P.T. "Le Phénomène Humain", ed. Du Seuil, (1955)

[5] Bruynseels, K., Vos, J., Vandekerckhove, P.: "Noösphere - a world of ideas on the web". Addendum to the proceedings of the Virtual Worlds conference (1998), Ed. Heudin, J.-C., Springer

[6] Selley, G., Hawkes, R., Prophet, J., Kind, A., Saunderson, J.: "Technosphere" http://tdg.linst.ac.uk/technosphere/

[7] Hirschberg, U., Gramazio, F., Papanikolaou, M., Tuncer, B., Stäger, B.: "phase(x)3" CAAD - ETH Zürich http://caad.arch.ethz.ch

[8] Matsumoto, F., Matsukawa, S. "Ginga" http://www.planet-arch.com/ginga.htm

[9] Cavallar, C., Dögl, D.: "Organizing information in 3D" proceedings of the Virtual Worlds conference (1998) p. 308-314, Ed. Heudin, J.-C., Springer

[10] Van De Moere, A..: "Lines - paths of knowledge", CAAD - ETH Zürich, http://caad.arch.ethz.ch/~bugajski/acadia/library.html

Integration of Simulation Tools in On-Line Virtual Worlds

Stéphane Sikora, David Steinberg, Claude Lattaud

LIAP5, Université René Descartes
45, Rue des Saints-Pères, 75006 Paris, France
{sikora, steinberg, claude.lattaud}@math-info.univ-paris5.fr

Abstract. This paper deals with the enhancement of virtual worlds by the use of simulation tools. It describes a plant growth model and its current integration in a virtual world. This model is based on a multi agent architecture, which allows an easy formulation of the processes occurring inside the plant. More generally, artificial life algorithms and biological models are used to define evolutionary processes applied on artificial entities. Virtual worlds provide an interface that allows the visualization of these model during their activity. In return, the integration of these models has an impact on the evolution of the simulated environment. As virtual worlds are open systems, environmental conditions are not precisely known, and this evolution tends to be less predictable and potentially more dynamic. Experimental results show the effect of different factors on the development of the plants.

1. Introduction

Though no strict definition exists, the term 'virtual world' generally refers to a digital space defined by two components:
- an environment containing the objects of the world [14],
- an interface linking the user and the environment.

A virtual world includes an environment that handles the relations existing between its objects by means of a set of laws. These laws, as well as physical laws, apply to the whole world, but their application depends on the characteristics of the objects. A particular kind of objects exists in the environment: the avatars. These avatars are the incarnation of users in virtual worlds.

A virtual world also provides an interface between the environment and the user, who acts through his avatar. This interface usually comprises a 3D graphical representation and allows the user to explore the world, to communicate with other avatars and to act on the environment.

Unfortunately, on-line virtual worlds are generally inhabited only by avatars. The purpose of this paper is to show how virtual worlds can be enhanced by the use of simulation tools. These tools belong to a wide variety of fields, like artificial life algorithms and multi-agent systems. This aspect and the underlying world model are detailed in section 2. This model, described in Section 3, is the first step of the development of a virtual garden in the 2nd World. Results concerning this work are given in section 4.

J.-C. Heudin (Ed.): VW 2000, LNAI 1834, pp. 32–43, 2000.
© Springer-Verlag Berlin Heidelberg 2000

2. World Model

Physics, biology and artificial life define models and algorithms that can be used within the framework of a virtual world. For example, the integration of simulated physical laws in a virtual environment renders this environment more realistic and dense, thus enhancing the experience of the users. Gravity is frequently used in virtual worlds, as it generally makes the world more understandable. In the same way, the immersion of autonomous entities, able to communicate and interact with the avatars, also enrich virtual worlds.

In the field of artificial life, research attempts to synthesize life-like phenomena, assuming independence between the complexity of these phenomena and the medium in which they occur [13]. Typically, artificial entities are designed and placed in simulated environments whose complexity is very variable. There's a wide range of these possible environments: from the most simple like Conway's game of life [9] to very realistic models featuring physical laws [12,21,22].

The behavior and structure of the entities is then studied, and adapted responses to particular problems are generally sought. As a total independence is assumed between the constituting elements of the entities and the behaviors they exhibit, artificial life works are quite general and can be applied in many domains. The use of artificial life algorithms in order to improve virtual worlds is the focus of interest of this paper. Indeed, multi-agent systems, genetic and evolutionary algorithms are some of the tools that could be used to build virtual ecosystems.

In the works conducted at the Artificial Intelligence Laboratory of Paris5 (LIAP5), the multi agent paradigm [5] is used to populate the environment with autonomous entities [16]. Each agent is a situated entity with a limited perception of its environment. It is able to perform several actions : move, exchange resources with the environment, communicate with other agents, etc. The resources of the environment can indirectly restrain the activity of the agents: a particular resource may be necessary to perform a specific action for example. The complexity of an agent's behavior depends on its control architecture. This control system creates the link between its sensors and its actuators and determines the agent's actions.

The agents possess a genotype, thus allowing the setting up of evolutionary mechanisms. Generally speaking, the genotype influences the shape, characteristics and behavior of the agent. The classical operators of genetic algorithms [10] (selection, crossover, mutation) are then implemented to explore the space of possible entities.

One of the most usual forms of selection is the death of an individual. In order to take this into account, the animat approach is used [23]. Each agent then has a viability zone in the space of his state variables. If his internal state goes out of this zone, the agent dies. The first goal of an animat is thus to survive in his environment, to find ways to use the environment's resources to stay in his viability zone. An agent that survives for a long time has a better chance to spread his genes, for example because it's considered to have more chances to reproduce.

The plant growth simulation is a part of the 2nd Garden project. This project is an attempt to build virtual gardens integrated in the 2nd World [1], a virtual community developed by Canal+. The biological data and models used in this project come from recent works of the Bioclimatology Research Unit of the INRA [6,7,8]. This work was inspired, amongst others, by the Nerve Garden project [2]. Nerve Garden is a virtual world composed of several island where users had the opportunity to plant seeds and see the resulting plants grow. In the current version, the growth process is determinist. Nerve Garden 2, still under development, should feature interaction between plants and their environment, and include genetic parameterization of the growth process.

3. Plant Growth Model

Biological models of plant development often consider plants as incremental structures constituted of known basic elements. According to the granularity of the model, these elements can be anything from cells to leaves or flowers. For example, L-systems are a mathematical formalism proposed by the biologist Lindenmayer in 1968 [15] in order to simulate plant development using parallel rewriting rules. They were first used to describe cellular growth and were then extended to simulate the growth of whole plants and their interactions with their environment [17,19,20]. L-systems are one of the most widely used model of plant development, both by biologists and computer scientists. Another model was developed by Colasanti and Hunt [3] to simulate the growth of single plants or entire populations from the artificial life point of view, using sets of simple rules. The study of plant morphogenesis being the main research theme of many laboratories, many other models have been developed by biologists.

3.1 Biological Model

This section briefly explains the choices made concerning the biological aspect of the model developed in this project. The first important choice is the scale used to represent the plants during the simulations. Plants are viewed as modular entities at several different levels, the basic constituting elements being different for each one. The lowest level that can be used to describe the growth of a plant is the cellular one: the chemical and energetic flows and interactions occurring between the cells are then modeled, as well as the mechanisms of cell creation and destruction. This leads to precise and complicated models, useful for in depth studies of plant morphogenesis but that can not be easily used to simulate the development of whole individuals. This level of description was for example used in the first works of Lindenmayer on L-systems. Another extreme level of description is used when one wants to simulate the evolution of whole fields. In this case, differential equations are used to render the mass and energy transfers occurring between the plants and their environment.

An intermediary level of description is used in this project: that of the organs (leaves, buds, flowers, etc.). Organs are the building blocks of this model: the plant is in fact a branching structure of organs.

The model presented in this paper uses five structures: apex, internode, leaf, bud and phytomer. The apex usually denominates the uppermost tip of a structure. In a plant the apex is the name of the apical meristem, the group of cells situated at the top of an axis that initiates the cells that will later become other organs. They are very small and are not usually visible. The apex are the only organs producing new matter in the part of the plant located on top of the ground. There is never more than one apex in a single branch. The activity of an apex mainly consists in the creation of groups of organs named phytomers. The phytomer is the basic, iterative, developmentally independent unit of the plant. Each phytomer includes the following organs: one internode and one or more associated leaves, each with an attached axilliary bud, see figure 1. An internode is a part of a stem situated between two leaves. Each bud has the possibility to turn into an apex, thus creating a new branch, according to endogenous and environmental factors. The roots of the plants are not considered in this model.

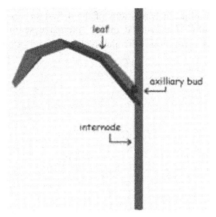

Fig. 1. A phytomer and its components

L-systems are the most widely used model of plant development. The next section presents a multi-agent approach based on L-systems, as well as the environment model used for the simulations.

3.2 Architectural Model

The model used in the simulations is a multi-agent reformulation of L-systems. L-systems are parallel rewriting systems that operate on strings used to describe branching structures of modules. When L-systems are used to simulate plant growth, modules usually represent organs of the plant such as leaves or internodes. The topology of the structure is described in the string: each branch is delimited by a pair of matching brackets. There are two main components in a L-system: a set of rules and an axiom. The rules describe changes that occur to the modules (size, orientation) as well as the creation or destruction of other modules during an iteration.

Example :
  axiom : F
  rule 1 : F → F [+F] [-F] F

At each discrete derivation step, these rewriting or production rules are applied to all the modules of the string, possibly replacing them with their successor modules. According to the type of L-system used, the conditions of application of the rules differ: they can be deterministic (in the most basic forms of L-systems) or stochastic [18], context-sensitive or not, and can depend on values of parameters.

Example : first three derivations of the L-system described above
    step 1 : F
    step 2 : F [+F] [-F] F
    step 3 : F [+F] [-F] F [+F [+F] [-F] F] [- F [+F] [-F] F] F [+F] [-F] F

Figure 2 shows a graphic interpretations of the 4 first strings generated by this L-System. The 'F' module is translated into a fixed-size segment. The '+' and '-' modules are interpreted as rotations of respectively +π/6 and -π/6 radians.

Fig. 2. Graphical interpretation of the first strings generated by the L-system.

As in L-systems, the model used in the 2nd Garden considers the organs as the basic structural elements of a plant. But instead of using general rules to describe the whole evolution, each organ has a different behavior. The overall growth is thus the result of independent processes described at a lower level. All these processes are synchronized and occur simultaneously at each iteration. The organs have different states, and their behaviors differ according to the state they are in. These behaviors determine the state the organs will be in at the next step, their own evolution (growth, death), and the creation of other organs. The states of the organs and the associated behaviors mainly reflect the physiological response of the plant to temperature and, at a lesser extent, to light and humidity.

Each plant has its own genotype, composed of genes affecting either the organ's behaviors or general responses of the plant to the environment. The genotype of a plant is composed of about fifty genes gathered in seven chromosomes. One of them is only used for the graphical aspect of the plant and has no effect on the simulation. Each chromosome is composed of genes that have influence on the same part of the model: initiation of phytomers by the apex, growth of leaves, etc.

Figure 3 shows the structure of chromosome #2, which is composed of five genes, all affecting the behavior of each apex of the plant. Each gene is composed by three values $<Mi,Ma,V>$. Mi and Ma are encoded as floats and define the range $[Mi;Ma]$ of the gene value. V is an unsigned integer necessary to calculate the real value of the gene. As V is encoded as a string of p bits (typically, $p=32$), gene value is computed as follow:

$$GeneValue = Mi + (Ma\text{-}Mi) \; (\; V \, / \, 2^p - 1)$$

Cross-over operator is permitted when two genotypes share the same gene ranges. In this case, the cross-over operator only changes V part of each gene. In the same way mutation operator is performed by changing one of the bits of V.

Gene #7	Gene #8	Gene #9	Gene #10	Gene #11
Duration of vegetative stage for the apex	Sensibility to photoperiod and temperature	Duration of inductive stage for the apex	Rhythm of initiation of phtyomer	Number of phytomers in a seed

Min	Max	V
100 dd	300 dd	0111111111

Fig. 3. Structure of chromosome #2. This chromosome has five genes affecting the behavior of the apex. The gene #7 is detailed, its unit is degree day[1]. For instance, with precision p=10, V represents the real value 199.90 dd.

The genetic code alone is not enough to predict the morphogenesis of a plant: variations of environmental factors at different stages of development might mark in an irreversible way the evolution of a plant.

An environment is composed of several parts (e.g. air, earth) and is populated with plants. It answers requests sent by plant's organs that need a local information (air temperature for example). These information can be either constant values or mathematical functions defined for the entire environment. For example, the temperature in a given point is calculated by a function of the distance to defined heat sources. Furthermore, the environment also has the capacity to find information concerning the plants. For example, the calculation of the luminosity received by an organ requires the calculation of the intersections between the plant and the light emitted by a given source.

3.3 Advantages of a Modular Architecture

Various reasons motivated the use of the multi-agent paradigm in this project. This approach allows easy communication between organs, by diffusion of qualitative or quantitative information. The transmitted signals are items that are sent or received by organs and are thus diffused in the plant, and that carry information. The speed of the transmission varies, as well as the way the plant's structure is traversed. Temporal or spatial multi-scaling may also be used. This reflects the fact that some structures are

---

[1] Physiological time is often expressed in units called degree-days. For instance: if a species has a lower developmental threshold of 8° C, and the temperature remains at 9°C for 24 hours, one degree-day is accumulated.

present in a plant at different levels of granularity, in the same way than fractals. An inflorescence is as complex as a whole plant, but is usually viewed as a simple organ. The structure of a multi-agent model is easy to modify and enhance. Modules can be broken up in smaller units implying modification of their structure (addition of attributes, etc.). Furthermore, although L-Systems limits haven't yet been reached, one sure thing is that each enrichment of L-systems results in the addition of parameters and symbols to the production rules. The writing and maintenance of these rules are thus made more difficult. In a multi agent model, the behaviors are easily maintained.

4. Results

The Second World is parceled into isolated places, called "cells", that can be reached easily by the avatars. Environmental parameters are associated with each of these cells, resulting to particular environmental conditions. During the first experiments, 5 similar greenhouses were   installed in the second world. Each greenhouse had a different ambient temperature, allowing to see the simultaneous response of similar plants to different parameters. Figure 4 shows such a greenhouse, characterized by an ambient temperature fixed at 16°C.

Fig. 4. Snapshots of a 2nd World cell, containing plants generated by the 2nd garden engine.

This part presents some examples of the growth of artificial plants and of their sensibility to their environment. In order to obtain a 3D graphic representation of the plants, VRML files depending on the geometric properties of the plants were generated. Two main factors have an influence on a given plant's evolution: its genotype and the environment.

4.1 Sensibility to the Environment

The following environmental factors are taken into account in the model: temperature, humidity and photoperiod. The temperature is by far the most used factor: it conditions the size of the plant (number of phytomers initiated, size of each phytomer), the duration of growth of leaves and internodes, etc. Humidity is used to determine the conditions needed for a plant to start its development and photoperiod has an influence on the number of phytomers present in the plant.

Fig. 5. Different steps in the development of a plant (scale used : days of simulated time)

Figure 5 shows the same plant at different time steps during its growth. In this example, a lot of leaves are initiated before the plant gains height. This is the result of a constraint imposed at the level of the organ that stipulates that internode elongation only occurs after a specific event: the end of initiation of phytomers by the apex. The branches are here symmetrical because the temperature was constant in the whole environment for this simulation. The genotype of this particular plant specifies that there are three leaves by phytomer (hence the three branches at the same height).

Figure 6 shows 10 individuals sharing the same genotype after 100 simulated days, but in different temperature conditions. The plants located at the right are in a hotter area than those located at the left. In this simulation, the temperature field is continuous. Some plants can't even start to grow or grow faintly because temperature is either too low or too high, whereas other ones located in a more suitable environment grow well. Not only the size but also the shape of the plants changes due to the difference of temperature. Temperature has a great influence on the rhythm of initiation of phytomers, therefore on the size of the plant. Furthermore, each plant has optimal, minimal and maximal temperatures specified in the genotype that condition their response to temperature.

A modification of environmental factors will have an influence on the way the plants grow. The ten plants shown on the figure 6 could be seen as various possible future states of a plant, according to the temperature chosen by the user. More subtle effects can be achieved by acting on factors that have less influence on the global growth of a plant, such as the duration of daily exposure to light.

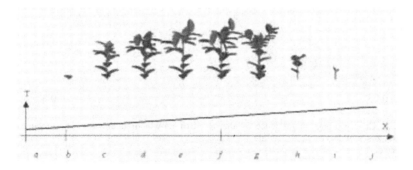

Fig. 6. 10 plants after 100 time steps, with the same genotype. The plants are placed at different positions in a continuous growing temperature field (the first plant is not visible).

4.2 Genetic Factors

As reported in the model, the genotype of a plant is composed of about fifty genes. Figure 7, 8 and 9 show the influence of three different genes. These figures were obtained after 150 time steps[2]. The temperature is homogenous, and fixed at 15°C. Figure 7 shows the effect of the gene #7 on the whole structure of the plant. With the duration of the vegetative stage increasing, the plant develops more branching structures. Figure 8 shows the impact of gene #31 on the size of the plant. In this example, the plant keeps the same complexity. Only the size of internodes is affected. Figure 9 shows an example with a gene directly encoding a property of the plant: the number of leaves and buds associated with each phytomer.

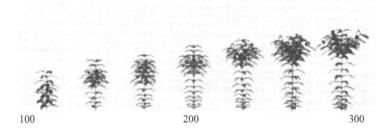

100   200   300

Fig. 7. Gene #7 controls the duration of the vegetative stage for an apex, encoded in degree day. During this stage, an apex initiates new phytomers.

These examples show the potentiality of a mutation operator applied on the plant's genotype. In the same way, a cross over operator was defined, in order to obtain a new offspring from selected plants. The main purpose of this operator is to diversify the individuals of the population. Figure 10 shows an example of several plants generated by the same two parents.

0.05   0.3

Fig. 8. Gene #31 has an influence on the speed of growth of internodes. The amount of phytomers and leaves produced are the same in all cases. Only the size of internodes is affected.

---

[2] E.g. 150 simulated days of growth.

Fig. 9. Gene #17 controls the amount of leaves by phytomer. The integer value associated with this gene ranges here from 1 to 5.

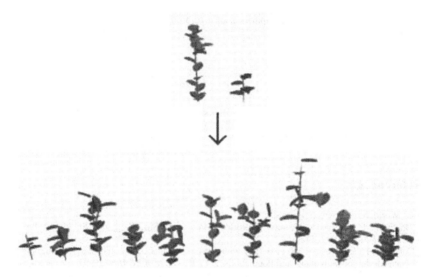

Fig. 10. 10 different plants generated by the same two parents. This offspring is the result of a crossover operator applied on the two parents.

5. Conclusion and Future Work

The model presented in this paper uses an original approach where the organs of plants are defined by agents. Fundamental steps of growth process in monocotyledon were implemented in the 2nd Garden engine. The architecture allows an easy formulation of the factors that will determine the plant's growth, as information is distributed in the different organ's behaviors and in the genotype.

Although these simulations are not realistic from a strict biological point of view, the results obtained are relevant. Due to the distributed architecture, plants present a coherent local answer to their environment, and particularly to the temperature field. Multi-agent model used in this application allows quick and easy improvements to the actual system, for instance the development of the root system. In addition to the enhancement of the architectural model, the focus has to be done on the communication process between organs.

This plant model is integrated in the 2nd World, and currently, the next step is to adapt the interface so as to allow avatars to act on the environment. The avatars being able to act directly on many factors, the environment can become less predictable. Avatars may affect the activity of other agents, and modify through their actions the gene pool present in the environment. Avatars could favor or disadvantage some individuals, for example by moving resources, or create new agents from chosen parents.

More globally, this work is the starting point in the construction of an online virtual ecosystem (i.e. a simplified artificial ecosystem integrated in a virtual world). One of the main goal of this project is to put into evidence emerging organizations at the level of the agents like the apparition of a trophic cascade between predators and preys [2].

Acknowledgments

The authors are grateful to Bruno Andrieu and Christian Fournier for their contribution on the biological model of plants. The experiences that have been described result from the activity performed at Canal+, thanks to Frédéric Lediberder.

References

1. 2nd World, http://www.2nd-world.fr.
2. Booth, G., Gecko : A Continuous 2D World for Ecological Modelling, in *Artificial Life Vol. 3:3*, MIT Press, 1997, 147-164.
3 Colasanti, R. and Hunt, R., Real Botany with Artificial Plants: A Dynamic Self Assembling Plant Model for Individuals and Populations, in *Proceedings of ECAL'97*, 1997.
4 Damer, B.: *Avatars*, Peachpit Press, 1998.
5 Ferber, J.: *Les Systèmes Multi-Agents*, Inter Edition, Paris, 1995.
6 Fournier, C., Introduction de réponses écophysiologiques à la température dans un modèle de plante à base de L-Systèmes, mémoire du DEA Fonctionnement Physique Chimique et Biologique de la Biosphère Continentale, INA P-G/Paris VI/ENS, 1995.
7 Fournier, C. and Andrieu, B., A 3D Architectural and Process-based Model of Maize Development, in *Annals of Botany* 81:233-250, 1998.
8 Fournier, C. and Andrieu, B., ADEL-maize : an L-system model for the integration of growth processes from the organ to the canopy. Application to regulation of morphogenesis by light availability, in *Agronomie'99*, INRA-Unité de Recherche en Bioclimatologie, 1999.
9 Gardner, M., The Fantastic Combinations of John Conways Game of Life, in *Scientific American* Vol. 223:4, 1970, 120-123.
10 Goldberg, D.: *Genetic Algorithms in Search, Optimization and Machine Learning*, Addison Wesley, 1989.
11 Heudin, J.C.: *Virtual Worlds : Synthetic Universes, Digital Life and Complexity*, Perseus Books, 1999.
12. Komosinski, M., Framsticks, http://www.frams.poznan.pl/.
13 Langton, C.: Artificial Life : Proceedings of the 1st Workshop on the Synthesis ant the Simulation of Living Systems '1987, C.Langton Ed., Addison-Wesley, 1989

14 Lattaud, C. and Cuenca, C., A Model for the Evolution of Environments, in *Lecture Notes in Artificial Intelligence n°1434*, J.C. Heudin Ed., Springer-Verlag, 1998, 218-228.

15 Lindenmayer, A., Mathematical models for cellular interaction in development, Parts I and II, in *Journal of Theoretical Biology*, 18, 1968, 280-315

16 Maes, P., Modelling Adaptive Autonomous Agents, in *Artificial Life : An Overview*, C. Langton Ed., MIT Press / Bradford Books, 1995, 135-162.

17 Mech, R. and Prusinkiewicz, P., Visual Models of Plants Interacting with Their Environment, in *Proceedings of SIGGRAPH 96*, 1996, 397-410.

18. Prusinkiewicz, P. and Lindenmayer, A.: *The Algorithic beauty of plants*, Springer-Verlag, New York, 1990.

19 Prusinkiewicz, P., Hammel, M., Hanan, J. and Mech, R.., Visual models of plant development, in Rozenberg, G. and Salomaa, A. Eds., Handbook of formal languages, Springer-Verlag, 1996.

20 Prusinkiewicz, P., James, M. and Mech, R., Synthetic topiary, in *Proceedings of SIGGRAPH 94*, 1994, 351-358.

21 Sims, K., Evolving 3D Morphology and Behavior by Competition, in *Artificial Life IV: Proceedings of the 4th International Conference on Artificial Life*, Brooks, R. and Maes, P. Eds., MIT Press, 1994, 28-39.

22 Terzopoulos, D., Tu, X.. and Grzeszczuk, R., Artificial fishes with autonomous locomotion, perception, behavior, and learning in a simulated physical world, in *Artificial Life IV: Proceedings of the 4th International Workshop on the Synthesis and Simulation of Living Systems*, Cambridge, MA, July, 1994, 17-27.

23 Wilson, S., Knowledge Growth in an Artificial Animal, in *Proceedings of the 1st International Conference on Genetic Algorithms and their Applications*, Grefenstette, J.J. Ed., 1985, 16-23.

Towards Digital Creatures in Real-Time 3D Games

Axel Buendia, Jean-Claude Heudin

IIMLab – International Institute of Multimedia
Pôle Universitaire Léonard de Vinci
92916 Paris La Défense Cedex – France
http://www.devinci.fr/iim
Axel.Buendia@devinci.fr
Jean-Claude.Heudin@devinci.fr

Abstract. This paper describes a preliminary experiment made at the IIMLab in order to design digital creatures in real-time three-dimensional virtual worlds. The aim of the project is to integrate state-of-the-art Artificial Life techniques with real-time 3D graphical engines in the framework of the next generation immersive 3D games.

1   Introduction

In the last few years, the gaming industry has become one of the most important market in information technology. Some game titles have been sold worldwide in millions of units. Forecasting of markets and applications show that the consumer spending on games will continue to grow in the next future. Therefore, computer games represent an ideal opportunity for the application and dissemination of the Artificial Life technologies. Most of existing games include the simulation of human or non-human creatures, but these creatures are generally characterized by a very low level of "Artificial Intelligence". In most cases, those intelligent behaviors are limited to the execution of a set of action scripts, each of them fired when a pre-defined event occurs. The resulting behaviors are generally predictable and far from realistic. A few number of recent games, like "Creatures" [1], have introduced the use of more sophisticated Artificial Life technologies in their design, but none of them has integrated state-of-the-art Artificial Life and real-time three-dimensional (3D) textured graphics.
In this paper, we will present preliminary experiments made at the IIMLab in order to design digital creatures in a real-time 3D virtual world. The aim of the project is to integrate state-of-the-art Artificial Life techniques with real-time 3D graphical engines in the framework of the next generation of immersive 3D games. The preliminary experiments reported in this paper focus on the behavioral approach used in the Nut project.
The paper is divided into three main parts. Section 2 briefly introduces the Nut virtual environment. Section 3 describes how the model used for the digital creatures fits for real time interaction. Section 4 describes preliminary experiments and discusses their results. The paper concludes by outlining the next steps of the Nut project.

J.-C. Heudin (Ed.): VW 2000, LNAI 1834, pp. 44-53, 2000.
© Springer-Verlag Berlin Heidelberg 2000

2   The Nut Virtual Environment

2.1   The Nut Environment

The Nut virtual world is a full 3D dynamical environment. A Nut world is basically made of *structural objects* grouped in a *map* and of non-structural objects called *entities*. Structural objects are static 3D shapes, which can be reshaped into walls, floors or ceilings, bodies of water, skies, etc. All these units can be grouped together in order to form a coherent 3D space (cf. figure 1).

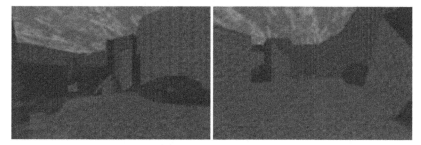

Fig. 1.   Two views of a map in the Nut Virtual World.

Entities include "physical" non-structural objects and "non-physical" non-structural objects. The first class includes animated objects that can move and respond to user-initiated events like a door for example. *Creatures* represent a special case of physical entities characterized by a bio-inspired model. The second class includes insubstantial and invisible objects like triggers, light sources and sound sources. Every entity has one or more properties like behavioral information and collision detection. Other examples are the brightness of a light source, the sound of a sound entity, the speed of a moving object, or the mass of an object for gravity simulation.

2.2   An Evolutionary Approach

The general model for Nut's creatures is based on an artificial evolution process. The idea is to design creatures and then let them co-evolve in their environment leading to an open-ended power and generating surprising consequences like efficient reactive behaviors or emerging cognitive capabilities.

The evolution principle is based on a classical Darwinian-inspired evolution cycle which can be briefly described as follow (cf. figure 2). A set of GTYPEs (Generalized Genotype [3]) generates a population of PTYPEs (Generalized Phenotype [3]) which interacts within the virtual environment. On the basis of their relative performance, some of these PTYPEs "survive" and reproduce, creating new GTYPEs. Then, a new generation of PTYPEs emerges out the interpretation of their respective GTYPE and this process continues [12].

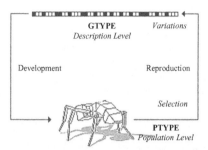

Fig. 2. This simplified diagram shows the relation between the generalized genotype, which is the encoded self-description of the creature, and the generalized phenotype, which is the resulting individual in the virtual environment.

2.3   Creature's Behavioral Model

The set of behaviors of a digital creature can be best described using a layered hierarchical model inspired by the subsumption architecture proposed by Brooks [10]. In this model, a given level relies on the existence of its sub-levels and all levels are intrinsically parallel. Unlike the subsumption model, the two elementary levels of each creature are its GTYPE and a *Primary Metabolism* (cf. figure 3). In biology, a metabolism is responsible for taking material from the environment and transforming it in order to create the form of the organism. The Primary Metabolism we refer to can be described as a recursive partially stochastic procedure responsible for self-creation (development), self-perpetuation (survival) and self-reproduction [11]. These three functions are strongly linked together and form the primary dynamics of any creature.

The sensori-motor and cognitive level relies on the existence of these two basic organizational levels. It is organized in parallel functions. Each function represents a goal. It is plugged to several actuators which help to reach its goal. Each function computes correct orders for these actuators and the current interest to active them. The orders (with their interest) are computed from sensors data, and are supposed to make the creature achieving the function's goal. Each actuator receives several orders, from different functions. They are responsible for final decision : the most interesting order is executed. Some actuators may be incompatible, a choice is then made between them using the simple rule "winner takes all" (the most interesting actuator is executed; the others, incompatible ones, are ignored).

Perceptions   **PTYPE**   Actions

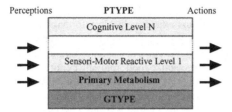

Fig. 3.   Theoretical layered model of a digital creature. Each level represents a set of "perception-computation-action" units that execute in parallel with the other levels.

3   Description of Experiments

3.1   Creature Implementation

Preliminary experiments were conducted in order to validate the behavioral architecture and to learn more about the technical constraints when integrating Artificial Life technologies in a real-time 3D environment such as Nut. We designed a simplified implementation of our model, focusing mainly on the Primary Metabolism and a single reactive behavioral layer (cf. figure 4).

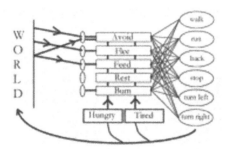

Fig. 4.   Schematic diagram of the reactive layer implemented in the preliminary experiment.

The metabolism of the creature is quite simple and includes two state variables, called attributes : *hungriness* and *tiredness*. These two attributes are cyclic and represent the need to feed and the need to rest. They are computed during each cycle of life. Their value is based on external factors (how many movements were made since the last resting) or internal (*tiredness* is based on *hungriness*).
The behavioral model is composed of a single reactive layer. This reactive layer is subdivided into five modules, each representing a primary reactive function of the creature. These functions are: *Avoid* obstacles, *Flee* predators, *Feed*, *Rest* and *Bum*

(wander) around to discover the world. Each function can sense the world through specific *sensors*. These sensors extract valuable information from the incoming data flow. The creature can sense the distance and the direction of entities and obstacles like walls. It can also perceive the color of the other creatures, which corresponds to a different specie. It can also recognize food from other entities.

The creature has also actuators. It can control directly its speed (walk, back walk or run), and its orientation (turn of 15° left or right per time step). Note that turning left and turning right are conflicting actions, registered as incompatible. In this experiment creatures have no muscles, thus the level of abstraction is quite high.

Each primary reactive function computes a set of orders for each sensed object, taking into account the state of the Primary Metabolism's variables. The orders are filtered and the most interesting one is executed. Conflicts between actions are solved by choosing the most stimulated one and ignoring the others. These actions modify the world and or some of the Primary Metabolism's attributes.

3.2   The Environment

For the purpose of the preliminary experiment, we have specifically designed a simple and dedicated virtual environment. It consisted in a cubic arena containing some food (cf. figure 5). The creatures were of two types: *preys* and *predators*. A prey can feed only on food and is afraid of predators. Note that when a creature is as the same location as the food is, it automatically feeds on it. A predator can feed on food and on prey and is never scared. Creatures were client side creatures and the experiments were run on several computers: a server plus one computer per creature. The arena contained only one portion of food which automatically reappeared 10 seconds after being consumed.

Fig. 5.   This view is a screenshot of the arena specifically designed for the preliminary experiment. The entity in the center of the image is a prey creature.

3.3   Single Prey vs. Single Predator

The main goal is to test the conflicting goals of getting food and fleeing a predator. The prey is controlled by a computer while the predator is controlled by a human.

The food is placed as shown on figure 6. The arena is composed of one prey and one predator.

First the prey is attracted by the food while the predator doesn't move. The prey gets the food and the predator starts to chase the prey. The predator blocks the prey against the north wall (right to its starting position) but the prey finally escapes to the east and is followed by the predator. The predator stands next to the food while the prey stays in the south west corner. The chase continues. The predator is in the south west corner while the prey get next the predator starting position. Finally the predator reaches there on the right while the prey flees to the south west next to the food position.

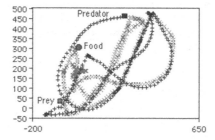

Fig. 6. This graph shows trajectories of both the prey and the predator for a single run. Numbers beside axes represent the x and y values corresponding to the location in the arena.

Figure 7 shows two diagrams depicting the excitation of each action of the prey during the course. Actions are grouped by conflicting ones. The first illustrates the actions that have an influence on the direction and the second on the speed. They represent the summary of the creature's reactive decision scheme. The excitation is the result of the computation of all sensors and attributes. These diagrams reproduce the prey's trajectory by applying the different most excited actions effects for each time step.

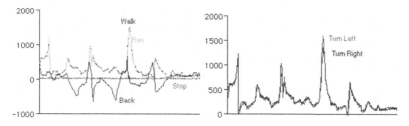

Fig. 7. Diagrams of the actions time series for the prey in a run with a predator in the arena.

The turn actions have quite similar excitations. This is due to the step angle used (15 degrees). The incidence between turning right or turning left is relatively small and so is the difference between excitations. For the speed actions it is the same. *Run* and *walk* are quite similar so are the excitations. *Stop* is not stimulated, except by the *Bum* function which provides a low randomized excitation. *Back* is different because it is almost like a U-turn. In the same way, the excitation of the *turn* actions and *walk/run* actions are similar. The slight difference is enough to allow the creature to choose the right action.

3.4   Metabolism's Influence

This experiment illustrates the role played by the metabolism's attributes (*hungriness* and *tiredness*) during the process of action selection.
Attributes weight the different functions by their value. This makes a function more or less suitable for the creature depending on its internal state.
The first attribute, *hungriness*, is cyclic, and decreases only when food is eaten. The first graph shows its evolution during a single run.

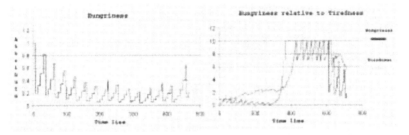

Fig. 8.   Evolution of *hungriness* during two experiments of 500 seconds.

Notice that the different collapses correspond to times when the creature eats. While the general look of this attribute corresponds to the cyclic process.
The second attribute, *tiredness*, is more complex. Its value is cyclic and depends on external factors (movements made so far), but also on another attribute : *hungriness*.
Regarding the second graph, it is significant that *hungriness* is an important factor. Successive collapses correspond to cycles that the creature spent to rest.
These attributes represent the role of the metabolism in action selection process. They are used as weights for functions, and thus are taken into account. Actions may modify them directly (as feeding or resting) or indirectly (as bumming to look for food).

3.5   Multiple Preys vs. Single Predator

The goal of this experiment was to study the interaction of creatures in a multiple prey facing a single predator. The group of preys can show flocking behaviors using the Reynolds rules [2]. Thus the prey has two more primary reactive functions, corresponding to the rules established by Reynolds : getting nearer the center of the group, aligning your speed on the speed of the group. The third rule (avoid others) is already implemented.

Fig. 9.   Three flocking creatures in grouping mode.

The *avoid* function invalidates actuators that make the creature move closer to the entity. The *center* function orientates the creature toward each entity of the same species. This results in the activation of the actuator that makes the creature the most closer to the center of the herd. The *speed* function orientates the creature to align it with each new entity of the same species. This function regulates also the speed of the creature in the same manner, matching the speed of each new entity of the same species.

During the experiments conducted we notice interesting behaviors :

- Even with one-entity-functions (each function takes only one entity into account for each evaluation), the correct flocking behavior emerges, due to actuator selection. This selection processes a kind of mean for all entities perceived during the cycle.
- If the *speed* function priority is too low, the creatures try to gather, but then turn around staying in the same area. Inversely if the *center* function priority is too low, the creatures do not gather but follow parallel paths. This is because both the *center* function and the *speed* function modify the direction of the creature. They are competitive and then must have similar priorities.
- Due to the small size of the arena, the primary functions (feeding, fleeing) tended to overpass the flocking functions. To show correct behavior, we introduce a minimal distance for feeding and fleeing functions. While out of the predator's range, the creatures evolve in concert, but when the predator approaches too closely they flee away from him and regroup further.

4   Discussion

The previous results show that the preliminary experiments were an important phase before dealing with more complex creature models and the implementation of the coevolution scheme. As a result of this preliminary phase, we can state that it allowed us to validate our approach and architecture.

Besides this validation, the preliminary experiments were conducted in order to learn more about the technological constraints of such a project. Most of previous works in Artificial Life have focused on evolving simple "block creatures" from random genetic codes, with non real-time rendering. One of the well known studies in this framework was done by Karl Sims on the evolution of 3D morphology and behavior by competition [7]. In contrast Nut is designed to run on a personal computer using a dedicated 3D engine. It enables to display in real-time virtual spaces inhabited by evolved digital creatures. The main constraint, real time processing, oriented all our work towards efficiency. This is why we favored connectionist methods rather than symbolic oriented ones. Our *functions* and *sensors* are simple mathematical entities, and the overall "intelligence" is only limited by their organization and number.

The real time constraint impacts also on the *sensors*. The determination of what is sensed by a localized creature and what is not, is a complex process which has been well studied by 3D game designers. But until now, this work has been only done for the main character. Computing these data for each creature requires a large amount of computing time. We had to pay attention to the environment design, and to implement some very efficient filters to eliminate unsensed data (issued from games design techniques). The real interest of these data is an important question. As an example, in the works done by Blumberg[6] the virtual creature (a dog) directly sensed energy of its environment and activates its actuators in response. It should have been more complex to sense geometry data (issued from game engine) and build a mental construct of the environment. A lot of the work is done before the cognitive process.

The behaviors showed in this paper are quite simple. *Functions* are still autonomous and can not yet influence each other as it is done in [6]. This is an important step to simulate more complex behaviors. *Functions* could be then organized as sets, each dedicated to a specific kind of tasks (moving tasks, memory tasks, feeding tasks etc.), thus enabling to design a hierarchy as in [6].

5   Conclusion and Future Works

In this paper, we have presented preliminary experiments made at the IIMLab that clearly establish the feasibility of integrating state-of-the-art Artificial Life techniques with real-time 3D graphical engines in the framework of the next generation of immersive 3D games. It has introduced the Nut virtual environment and architecture. Then, it has described our preliminary experiments and has given its first results in term of architecture validation and technological constraints for future game design. These experiments provide us with a more precise and modular conception. This lets us imagine that it is possible to build basic components that could be used to design digital creatures and their behaviors.

We can sum up the main technologies which appear to be central in the design of our environment. Modularity was our main concern and was obtained using object-oriented event driven programming. The 3D rendering engine needs improvements, it handles only sprites for creatures. For the next experiments (concerning motor control) we will need also a more realistic dynamic engine, and to improve the current behavioral model.

The next phase of the project will focus on motor control problem. We have to integrate a dynamic engine in Nut. The creature will then be able to sense physical stimuli. Then we have to extend the behavioral model (influence between *functions*) and to develop a structure, able to control the actuators correctly. The second phase will focus on more cognitive capabilities as emotions [8], memory, environment representation and communication.

6   Acknowledgements

We wish to acknowledge the students of the IIM school for their help in designing the Nut Virtual Environment, especially Gregory Champoux and Dominique Bossu, and also to thank Xuân Nga Cao for her reading.

7   References

1. Cyberlife: *Creatures*. Technical notes, Cyberlife Technology Ltd, 1996
2. Reynolds, C.W.: Flocks, Herds, and Schools : a Distributed Behaviorial Model. Proceedings of SIGGRAPH 87 (Anaheim, CA, July 27-31, 1987). In Computer Graphics 21, 4, July 1987, 25-34
3. Langton, C.G.: Artificial Life. In *Artificial Life*, edited by C.G. Langton, SFI Studies in the Sciences of Complexity, Addison-Wesley, Reading (MA), **6**, 1, 1988
4. Goldberg, D.E.: *Genetic Algorithms in Search, Optimization and Machine Learning*, Addison-Wesley, Reading (MA), 1989
5. Koza, J.R.: 1992, *Genetic Programming – On the Programming of Computers by Means of Natural Selection*, MIT Press, Cambridge (MA), 1992
6. Blumberg B.M.: Action-Selection in Hamsterdam : Lessons from Ethology. In *Third International Conference on the Simulation of Adaptive Behavior*, MIT Press, Brighton, 1994
7. Harvey, I.: Evolutionary Robotics and SAGA: The Case for Hill Crawling and Tournament Selection. In *Artificial Life III*, edited by C.G. Langton, SFI Studies in the Sciences of Complexity, Addison-Wesley, Reading (MA), **17**, 299, 1994
8. Loyall A.B., Bates J.: HAP : A Reactive Adaptive Architecture for Agents. Technical Report CMU-CS-91-147, School of Computer Science, Carnegie Mellon University, Pittsburgh, PA, June 1991
9. Oppenheimer, P.: The Artificial Menagerie. In *Artificial Life*, edited by C.G. Langton, SFI Studies in the Sciences of Complexity, Addison-Wesley, Reading (MA), **6**, 251, 1988
10. Brooks, R.: Challenges for Complete Creature Architectures. *From Animals to Animats*, edited by J.A. Meyer and S.W. Wilson, MIT Press, Cambridge (MA), 1991
11. Heudin, J.C.: *La Vie Artificielle*. Editions Hermès, Paris, 1994
12. Heudin, J.C.: *Virtual Worlds* in Virtual Worlds Synthetic Universes, Digital Life, and Complexity, edited by J.C. Heudin, Perseus Books, Reading (MA), 1998, 16-22

A Framework to Dynamically Manage Distributed Virtual Environments

Yoann Fabre, Guillaume Pitel, Laurent Soubrevilla, Emmanuel Marchand,
Thierry Géraud, and Akim Demaille

EPITA Research and Development Laboratory, 14-16 rue Voltaire,
F-94276 Le Kremlin-Bicêtre cedex, France,
thierry.geraud@epita.fr,
http://www.lrde.epita.fr/

Abstract. In this paper, we present the project URBI ET ORBI, a framework to dynamically manage distributed virtual environments (DVEs). This framework relies on a dedicated scripting language, *Goal*, which is typed, object-oriented and dynamically bound. *Goal* is interpreted by the application hosted by each machine and is designed to handle efficiently both network communications and interactivity. Finally, we have made an unusual design decision: our project is based on a functional programming language, *Objective Caml*.

1   Introduction

This paper presents the current state of the URBI ET ORBI project, a framework to dynamically manage distributed environments, whose principle applications are virtual worlds. Virtual worlds are virtual 3D scenes inhabited with common objects (houses, trees, etc.) and avatars, in which one may walk around and interact. In addition, this virtual world is *distributed*: its full description is spread over several computers, connected via a network. There is no need for a single host to have full knowledge of the world.

As Das *et al.* (1997), we focus on virtual worlds for a large audience, therefore there are no other material requirements than a standard personal machine, with a connection to a local network or the Internet. Windows and UNIX platforms are supported. Scalability is required.

Compared to related projects the main characteristics of URBI ET ORBI are:

- **full distribution.** To support large scale environments, no host can be privileged. Therefore, we exclude the client/server paradigm; each machine hosts the same application and data is fully distributed.
- **mostly asynchronous.** Because there is no guarantee of network responsiveness, because the core of a DVE is essentially dealing with non deterministic events, all the communications in our implementation are asynchronous, including data management within each local application.

J.-C. Heudin (Ed.): VW 2000, LNAI 1834, pp. 54–64, 2000.

- **data management.** While developing our own virtual world we felt the need to supply the objects with rich semantics (type, behavior, etc.) in addition to the usual geometric descriptions. Therefore we developed a language, *Goal*, to describe the objects and their behavior including their distribution policy.
- **functional ground.** Finally, the whole architecture, from the distribution engine to the *Goal* interpreter, is implemented in a functional programming language, *Objective Caml*.

This paper is structured as follows. In section 2, we give an overview of our framework. We expose the way the information is structured and distributed. In section 3, we present the language *Goal*. We explain how it satisfies our requirements concerning the data structure; we point out its relationship to our distributed system, and we describe the software architecture in which the *Goal* interpreter plays a key role. Finally, section 4, presents our conclusion and future work.

2   Overview of the Framework

A very popular way of building virtual worlds is to use the VRML language; a working group has specified an architecture for multi-user distributed VRML worlds, *Living Worlds*, which has already been implemented by Wray and Hawkes (1998). Another way is to reuse a dedicated language like NPSOFF by Zyda (1993). Unfortunately, both solutions do not meet our requirements: we want extra object attributes without geometric semantics, we want complex relations between objects, and we want a strong control on object distribution.

2.1   Structure of the Information

We want to describe virtual worlds with rich semantics: forests are composed of trees, of which there are several types, an object such as a house has an inside and an outside, etc. We also want to avoid the *3D bias*: virtual worlds should be thought of as an abstract idea. Hence, thanks to a text terminal it should be possible for the user to walk around and interact with the world *textually*. With our approach, the world has enough semantics for a terminal to represent it faithfully, whatever its nature: textual, 3D rendering, etc. Currently, we have a textual terminal, which is actually a shell to the *Goal* interpreter, and a 3D rendering engine that uses an *OpenGL* display.

Another benefit of rich descriptions of scenes is that a lot of extra optimizations can be performed, for instance related to the distance. Imagine a forest far off on the horizon: there is no need to compute the graphic rendering of every single tree, since it will most probably result in a green spot. The traditional answer is level of details (*lods* for short) generated by mesh simplification: objects present different lods according to the distance from the observer. Here, using

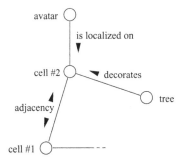

Fig. 1. Part of a conceptual graph.

a richer semantics, such as the variety of the trees and some of their characteristics, we may provide different views, ranging from the green spot to the fully detailed rendering, through approximations based on functions depending upon the nature of the trees and their spatial disposition, etc. The nature of the flat green spot is very different from the fully detailed description of the forest. Our "levels of details" not only imply a quantitative change of the semantics of the objects, but also a qualitative change. And again, since the observer may not have a 3D rendering engine, the type of the object, here "forest", can be used to deduce the fact we don't need to request further details.

The natural implementation of values with specific semantics leads to the typing of values, more specifically, to the typing of the objects and their attributes of our worlds. It is well-known in compilation that the more you know about the semantics of the objects (which means the richer your typing system is) the more opportunities the system has to perform optimizations.

We need a flexible type system which allows us to define families of objects with different attributes, hence we need classes. We want to be able to specialize some concepts, so we want inheritance.

In addition to the nature of the objects of the world, we also need relations between them. Of course, we need relations such as "is on" or "is adjacent to" but we also need non-spatial relations such as "is composed of" or "activates". We are therefore naturally led to the notion of *conceptual graphs*. Again, such relations should be typed, which simply means that attributes, or slots, of our objects must be typed.

Figure 1 illustrates a partial view of the world's state: there are two geometrical cells, i.e. regions or zones of the world, a tree decorating cell 2 and an avatar somewhere in this cell. Yet in this simple example, there are three different relations involved: the link between the two cells stating that we may reach one from the other, the oriented edge "is localized on" specifying the presence of the avatar on a cell, and finally "decorates" which is similar to the previous relation but slightly different. "decorates" gives additional information: the tree

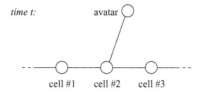

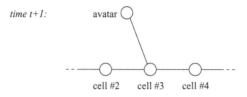

Fig. 2. Global graph modification and local evolution.

is unessential and can be passed over at first approximation (for instance because some more urgent updates need to be performed).

Because the world changes, the graph is constantly modified. The updates must be reflected in each local partial view of the world. They must be distributed.

The prototypal example of a graph incremental update is when an avatar moves and changes cell. Figure 2 shows such an example. The machine hosting the avatar has then to inform the world (namely the users seeing these cells) of the moves, to fetch needed information such as cell 4 and to flush useless information such as cell 1. There are two operations: the graph of the world is changing and the local graph of each host is evolving.

Please note that this approach is fully compatible with current solutions to reduce the volume of information flow: a hierarchical description of the world as proposed by Sugano *et al.* (1997) and/or an aura management as proposed by Hagsand and Stenius (1997) or by Hesina and Schmalstieg (1998). The nature of the data can depend on the scale on which the graph is consulted; the world must be also represented by a multi-scale graph.

2.2   Distribution Management

Our aim in the design of URBI ET ORBI is to provide a completely distributed environment. This approach is similar to the ones of Frécon and Stenius (1998) in DIVE, and of Greenhalgh and Benford (1995) in MASSIVE. It contrasts with client-server architectures.

In order to reduce the amount of network communication, we have preferred, like Tramberend (1999), group communication to multicast and broadcast solutions. Group communication is a way of implementing the notion of aura in

DVEs, and allows us to define various groups equipped with different quality of service. To this end, we rely on *Ensemble* [1], a group communication toolkit developed at Cornell University by Hayden *et al.* (1998):

> "For a distributed systems researcher, Ensemble is a highly modular and reconfigurable toolkit. The high-level protocols provided to applications are really stacks of tiny protocol layers. These protocol layers each implement several simple properties: they are composed to provide sets of high-level properties, such as total ordering, security, virtual synchrony, etc. Individual layers can be modified or rebuilt to experiment with new properties or change the performance characteristics of the system. This makes Ensemble a very flexible platform on which to do research."

As mentioned by Macedonia and Zyda (1997), system requirements such as strong data consistency, strict causality, very reliable communications and real-time interaction imply tough penalties on scalability. Consequently we decided to relax these requirements and to rely on different qualities of services provided by *Ensemble*. In particular, it is easily feasible with *Ensemble* to test distribution models like, for instance, the one proposed by Ryan and Sharkey (1998). We also observe that combining group communication with asynchronous and partially reliable transfer protocols results in low-cost and efficient data exchange mechanisms.

When a user enters the world, she first joins a spatial group and some other user within this group is elected to inform the newcomer of the current state of the world, more specifically of the current state of the view of world pertinent to the newcomer. An economic consistency of the knowledge is obtained thanks to different policies on the distribution of the messages. For instance, elections are made with an extreme care, some actions require a causal ordering, and finally some unimportant tasks are just multicast with almost no quality of service. Furthermore, the possibility of choosing the protocol is a means to control the load imposed on the network: urgent messages which must be delivered safely obtain most of the bandwidth at a given time, while messages of little importance may be delayed or even lost.

Note finally that the notion of group also helps in the design of the virtual world, since they constrain the programmer to structure its description and to partition it properly.

3   The Language *Goal*

Our requirements pertaining to the structure of the information and to the distribution system drove us to build a new language. The additional requirement that world management must be programmer-friendly naturally led to the concept of a scripting language: *Goal*. "High level" *Goal* is used between the user

---

[1] http://www.cs.cornell.edu/Info/Projects/Ensemble

and the environment to describe and modify the world, whereas "low level" *Goal* is exchanged between the machines through the network and between the different modules which constitute the user application.

3.1   Features of *Goal*

Strongly typed. When *Goal* instructions are introduced in the environment, the *Goal* interpreter checks for errors before executing them and modifying the environment. The strong typing policy is a fundamental help in developing the complex features of the project, leading to safer code.

Frame-oriented. *Goal* is a frame language implementing the concept of class and inheritance. Since *Goal* is strongly typed the notion of conceptual graph (Cf. section 2.1) is implicitly supported by objects containing references to other objects. Each slot of the objects may be equipped with a daemon, i.e., a routine triggered when its slot is modified. Here, objects help modularize world descriptions and daemons help divide the tasks: when values are updated, there are usually a collection of actions to take, but some of them imply a global side-effect for several users spread over the network while others are purely local.

Distribution/replication-oriented. In a distributed environment, objects are usually replicated over the network and, when a user acts on such objects, a *Goal* routine is executed which may contain code for sending messages to distant replicates. Furthermore, objects can belong to several groups, which implies that objects' behavior at run-time may use several communication channels. Group communication (Cf. section 2.2) should be a primitive of the environment provided to the programmer. *Goal* provides a high level interface to *Ensemble*.

Dynamic. *Goal* has been designed to make the virtual environment evolve. It allows to dynamically insert objects in the environment as easily as a web page is published on the Internet. Similarly, a new class can be defined by a user and loaded dynamically in the environment while running; this new class can then be accessed by another programmer and reused.

Reflectivity. All *Goal* entities can be introspected. With a class name, we can know the list of its attributes and methods; with a given object, we can get the name of its class and the values of its attributes.

Efficiency. Although *Goal* is an interpreted language, we have a very efficient virtual machine, built on the top of the one of *Objective Caml*, a strongly-typed functional programming language from the ML family; see Leroy, Rémy *et al.* (1999) for a description of this language.

3.2   Interpretation and *Objective Caml*

Scripting languages have proven to be extremely useful both for extensions of the system and for programmer interface (e.g. shell scripts, TCL, etc.) The fact that scripting languages are interpreted is part of their success: they ensure very easy prototyping, dynamic extensions and modifications (no need to recompile and reinstall the software, which is ideal for distributed systems) and an extreme comfort for the programmer thanks to the interaction with the interpreter.

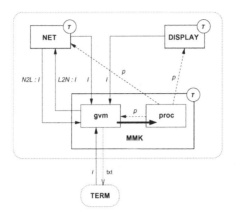

Fig. 3. Software architecture.

The interpreted nature of *Goal*, together with the ease of extension, made it possible to have different types of terminals: obviously, a 3D terminal in charge of rendering the *OpenGL* information, but also a text terminal which is able to listen to the world, change it, control it, etc. Other kinds of terminals will be easy to develop; in particular, inferfaces with VR devices such as datagloves or head mounted displays. Please note that *Objective Caml* can be easily interfaced with other languages; for instance, the 3D rendering in URBI ET ORBI is performed in C code.

The functional paradigm has proven to be suitable to implement most of the transformations we apply on the distributed data, helping us to isolate the areas where imperative instructions are truly needed. The development environment is also attractive: thanks to the ability to mix compiled and interpreted code it is fairly easy to observe the behavior at run-time. Finally, the performance of the compiled executable outperforms *Java*.

In addition, since our project is based on *Objective Caml*, *Ensemble*, also based on *Objective Caml*, appeared as an attractive choice for the distribution layer.

3.3   Overview of the Software Architecture

A major issue in DVEs design is to ensure that network communication does not degrade the interactivity between the machine and the user.

With this aim in view, our application is composed of three active modules, depicted by a bold rectangle in figure 3. Each module is responsible for an independent task, and offers particular services.

MMk (or kernel) is the core of our software; it receives a flow of instructions, schedules their execution and manages the resources (files, memory, display and communication). MMK includes the Goal Virtual Machine (GVM for short) to process *Goal* instructions.

NET is in charge of the communications through the network; it handles the connection/disconnection and information transfer. This module can be seen as a layer over *Ensemble*.

DISPLAY (or renderer, or navigator) provides the user with "read" access to the state of the world as known by MMK, and with "write" access: when a user moves or activates an element of the world, the display sends information to MMK. For sake of simplicity the data circuit is not represented in figure 3 and it will not be discussed touch.

Each task runs in a separate *thread* (symbolized by the letter T in figure 3). *Goal* is expressive enough for programmers to introduce bugs in their programs, such as deadlocks. However, the implementation, based on time slots, still guarantees that the system is fair: each task will be provided with the ability to make a step.

In figure 3, the arrows represent *channels*, i.e., queues of messages/requests, and not function calls. When a *Goal* instruction requires services (network, display etc.), the interpreter delegates the procedure call to the module proc. proc then sends the *procedure p* to the proper module. Technically, *p* is a closure: it contains both the procedure and the environment it needs. Then the module applies the closure: once the whole environment is filled, the procedure is executed. The receiving module is not blocked while awaiting further data: it still executes other routines. This mechanism could be considered as an *asynchronous execution transfer*.

The TERMinal is also represented; it is a shell (command interpreter) which allows direct textual communication with MMK, via *Goal* instructions.

Several other projects have based their approach upon a kernel, such as MAVERIK by Hubbold *et al.* (1996). One of the most striking differences between the two projects lies in the fact that their approach is based upon modules, while we stress the importance of the high level language, *Goal*. A detailed description of our architecture is given by Fabre *et al.* (2000).

3.4   Example

A sample file containing few *Goal* instructions is given in figure 4. It defines the interactive windmill depicted in the virtual landscape of figure 5.

The symbol @ indicates that the instruction is only sent to the local virtual machine (alternatives are . and ! to broadcast the instruction to the members of the communication group, respectively including and excluding the local machine). Lines 1 to 4 define the mill, lines 5 to 8 the sails, and lines 9 to 13 a rotator to make the sails turn and to manage their speed.

Goal provides distribution primitives. Distributing data is the major challenge in large distributed worlds: ideally, any data that has to be shared or

```
// file windmill.goal
@mill_shape = New Shape;                    //  1
@mill_shape <- Set file3DS = "mill.3ds";    //  2
@mill = New 3DGridObject;                    //  3
@mill <- Set shape = shape_mill;             //  4
@sails_shape = New Shape;                     //  5
@sails_shape <- Set file3DS = "sails.3ds"; //  6
@sails = New 3DGridObject;                    //  7
@sails <- Set shape = sails_shape;           //  8
@rotator = New Rotator;                       //  9
@rotator <- Set target = sails;              // 10
@rotator <- Set delay = 0.02;                // 11
@listener = New RotatorListener;             // 12
@listener <- Set eventTarget = sails;        // 13
```

Fig. 4. Code sample.

transmitted between hosts should be distributed. But, in order to perform an efficient distribution of the data we first have to classify it.

Oversized objects, e.g. textures or classical 3D models (like the mill in the example of the previous section), are considered as part of a standard library that members must have available on their hosts (maybe via standard point-to-point file transport protocols). Since we aim at large distributed systems (several hundreds or thousands of participants), it is unreasonable to distribute such huge constant values to each newcomer.

All other values are truly distributed values, that is created somewhere and then propagated via the network. Nevertheless, for the sake of the bandwidth economy, the remaining data is classified per priority. A high priority data is more likely to be updated than low priority data. The priority of the various attributes/objects is specified as part of their type: it is therefore completely and cleanly integrated into *Goal* and handled seamlessly by the VE application. For instance, a **3DGridObject** is an object that decorates a grid cell; its priority is medium.

Without entering the gory details, we also noted that shared values have a completely distinct status from replicated values. In particular, it is forbidden in *Goal* to set a shared value: one has to ask the object containing this value to perform that task. Then, the usual daemon mechanism is launched. This simple limitation, voluntarily introduced in *Goal*, appeared to save the VR-programmers from many errors, leading them to question the status (replicated or shared) of their values in a distributed world: there is a natural tendency to use parsimony. In the example, the sails of the windmill have a fully predictable behavior (they turn!) and frequent updates of their position would waste the bandwidth. So, the *replication* is a natural solution, and each host has a local timer.

Fig. 5. A virtual landscape with a windmill.

4 Conclusion and Criticism

We have presented our project URBI ET ORBI, its motivations, the rationale for unusual design decisions. Specifically, we have detailed why we think that the *ad hoc* language that we have developed, *Goal*, is suitable to describe large and complex interactive virtual worlds. *Goal* is the natural high level interface to a distribution kernel, the MMK, which makes heavy use of *Ensemble* in order to ensure the coherence of the partial views each host has of the world.

The architecture of URBI ET ORBI is designed to face such difficulties while ensuring real-time rendering. Conceptors of worlds can then take care over the graphical aspect. To get immersive capabilities with URBI ET ORBI, the end-user can today buy cheap commercial 3D glasses which rely on *OpenGL* to produce 3D sensations. Our experiments were limited to a fast LAN (Ethernet 100MB) with PC equipped with 3D video cards: we typically reach 25 frames per seconds with high quality images (see figure 5) and excellent interactivity.

A key aspect of our projet is the intensive use of the functional language *Objective Caml*, which allows the developers to leverage powerful language support to attain high performance and flexibility. URBI ET ORBI differs from other systems in that it is mostly scripted. The advantage is twofold. This feature addresses the real need of being able to develop components that may be dynamically inserted into a distributed virtual environment, and it also allows to dynamically adjust the configuration of the environment.

Many tasks remain to be fulfilled. The priority management has not yet been implemented; the number of groups, their nature and qualities of services have not been completely established. These elements should be fixed in our current re-engineering of the prototype. Tests have only been carried out on a high speed local network; a full scale test, with an environment spread over large distances, still have to be performed. Nevertheless, the prototype behaves in a very satisfactory manner.

References

[1997]Das, T.K., Singh, G., Mitchell, A., Kumar, P.S., McGee, K.: Developing Social Virtual Environments using NetEffect. In Proceedings of the 6th IEEE Workshops on Enabling Technologies: Infrastructures for Collaborative Enterprises, IEEE Computer Society Press. (1997) 148–154

[2000]Fabre, Y., Pitel, G., Soubrevilla, L., Marchand, E., Géraud, T., Demaille, A.: An Asynchronous Architecture to Manage Communication, Display, and User Interaction in Distributed Virtual Environments. Submitted to the 6th Eurographics Workshop on Virtual Environments, Amsterdam, The Netherlands. (2000)

[1998]Frécon, E., Stenius, M.: DIVE: A Scaleable Network Architecture for Distributed Virtual Environments. Distributed Systems Engineering Journal (special issue on Distributed Virtual Environments). **5(3)** (1998) 91–100

[1995]Greenhalgh, C., Benford, S.: MASSIVE: a Distributed Virtual Reality System Incorporating Spatial Trading. In Proceedings of the 15th International Conference on Distributed Computing Systems, IEEE Computer Society Press, Vancouver, Canada. (1995) 27–34

[1997]Hagsand, O., Stenius, M.: Using Spatial Techniques to Decrease Message Passing in a Distributed VE System. In VRML'97.

[1998]Hayden, M.: The Ensemble System. Technical Report TR98-1662, Cornell University. http://cs-tr.cs.cornell.edu/Dienst/UI/1.0/Display/ncstrl.cornell/TR98-1662 (1998)

[1998]Hesina, G., Schmalstieg, D.: A Network Architecture for Remote Rendering. In Proceedings of the 2nd International Workshop on Distributed Interactive Simulation and Real Time Applications (DIS-RT'98), Montreal, Canada. (1998) 88–91

[1996]Hubbold, R., Dongbo, X., Gibson, S.: MAVERIK – The Manchester Virtual Environment Interface Kernel. In Proceedings of the 3rd Eurographics Workshop on Virtual Environments. (1996)

[1999]Leroy, X., Rémy, D., Vouillon, J., Doligez, D.: The Objective Caml system. Manual Report, INRIA, Rocquencourt, France. http://caml.inria.fr/index-eng.html (1999)

[1997]Macedonia, M.R., Zyda, M.J.: A Taxonomy for Networked Virtual Environments. IEEE MultiMedia. **4(1)** (1997) 48–56

[1998]Ryan, M.D., Sharkey, P.M.: Distortion in Distributed Virtual Environment. In Proceedings of the 1st International Conference on Virtual Worlds. Paris, France. (1998) 42–48

[1997]Sugano H., Otani, K., Ueda, H., Hiraiwa, S., Endo, S., Kohda, Y.: SpaceFusion: A Multi-Server Architecture For Shared Virtual Environments. In VRML'97.

[1999]Tramberend, H.: Avocado: A distributed Virtual Reality Framework. In Proceedings of the IEEE Virtual Reality International Conference, Houston, USA. (1999)

[1997]VRML'97: Proceedings of the 2nd International Conference on the Virtual Reality Modeling Language. (1997)

[1998]Wray, M., Hawkes, R.: Distributed Virtual Environments and VRML: an Event-Based Architecture. Computer Networks and ISDN systems. **30** (1998) 43–51

[1993]Zyda, M.J., Wilson, K.P., Pratt, D.R., Monahan, J.G., Falby, J.S.: NPSOFF: An Object Description Language for Supporting Virtual Worlds Construction. Computer and Graphics. **17(4)** (1993) 457–464

Using GASP for Collaborative Interaction within 3D Virtual Worlds

Thierry Duval and David Margery

IRISA — SIAMES project,
Campus de Beaulieu, F-35042 Rennes cedex
{Thierry.Duval, David.Margery}@irisa.fr

Abstract In this paper, we present GASP, a General Animation and Simulation Platform, whose purpose is to animate autonomous or user-driven agents, and we explain how it can be used for Collaborative Virtual Reality. First, we explain its architecture, based on the notion of simulation objects (or agents) associated with a calculation part (the behavior). Then we describe how it is possible to distribute efficiently our agents upon a network in order to share the amount of calculation between several computers. Finally, as the visualization of a simulation is also a simulation object, we show that our architecture allows us to distribute several visualizations upon a network to share a 3D interactive simulation between several users.

1 Introduction

The construction of 3D virtual worlds full of intelligent or human-driven entities (or agents) may be a very complex task, which requires many complementary skills, such as 3D graphic programming for the visualization, artificial intelligence knowledge for the entities' behavior, network programming in order either to distribute the computational weight, or to share the virtual worlds between several users, and software engineering for the global architecture of the system.

In order to reduce the complexity of the task, we believe that a framework should be provided to specialists of behavioral animation so that they can concentrate on the programming of the entities to be included in the virtual world. A run-time platform dealing with the other problems (3D visualization, interaction and network distribution of the entities) should be associated with that framework. GASP is our attempt to achieve this goal.

The framework presents itself as basic classes a programmer has to reuse by inheritance to write his virtual world entities. Then, using a configuration file, he can decide to deploy these entities upon a network of workstations, and optionally act upon them using several interactive visualizations located on different workstations. The associated platform uses this configuration file to start the virtual world and ensure proper scheduling of the different entities as well as all the distributed aspects of the simulation and synchronization.

With the associated platform, it is possible to distribute calculations to animate a complex virtual world and, at the same time, to distribute interactive

J.-C. Heudin (Ed.): VW 2000, LNAI 1834, pp. 65–76, 2000.

visualizations to interact with this world on a collaborative base. Within our framework, the same platform is used for both aspects. This contrasts with most of the work in the distributed virtual reality field which concentrates on collaboration (DIVE [1], MASSIVE [2], Community Place [3] or ARéVi [4]). This enables us to populate the world with more entities with complex behaviors than it would have been possible with frameworks where the only computing power available is the one available on the different users' workstations.

Our main concern in the conception of our platform is performance of interactive virtual worlds at run-time, unlike ARéVi [5] which addresses prototyping of virtual worlds during conception phase.

This paper is organized in the following way. First, we describe the framework provided and the associated concepts for distribution. We then talk about the way the platform distributes entities and visualizations over the network, in order to share the calculation weight of the simulation between several workstations and the interactions between several end-users. Finally, we talk about its technical aspects and possible improvements.

2   GASP Framework Overview: The Entities

The GASP [6] framework is an object oriented development environment allowing real-time simulation and visualization of complex systems.

2.1   A Simulation: A Set of Entities with Different Frequencies

Each entity in the system is composed of one or more simulation objects. These simulation objects are composed of a set of named outputs, inputs and control parameters which constitute the public interface of the entity and of a calculus which is in charge of their evolution. This evolution happens at the frequency associated with each object or family of objects. Indeed, each simulation object may need its own frequency. For example a mechanical model of a car will need a 50 Hertz frequency to obtain a realistic mechanical simulation, but a behavioral model such as a car driver may only need a 5 Hertz frequency to simulate human behavior. We believe this aspect is important for virtual worlds populated with entities (in our example a car entity) made out of components of different nature and is to our mind one of the main differences between GASP and other distributed environments. Indeed, this enables a modular approach to building complex entities.

At each simulation step of an object, the calculus part will read the inputs it needs and calculate new outputs and a new private state for the object. Inputs can be connected to outputs of other objects at different stages in the simulation by either naming the objects to connect to or asking the controller for an object of the correct class. In other words, the evolution of a simulation object can be function of the entity's changing environment. Figure 1 shows a typical exchange between two simulation objects in the same simulation process: for each calculation, the CB object will ask its input for a new position value, maybe

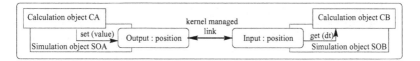

Fig.1. Typical exchange between two simulation objects in the same process

in order to follow the SOA simulation object. The kernel is in charge of ensuring that the value provided to the object is coherent with the value from the output. In the current implementation of GASP, this is done by fetching the value, but this could change without affecting the programming framework.

Due to the different frequencies the simulation object may have, an object may be asking for a value at a date where no value was produced. Therefore, every output is automatically able to provide a value at any asked date. This value is either calculated (by interpolation or extrapolation) or exact. Naturally, it is always possible for the asker to know if the answered value is an exact one or if it is a calculated one. In this last case, the system provides the difference between the date for which the value was asked and the date associated to the nearest (by mean of time) exact value produced by the calculation.

With such a mechanism, entities can ask for the value of other objects at the current simulated time. If the value has not yet been produced, an approximation will be calculated. This enables a modular approach, as simulated entities can be conceived without prior knowledge of their place in the simulation chain. This is quite different from traditional animation models such as those used in VRML [7] where the complete animation chain must be completely redesigned for each virtual world. This is of particular importance when cyclic dependencies are used which is the case in most multi-agent inhabited virtual worlds. For fine grained tuning, our simulation platform still enables VRML style coding, but we believe that for complex worlds, this is not a scalable approach.

2.2   The Distribution: Referentials and Mirrors

Our entities can be dispatched, at run time, across a network of heterogeneous workstations, in order to distribute the computational weight.

Each of the workstations will own one or several process making the calculations or watching some of the results produced by the global simulation.

Each process belonging to a simulation will own a particular simulation object: a controller, which schedules all the local simulation objects. This schedule is achieved by using several simulation frames, filled with references to the objects to simulate, according to their frequency.

So, within each process, there will be none, one or several "real entities": we call them "referentials", and none, one or several "ghost entities": we call them "mirrors", other people may call them "proxies" or "ghosts".

The presence of mirrors in a process is function of the inputs needed by the referentials of this process: if there is a referential B that needs for input the output of a referential **A** located within another process, then there will be a mirror of **A** within the process where **B** is located.

Mirrors are linked to their referentials with a data-stream connection: at each step of the simulation, a referential sends up to date values to all of its mirrors. Figure 2 shows a typical exchange between two simulation objects owned by two different simulation process: at each calculation step, a GASP mechanism of "pushing" will provide new output values to the **SOA** mirror, in order to enable the **SOB** referential to obtain its input value.

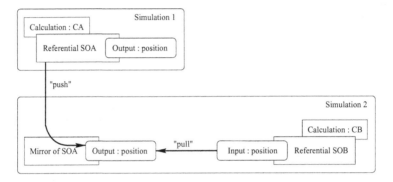

Fig.2. Typical exchange between two simulation objects in two different process

3   The Exchanges between Referentials and Mirrors

We are now going to explain the way referentials and mirrors communicate: this communication is valid because of the interpolation and extrapolation mechanisms we talked about in section 2.1. Thanks to them, we do not need a strong synchronization between our different processes.

3.1   The Exchanges Are Synchronous

The data-stream connection is a synchronous one.

Our aim is to ensure the realism of our virtual worlds in term of consistence between the referentials and their mirrors in the different process, in order to avoid the distortion caused by the network latency as presented in [8] for the interactions. The proposed solution of [8] consists in placing the object to interact with on the same workstation than the end-user involved in this interaction. It is not enough for us, because we need consistency between referentials and mirrors in a more general way for the realism of the entities behavior, and because several users may want to share an interaction with the same virtual object (interaction level 3.2 of [9]).

This consistence is achieved by updating the data of the mirrors at each simulation step. To enable high interactivity, this updating typically occurs 50 times a second. This means that we need a large bandwidth network, as the amount of data that will have to transit on the network will be very important. It also means we cannot adopt a wide area network dead-reckoning approach such as in NPS-NET [10] or ARévi[4]. GASP ensures that the mirrors will always be the more "up to date" possible, by slowing faster process to adjust to the frequency of the slower one. So GASP approach is synchronous: at t time, each mirror will always own the referential values of the t - (dt + latency) time, where dt is the simulated time between two simulation steps for the referential, and where latency is the simulated time messages spend on the network. This latency can be parameterized to optimize the synchronization (latency can be positioned equal to zero to obtain a perfect synchronization, even if it will slow the global simulation).

Thanks to these data stream connections between referentials and mirrors, a mirror can always instantaneously provide the best values available to the referentials interested in them, without neither having to wait for the data to come from its referential, nor having to ask the referential to provide a new value (as we could do using a CORBA mechanism) which cost could be at least twice the cost of the network latency.

3.2   The Controllers Look for Informations

We use a subscription mechanism to ensure the synchronization between all our controllers. During the initialization step of a simulation, each mirror will ask its controller to subscribe to its referential's controller.

So, a controller will know that it must receive informations from a set of other controllers, and at each step of simulation, it will look at the latest information from these controllers.

If a date associated to the last reception of information from a particular controller is too old, the controller will decide that newer informations from that controller are needed, and it will put that controller in the set of the controllers from which he absolutely must receive something before going on.

Then the controller will look at all the messages waiting for it from all the existing controllers (because some asynchronous informations such as events and messages may have been sent to it), and it will update the set of the controllers from which information is lacking, because it may have received some.

After that, if some informations from some controllers are still lacking, the controller will now wait for them, and only for them, then it will be able to go on the next simulation step.

3.3   Nearly Every Controller Subscribes to Another One

As process without mirrors could never have to wait for other controllers, their advance could become too important, so it would be problematic to dynamically add mirrors in such controllers, because this addition should then wait until other controllers have join them.

So, in order to slow down these controllers and then to synchronize them with the other ones in the same shared simulation, they subscribe to each controller owning a mirror of one of their referentials. In such a case, the only information they will be waiting for is the date of the latest simulation step of these other controllers.

This does not solve the problem of a controller who would only own referentials without any mirrors anywhere. But what would be the use of such simulation objects in a shared simulation ? Of course, it could allow for example to dynamically make separations between a controller (or a group of controllers) and the rest of the simulation, so with our communication paradigm, one group could take some important advance on another one. To avoid this, we could force each controller to subscribe to a global scheduler, which would provide clock tics, or we could provide a new paradigm for distributed objects to complete the referential/mirror paradigm.

Another problem is the asynchronous diffusion of events and messages: as they are asynchronous, a controller does not know when it will receive such informations, so, at this time, we can only offer the guarantee that the time messages and events will take to reach their targets will be at most (dt + latency), where dt is the time between two simulation steps for the receiver's controller.

4 Sharing 3D Virtual Worlds

Each entity can be associated to a geometry (a visual 3D representation), and entities can be a compound of other entities ; in such a case, the visualization of the compound entity results from the visualizations of its parts.

We provide a special simulation object called "Visualization" which is in charge of the graphical representation of the objects of a simulation. It also allows the end-user to take control of some of the simulation objects.

With this simulation object, we can then instantiate several visualization objects that can also be distributed upon the network on several workstations, not only in order to allow several people to see a graphical representation of the simulation, but also to allow these people to interact with the simulation, and therefore to cooperate in a shared 3D virtual world.

We have worked on a way to integrate interactors entities within visualizations, so that they could pilot the inputs of some simulations objects to benefit from our referential/mirror paradigm for synchronous interactions between several remote users of the same shared virtual environment. Now, it is possible to add interactors to simulation objects, so that these interactors can control the behavior of these objects, and then to share an interactive virtual world between several end-users. The way we do it is by dynamically adding some inputs to the simulation objects, and by linking these inputs to the outputs of some interactors. We use a generic way to achieve it nearly automatically, using the

C++ inheritance mechanism, so that as many simulation objects as possible can benefit from these interactors.

5   How to Use GASP

Here, we are going to make a short state of the art about how to use GASP to develop a simulation application and how to distribute it upon a network.

5.1   From the Simulation Object Point of View

The GASP controllers' main task is to create and then to schedule a set of simulation objects, asking each of them to evolve. These simulation objects are instances of C++ classes which inherit from the GASP PsObjetSimul class.

This class provides some virtual methods that its subclasses must redefine:

- PsCalcul * creerCalcul () ;
  creation of the associated calculation object, an instance of a subclass of the PsCalcul class.
- void initTableEntrees () ;
  declaration of the inputs.
- void initTableSorties () ;
  declaration of the outputs.
- void initTableParams () ;
  declaration of the control parameters.
- void traiterEvt () ;
  management of the asynchronous events and their associated messages coming from any object of the simulation.

Inputs, outputs and control parameters types can be provided by GASP (basic types such as integer, float, long integer, long float, string) or extended by some simulation object to obtain complex types such as 3D referentials or quaternions.

A simulation object evolves thanks to its PsCalcul associated object, which provides also some virtual methods that its subclasses must redefine:

- virtual void init () ;
  initialization of the internal data of the calculation object, this method enables the static connections between the inputs of its simulation object and the outputs of other objects.
- virtual void calculer () ;
  calculation of the new internal state and of the possible outputs of its simulation object from the previous internal state and from the values of the inputs of its simulation object.

5.2   From the Simulation Application Point of View

The main function of the simulation process must now be able to create new instances of the new classes that have been defined for the new simulation.

This is done by defining two methods of the `PsnControleur` class:
- `void initListeObjetsDerives () ;`
  responsible for the correspondence between the names (strings ...) read from
  the configuration file and the real simulation objects types.
- `PsObjetSimul * associerCode (int i) ;`
  responsible for the creation of the effective simulation objects types according
  to their type (represented here by an integer).

The name of the configuration file will then be provided to the main GASP
function on the command line. This file describes the types and the names of
the simulation objects initially in the simulation, their calculation frequency, and
the process responsible for their evolution.

This file describes also the association between process and workstations (a
workstation may "own" several process, a process can only be associated with
one workstation).

So, the distribution of the simulation objects is only decided at run time, and
can easily be changed, without needing any new compilation or binding.

5.3   From the Visualization Point of View

In order to be visualized by our visualization objects, a simulation object must
inherit from a particular subclass of `PsObjetSimul: PsGeoMeca`, and must be
associated with a geometrical file.

5.4   Example Use of GASP for a New Simulation

Design of the New Simulation Package Assuming that the scheduler provided by the GASP kernel is only able to schedule simulation objects associated
with a calculation object, the programmer of a new simulation object will have
to create new classes that will inherit from this two classes: `PsObjetSimul` and
`PsCalcul`, which are represented figure 3 by the `SO` and `C` classes provided by
the GASP API.

First, if this programmer does not need visualization, he can directly inherit
from these classes, as for the `SO4` class of the figure 3.

Then, if he needs to provide visualization or interaction for some of the new
simulation objects, he can create new classes that will inherit from the `PsgeoMeca`
class, represented figure 3 by the `SOIG` class (Simulation Object with an Interface
for Geometry) which provides an interface to act upon its geometrical representation in terms of position, orientation and scale: it is possible to act upon a
particular Performer DCS node associated to the geometry. That is the way the
`SOIG1` and `SOIG3` classes have been created here, and then can be associated
with some geometry.

Thanks to the classes provided by the GASP basic visualization (such like the
`SO'IG` class), it will then be possible:
- to visualize the geometries of the simulation objects,
- to see their dynamic evolution (modification of a Performer DCS node),
- to interact with these objects.

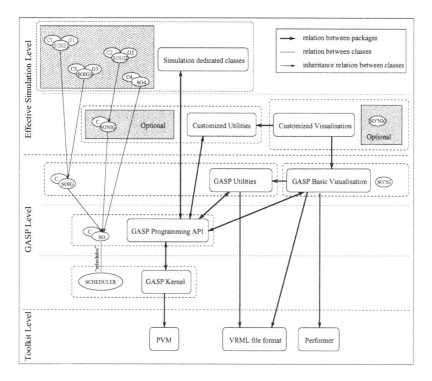

Fig.3. Example of a creation of a new simulation

If the programmer needs some new ways to visualize or to interact with the simulation objects, he will be allowed to create its own classes, by providing new interfaces to the geometries. This possibility is illustrated figure 3 by the SONIG class (Simulation Object with a New Interface for Geometry) of the customized utilities and the SO'NIG class of the customized visualization. For example, this new interface could allow to act upon a Performer color node associated with the geometry.

The Simulation at Run-Time If the simulation is a very simple one, that is to say that the configuration file places all the simulation objects in the same process, with no visualization, there will be only one simulation process, which scheduler will have to schedule all the simulation objects.

For example, figure 4 shows seven simulation objects, called A, B, C, D, E, F and G and a scheduler. As there is only one process, the simulation objects are referentials, that is why they are presented as rA, rB, rC, rD, rE, rF and rG.

In order to visualize this simulation and then to allow two end-users to cooperate with the simulation objects, the configuration file will need the declaration of two visualizations, upon two different process on two different workstations.

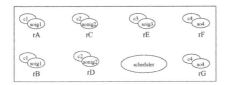

Fig.4. Run-time for a simple simulation

The result is shown figure 5: the two visualization process only own mirrors (with no calculation part), presented as mA, mB, mC, mD and mE, as the F and G objects do not own a geometry and then are not visible.

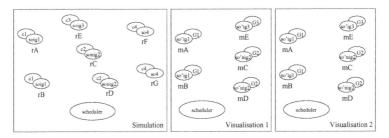

Fig.5. Run-time for a simple simulation with visualizations

Finally, this result can also be achieved by distributing the simulation objects upon several process on several workstations or CPU. Then, on each process, there will be a scheduler responsible for the referentials of its process, maybe some referentials (for example, the visualization process will not own any referential for A, B, C, D, E, F or G), and maybe some mirrors, if the outputs of the simulation objects associated with these mirrors are needed by some of the referentials of the process.

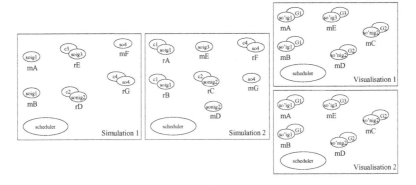

Fig.6. Run-time for a distributed simulation with two visualizations

A possible result is shown figure 6, where the first simulation is responsible for the D, E and G simulation objects, and the second simulation is responsible for the A, B, C and F simulation objects.

We suppose here that none of the D, E and G simulation objects are interested in the outputs of the C object, that is why there is no mirror of C in the first simulation process.

6   Technicals Aspects of Our Platform

This platform relies on Performer for the real-time visualization. Is is currently developed with Silicon Graphics workstations.

Distribution of calculations can rely on REACT (only on SGI multi-processors hardware) or on PVM for heterogeneous hardware UNIX platforms.

The mechanisms of communications between referentials and mirrors we have described here are based on PVM (Parallel Virtual Machine), it is that way we ensure the distribution of visualizations.

To visualize our simulation objects, we associate them to a geometry, which is a VRML 1.0 description.

All the calculations of the simulation objects are written in C++.

Previous versions of the GASP kernel have already been ported upon many UNIX systems and upon Windows NT, the only difficulty is for the visualization, because of Performer, which is currently only available for SGI and Linux workstations.

7   Further Work

7.1   About the Use of User-Defined Predictive Models

For a distributed simulation, the amount of data transmitted between the different nodes and the way concurrency between communication and calculation are handled are critical aspects of the overall performance. If a good approximation of the output values can be calculated, then the amount of data transmitted can be reduced and better concurrency can be achieved. In the current implementation of our simulation platform, these approximations are type based and system provided. We are now focusing on enabling user defined predictive models for these calculations. This will be possible on user-defined input/output type level or on an entity level.

7.2   About Physically Shared Collaborative Interactions

As we own a SGI reality center which allows group immersion, we are also studying the possibility to allow several users to interact with each other in front of the same physical visualization, to benefit from a real collaborative immersion in a physically shared virtual environment. This is going to be realized by using techniques similar to these used for multi-modal applications.

8 Conclusion

We have presented here the architecture of GASP, our platform for animation and simulation. This platform can be useful for multi-agent simulations, as it allows a designer and a programmer to focus on the interesting part of the development of a virtual world : the behavior of the entities that populate that world.

As GASP allows entities to be distributed upon several workstations, it enables the construction and the execution of complex virtual worlds, with a lot of entities with complex and heavy weight calculation behavior.

What is very interesting here is that this programmer does not have to worry about the distributed aspects.

As GASP provides a generic 3D visualization which is a simulation object that can also be distributed, we allow several end-users to share the same 3D virtual world, each of them has its own point of view and is able to interact with the entities of the world, so they can share interactions and then collaborate.

References

[1] C. Carlsson and O. Hagsand, "DIVE — A platform for multi-user virtual environments," *Computers and Graphics*, vol. 17, pp. 663–669, Nov.–Dec. 1993.

[2] C. Greenhalgh and S. Benford, "MASSIVE: A distributed virtual reality system incorporating spatial trading," in *Proceedings of the 15th International Conference on Distributed Computing Systems (ICDCS'95)*, (Los Alamitos, CA, USA), pp. 27–35, IEEE Computer Society Press, May30 June–2 1995.

[3] R. Lea, Y. Honda, K. Matsuda, and S. Matsuda, "Community place: Architecture and performance," in *VRML 97: Second Symposium on the Virtual Reality Modeling Language* (R. Carey and P. Strauss, eds.), (New York City, NY), ACM SIGGRAPH / ACM SIGCOMM, ACM Press, Feb. 1997. ISBN 0-89791-886-x.

[4] T. Duval, S. Morvan, P. Reignier, F. Harrouet, and J. Tisseau, "Arévi : une boîte à outils 3d pour des applications coopératives," *Numéro spécial de la revue Calculateurs Parallèles (coopération)*, pp. 239–250, juillet 1997.

[5] P. Reignier, F. Harrouet, S. Morvan, J. Tisseau, and T. Duval, "Arévi : A virtual reality multiagent platform," in *Proceedings of the First International Conference on Virtual Worlds (VW'98), Paris, Lecture Notes in Computer Science, Artifial Intelligence series (LNCS/AI 1434)*, pp. 229–240, juillet 1998.

[6] S. Donikian, A. Chauffaut, T. Duval, and R. Kulpa, "Gasp: from modular programming to distributed execution," in *Computer Animation'98, IEEE, Philadelphie, USA*, pp. 79–87, juin 1998.

[7] G. Bell, R. Carry, and C. Marrin, "VRML 2.0 final specification," 1996.

[8] M. Ryan and P. Sharkey, "Distortion in distributed virtual environments," in *Proceedings of the First International Conference on Virtual Worlds (VW'98), Paris, Lecture Notes in Computer Science, Artifial Intelligence series (LNCS/AI 1434)*, pp. 42–48, juillet 1998.

[9] D. Margery, B. Arnaldi, and N. Plouzeau, "A general framework for cooperative manipulation in virtual environments," in *Virtual Environments '99* (M. Gervautz, A. Hildebrand, and D. Schmaltsieg, eds.), pp. 169–178, Eurographics, Springer, 1999.

[10] M.R. Macedonia, *A Network software Architecture For Large Scale Virtual Environnements*. PhD thesis, Naval Postgraduate School, Monterey, California, 1995.

Generic 3D Ball Animation Model for Networked Interactive VR Environments

Hansrudi Noser[1], Christian Stern[1], Peter Stucki[1], Daniel Thalmann[2]

[1]Institut für Informatik der Universität Zürich, Winterthurerstr. 190
CH-8050 Zürich, Switzerland
{noser, stern, stucki}@ifi.unizh.ch
[2]Computer Graphics Lab, Swiss Federal Institute of Technology
CH-1015 Lausanne, Switzerland
thalmann@lig.di.epfl.ch

Abstract. This paper describes a versatile, robust, and parametric ball animation model that can be used in many types of interactive Virtual Reality (VR) environments. The generic model is particularly useful for animation of ball-like objects such as tennis balls and footballs in networked collaborative environments where low frame rates, network delays and information losses complicate collision detection of fast moving objects. The ball animation model includes a multi-level physical modeling as well as collision detection and treatment. Finally, the parameterization of typical applications is discussed.

1 Introduction

In most cultures many popular ball games exist. Therefore, their use in VR applications is of interest. Moreover, fast balls and user driven rackets are a challenge for networked VR systems suffering mostly from low frame rates and delays. The general problem of ball animation in distributed VR environments is not extensively treated in literature. In [1, 2, 3] tennis game modeling with autonomous actors and interactive users is presented. The authors used a physics-based particle system approach for the ball animation. In [4] a networked VR application of a tennis game is described, where parts of the ball-model described in this work have been used. However, the ball-model itself is described only marginally.

Particle dynamics, as it is used for ball animation, is extensively treated in literature. Differential equations of particles and their analytic solutions can be found in [5]. Similarly, there exist many books on collision detection. Our work is inspired from a method described in [6].

The main problems of ball physics such as dynamics as well as collision detection, and treatment are solved. However, ball animation in distributed VR environments implies some VR specific problems due to real-time constraints, interactivity, as well as update-delays and possible update-losses.

In general animated balls are fast moving objects colliding with static obstacles – such as the floor, nets, or walls – or with other fast moving objects such as feet, fists, or rackets. As in distributed environments frame rates and update rates of the position of balls and interactively moved objects can be low (~6 – 15 Hz), well defined

J.-C. Heudin (Ed.): VW 2000, LNAI 1834, pp. 77-90, 2000.

trajectories of the objects are missing making it difficult to calculate collisions and collision responses. In such cases force field based ball models with numerical integration of the differential equations [2] will fail, or considerably slow down the speed of the animation process.

Another important problem for an interactive player in VR is to hit the ball, as in general his radius of action is limited, and the exact 3D localization of the ball depends strongly on the quality of stereo-view, 3D immersion, and animation rate.

All these limiting factors of a distributed VR environment require a specialized ball animation model. In this paper we propose a generic ball animation model including multi-level physics as well as collision detection and treatment, optimized for a networked VR environment, where the ball model can be adapted to VR display quality, network speed, game type, and game levels.

2 Physical Model of Ball Animation

In this article we describe some basic elements of a virtual environment for games with ball-like objects, the floor, a net, and racket-like objects that can hit the ball. In a VR application these elements can be combined easily to a variety of interactive ball games.

We suppose interactive users or autonomous actors are animating the racket-like objects in an attempt to hit a ball. In order to simplify certain calculations, we can fix a coordinate system with gravity acting in y-down direction and a flat ground aligned to x, z coordinate axes with the origin at a court edge (see Fig. 1). The net is supposed to be vertical and parallel to the z-axes. Most ball game environments can easily be mapped to this orientation by using elementary transformations.

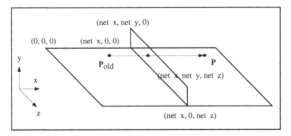

Fig. 1. Orientation of the court

2.1 Ball Dynamics

Our model approximates the ball movement by simplified physical laws. In most games the vertical ball movements are in general slow compared to the horizontal movement. Therefore, we can neglect the air friction term for the vertical ball movement. This approach simplifies certain subsequent calculations. The differential equation is given by equation 1. Vectors are indicated by bold letters.

m:	mass of ball	$\mathbf{g}$:	gravity acceleration
$\mathbf{Y}$:	vertical ball position	t:	time

$$m \cdot \ddot{\mathbf{Y}} = -m \cdot \mathbf{g} \tag{1}$$

Air resistance, however, which is proportional to the horizontal velocity, influences the horizontal ball movement. This term is necessary for a natural looking ball animation. The corresponding differential equation is given by equation 2.

$\mathbf{X}$: horizontal position of the ball	ß:	air friction
$\mathbf{V}$: horizontal velocity of the ball	$\mathbf{V}_o$:	initial velocity of the ball

$$m \cdot \ddot{\mathbf{X}} = -\beta \cdot \dot{\mathbf{X}} = -\beta \cdot \mathbf{V}, \qquad b = \frac{m}{\beta} \tag{2}$$

Finally, the complete ball movement is governed by the superposition of the horizontal and vertical movement. The analytic solution of the above differential equations 1 and 2 is given by equation 3.

$$\dot{\mathbf{P}}(t) = \begin{pmatrix} V_{ox} \cdot e^{-t/b} \\ V_{oy} - gt \\ V_{oz} \cdot e^{-t/b} \end{pmatrix}, \qquad \mathbf{P}(t) = \begin{pmatrix} X_0 + V_{0x} \cdot \left(1 - e^{-t/b}\right) \cdot b \\ Y_0 + V_{0y} \cdot t - 0.5 \cdot g \cdot t^2 \\ Z_0 + V_{0z} \cdot \left(1 - e^{-t/b}\right) \cdot b \end{pmatrix} = \mathbf{X}(t) + \mathbf{Y}(t) \tag{3}$$

For high level game modes, we also take into account the ball spin. We suppose that the spin damping during the ball flight in the air lasting t seconds is given by equation 4.

$$\text{spin AirDamping} = sDamp / (sDamp + t) \tag{4}$$

sDamp: spin damping factor for the ball moving in air.

We use only a simplified physical model for the game, which neglects secondary effects. For example, we ignore the small influence of the ball spin on the ball's trajectory, but on the other hand, we treat the response when bouncing on the floor or when colliding with a racket.

The rackets are important elements of the ball animation model. By hitting the ball, they can modify its trajectory determined by the physical laws. In the computational model the rackets are geometrically represented by discs of a given radius r_{disc}. In the virtual environment, however, they are generally represented by nice looking triangulated complex surfaces. All we have to do for collision detection is to map them to the corresponding discs of the computational model.

As already mentioned, interactive players or autonomous actors determine the racket's position and orientation. 3D tracking devices such as the Flock of Birds (FOBs) or SpaceBalls, for example, capture their movement. The resulting information describing these movements is transmitted over the net to the ball server and potential other clients. The ball server memorizes the last n (typically n=3) racket positions and orientations in order to estimate, interpolate, or extrapolate actual racket positions, orientations, and velocities that are needed for collision detection.

2.2 Collision Detection and Response

In our model the ball collides only with the floor, the net and the rackets. Therefore, these are important elements of the ball model. Collision detection with further objects of the virtual environment could be added, but it would slow down the animation speed.

The floor and the net are static objects. Therefore, collision detection with these static objects is relatively simple to simulate. The rackets, however, are dynamic objects with sampled position and orientation. Collision detection between the ball and the rackets needs some special consideration and is discussed in the next sections.

Each time a collision event is detected, we first calculate the actual velocity of the ball, which serves as the actual velocity value for subsequent collision response calculations. Then we reset the time to zero, and the collision response determines the initial ball position and velocity for the evolution after the collision. After a collision and at the beginning of the animation the initial ball position and velocity are in general indexed by zero, i.e., P_0 or V_0.

Ball - Floor. The ball - floor collision detection is immediate according to Fig. 2. When the actual position P of the ball is below floor level ($P_y <$ floor_level), then collision occurs. The new initial position P_0 after the collision event is simply adjusted to the floor level to avoid floor penetration. This correction simulates a slight gliding of the ball on the floor when bouncing with some additional horizontal speed. The corresponding collision response is given by equation 5.

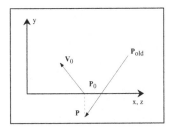

Fig. 2. Ball-floor collision detection

$$f = e^{-t/b}$$

$$\mathbf{P}_0 = \begin{pmatrix} P_x \\ floor\_level \\ P_z \end{pmatrix} : \text{new initial position}$$

$$\mathbf{V}_0 = \begin{pmatrix} V_{0x} \cdot f \cdot floorDamping \\ -(V_{0y} - g \cdot t) \cdot floorDamping \\ V_{0z} \cdot f \cdot floorDamping \end{pmatrix} (+\mathbf{V}_{spin\_floor}) : \text{new initial velocity}$$

$$t = 0$$

(5)

The ball-floor collision event provokes a collision sound if V_{0y} > sound_threshold. The sound feed back for indicating collisions is an important element for the user's quality of immersion. Each time a collision is detected, the ball server broadcasts a corresponding sound event to all participating clients.

In equation 5, the vertical speed is set to zero if V_{0y} > bounce_threshold. This last correction avoids infinite small bounce movements of the ball that are due to the gravitation force acting constantly to the ball and pushing it repeatedly into the floor. The floorDamping factor simulates a loss of energy at each bounce on the floor. It can be used to model floor and ball properties. If ball spin is considered, the corresponding velocity contribution V_{spin_floor} of equation 13 has to be added.

Ball - Net. Ball-net or ball-wall collisions represent another important class of collision events. We treat only the ball-net case as ball-wall collisions can be treated with only minor modifications. Moreover, the effect of dribbling over the top of the net is not considered.

The collision point **Q** of the line through the actual ball position **P** at time t and the previous one P_{old} at time t-dt is given by the pseudo code of Fig. 3 that refers to Fig. 1. The corresponding response of a ball-net collision is given by equation 6.

$$if\left(P_{oldx} = P_x\right) \text{then } \textbf{no collision} \text{ as line segment and net plane parallel}$$
$$else \quad \textbf{Q} = \textbf{P}_{old} + s \cdot \left(\textbf{P} - \textbf{P}_{old}\right)$$
$$Q_x = net\_x = P_{oldx} + s \cdot \left(P_x - P_{oldx}\right)$$
$$\Rightarrow s = \frac{net\_x - P_{oldx}}{P_x - P_{oldx}}$$
$$if \quad s \notin [0..1] \text{then } \textbf{no collision} \text{ as } \textbf{Q} \text{ not on line segment } \textbf{P}_{old}\textbf{P}$$
$$else \quad calculate \quad \textbf{Q} = \textbf{P}_{old} + s \cdot \left(\textbf{P} - \textbf{P}_{old}\right)$$
$$\Rightarrow \textbf{collision} \text{ if } Q_z \in [0..net\_z] \wedge Q_y \in [0..net\_y]$$

Fig. 3. Ball-net collision detection

$$f = e^{-t/b} \qquad \textbf{V}_0 = \begin{pmatrix} -V_{0x} \cdot f \\ V_{0y} - g \cdot t \\ V_{0z} \cdot f \end{pmatrix} \cdot netDamping \text{ : new initial velocity}$$

$$t = 0 \qquad \textbf{P}_0 = \begin{pmatrix} V_{0x} \cdot \Delta t \cdot shift \\ 0 \\ 0 \end{pmatrix} + \textbf{Q} \text{ : new initial position} \tag{6}$$

The new initial position is slightly moved in direction of the new velocity after the net collision. This shift avoids multiple consecutive collisions with the net and places the ball slightly outside the net. In fact, with the netDamping factor we can model the collision behavior. If the factor is close to zero, we simulate a net that absorbs much of the ball energy. If the factor, however, is close to one, we have a typical ball-wall collision. Note that in equation 6 the time t represents the time passed since the previous collision event.

Ball - Racket. Ball-racket collisions are the most critical ones. In general both objects are moving fast. Additionally, the racket trajectories are mostly represented by sampled noisy data produced by 3D tracking devices and transmitted with certain delays at low sampling rates (typically 2 to 12 frames per second) through the network.

Simple collision detection, for instance, can be realized by calculating the distance of the ball from the racket center. If the ball is closer than a certain collision distance, we assume a collision. This collision detection method is not precise, but it is very robust and could be used in a low-level game mode, or in cases, where the racket data is very noisy at low frame rates. In this case the ball position **P** at time t is the collision point **Q**. This approach, however, detects not all ball-racket collisions. If the ball and the racket move so fast that the distances traveled between two consecutive frames is bigger than the collision distance d_{coll}, a potential collision is ignored.

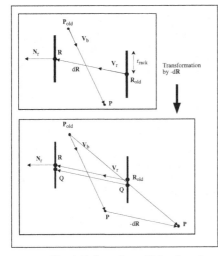

r_{rack}: radius of racket

R: racket position at time t

R_{old}: racket position at time t-dt

V_r: racket velocity

N_r: racket normal

P: ball position at time t

P_{old}: ball position at time t-dt

V_b: ball velocity

Fig. 4. Ball - racket collision detection using a disc like racket surface

A more precise collision detection method is presented now. In a first step, the actual ball position **P** is transformed into the moving coordinate system of the racket where the collision detection can be calculated such as illustrated in Fig. 4. We use two consecutive ball and racket positions of two consecutive frames. The transformed ball position **P'** is shifted by the negative movement of the racket (-d**R** = R_{old} - **R**). In this coordinate system the racket is static, and therefore, we can now calculate the intersection of the racket disc with the line segment given by **P'** - P_{old}. This method is described by the pseudo code of Fig 5.

This mode of collision detection considers the racket normal that is orthogonal to the racket surface. Consequently, the player has to control also the racket orientation during a game. To simplify the game, a player can switch off the racket orientation sensibility, and choose the racket normal to be aligned with the racket velocity. When the racket is not moving, the current racket normal has to be taken. This mode is easier for the player as he may neglect the racket's orientation. Therefore, he can concentrate completely on the ball and his stroke.

$dist = \|\mathbf{P'}-\mathbf{R}\|$

if $(dist > clippingFactor)$ then there is **no collision**

else $\mathbf{d} = \mathbf{P'}-\mathbf{P}_{old}$

$\quad\quad c = -\mathbf{N}_r \cdot \mathbf{R}_{old}$

$\quad\quad divisor = \mathbf{N}_r \cdot \mathbf{d}$

if (divisor = 0) then there is **no collision**

$\quad\quad\quad\quad$ as the ball movement is parallel to the racket plane

else $\quad t = \dfrac{-(\mathbf{N}_r \cdot \mathbf{P}_{old} + c)}{divisor}$

$if\,(t \in [0..1])$ then there is **intersection** with the racket plane and the line segment

$\quad\quad$ dist $= \|\mathbf{Q'}\text{-}\mathbf{R}_{old}\|$

if $(dist > racketRadius)$ then there is **no collision**

else $\mathbf{Q'} = \mathbf{P}_{old} + t \cdot \mathbf{d}$

$\quad\quad \mathbf{Q} = \mathbf{Q'} + d\mathbf{R}$ the **collision point**

Fig. 5. Ball-racket collision detection

2.3   Response after Ball - Racket Collision Detection

In order to compensate certain network induced problems and to allow multiple game levels, we propose several methods for the ball-racket collision response. These methods range from user friendly "missile like" balls flying automatically to the partner's racket, to physically based collision response with ball spin effects for advanced players on high performance networks and computers. In this section, we present the following collision response methods:

- racket determined: determined only by racket velocity
- autonomous ball: missile like; it flies to a given goal
- mixed response: mix of the above methods
- physical response: approximation based on physical laws

Racket Determined. To facilitate the game, one possible response is to force the ball to fly into the direction of the racket velocity during the hit. Moreover, as the user defined racket movements can be very fast it is useful to clamp the initial velocity to a certain range. The speed clamping avoids unrealistic strokes, and allows the application to predefine certain game levels. In this method, immediately after the stroke, the initial position of the ball is placed slightly in front of the racket collision point according equation 7.

$$\mathbf{P} = \mathbf{Q} + \mathbf{V}_0 * dt \tag{7}$$

This measure helps to avoid multiple collisions with the racket. Multiple collisions can happen if the racket is accelerating during the stroke. Then, it can strike consecutively the ball several times. It may even happen that the ball bounces into the racket from behind when the racket is overtaking the ball. Therefore, after a ball-racket collision, we stop collision detection during the next two or three frames in order to avoid such multiple collisions.

Autonomous Ball. The autonomous ball flies to the racket of the partner independently of the hit executed by the player such as illustrated in Fig. 6.

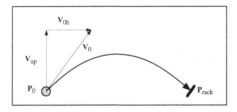

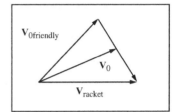

Fig. 6. "Friendly" ball flying to the partners racket   **Fig. 7.** Mixed collision treatment

To simplify the calculation of the initial velocity of the autonomous ball, we suppose that the height of the goal point corresponds to the height of the ball position at the moment of the stroke. Given a vertical velocity V_{up} we can calculate the time t_0 the ball needs to mount and descend at the height immediately after the hit. Equation 8 shows the details.

$$\mathbf{P}_{rack} = \begin{pmatrix} P_{rackx} \\ P_{racky} \\ P_{rackz} \end{pmatrix} \qquad \begin{aligned} P_{0y} &= P_{racky} \\ V_{up} \cdot t - 0.5 \cdot g \cdot t^2 &= 0 \\ t_0 &= V_{up} \cdot 2 / g \end{aligned} \qquad (8)$$

In consequence, this time t_0 determines the horizontal velocity V_0 according to equation 9.

The vertical speed V_{up} can be chosen freely, or it can be matched to the actual vertical speed of the racket in order to have some limited influence of the player on the resulting ball trajectory. Finally, we can multiply the ball velocity V_0 by a factor that we call friendlyFactor. When this factor is one, the ball flies automatically to planned point. If it is smaller than one, it will bounce first in front of the planned point. If it is larger than 1, it will fly over the given goal. Thus, the degree of "friendliness" of the ball can be adjusted easily according the taste of the players.

$$P_{0y} = P_{racky}, \quad d_1 = P_{0x} - P_{rackx}, \quad d_2 = P_{0z} - P_{rackz}, \quad dist_h = \sqrt{d_1^2 + d_2^2}$$

$$V_0 = \frac{dist_h}{b\left(1 - e^{-t_0/b}\right)},$$

$$f = \frac{V_0}{dist_h} = \frac{1}{b\left(1 - e^{-t_0/b}\right)}$$

$$\Rightarrow V_0 = \begin{pmatrix} d_1 \cdot f \\ V_{up} \\ d_2 \cdot f \end{pmatrix} \cdot friendlyFactor \qquad (9)$$

Mixed Treatment. On the long run, the response of the autonomous ball is boring for advanced players using fast networks and powerful computers, because the ball always flies to the opponent, nearly independently of the actual stroke of the player. To improve the response behavior we can make a mixed collision treatment by taking into account the racket velocity.

$$V_0 = V_{0\,friendly} + \left(V_{racket} - V_{0\,friendly}\right) \cdot \left(1 - friendlyFactor\right) \qquad (10)$$

As indicated in Fig. 7 we can calculate the difference vector between the autonomous ball velocity and the racket velocity. According to equation 10 we can adjust the behavior of the response with the "friendlyFactor", having a value between zero and one. When the friendlyFactor is 1, then the ball flies directly to the partner's racket. If the friendlyFactor is 0, the racket speed will completely determine the ball's response. With values between zero and one we can choose a mixed behavior between the two extremes.

Physical Response. For advanced players using fast networks and powerful computers, a physical collision response model is convenient. The model we present now is not an exact physical model, but it is based on physical collision principles in order to simulate real ball-racket collision responses. We consider also possible spin effects, which are produced if the racket normal and the racket speed at the collision are not parallel.

We make the following assumptions:

- The new spin of the ball is determined only by the racket velocity component which is orthogonal to the racket normal.
- The spin response on the racket is proportional to the difference of the ball spin and the new spin induced by the racket movement
- In order to be able to hit with both racket sides, the racket normal is always in direction of the previous ball position if a collision is detected. If a collision is detected, the actual ball position and the previous one are at different sides of the racket. This means that the racket plane normal has to be inverted if $dP*n_{racket} < 0$ (see Fig. 8).

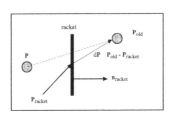

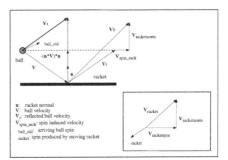

Fig. 8. Racket normal inversion   **Fig. 9.** Mixed collision treatment

The response calculation is illustrated by Fig. 9. The velocity $\mathbf{V}$, the spin $\mathbf{S_{ball\_old}}$, the racket normal $\mathbf{n}$, and the racket velocity $\mathbf{V_{racket}}$ are given values of the arriving ball. From these values we deduce according to equation 11 the resulting velocity $\mathbf{V_0}$ after the hit which is influenced by a bounce component (or reflected velocity) $\mathbf{V_r}$, by the racket velocity $\mathbf{V_{racketnorm}}$ in direction of the racket normal and a spin induced component $\mathbf{V_{spin\_rack}}$. The ball spin after the collision and its response at a bounce are given by equation 12 and 13. Additionally, after a bounce the ball spin is also damped by a given factor according to equation 14.

$$
\begin{aligned}
\mathbf{V}_0 &= \mathbf{V}_r + \mathbf{V}_{racketnorm} + \mathbf{V}_{spin\_rack} \\
\mathbf{V}_r &= \mathbf{V} - 2 \cdot (\mathbf{n} \cdot \mathbf{V}) \cdot \mathbf{n} \\
\mathbf{V}_{racketnorm} &= (\mathbf{n} \cdot \mathbf{V}_{racket}) \cdot \mathbf{n} \\
\mathbf{S}_{racket} &= \mathbf{V}_{racket} \times \mathbf{n} \\
\mathbf{V}_{spin\_rack} &= (spinAirDamping \cdot \mathbf{S}_{ball\_old} - \mathbf{S}_{racket}) \times \mathbf{n}
\end{aligned}
\tag{11}
$$

$$
\mathbf{S}_{ball} = spinRackDamping \cdot \mathbf{S}_{racket}
\tag{12}
$$

$$
\mathbf{V}_{spin\_floor} = spinFloorDamping(spinAirDamping \cdot \mathbf{S}_{ball}) \times \mathbf{n}
\tag{13}
$$

$$
\mathbf{S}_{ball} = spinFloorDamping \cdot \mathbf{S}_{ball}
\tag{14}
$$

3   Parameterization

In networked shared environments with asynchronous process communication we typically use a ball server managing dynamics and collisions of the ball. It communicates with game clients delivering positions of objects susceptible to hit the ball. Its task is to broadcast the updated ball and shared object data. In such a configuration we always have to deal with update delays of object positions and orientations which can range from milliseconds to one or several seconds in extreme cases. When the objects in the virtual world are moving slowly, the effects of the network delays do not disturb the animation. If, however, the objects are moving fast, such as a tennis ball, or a racket hitting a ball, then these delays can become disturbing, because each participant client displays temporarily a different object configuration. Especially, when collision detection between the fast moving ball and rackets has to be done, some consistency problems arise. Fig. 10 shows a typical example of a ball-racket collision detected in the environment of the ball server. In the player client, however, the racket passes in front of the ball without touching it. Despite of this fact, the ball reacts as if being hit by the racket. This effect results from the fact that the ball movement is calculated in the ball server and the racket movement is captured in the player client. Both clients broadcast their object positions through the network. In our example the ball server gets the racket position with a delay of one frame. Similarly, the racket client gets the ball position also with a delay of one frame.

Update losses represent another type of problems. If racket clients send asynchronously a lot of update information to the server, they can overload it. Then, it cannot broadcast each update in time. The next time, when it finally broadcasts the update information, it will take only the last update for a given object. Consequently, the more recent updates are ignored. This effect can lead to discontinuous ball and racket movements making collision detection and response difficult.

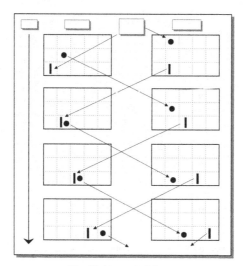

Fig. 10. Network delay

To minimize these delay problems we propose the following measures:

- Adjustment of ball speed and update rate to the network performance
- Extrapolation of racket movement
- Introduction of game levels

In networked applications it makes sense to include an absolute frame rate control which allows us to adjust the frame rate to the network performance. We measure the time a single frame takes for being calculated and force the process to sleep the rest of the given frame time interval. Independently of this real time frame rate control, we can adjust the time base of the animation, which allows us to adjust the ball speed.

The second step for minimizing network delays is the extrapolation of the racket positions in the ball server. An extrapolation can only work well for correlated movements. When the player makes fast, random or uncorrelated movements, then a prediction is impossible, and the resulting visual effects are worse than without an extrapolation. When the racket, however, executes a hit, generally the movement at the moment of the collision is correlated and extrapolation is possible. We use only linear extrapolation by adding an estimated offset to the actual racket position as given by equation 15.

$$\mathbf{P}_{extrapolation} = \mathbf{P}_{current} + \mathbf{V}_{current} \cdot extrapolationTime \qquad (15)$$

The third possibility to deal with network problems is the introduction of game levels and simplifying approximations for the racket-ball collision detection and response. These measures allow inexperienced players to play with a certain success rate even at a low network performance.

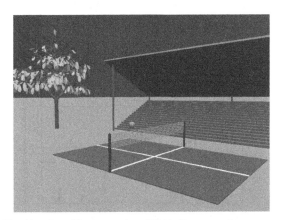

Fig. 11. A Rewriting system based VR ball game environment

The described models of the ball animation contain many parameters which can be used to define game levels, or/and to adjust a game to actual network and computer performances. The following list describes parameters acting on the ball dynamics, fixing its actual behavior.

- mass of the ball
- time step of the ball animation
- velocity and spin damping at collisions
- air friction
- the racket size for collision detection

Other parameters are useful to adjust the game to network performances and game-levels.

- Collision detection sleep rate (number of frames where no collision detection is done immediately after a collision (avoids multiple collisions))
- threshold values for collision sound and floor-ball collision detection
- frame time
- racket speed clamp values
- ball-racket collision detection mode (sphere, disc)
- ball collision response type (friendly, mixed, physical)

For game applications these parameters should figure in configuration files and/or in interactive menus. For an easy game level on a slow network, we can use the distance dependent collision detection with an autonomous ball response and a friendlyFactor of one (see equation 10). A mid game level configuration corresponds to a collision detection with the racket where the normal is defined by the velocity, as well as a mixed collision response with a friendlyFactor of 0.8. Finally, an advanced game level on a ATM network, for example, with fast computers at each end could use a geometrical collision detection between the ball and a racket where the racket normal corresponds to the real racket normal and a spin dependent physical collision response.

Parts of the generic ball model were successfully used in a networked VR tennis game described in [4]. At present it is implemented in a rewriting system based VR system [7, 8] at the Multimedia Laboratory of the University of Zurich, and it serves as a test-bed for networked VR ball games (see Fig. 11).

4 Conclusions

One of the difficulties of networked ball game models is the presence of fast moving objects. Whereas slow moving objects can be animated without problems, the fast moving ball and rackets require the use of special techniques, since we have to deal with low update rates and information losses.

For the ball animation we use simplified collision detection mechanisms as well as analytical movement and collision response calculation. These different techniques can be used to introduce game levels as well as to compensate network and performance problems.

Acknowledgments

Important parts of the research were realized at the Computer Graphics Laboratory (LIG), directed by Prof. D. Thalmann at EPFL, in close collaboration with MIRALAB, directed by Prof. N. Magnenat-Thalmann, at the University of Geneva. The authors would like to thank the directors and all members of both labs for their support and collaboration.

References

1. H. Noser, D. Thalmann, Sensor Based Synthetic Actors in a Tennis Game Simulation, Proceedings Computer Graphics International 1997, Hasselt, Belgium, June 24-28, 1997, pp 189-198
2. H. Noser, I. S. Pandzic, T. K. Capin, N. M. Thalmann, D. Thalmann, *Playing Games through the Virtual Life Network*, ALIFE V, Oral Presentations, May 16-18, 1996, Nara, Japan, pp. 114-121
3. D. Thalmann, H. Noser, Z. Huang, Chapter: *How to Create a Virtual Life ?*, in Interactive Computer Animation, eds. N.M. Thalmann, D. Thalmann, Prentice Hall Europe, 1996, pp 263 – 291
4. T. Molet, A. Aubel, H. Noser, T. Capin, E. Lee, I. Pandzic, D.Thalmann, N.M. Thalmann, Sannier, *Anyone for Tennis?*, Presence, Vol. 8, No. 2, April 1999, 140-156
5. R. Bronson, *Modern Introductory Differential Equations*, Schaum's Outline Series, McGRAW-HILL, Inc, 1973, Chapter 9, and 17
6. Priamos Georgiades, Signed Distance from Point to Plane, in Graphics Gems III, Ed. D. Kirk, Academic Press, Inc. 1992, pp. 223-224
7. H. Noser, D. Thalmann, *The Animation of Autonomous Actors Based on Production Rules*, Proceedings Computer Animation'96, June 3-4, 1996, Geneva Switzerland, IEEE Computer Society Press, Los Alamitos, California, pp 47-57
8. H. Noser, D.Thalmann, *A Rule-Based Interactive Behavioral Animation System for Humanoids*, IEEE Transactions on Visualization and Computer Graphics, Vol. 5, No. 4, October-December 1999

An Overview on Virtual Sets

Antonia Lucinelma Pessoa Albuquerque[1,2], Jonas Gomes[2], and Luiz Velho[2]

[1] VISGRAF Laboratory, IMPA–Instituto de Matemática Pura e Aplicada
Estrada Dona Castorina, 110, 22460-320, Rio de Janeiro, RJ, Brasil
{nelma,jonas,lvelho}@visgraf.impa.br
[2] TecGraf - Grupo de Tecnologia em Computação Gráfica
Departamento de Informática, PUC-Rio
Rua Marquês de São Vicente 255, 22453-900, Rio de Janeiro, RJ, Brasil

Abstract The combination of real and virtual worlds opens up many interesting applications of computer graphics technology. This work focus on virtual sets. We present a conceptual overview of the problem, which enables us to understand the techniques and identify current trends. The paper outlines our initial implementations and presents future plans.

1 Introduction

The integration between real and virtual worlds offers interesting possibilities of applications in the near future. Currently, some of these applications have already appeared in the commercial market. We will discuss one of these applications in this paper: virtual sets.

Virtual sets or *Virtual studios* are denominations given to the integrated use of computer generated elements with real actors and objects in a studio.

Its main advantages are: more flexibility in changing the scene, risky scenes can be made safely, allowing the production of complex special effects and also provides economy in the production of sophisticated designs along with flexibility in making quick changes. With the advent of high speed network, there is the possibility of remote operation.

Real–time virtual sets is a very recent area in computer graphics, which has potential applications in the film and television industry. The literature about this topic is scarce, although there are few commercial systems available.

This work focus on the concepts and correlated technologies behind virtual sets. Current trends will be discussed and new research directions will be pointed out.

2 Virtual Sets

When integrating real and virtual worlds in a virtual set, there are requirements other than immersibility. We should remark that there are two different kinds of users of the system: the autonomous actor who will "interact" with the virtual world, and the audience that will see the result of the combination. The final goal of a good virtual set system is to attain total integration between real and virtual worlds: a person from the audience should not distinguish one form the other.

J.-C. Heudin (Ed.): VW 2000, LNAI 1834, pp. 91–98, 2000.

In general, we could say that a virtual set is one where the real, autonomous, actor does not interact with. Examples of virtual sets are present when filming with miniatures. In this paper we are interested in *synthetic virtual sets*, that is, virtual sets generated by the computer.

The current computer graphics imaging technology has enabled a good degree of integration as can be seen on the special effects used in the movie industry: it is very difficult to distinguish between a real set and a computer generated one.

Nevertheless, the integration between the real and the virtual in the movie industry does not have the requirement of real time. Virtual sets for television applications in general demand real time for two main reasons:

- Costly post-productions are not affordable in the television industry;
- For live applications, such as news and talk shows, real time is mandatory.

From now on, we will use the term virtual set to mean *real time synthetic virtual set*, that is, the mixing of real and synthetic world to generate combined images, in real time, with a high degree of integration.

Note that this is distinct from virtual reality or augmented reality applications. In virtual set applications there is no user's immersion in the virtual environment. The viewer, who is the final user of these systems, does not need to wear an optical device. The main target is to make the virtual scene appear to be as real as possible, in the way that the actor seems to be part of that environment.

Figure 1 shows the components of a virtual set system, as follows:

- Data is captured from real world. Video cameras and sensors are used in this process in order to capture images and features of the real world;
- A synthetic world is generated by a computer. In general a high performance graphics workstation is used;
- The combination of the synthetic world and the real world is attained to generate the final image.

It should be noted in the diagram the communication paths between the computer and data capture devices. This communication is essential to produce the combination of real and synthetic data.

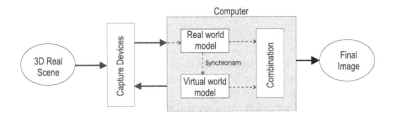

Fig.1. Virtual Sets' functional scheme

Based on the diagram of Figure 1, we can pose the three main problems on a virtual set system:

1. Attain a good spatial and temporal registration of the real and synthetic data;
2. Rendering of the synthetic world;
3. Combination of the real and synthetic worlds.

Registration: An important component of the spatial and temporal registration is the synchronization between the real camera, that captures real world images, and the virtual camera, used to generate images of the synthetic world. The intrinsic and extrinsic parameters of these two cameras must match in order to get a good spatial alignment, moreover, this synchronization must occur along the temporal dimension. It turns out that this does not reduces to the classical problem of camera calibration since camera parameters must be tracked along the time.

Rendering: The indistinguishable integration between the real and synthetic images put strong demands on the system: photorealistic rendering in real time. This is the Holy Grail of the computer graphics research effort, and it is a difficult goal to accomplish.

Combination: When the real and virtual worlds have a clear segmentation in foreground / background images, the combination is easily attained using digital compositing with the α-channel [1]. But this is not always the case in the virtual sets applications, therefore different combination techniques must be used.

In what follows we will discuss each of these problems in more detail.

3   Rendering

The rendering process is responsible for the virtual scene generation. Photorealistic rendering techniques must be used for satisfactory results. In live broadcasting the scene must be rendered in real time, demanding high computational performance. The trade off between quality and efficiency is the critical aspect in the system design.

Therefore, two criterias are essential to a rendering system:

- **Photorealistic look.** The ability to synthesize computer generated images with comparable quality to the images captured from a real camera is called photorealism. The need of floors using marble or wood, walls with special paintings, sophisticated illumination, chrome furniture with reflection; all this makes photorealism a priority. But that goal puts strong demands both in modeling and rendering.
- **Real time performance.** In virtual sets, the scene must be rendered at video rates and updated to match camera motion and actors performance. From there, one can conclude the importance of time in the rendering process.

3.1   Model-Based Rendering

The virtual scene passes initially by the modeling process to generate the $3D$ model, the illumination must be part of this model and be compatible with the studio's illumination. After the $3D$ model generation, the scene is rendered using a proper illumination model and rendering algorithm. This stage can be used to visualize the scene and also for planning; but in live broadcasting, the scene needs to be rendered in real time and be synchronized with the real camera. In the $3D$ model-based scenes the limitations to real camera movement are constraints imposed by the system control and not because of the modeling.

3.2 Image-Based Rendering

The process of image-based rendering is based on photographs taken from different points of view. It is necessary then to determine the real depth, z, of each pixel corresponding to its $3D$ location obtaining thus a depth map of all images. Knowing this information, images may be reprojected to different perspectives, in another view. Images are transformed using warping techniques. Camera operations can be simulated by perspective transformations applied to regions over the image. A conceptual approach for this area can be found in [2].

An advantage of image-based rendering is that computational complexity is related to pixels. Therefore, rendering time is bounded by image resolution, and not by the size of the model. A limitation is the difficulty to generate a virtual environment that would be freely navigable, since the acquisition of many photos of an environment can become impracticable. As a consequence, there are limitations in the camera motion in order not to view areas where there is no data available.

3.3 Hybrid Solutions

Image-based and model-based can be used together [3]. In that way, simple geometric models could be enriched with images to compose a scene. The pictures are used also to guide the construction of the model geometry and as textures that depend on the point of view – they are called view-dependent textures.

We propose that hybrid rendering systems would be very interesting solution for virtual sets, because it is a propitious technique to reproduce famous and sophisticated environments such as museums and churches. The construction of such data bases would be a valuable asset, nevertheless there is no commercial system for virtual sets using this technique.

4   Compositing in Virtual Sets

Traditional analog compositing techniques are: Matte Painting, Back Projection and Front Projection [4].

Digital compositing brought new techniques to the area, such as alpha channel and depth compositing. For synthetic images it is simple to get the alpha mask and the depth buffer. For video images this information is not directly available. Blue Screen is the technique used to determine the alpha channel in video images. Stereographic techniques are used to determine the z depth of the images [5].

Alpha and depth compositing when treated separately do not constitute a good solution for virtual sets. This is because each technique alone does not meet the two requirements for combining virtual and real elements: (a) match elements in arbitrary order; (b) maintain temporal registration [6].

Alpha blending assumes that an object in the real world is always in front (foreground) of the synthetic scene (background). In virtual sets this assumption is not always true. In order for the actor to be really immersed in a virtual environment, he needs to be able to occupy any spatial position in the scene. Depth information is necessary to carry through this effect, but alpha mask is also necessary to separate the actor from the studio environment.

Chroma key is still the basic technique used for compositing in a virtual studio, but new components become essential for better results. There is the need to be able to place elements in front of actors and this type of compositing is not possible using only alpha masks. Another problem is matching shadows and illumination. Furthermore, real-time compositing eliminates the possibility of post-production resources.

The knowledge of depth information for actors and scenes, real and virtual images, becomes essential for compositing in non-conventional order.

In terms of compositing in virtual sets it is as if we were today in the digital stage of "traveling mattes", searching to allow freedom of movements to the actor and camera. What it is lacking? Interactivity and Immersion. The actor being able to see synthetic elements, better yet, to feel more integration with the scene. These are far reaching goals that should be pursued.

5 Synchronism

The synchronism consists of getting a perfect correspondence between the parameters of the real camera and the virtual camera, this is equivalent to say that the position and orientation of the virtual camera must be the same as the real camera. This correspondence needs to be maintained during the whole process, in real time.

The camera concept varies for each type of application. In virtual reality and augmented reality, see-through displays give the viewer line of sight matched by the computer. In virtual sets the real camera is the camera used in the film set.

The synchronism has two important stages: calibration and tracking.

5.1 Calibration

Initially the alignment of the real image and the synthetic image needs to be adjusted until the desired match between them is obtained. This is only possible knowing the position, orientation (extrinsic parameters) and focal length (intrinsic parameters) of the real camera. This first stage is called camera calibration. The parameters are derived from objects in the image and 3D information about these objects. In order to maintain temporal synchronism this process has to be repeated at every frame.

5.2 Tracking

Synchronization techniques requires finding, at every frame, the real camera parameters that determine the virtual camera, this stage is called camera tracking. Therefore, the synchronism in virtual sets requires temporal synchronism achieved by tracking the camera, as well as, spatial synchronism achieved through camera calibration.

Currently there are some algorithms using tracking techniques. Nonetheless, a complete solution that takes care of all types of camera movements has not been developed yet [7]. A study about tracking for head mounted display systems can be found in [8].

5.3   Tracking Systems in Virtual Sets

In the existing systems for virtual sets, there are two kinds of tracking solutions: some use sensor-based techniques [7], while others use vision-based techniques [9]. In the existing literature, the first ones are called electromechanical tracking and the second ones optical tracking.

But, these denominations are not adequate for our framework of the virtual sets. Therefore we present the following taxonomy for tracking in virtual sets: monitored tracking and algorithmic tracking [10].

Monitored Tracking These systems are the most popular in the industry. They use optical or mechanical devices which are not part of the scene. Their function is to control and capture the camera movement.

Sensors can be active or passive. Active sensors control the camera, while passive sensors monitor the camera movement.

An advantage of this type of system is fast and accurate measuring. In TV studios the camera needs to be on a mobile platform so that the physical coupling does not represent a problem [11].

A commercial system using monitored tracking is The Memory Head by the Ultimate Corp. This system uses "pacing motors" of high accuracy to measure and to send camera elevation, pan, tilt and roll angles, as well as zoom and focus data to the computer [12].

Algorithmic Tracking These systems are the most flexible. They use algorithms to recover camera parameters. An advantage of this type of system is that, because they are based on pattern recognition, there is no restriction on the camera.

Vision techniques extract the camera parameters from image patterns. The pattern could be a grid painted on the blue wall of the studio. These techniques demand camera calibration in order to give accurate results. Moreover, proper illumination is required to make the pattern apparent. The complexity of the algorithms makes the system response below real-time rates.

Normally, applications developed to insert virtual elements in real images require the availability of a sequence of real images, in order to recover the real camera parameters. Consequently, they are not real time applications as [13] and [14].

6   Synchronization Using Incremental Calibration

Real time applications demand calibration along the time. In general, the camera calibration methods are static and consider the parameters that were calculated in one determined instant, assuming that these keep constant for one determined period, after which a new calibration needs to be made. This fact makes difficult to attain a continuous camera movement. Some methods interpolate the intermediate positions in order to get movement.

Tracking camera motion makes possible the use of incremental calibration techniques that are computationally more efficient. In our opinion, this solution is the best choice for real-time synchronism. Below we outline our proposal solution.

In [15], an optimization technique is presented that allows manipulation of a virtual camera by constraining image points seen through the camera lenses.

The technique has the following steps:

1. expresses image points **p** in terms of camera parameters **c**;
2. given the velocity of **p**, determines the rates of **c**;
3. the function **p**=**f**(**c**) is derived with respect to **c**, obtaining the Jacobian **J**;
4. finds the optimal solution for the equation: $\dot{\mathbf{p}} = \mathbf{J}\dot{\mathbf{c}}$;
5. the computed value $\dot{\mathbf{c}}$ is used to update the camera state, solving, numerically, a system of ordinary differential equations.

Based on that differential approach, our solution combines calibration and tracking in an incremental form. The virtual camera will follow the real image features, in real time, trying to reproduce the cameraman movements.

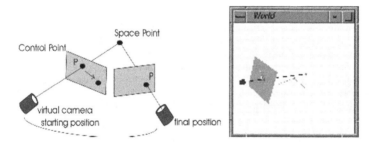

Fig.2. Incremental Tracking

This algorithm focuses on the virtual camera control instead of the real one. Based on a quaternion camera model [15] and a numerical method for integration, the virtual camera attain continous and smooth movements.

Tracking using this technique controls the virtual camera motion by following image points from frame to frame. The recovery of camera parameters uses constrained optimization. The methodology has two great advantages: it linearizes the optimization problem and also calibrates the camera in incremental form.

This solution can be applied to insert virtual elements in a real video sequence, in real time, and also to track a real element in a scene to be inserted in a virtual one.

7   Conclusions and Future Work

Virtual sets is a promising area that involves new technologies. In this paper we developed a conceptual framework for the area. This analysis is important to make possible a complete understanding of the problems to be solved, as well as to guide the research of new techniques.

Based on our experiment which we called *cameraman paradigm*, our plan is to develop a system using this approach [15], in which the virtual camera will be controlled with intuitive commands in order to obtain an incremental continuous synchronism.

References

1. Smith, Alvy Ray and James F. Blinn: Blue Screen Matting, SIGGRAPH 96 Conference Proceedings, Annual Conference Series, 1996, 259-268.
2. Gomes J., Darsa L., Costa B. and Velho L.: Warping and Morphing of Graphical Objects, Morgan Kaufmann Publishers, Inc., 1998.
3. Debevec, Paul E. and Yizhou Yu and Borshukov, George D.: Efficient View-Dependent Image-Based Rendering with Projective Texture-Mapping, Eurographics Rendering Workshop 1998, pp. 105-116 (June 1998, Vienna, Austria).
4. Raymond Fielding: The Technique of Special Effects Cinematography, Focal Press, 1985.
5. T. Kanade and K. Oda and A. Yoshida and M. Tanaka and H. Kano: Z-Key: A New Method for Creating Virtual Reality, http://www.cs.cmu.edu/afs/cs/project/stereo-machine/www/z-key.html, 1996.
6. Gomes, J. and Velho, L.: Image Processing for Computer Graphics, Springer-Verlag, 1997.
7. Radamec Broadcast Systems: Virtual Scenario Studio System, http://website.lineone.net/~radamec_broadcast/virt1.html, 1995.
8. Bhatnagar, Devesh Kumar: Position trackers for Head Mounted Display systems: A survey, Technical Report, University of North Carolina at Chapell Hill, 1993.
9. Orad: Virtual Sets, http://www.orad.co.il/virsets/index.htm, 1998.
10. Albuquerque, Antonia Lucinelma Pessoa: Virtual sets with a study of camera syncronization. Master Thesis (in portuguese), PUC-Rio, Brazil, April, 1999.
11. Oschatz, Sebastian: Grundlagen eines echtzeitfähigen Systems zur Verwendung virtueller Fernseh-Studio-Kulissen, http://www-cui.darmstadt.gmd.de/visit/Activities/Vist/ Diplomarbeit.oschatz/, 1994.
12. Ultimate Corp.: Memory Head Operations Manual, http://www.audiovideo.pt/ibertelco/Ultimatte/MemoryHead_i.html, 1993.
13. Jancène P. and Meilhac C. and Neyret F. and Provot X. and Tarel J. P. and Vézien J. M. and Verroust A.: Réalité Enrichie par Synthèse, INRIA, 1996.
14. REALViZ S.A.: Applications of computer vision to the industry of special effects, http://www.realviz.com/products/matchmover/index.htm. Sophia Antipolis Cedex - FRANCE.
15. Gleicher, M. and Witkin, A.: Through-the-Lens Camera Control, SIGGRAPH'92, 1992.

Creating Emotive Responsive Characters
Within Virtual Worlds

Ken Perlin

Media Research Laboratory
NYU Department of Computer Science
perlin@nyu.edu

Abstract. Virtual Worlds can seem to come to life when they have virtual characters in them. On the other hand, if these characters are not "believable" they can actually damage the sense of presence and immersion for a human participant. This problem is not purely one of engineering or of artistic judgement, but rather it calls for a combination of both. How do we combine technology and artistic content effectively to create believable interactive virtual characters? We will look at several examples from our own research and try to extrapolate some principles.

1 Introduction

Virtual worlds should be fun, engaging places, where participants' sense of humor, adventure and playfulness (and therefore their sense of imagination) are allowed to flourish [22]. One of the key components of such worlds are believable, engaging interactive characters.

It has long been a goal of the animated agent community to bring embodied agent technologies out of the research labs and into the hands of authors and designers who may put them to practical use. Improv is a set of tools and techniques developed at NYU which make it possible to create applications involving animated agents that behave, interact and respond to user input in ways that convey mood and emotion. These tools can be used without prior experience in computer programming, cognitive science or ergonomic simulation, while still allowing creation of animated agents who exhibit behavior which has the lifelike, somewhat unpredictable feel of human behavior, yet remains consistent with a character's personality and defined goals.

The goal of this research has been to make improvisational animation accessible to experts with minimal expertise in animation and dramatic performance, and to enable researchers and educators to exploit these technologies without relying on expensive production efforts. These are clearly two of the most important steps toward the widescale acceptance and use of animated agents for education and training, social simulation and collaborative environments.

J.-C. Heudin (Ed.): VW 2000, LNAI 1834, pp. 99-106, 2000.

In this paper we describe some of the experiments we have done to combine artistic design with technological innovation toward this goal.

2 Goals

Our research goals in this area have focused on building and testing examples that can run on the current World Wide Web and that demonstrate or embody interesting ideas. Our experiments are mainly in the area of interactive character animation.

Other than the historical examples, all of the experiments shown are Java 1.0 compatible applets. This lowest-common-denominator platform was chosen because it allows the broadest available flexibility in making on-line experiments simultaneously available to large numbers of users.

2.1 Animation Modeling

One question to ask is "how simple and intuitive can a system be, so that the user/participant can be given authoring powers?"

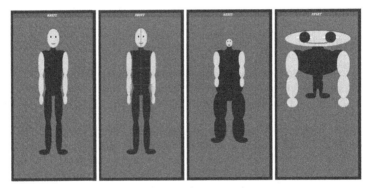

Figure 1. How simple can we make it for people to design customized animated characters?

The figures above are from an interactive applet designed to investigate the question "how simple can we make it for people to design customized animated characters?" The "character" on the left actually contains seven interactive zones. Dragging the mouse within any of these zones causes certain regions of the body to change shape so as to follow the mouse movement. Certain parts are coupled together, so that dragging one always causes the other to change as well.

This interface was designed to be intuitive to the extent that even a small child could design their own character. Experiments showed that this goal was achieved: Children as small as four years old were successful in creating their own custom character models, with no prior instruction.

We can view this as a very simple example of a smart virtual world object that leverages on multiple layers. The base substrate provides the potential for deformable shapes and for deformations to drive other parameters (including other deformations, and perhaps modes of action, or even personality traits). The example body is simple enough to be designed or customized by a user with nearly any level of drawing expertise. Expert-created rules can then be applied, which might be stored in a series of humanoid rule sets (for deformations and correspondences) between which the individual author/user can select and blend.

2.2   Human Character Animation Design

In the case of design of movement for virtual world avatars, layers of expert-created rules can provide a non-expert user with individual movements to include or overall stylistic guidance. For each virtual avatar, this work can happen on the level of direct manipulation of the avatar's character and other parameters.

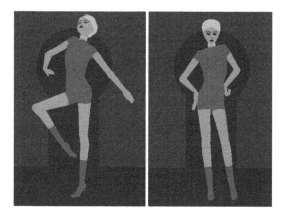

Figure 2. Attitude control.

The above figure was created using a prototype applet that allows an animator to work on a higher level of "attitude" control, somewhat as though the graphical puppet were a human actor being given motivational instructions.

We are not primarily interested in simply creating characters and movements, but in answering some specific questions about the authorability of character movements. Questions we are researching include: What are the limits of naive and simple "command-level" control? For example, could this figure be "taught" by naive users, using only simple gestures? How high level can control of an animated avatar be? How dow we construct an intuitive meta-authoring environment that allows experts to add to this user-control vocabulary?

2.3 Cognitive Modeling

We have also extended the principles of layered easily authorable animation to facial expression.

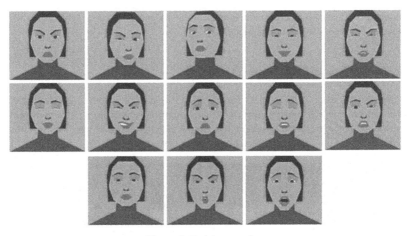

Figure 3. Facial expression.

In our improvisational animation work, we have shown how to make an embodied agent react with responsive facial expression, without using repetitive prebuilt animations, and how to mix those facial expressions to simulate shifting moods and attitudes. The result is real-time interactive facial animation with convincing emotive expressiveness.

The eventual goal of this research is to give computer-mediated worlds the ability to represent the subtleties we take for granted in face to face communication, so that they can function as agents for an emotional point of view.

In an experiment to discover a viable vocabulary for such a capability, we isolated the minimal number of facial expression elements that will produce a "convincing" impression of character and personality. Of course this is just a subset of the full range of expression of which the human face is capable. Paul Ekman's pioneering work on the Facial Action Coding System gives a functional description of the full range of expression of which the human face is capable.

The questions we are researching in this area include: How complete is this subset of expressions for creating believability? How best can such an emotive face be integrated into computer-mediated worlds in order to add connotative information? What sorts of meta-information are needed in a computer-mediated world to make this capability most useful?

3 History

The history of our Improv research has gone through several stages. In 1987, we did some preliminary work in using controlled random control signals to animate computer generated figures. When such signals were properly tuned, the sense of belie ability and engagement of these figures could be striking, given their simplicity. By 1994, we had advanced to the creation of layered animated dancer (below left), by 1995 to a shared interactive simulated social world (below center) and by 1996, to an immersive virtual simulated world which gave the participant the ability to walk around and interact with responsive story-telling characters (below right).

Figure 4. Animated dancer.

One of our main efforts has been the creation of entire theatrical troupes of interactive virtual performers. At the SIGGRAPH 95 conference, we presented what may have been the longest continually running film in history - in which a troupe of virtual actors hung out with each other socially for a week. Participants could enter the scene and interact with the characters, or they could be left to their own devices, in which case they would improvise social interactions with each other. In the image below, taken from this project, the two tall characters are telling a joke at the expense of the shorter character, and he is responding to his corresponding loss of social status.

Figure 5. Project shown at SIGGRAPH 95.

The need for highly distributed simulations led to a web-enabled Java version of our Improv system, which could be run collaboratively over the World Wide Web.

Figure 6. Sid & The Penguins.

Created by a group of programmers and artists at New York University's Media Research Laboratory and Center for Advanced Technology, "Sid & The Penguins" debuted at the Siggraph '98 Electronic Theatre. Sid & the Penguins is not a film. It's a live theatrical performance that is computed and displayed in real-time. The actors are virtual. Upon launching they are directed to act out a scene together, but each actor has autonomy to figure out how to play their part, and to improvise.

The camera is also an actor. It watches the other actors, and based on what they do during any given performance, it chooses shots and decides how to follow the action. Each actor contains a layered set of responsive content and styles, so that it can customize its response at each moment, based on what the other actors in the scene are doing. Thus, no two performances are exactly alike. Each performance contains unique decisions by the virtual actors as to how they will coordinate and block out the theatrical scene they are playing.

4 Conclusion

Each of the experiments shown above was a different approach to creating engagement, persistence and/or believability within a shared virtual world. Experiments such as these give insight into work to be done in shared virtual worlds in a number of areas, including animation design, animation modeling, cognitive modeling, pedagogical presentation and organization, information search and retrieval, and scientific visualization. These experiments are a merely snapshot of work in progress, and there is clearly much more to learn in this area. Arising from this research, robust tools for creation of responsive animation are currently being developed at http://www.improv-tech.com. By using such tools, virtual worlds can be more engaging and believable, for in the long run, engagement and believability in virtual worlds come from making accessible interfaces that can be used by creative people.

References

1. N. Badler, B. Barsky, D. Zeltzer, Making Them Move: Mechanics, Control, and Animation of Articulated Figures Morgan Kaufmann Publishers, San Mateo, CA, 1991.
2. N. Badler, C. Phillips, B. Webber, Simulating Humans: Computer Graphics, Animation, and Control Oxford University Press, 1993.
3. J. Bates, A. Loyall, W. Reilly, Integrating Reactivity, Goals and Emotions in a Broad Agent, Proceedings of the 14th Annual Conference of the Cognitive Science Society, Indiana, July 1992.
4. B. Blumberg, T. Galyean, Multi-Level Direction of Autonomous Creatures for Real-Time Virtual Environments Computer Graphics (SIGGRAPH '95 Proceedings), 30(3):47--54, 1995.
5. A. Broderlin, L. Williams, Motion Signal Processing, Computer Graphics (SIGGRAPH '95 Proceedings), 30(3):97--104, 1995.
6. R. Brooks. A Robust Layered Control for a Mobile Robot , IEEE Journal of Robotics and Automation, 2(1):14--23, 1986.
7. J. Chadwick, D. Haumann, R. Parent, Layered construction for deformable animated characters . Computer Graphics (SIGGRAPH '89 Proceedings), 23(3):243--252, 1989.
8. P. Ekman, Facial expression of emotion. American Psychologist, 48, 384-392.
9. M. Girard, A. Maciejewski, Computational modeling for the computer animation of legged figures. Computer Graphics (SIGGRAPH '85 Proceedings), 20(3):263--270, 1985.
10. B., Hayes-Roth, and R., van Gent, Improvisational puppets, actors, and avatars, in Proceedings of the Computer Game Developers' Conference, Santa Clara, CA, 1996.
11. J. Hodgins, W. Wooten, D. Brogan, J O'Brien, Animating Human Athletics, Computer Graphics (SIGGRAPH '95 Proceedings), 30(3):71--78, 1995.
12. M. Johnson, WavesWorld: PhD Thesis, A Testbed for Three Dimensional Semi-Autonomous Animated Characters , MIT, 1994.
13. P. Maes, T. Darrell and B. Blumberg, The Alive System: Full Body Interaction with Autonomous Agents in Computer Animation'95 Conference, Switzerland, April 1995 .IEEE Press, pages 11-18.
14. M. Minsky, Society of Mind , MIT press, 1986.
15. C. Morawetz, T. Calvert, Goal-directed human animation of multiple movements. Proc. Graphics Interface}, pages 60--67, 1990.
16. K. Perlin, An image synthesizer. Computer Graphics (SIGGRAPH '85 Proceedings)}, 19(3):287--293, 1985.
17. K. Perlin, Danse interactif. SIGGRAPH '94 Electronic Theatre, Orlando.
18. K. Perlin, Real Time Responsive Animation with Personality , IEEE Transactions on Visualization and Computer Graphics, 1(1), 1995.
19. K. Perlin, A. Goldberg, Improv: A System for Scripting Interactive Actors in Virtual Worlds, Computer Graphics; Vol. 29 No. 3. 1996.
20. K. Perlin, Layered Compositing of Facial Expression, SIGGRAPH '97 Technical Sketch, Los Angeles. 1997.

21. K. Perlin, A. Goldberg, Sid and the Penguins, SIGGRAPH '98 Electronic Theatre, Orlando. 1998.
22. K. Perlin, Responsive Actors in Shared Virtual Worlds, 2000 International Conference on Virtual Worlds and Simulation, San Diego.
23. K. Sims, Evolving virtual creatures . Computer Graphics (SIGGRAPH '94 Proceedings), 28(3):15--22, 1994.
24. N. Stephenson, Snow Crash Bantam Doubleday, New York, 1992.
25. S. Strassman, Desktop Theater: Automatic Generation of Expresssive Animation, PhD thesis, MIT Media Lab, June 1991. (online at http://www.method.com/straz/straz-phd.pdf)
26. D. Terzopoulos, X. Tu, and R. Grzesczuk Artificial Fishes: Autonomous Locomotion, Perception, Behavior, and Learning in a Simulated Physical World, Artificial Life, 1(4):327-351, 1994.
27. A. Witkin, Z. Popovic, Motion Warping Computer Graphics (SIGGRAPH '95 Proceedings), 30(3):105-108, 1995.

Avatar Physics and Genetics

Jeffrey Ventrella

jeffrey@ventrella.com

Abstract. A technology for creating avatars (virtual humans), and the principles behind its design are described. Avatars in this system are generated entirely through computer programming. Variation is enabled through the specification of hundreds of parameters, which are treated within a genetic paradigm. Animated motion is achieved through a combination of forward dynamics and parametric motion control algorithms. This paper demonstrates how the design of a virtual human can be achieved through simulation based on natural laws, such as in physics and biology.

1 Introduction

While there have been many advances in rendering and animation of humans for virtual reality, there is still a long way to go before these beings become expressive and exhibit a rich repertoire of behaviors. In this paper, I describe how attention to laws of nature (physical and biological) can help facilitate the making of a variety of dynamic and expressive avatars.

Our world is rich and varied, not only because of the visual detail, color, texture, and movement we perceive in it, but also because of our biological and emotional connection to living things, human and non-human. Our world is also rich because of the emergent properties of physical process. A belief expressed in this paper is that a rich virtual reality experience can be achieved through building a foundation of naturalistic laws, whereby more complex, realistic, and expressive levels of detail can emerge easily. With this underlying premise, a prototype of a virtual human has been developed, built entirely out of software, appropriate for a large-scale virtual world.

Many of the established techniques for designing virtual humans are descendants of the tools of computer-aided design and 3D modeling, which is the prevailing paradigm for building virtual world objects. Techniques and principles from traditional art and design have become incorporated into such modeling systems to make the process of human modeling more intuitive [3].

For constructing virtual worlds, standards such as VRML have spawned many technical variants, as well as a culture of users. While including functionality for designing virtual worlds, these paradigms rely heavily on polygonal model representations. Emphasis on polygonal models and rendering is referred to here as the "computer graphics paradigm". In this paradigm, the representation of a human is influenced by the specific nature of 3D modeling and animation software.

This paradigm has been augmented by many other fields as in the extensive human modeling research of Thalmann [5]. This work represents a thorough study in repre-

J.-C. Heudin (Ed.): VW 2000, LNAI 1834, pp. 107-118, 2000.

senting human anatomy, motion, and clothing, including facial modeling. Of note is the detailed modeling of hands, which, like faces, are important for expression.

The approach to virtual human design described in this paper places importance on physics and genetics, and places rendering towards the end of the pipeline. This approach is intended to scale up such that each avatar is unique yet related to the same humanoid gene pool, able to render itself in 3D, and equipped with all the physical laws necessary to land in the virtual world "running".

1.1 Avatars

When you chat in a 3D online world or play one of many 3D computer games, you are operating a synthetic character: an avatar. An avatar is defined here as a synthetic human represented graphically in a virtual world, which is controlled by a real human, and which represents that human's identity. For purposes of this discussion, it is assumed that a virtual camera is positioned near the avatar, (usually behind, in third-person view), and that the camera can be manipulated for alternate views, including first-person view.

We are approaching a time when many of us will have our own avatar online, perhaps multiple avatars. Each will be distinct from every other, able to be customized, able to interact with other avatars and increasingly complex virtual worlds. It will even be possible for avatars to be bred and to reproduce their virtual genes online for future generations. Most of the basic research has been done to achieve this. All that is needed are the appropriate technologies and interfaces.

What makes for an interesting and effective avatar? It depends on its purpose, of course. In the case of a virtual world where communication is important, facial features and expressiveness must be well supported. In the case of action games, physics and interaction with the world must be well supported. In the case of hardcore violent action games, viscera and bodily fluids may be necessary – although that is not the focus here. In fact, this is a rather non-visceral approach to what it means to be or to interact with a human. Having said that, however, the experience of moving around on a terrain or floor, having a sense of balance, and other physical aspects of being a human in the world, are important in this representation. Thus, these avatars can be seen as supporting two major needs: social and physical. Where genetics comes into play is mostly in the service of social needs: the diversity and manipulable aspects of genetic customization are important components to having a unique avatar in a virtual world, and in being a part of a large, diverse community.

1.2 Parametric Motion

In setting out to design a virtual human, this method assumes the problem as a matter of simulation. Physically based modeling techniques have become common tools in computer game engineering, and are useful ingredients for building rich, immersive virtual worlds. Techniques inspired by the biological bases of motion control are proven useful as well [1]. In the work of Hodgins [2], there is detailed attention to human motion, in which biomechanics data are used to drive physically-based models.

Motion Capture systems are very useful for visualizing the motions of humans, and are used widely in computer games. But while motion capture data provide realistic motions, they are not adaptive, like the cerebellum, and cannot be scaled easily to handle any situation, such as complex terrains, collisions with varieties of objects, and variations in user control.

Techniques for "gluing together" separate motion scripts have become sophisticated, but the amount of glue and kinds of glue necessarily grows with each new inclusion of a motion script. In contrast, a parametric, reactive system for handling the motions of humans has potential. While a large amount of work must be done up front to get it right, the payoffs are big.

1.3 The Body: Three Aspects

There are three main aspects to the avatar's physical body:

Bones
The body geometry is based on a hierarchical tree structure of bones (the skeletal system) comprised of rigid rods connected at joints. At the base of the hierarchical tree is the *pelvis* node. Each bone possesses a complete orientation matrix with 3D rotation values.

Motion Control
All animation procedures operate on the avatar's skeleton, and consist of translating and rotating the pelvis (i.e., the avatar), and rotating individual bones. Motion is controlled by a combination of physics, procedural animation, and user input. Facial points constitute non-skeletal geometry, and are also dynamic.

Surface
An outer surface is rendered around the bones, to visualize skin and clothes. A combination of rendering techniques have been prototyped – a few are discussed below.

There are of course many more components than these. It is important to note that the order of these components is significant, and critical to the notion of designing a human "from the inside out". In many human modeling systems, the outer surface is the first thing that is modeled, using a 3D modeling application. This is useful for artistically specifying a desired shape, but causes difficulty when the animation system requires a skeleton. In a technique described by Thalmann [5], after designing the polygonal surface of a human model, the bones had to be "tediously" placed within the confines of the vertices.

The approach developed here makes a trade-off: by creating a completely code-based model, it is not possible to design the outer shape of the avatar with the ease that advanced modeling systems provide. However, it is possible to design in "parameter space", in such a way that the geometry and the motion are determined on a more fundamental level. By working hard to set up intuitive interfaces, and carefully-chosen parameters, what is provided is a rich palette for creative control.

2 Physics

Having a physical presence in a virtual world is a basic property of being a 3D avatar. It is also a basic ingredient of the most primitive of computer games. Near the low end of the spectrum is something like Pac Man, a sprite whose physical properties consist simply of 2D location and orthogonal movement. Moving up through the history of computer games, we encounter higher-level physical identities, incorporating three dimensions, deeper physics, articulated bodies, and realistic interactions with environmental factors, such as terrain. There is almost no end to the levels of detail that can be added to this list, as we project into the future of experiencing a virtual reality through our virtual selves.

As far as avatars are concerned, there is no one correct physical model: physics is simply a tool to aid in utility and experience, and there are many levels of physical simulation that can be implemented for different purposes. Deep physics, such as an intensive forward dynamics simulation, may not be the most appropriate for all situations, as discovered in early experiments. The solution found was to use a hybrid, pseudo-physics model, with a variety of motion-controllers. Just as Marvin Minsky suggested that intelligence cannot be characterized with one elegant algorithm, suitable for a single AI model, the human body's ensemble of motions is likewise a collection of many layers and styles of control.

However, if at some low level a Newtonian model is at work, many things will come for free. In this model, the position and orientation of the (standing/walking) avatar are determined by a forward dynamics model, as illustrated in Figure 1:

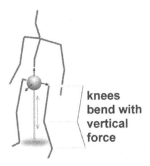

Fig. 1. Forces affecting standing/walking avatar

Two forces act upon the avatar body to affect its linear velocity and angular velocity: 1) the *knee force*, and 2) the *gyroscope*.

The knee force acts upon the vertical component of the avatar's velocity. Essentially, if the vertical distance from the ground to the avatar's position is less than the avatar's leg length, then a force is added to the avatar's vertical velocity, pushing it upward. There is also a friction constant which dampens the vertical velocity. The effect is much like the force the knees have on the body in order to keep it above the ground. When you jump out of a tree and land on your feet, there is some give, and you spring back into the standing position. The gyroscope is a force which acts upon the angular velocity of the avatar by applying rotational forces which keep the upper body in an approximate upright orientation.

These two forces affect the position and orientation of the avatar's body. Using this representation, the avatar can be affected by gravity, always being kept approximately leg-length above the ground, experiencing (soft) collisions with the ground, and correcting itself from angular perturbation, as indicated in Figure 2.

Fig. 2. Avatar interacting with terrain.

When an avatar is weakened, the knee and gyroscope forces decrease, thus the avatar's knees bend more and the body has less energy to stay upright. A dead avatar has zero knee-spring and gyroscope forces – it is essentially a passive Newtonian object, no longer exerting any life-force.

A few of the ways in which the positions and orientations of the individual bones are updated, in relation to the above-mentioned physics, are described below.

2.1 Walking

Avatar locomotion is controlled by a computer mouse and/or keyboard, used to specify two forces: forward, and turning. Forward control adds forces to the avatar's linear velocity along the avatar's forward axis. Turning control adds forces to the avatar's angular velocity about the avatar's up axis. As secondary forces, small amounts of pitching and rolling are caused by forward and turning forces, respectively (for effect, not necessarily for realism). When the avatar is on the ground (i.e., the vertical distance between the pelvis and the ground is less than or equal to leg length), *and* the avatar's horizontal speed is larger than a small threshold, the avatar is set to "walking mode", and is then animated by way of a walking system. The walking system has three components:

1. Foot Step Animator
The foot step animator directly moves two ideal heel positions through space, corresponding to the positions the heel would be in if the avatar were walking. The distance of each forward step and the period of the stepping cycle are determined by the horizontal speed and the lengths of the legs.

2. Inverse-Kinematic Leg-Bender

The inverse-kinematic leg bender sets the orientations of the thighs, shins, and feet, so that the heel is placed as close as possible to the ideal position as determined above.

3. Periodic Body Part Oscillator

The periodic body part oscillator transforms non-leg body parts according to periodic waves whose frequencies are determined by the step cycle, and whose amplitudes are determined by the horizontal speed. Various parts of the body are oscillated to create distinct walking styles. These parts include the neck, the hips, the shoulders, the arms, and many others. About a dozen parameters for these body part oscillations are controlled by genes, and they are responsible for a large variety of gaits.

2.2 Animal Physics and Topology

A technique used for non-human physics is similar in principle to that of the avatar, except that the number of point masses, springs, types of springs, and topology may vary. As an example, a small mammal's body may be represented as two main point masses (pelvis and chest) connected by a high-friction spring, and supported above the ground by two vertical knee forces, similar to the one used for the avatar, as illustrated in Figure 3.

Fig. 3. Four-legged mammal physics

The head and neck complex may be built either with springs or with rigid body dynamics. In either case, each "body sphere" possesses a position, a radius, and a complete orientation matrix defined in the world coordinate system.

While Newtonian physics are affecting the point masses in fairly realistic ways, the animal imparts *intentional* forces on these parts as well. These can come in a great variety, depending on the animal and depending on the mental state of the animal.

2.3 Interacting with the World

I will not go into much detail on the topic of how avatars interact with objects in the world other than the ground. The avatar, for most purposes, is defined physically as a point mass with position and velocity, and also having a radius, orientation, and rotational velocity. Thus it is also possible to detect simple collisions with other objects and to apply forces to the avatar and/or the other objects appropriately. Higher detailed collisions with objects can be calculated on individual body spheres (occurring at the joints of the skeleton), each of which possess a position, radius, and implied velocity. Higher-detailed collisions (i.e., on arbitrarily-shaped body part volumes), while important for intimate interactions, are beyond the scope of this exploration.

One basic example of interacting with objects in the world is an inverse-kinematic arm controller, which handles placement of the hands on certain objects, and calculates appropriate arm orientations. This is similar to the inverse-kinematic leg-bender of the walking system described above.

3 Genetics

Parametric representations naturally lend themselves to a genetic interpretation. The design methodology of the avatar includes identifying variations in the parameters used in the computer code, setting ranges for these parameters, and placing them into an array, which can be manipulated in a variety of ways. This array is called the *genotype*, and every avatar has one.

3.1 Genotype

The genotype consists of an array of values that determine various attributes of an avatar. The gene ranges provide an overall genetic space within which all possible avatars can exist. While some of the remote regions of this genetic space are occupied by some freaky-looking monsters, the space is largely occupied by reasonable-looking humanoids. Figure 4 shows five ethnic types, each existing within the genetic space.

Fig. 4. Avatar faces showing genetic variety

3.2 Genetic Customization

Figure 5 shows some examples of avatar faces that were made with the *Genetic Customization Tool*. With this tool, one can manipulate about 60 of the more than 100 genes which describe an avatar. These genes affect body shapes, colors, motions, facial proportions, and walking styles. The number of genes and the manner in which they interact, is such that many possible avatars can be generated within one system.

The Genetic Customization Tool allows users to interactively tweak genes in a continuous manner and to see the changes in real time. This is done "online" within the virtual world with physics continually running. One does not have to remove the avatar from the world and place it into a separate application. While customizing, one can rotate the avatar and move the camera closer to the face or away to see the whole body. This interface is similar to the real-time genetic tweakers used in two previous research projects: the *Character Evolution Tool* [6] and *Darwin Pond*, [7] (www.ventrella.com).

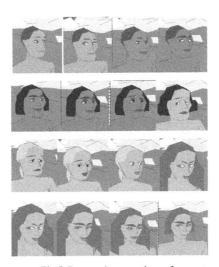

Fig.5. Progressive mutations of an avatar

With this genetic representation of avatars in place, it is possible to later apply genetic operators and use a variety of genetic manipulations, including cross-over from sexual reproduction.

4   Social Aspects

4.1   Intentional vs. Newtonian Motion

Physical simulation has become a common ingredient in many animated media and it has made a difference in the level of realism possible. But when modeling humans, it is not enough to build a human-shaped 3D object and simply to apply some Newtonian mechanics to its parts so that it moves according to physical laws. Humans do not roll down hills like spheres and they do not topple over passively when hit (unless they're dead). Humans, like all agile animals, have a way of overcoming many of the constraints of physics, transcending it, exhibiting motions and behaviors which can be complex, goal-directed, often linguistic in nature, and often opposing the laws of gravity (as in the finer moments of dance and sport). This is why inverse kinematics is such a useful technique for humans and animal animation: we have neuromuscular systems for positioning parts of our bodies in precise ways.

As part of a methodology for designing avatars, one might begin with the premise that the avatar is two things: 1) a physical object (obeying the laws of physics) and, 2) an intentional object (obeying the laws of biology, psychology, sociology, and culture). This is especially important since most avatars are instruments of expression and communication within online worlds where community and communication rule.

4.2 What's in a Face?

An example of this principle in this implementation is the design of the face. The avatars described here are designed for optimal communication, expression, and individuality. Rather than consider the face as a physical surface made out of teeth, hair, and skin, the design of the face is approached from a visual expression point of view. To most of us, a face is a giver and taker of expression, and the locus of identity. It is a dynamic, expressive sign – an animated visual signal, possessing distinct visual elements which are evolved for message-giving, and message receiving. Faces are unique among objects in the universe which are perceived and responded to by humans. Not only are our eye/brain systems highly tuned to faces, but we tend to filter out noise in the background, where mouth, eye, head motion, etc., compromise the salient features to which we respond. For this reason, a face was developed which dedicates computation to the behaviors and geometry of mouths, eyes, and head motions.

These faces are dynamic, in that every avatar's expressive state from moment to moment can alter the geometry of the face, procedurally. In addition to this, individual genetics determines a great variety. For these reasons, a *procedural* head was designed, generated in software, along with the control functionality necessary for operation, instead of using a pre-existing model. Figure 6 shows four examples of facial expressions. The rendering style here uses flat shading and real time-computed silhouettes: outlines – basic ingredients in cartoon art. This rendering style eliminates most of the modeling aspects that are not relevant to expression, and may be a distraction.

Fig. 6. Some facial expressions

4.3 Head Orientation

One of the most salient indicators of sentience in animals is the orientation and rotation of the head. Looking and listening are often accompanied by orienting and re-orienting the head, as the animal moves through reality, encountering other animals along the way. Avatars in a social world must engage with each other, sometimes in flirtatious situations. To simulate the effect of aiming the head and gazing, a form of inverse-kinematics is applied to the head, except, unlike most inverse-kinematic techniques, which simulate physical forces as applied to articulated bodies, this one simulates a psychological force.

To create an upright position of the head, under normal conditions, a head gyroscope is applied: while the head can turn (or "yaw", rotating around the global vertical axis), the head cannot tilt forward or from side to side as a result of the neck (its parent part) rotating. This breaks the parent-child constraint of hierarchical modeling. Essentially, this means that unless the avatar is specifically rotating its head as part of an expression or a gaze, the head remains upright, its *up* vector always pointing in the global *up* direction, as illustrated in Figure 7.

Fig. 7. The head gyroscope makes avatars look more alive

I remember when I implemented this simple constraint. Many people noticed a marked difference, noting that the avatars seemed more alive, although they could not say why.

5 Visualization

With this approach, avatars are seen as synthetic personas that lie outside of reality, yet refer to our reality, in a stylized manner, where some things are left out, and other things are exaggerated. For instance, eyes are a little larger than normal, genetic variation is extreme, and walking motions are exaggerated. To represent avatars visually, a cartoon-style outline renderer is used. It displays 3D polygonal models with flat-shading and outlines.

The outline renderer displays lines only on the silhouette, or *horizon* edges. The avatar head shown in Figure 8a is drawn *without* the outline renderer eliminating non-silhouette edges, to show a contrast to the faces shown in previous figures, which demonstrate the effect of the outline renderer. The outline renderer only displays the edges whose shared triangles lie such that their surface normals satisfy the following condition: One surface normal (A) points towards the viewpoint, and the other (B) points away (determined by calculating the dot product of the line of sight with each normal), as indicated in Figure 8b.

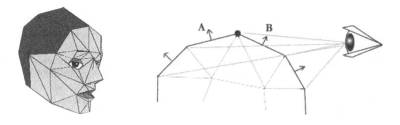

Fig. 8. a) Facial geometry showing all edges, b) silhouette edge detection

5.1 Level of Detail

An important aspect of the avatar design, as is true with the design of any object in a virtual world, is Level of Detail. At any given time, an avatar is rendered using one of many possible levels of detail – as dictated by the distance from the viewpoint to the avatar. Each of these rendering levels has been designed separately. Level of detail in an online community takes on a more complex meaning when it includes not just mere viewing distance, but also "importance" in a given situation, as well as crowd considerations.

6 Conclusion

The avatar system which I have described demonstrates an intensive software-oriented view towards modeling humans. It may seem "anti-art" to some readers, since it essentially eliminates the "traditional" character animator and 3D modeler from the process. But, this conclusion would be far from the truth. The belief is that the art is in the software, and is located in the details of how the physical laws, genetic parameters, and motion controllers are defined, such that human-like expression and genetic variety emerge. Computer simulations allow us to speak a language akin to the dynamics of nature – involving the elements of time, physics, adaptive behavior, genetic inheritance, interaction, and communication. An avatar technology which is built upon these principles, and in which 3D rendering effectively expresses these underlying principles, has potential for generating continuous novelty and variety, as virtual worlds grow larger and more complex.

Acknowledgements

I would like to thank Dr. Will Harvey for his technical help and conceptual contributions in designing avatars, and for supporting my research into new technologies. Thanks also goes to Ben Werther, Tim Nufire, and Amy Morris. Thanks also to Tom Melcher for his support. And finally, thanks to my wife, Nuala.

References

1. Badler, N., Barsky, B., Zeltzer, D. Making Them Move. Morgan Kaufmann, 1991.
2. Hodgins, Jessica. Simulating Human Motion, web site:
   http://www.cc.gatech.edu/gvu/animation/Areas/humanMotion/humanMotion.html,   Graphics, Visualization, and Usability Center, Georgia Institute of Technology, (3/2000)
3. Ratner, Peter., 3-D Human Modeling and Animation. John Wiley & Sons. 1998
4. Reynolds, Craig. Flocks, Herds, and Schools: A Distributed Behavioral Model. Computer Graphics, Vol 21, Number 4, July, 1987
5. Thalmann, Nadia, and Moccozet, Laurent. Virtual Humans on Stage. In Virtual Worlds (ed. Jean-Claude Heudin). Perseus Books, 1998. (pages 95-125)
6. Ventrella, J. Disney Meets Darwin – An Evolutionary-based Interface for Exploration and Design of Expressive Animated Behavior. MIT Master's Thesis. MIT Press, 1994
7. Ventrella, Jeffrey. *Darwin Pond*, artificial life software, 1997. www.ventrella.com

Virtual Living Beings

Michel BRET

Université PARIS 8
2, rue de la Liberté 93526 Saint Denis - France
Michel.Bret@univ-paris8.fr

Abstract. The body of 3D synthesis has long been described as an «object». Scientists and artists alike are today reconsidering the subject of life and reality through virtual simulations. We must move beyond the real-virtual duality (which encompasses the body-mind duality) towards a redefinition of both terms: That which is real must henceforth integrate a virtual component (since we perceive that which is virtual) and that which is virtual is unable to exist outside the sphere of reality, since it is expressed through physical machines.The living body is a pluridisciplinary subject, being influenced both on the scientific side by medicine and biology and from the sphere of arts by philosophy and its ties to the mind. Thus, it can not be dealt with adequately by a unilateral approach. Various analyses of this problem will show that an analytical method alone is insufficient and that approaches which call upon the concept of emergence are necessary.

1 Introduction

The body, considered as the object of perception can be geometrically modeled in 3D and be restituted by a virtual camera. But to do so is to privilege the visual sense, and moreover, the view of a sole observer who is external to this body. However the body is the center for multiple perceptions, not only of its environment, but also of itself, by means of modeling and simulation: The nervous system, simultaneously simulates and acts upon a scene which it virtualizes in an interactive manner so as to be better able to predict. It is thus both witness and actor.
Dynamic models simulating movements by their causes enable the animation of a physical body (weights placed in a forcefield) in interaction with an environment governed by the laws of mechanics.

Behavioral models allow us to give an account of the voluntary interaction of a body with its environment, but only as a pre-programmed automaton.

The autonomy shown by living beings is to be sought not in a construction pre-dating their existence, but in the very process of their creation: The properties which define an auto-organization as living transpire from the auto-organization itself.

Connectionist models such as neural networks do indeed show this type of emerging behavior. The living body is located in history, and partakes in a certain evolution. The ontological study of the of the individual's past must be paralleled with the phylogenetic study of the species to which he belongs. The evolutionary models, such as genetic algorithms and macros, will help us to make an account of this dimension.

J.-C. Heudin (Ed.): VW 2000, LNAI 1834, pp. 119-134, 2000.
© Springer-Verlag Berlin Heidelberg 2000

The modeling of a defined body as object, acting body, body capable of behavior body capable of learning and finally the evolving body will be studied in turn. Each level of description will lead us to the next: Thus, the inadequacies of modeling by databases imply the necessity to have recourse to a constructive rather than a descriptive one, which will lead us to evoke the notions of actors and behavior. The most evolved behaviors, those acquired rather than inherited, require the notion of learning and are modeled by means of neural networks. Finally, the construction of physical models, both behavioral and neural, is not achieved by means of a description pre-dating the existence of the subjects, but rather emerges from the evolution of a population of such subjects.

2 Previous Work

2.1 Of Animation in General

The simulation by traditional methods of animation has been and remains predominant, especially in the sphere of production. This probably due to maximizing immediate returns. Indeed, it is easier to follow in a well-beaten path than it is to innovate.

However, since the eighties, research has oriented towards the use of dynamic models, and in the nineties, towards the use of connectionist models.

Renewing the old conception of representation as «mimesis», these new approaches aim to simulate their functioning rather than render their appearance. Dynamics simulate the world of things and connectionism that of beings. In the next few years, techniques of animation will integrate this new knowledge stemming from «Artificial Life» [23], [30], [13].

2.2 Dynamic Modeling of a Body

David Zeltzer [39] has been using the idea of a «control motor» since 1982 to manage the animation of articulated structures, to which he joins the movement processor which is a pre-figuration of what behavior will be.

While not dealing specifically with living bodies, the work of Demetri Terzopoulos is at the base of the dynamic animation of soft surfaces used to model muscles and skin [34].

Gavin Miller [20] has introduced the use of springs in the simulation of motor muscles to animate snakes and worms.

Armin Bruderlin [7] described human locomotion by a dynamic model of leg movement which he associated with a «goal»oriented direction. By doing so, he anticipated work on the intentionality.

Michael McKenna [19] animated articulated figures by applying Newtonian mechanics and also introduced the ideas of « control center of walking» and «motor program».

Marc Raibert [22] applied robotics to the dynamic control of bipedal artificial beings.

Jessica Hodgins [15] simulated athletic behavior such as running, cycling and jumping by dynamic models compatible with biomechanical facts. She also adapted these behaviors to random actors. [16].

2.3 Anatomical Modeling of the Body

Keith Waters [38] introduced a method of parametrizing a facial model which simulated the superficial action of facial muscles so as to synthesize expressions.

Yuencheng Lee [42] took this method and automated it by associating a dynamic model with it. Zajac [40] [41] developed the first model of muscles applied to the synthesis of the human body.

John Chadwick [8] developed a system designed to aid traditional animation of people based on a layered structure which provided various layers of control.

David Chen et Zeltzer [6] proposed producing the deformations of a mobile body by simulating the action of muscles and the associated forces they exert on the skeleton. In order to do this, they had developed a model based on biomechanics and the method of finite elements which had been destined for the use of animators and specialists of the functional study of muscles.

Victor Ng Thow Hing [14] provided a dynamic model of muscles and tendons to control the movements of an articulated body.

Ferdi Scheepers [28] and his collaborators describe a modeling system of the body based on the deformation of muscles induced by skeletal motion.
Jane Wilhelms [37] automatically models skin by voxelising the body mass from which a polygonal isosurface
which is anchored to the muscles by means of springs.

2.4 Behavioral Animation

Craig Reynolds was the first to introduce the concepts of «actor» [24] and «behavior» [25] which were then taken and improved upon by numerous authors.

Xiaoyuan Tu et Terzopoulos [33] synthesized a virtual marine world based on physical model and inhabited by artificial fish, defined as autonomous agents, whose behavior responds to intentions by activating control motors.

In the same way, Radek Grzeszczuk et Terzopoulos [12] built artificial animals which learned by trial and error to move in a virtual environment.

Bruce Blumberg [3] synthesized autonomous virtual creatures capable of behaving in a given environment, but which would also accept exterior control at the level of intention, and at the level of the execution of a motor task.

2.5 Applications of Connectionist and Evolutionary Models

Michiel Van de Panne and Eugène Fiume [35] [36] used neural networks of which the inputs are the values of sensors and of which the outputs set off locomotion motors so as to build the creatures which could discover the processes involved in walking.

Karl Sims [29] used selection, variation and mutation techniques on LISP expressions (inspired by genetic programming [18]) to create complex structures such as plants, textures and movements etc...

Karl Sims [30] used neural networks generated by genetic algorithms to control the muscles of artificial creatures with goal oriented behavior such as swimming, walking and jumping.

3 The Body as an Object

3.1 Modeling of Appearances and Functional Modelling

We will call «modeling of appearances» any abstract construction procedure by which a physical perception is simulated. For example, perspective projection transforms an object into a 2D representation, isomorphous to the retinal image. In the same way, laser data capturing by means of «cyberware» digitizes the visible surfaces of objects.

If the representation is an analytical one rather than a perceptual one, we will speak of a «functional modeling». For instance, instead of seizing the body's external surface, skin, an automatic anatomical and biomechanical is carried out by defining a skeleton, a dynamic system of muscles and fatty tissues, and then a laser data capture of this abstract model so as to be able to build a model of adaptive skin.

To make this abstract representation «work» enables us to dynamically reconstruct the skin frame by frame and thereby allows us to synthesize any movement. While the laser data capture can only provide us with samples of surfaces that are difficult to animate, except to digitize all positions (3D camera), it thus limits the animation to the capturing of real movements.

3.2 Deep and Visible Layers

The *skeleton* is defined as an articulated structure made up of rigid elements, bones, and subject to both positional forces (at the attachment points) and angular ones in the shape of possible movements. The root of the associated tree is the supporting bone, for instance, a bone in the foot in contact with the ground. The changing of this bone, as in walking, supposes a dynamic reorganizing of the root of anchorings-the calculation of new links when the root changes). *Muscles* are defined by a dynamic system made up of elements of a certain elasticity, in this case springs, which are submitted to positional forces and constraints at the bones, the attachment points, and of shape (limited elongation and compression, constant volume [21] [26] [32].

Fatty tissues and organs dynamically attached to the bones and muscles complete this corporal mass.

Lastly, *Skin* is obtained by a virtual laser which analyses this complex structure so as to determine a supple surface enveloping the entirety of preceding parts. Openings such as the mouth, eyes and nostrils allow a partial view of the body's interior.

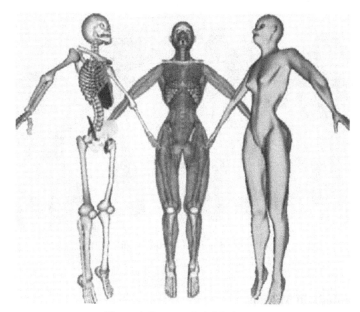

Figure 1: Deep and visible layers

3.3 Skin Generation

A virtual laser is defined by a cylindrical mail-clad surface on which each summit features a position which emits light towards the cylinder's axis. The intersection of this beam with the anatomical model provides an element (n,f,x,y) with :

n = the identifier of the body part intersected (bone, muscle, fatty tissue or organ).

f = the side intersected.

x, y = barycentric coordinates of the intersection of that side.

The object made up by these elements features the projection of the cylinder on the body.

A spring is then attached between each element and the corresponding summit of the cylindrical surface, and is then dynamically left to find its own balance point by the method of relaxation by preventing it from crossing the body which is considered an obstacle. The skin will readjust itself automatically for each body movement to the new configuration of the anatomical model.

Since it is programmable, the virtual laser is far more flexible than its real life equivalent.

1) The surface defined by the laser is not necessarily cylindrical but can at least adapt to the overall shape of the body.

2) It can visit hollows. For this, it is only necessary to avoid aiming for the axis of the cylinder but rather in body's general direction.

3) Its precision can be adjusted depending on the wealth of details of the surface to be analyzed.

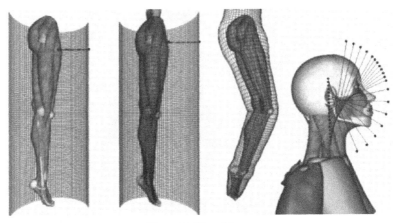

Figure 2. Virtual laser

4 The Body in Motion

4.1 Dynamic Modelling

A dynamic articulated skeleton placed in a vertical force field will collapse to the ground (if the ground is considered an obstacle) (see fig. 3). A living body endowed with certain properties (*mass, elasticity*, the non penetration of its parts) placed in a force field will start moving under the influence of these forces and also the forces that it itself impresses on its *muscles* (see fig. 4)

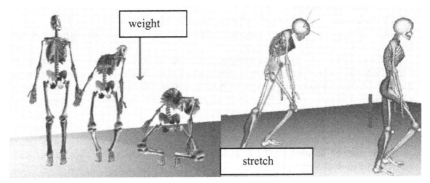

Figure 3: Collapsing   Figure 4: muscular control

Mechanisms of reflex compensation allow the body to maintain a posture, for instance standing, when a force such as gravity counteracts the posture. The length of the muscle and the amplitude of these forces are regulated by a negative retro-feedback loop. A stop point having been defined, the manipulated parameter is measured by means of a sensor, and the contraction is modified so as to minimize the discrepancy between the observed and expected values. (See fig. 5).

Furthermore, movement macros translate these complex movements, the expression of conscious will. The running of these implies anticipated postural adjustments and the compensation for overbalancing. (See fig. 6).

These voluntary movements are distinguished from reflex movements in that they are acquired during a learning period.

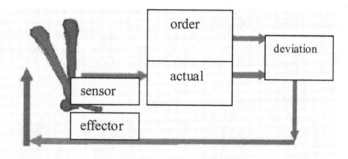

Figure 5: Reflex control.

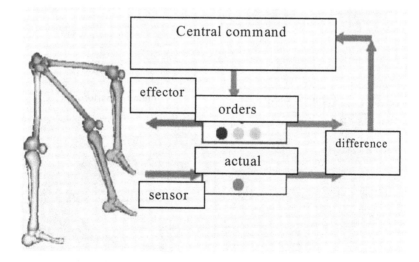

Figure 6: Voluntary control

A *dynamic* model which explains the physical behavior of an inert body must be paralleled by a *behavioral* model which explains the voluntary reactions of this body to its environment.

4.2 Biomechanical Modelling

Muscles, considered as dynamic elements, are comparable to *springs* of variable stiffness and elasticity, which are submitted to forces of compression and elongation. Thus, the skeletal muscles are connected to bones which function as levers, for instance, the biceps controls the radius relative to the humerus. The *total force* exerted on a muscle is equal to the sum of the *force of elasticity* of the return spring which is equivalent to a spring varying in an exponential way with its elongation. The energy built up by the stretching of the extensor muscle is unleashed in the shape of a elastic return which brings about extension. [11].

The movements of a limb results from the interplay between the return forces of the extensor and contractor muscles (which are considered as springs) and the forces exerted on the tendons under the control of the nervous system.

4.3 Examples of Muscles

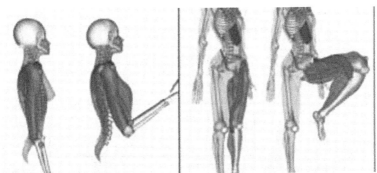

Figure 7: Biceps   Figure 8: Sartorius

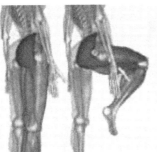

Figure 9: Gluteal muscles   Figure 10: Head and neck

5 Behavioural Model

5.1 Perception and Action: The Role of the Brain

The sense organs provide the brain with information on the outer world and on the state of the body itself. The analysis of this information must first go through a series of relevant sensors. For instance, when we look at the world with our heads cocked, we still continue to see the horizon as level as our visual information is corrected by that coming from the inner ear. Alain Berthoz [2] talks about *the sense of movement* as a multisensorial perception by which the body correctly judges its position and movements.

The role of the brain is threefold :

1) Firstly, it constructs a predictive model of what the state of the body-environment system will at a later date.

2) Then it starts up a simulation based on this model.

3) Lastly, it ensures a permanent interactive control between the simulation and reality by adjusting the first to the second if necessary.

5.2 Adaptative Behaviour

Let us take the case of a falling ball which we wish to catch. For a very short space of time, the brain analyses the situation and calculates the ball's velocity (the difference between these two close positions), its probable trajectory (which depends on its weight which is inferred from the visual analysis of its texture and prior knowledge). From this, it deduces a strategy for moving its arm, forearm and hand so that the latter can be in close vicinity of the ball at a later stage. This strategy is then carried out by the sending of orders to the muscles in the arm, and compared frame by frame as it were, to the real positions of the hand and the ball.

In the case of any discrepancy, the strategy is consequently amended (see fig. 10).

Such behavior can be implemented by a *states machine* responsible for commanding a series of elementary orders of which the sequence is determined by the values of the sensors.

For instance, walking on an irregular surface can be simulated by a periodical series of swinging gestures of the legs producing a step. To place a foot on the ground activates a pression sensor which activates the next step. In this way, the body can climb stairs. A *knowledge database* allows it to deal with particular situations such as ascending, rotating, descending, running etc.

Whatever the complexity of the implemented behaviors, whatever the wealth of knowledge in the database, the body will always act according to a program set in stone, and will only ever be able to adapt to the environment for which the program was written. To be able to deal with any new situation, the body must be capable of *learning*.

World: detailed analysis ----> Simulation: (velocity, trajectory, strategy)

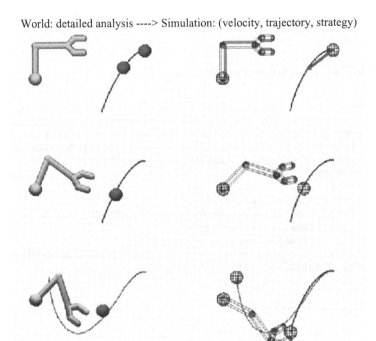

Unforeseen change ----> Strategy modification

Figure 10: Adaptive behavior.

6 Connectionnist Model

6.1 Neural Networks

Rather than seeking an algorithmic solution to a complex problem, a neural network is built and put in the company of this problem in "question and answer" or again "trial and error" mode letting it autoconfigure so as to best respond to examples. This is called supervised learning. The property of *generalization* of a neural network ensures that it can react suitably to examples not previously encountered. [5] [1] [4]. An unsupervised learning can be carried out by Kohonen's auto-organization algorithm. [27].

6.2 Applied Example

Influenced by the work of Van de Panne and Fiume [35] as well as that of Karl Sims [29], we implemented the *back-propagation* algorithm on neural networks endowed with an input level, one or more hidden levels, and an output level, and of which the relative strength of connections have been randomly initialized.

Sensors of different kinds are connected to the inputs. These will be for instance pression sensors for the carrying foot or angular sensors for determining the relative positions of the limbs etc.

The outputs send orders to contract to the *motors* to which they are connected.

Learning pairs (I,T) are presented successively to the network, T being the theoretical response corresponding to input I. The network calculates a response R from I, and the T-R difference is used to correct the weights so as to minimize this difference.

In practical terms, the inputs (I) are positions of imbalance and the theoretical responses (T) are the forces which have to applied to the muscles so as to re-establish balance. With a network of twenty or so neurones and the same number of pairs (E,T), 20000 trials were necessary for the network to restabilize. For non-learned I' inputs, the corresponding R' responses were correct in that the learning pairs constituted a sufficiently representative sample of the infinite totality of possible situations. Random I inputs can be given to the network to train and check that the R responses obtained do indeed restore balance. If not, the correct R' response must be sought and the process repeated, adding the (E, R') pair to the totality of (E,T) pairs. An automatic calculation of this correct R' response is desirable so as to make the process entirely autonomous. In the example of restoring balance, the forces required by some of the major muscles can be calculated so as to displace projection of the skeleton's system center of gravity towards the base.

Input -> Hidden level -> Output

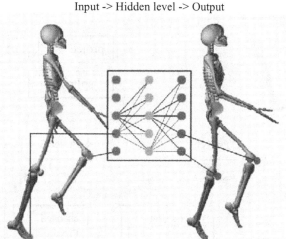

Sensors (pression, angle, position) -------> Dynamic pairs.

Figure 11:Supervised learning by a network of neurons.

6.3 Outputs in the Shape of "Projects"

For more elaborate actions such as walking, a unique reflex action is no longer sufficient. We have then defined outputs in the shape of *projects* in this case, dynamic triplets (C0,C1,C2) interpolated by a spline, C0 being the value of the pair in the project running at the time of impulsion, C1 and C2 defining the continuation of the project. Such a project is made «tangent» to the current project so as to avoid first order discontinuities (see fig. 12).

These forces are sent directly to the muscles, and at each moment, the input sensors give information about the gesture motioned by the body. In case of too great a discrepancy, the project is corrected so as to minimize it. The end of the project which is running or an external event such as the foot coming into contact with the ground or a step for instance, will start a new activation of the network analyzing the sensors and deducing a new project.

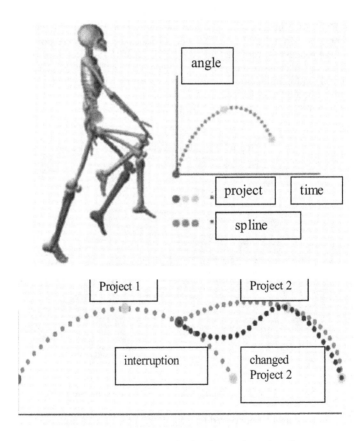

Figure 12: Outputs in the shape of "projects".

7 Evolutionist Model

7.1 Evolution by Genetic Algorithms

The genetic algorithms initially developped by John Holland [17], are exploration algorithms based on natural and genetic selection, making use of psuedo-random processes. Aside from their simplicity, they are characterised by their remarkable robustness and demonstrate adaptive behaviour close to that of humans [10][9].

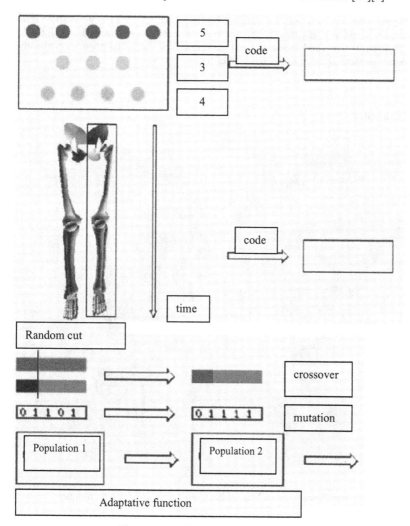

Figure 13: Evolution by genetic algorithms.

7.2 Impementation

Building on the ideas of Karl Sims [31], we formed a population of individuals whose genetic material contained the description of the neural network used during learning and the general description of the body. The construction of these body elements, considered as actors, had been parameterized.

We then defined an *adaptative function* which it was necessary to optimize, for instance for a distance covered by walking. Lastly, we made this population evolve by *crossover* (mixing the genetic material) and *mutation* (random variations) by selectively breeding the better-adapted individuals [10].

Despite the intensity of time and effort required, as in each generation it is necessary to run an animation during which it will exhibit a greater or lesser aptitude for walking, this method seems to yield good results if the initial population already responds sufficiently well to the assessed criterion.

7.3 Examples

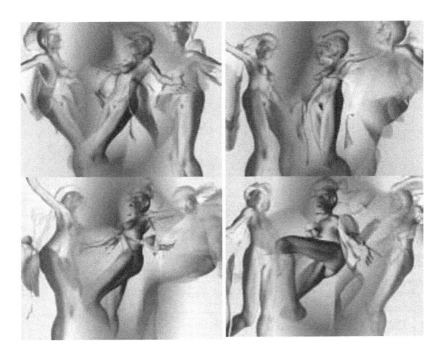

Images from films of Michel Bret generated with such tecnniques

8 Conclusion and Future Work

We have shown that the living body, as a transversal subject, does not admit a unique model stemming from exhaustive analysis. Its simulation, aside from classical 3D geometrical, dynamic and behavioral models, demands a connectionist approach which endows it with the ability to learn, that is, to be able to adapt to a changing environment. Aside from that, the construction of such models is facilitated by the use of populations which conform to the laws of evolution, from which optimized individuals will eventually emerge.

We are currently studying the real-time implementation of these ideas which we intend on applying to choreographic shows in which dancers and virtual intelligent actors would interact.

References

1. Hervé Abdi: Les réseaux de neurones. Presses Universitaires de Grenoble , France (1994)
2. Alain Berthoz: Le sens du mouvement. Éditions Odile Jacob Sciences, France (1997)
3. Bruce M. Blumberg, Tinsley A. Galyean: Multi-Level Direction of Autonomous Creatures for Real-Time Virtual Environments. in Computer Graphics, USA (1995) 47-54
4. Ramachandran Bharath, James Drosen: Neural Network Computing. Windcrest/McGraw-Hill (1994)
5. P. Bourret, J. Reggia, M. Samuelides: Réseaux Neuronaux. Tekena, France (1991)
6. David T. Chen, David Zeltzer: Pump It Up: Computer Animation of Biomechanically Based Model of Muscle. in Computer Graphics Vol. 26(4), USA (1992) 89-98
7. Armin Bruderlin, Thomas W. Calvert: Goal-Directed, Dynamic Animation of Human Walking. in Computer Graphice Vol. 23(3), USA (1989) 232-242
8. John E. Chadwick, David R. Haumann, Richard E. Parent: Layered Construction for Deformable Animated Characters. in Computer Graphics Vol. 23(3), USA (1989) 243-252
9. Jean-Louis Dessalles: L'ordinateur génétique. Hermes, France (1996)
10. David E. Goldberg: Algorithmes Génétiques. Addison-Wesley (1991)
11. Francis Goubel, Ghislaine Lensel-Corbeil: Biomécanique, éléments de mécanique musculaire. Masson France (1998)
12. Radek Grzeszczuk, Demetri Terzopoulos: Automated Learning of Muscle-Actuated Locomotion Through Control Abstraction. in Computer Graphics, USA (1995) 63-70
13. Jean-Claude Heudin: La Vie Artificielle. Hermes France (1994)
14. Victor Ng Thow Hing: A Biomechanical Musculotendon Model For Animating Articulated Objects. Thesis, Departement of Computer Science University of Toronto Canada, (1994)
15. Jessica K. Hodgins, Wayne L. Wooten, David C. Brogan, James F. O'BrienR: Animating Human Athletics. in Computer Graphics, USA (1995) 71-78
16. Jessica K. Hodgins, Nancy S. Pollard: Adaptating Simulated Behaviors For New Characters. in Computer Graphics, USA (1997) 153-162
17. John Holland: Adaptation in natural and artificial systems. Ann Arbor; The University of Michigan Press, USA (1975)
18. J.R. Koza: Genetic evolution and co-evolution of computer programs. in C.G. Langton (Ed.), Artificial Life II, Addison-Wesley, (1991) 603-629
19. Michael McKenna, David Zeltzer: Dynamic Simulation of Autonomous Legged Locomotion. in Computer Graphics Vol. 24(4), (1990) 29-38
20. Gavin S.P. Miller: The Motion Dynamics of Snakes and Worms. in Computer Graphics Vol. 22(4), USA (1988) 168-178
21. Arrnould Moreaux: Anatomie Artistique de l'Homme. Maloine, France (1959)

22. Marc H. Raibert, Jessica K. HODGINS: Animation of Dynamic Legged Locomotion. in Computer Graphics Vol. 25(4), USA (1991) 349-358
23. Thomas S. Ray: Evolution, complexity, entropy, and artificial reality. in Physica, (1994) 239-263
24. Craig W. Reynolds: Computer Animation with Scripts and Actors. in Computer Graphics Vol. 16(3), USA (1982) 289-296
25. Craig W. Reynolds: Flocks, herds, and schools: A distributed behavioral model. in Computer Graphics Vol. 21(4), USA (1987) 25-34
26. Paul Richer: Taité d'Anatomie Artistique. Bibliothèque de l'Image, France (1996)
27. Olivier Sarzeaud: Les réseaux de neurones, contribution à une théorie. Ouset Editions, France (1994)
28. Ferdi Scheepers, Richard E.Parent, Wayne E.Carlsom, Stephen F.May: Anatomy-Based Modeling of the Human Musculature. in Computer Graphics, USA (1997) 163-172
29. Karl Sims: Artificial Evolution for Computer Graphics. in Computer Graphics Vol. 25(4), USA (1991) 319-328
30. Karl Sims: Evolving Virtual Creatures. in Computer Graphics, USA (1994) 15-22
31. Karl Sims: Evolving 3D Morphology and Behavior by Competition. in Artificial Life IVProceedings, MIT Press, USA (1994) 28-39
32. András Szunyoghy, György Fehé: Grand Cours d'Anatomie Artistique. Konemann France (1996)
33. Xiaoyuan Tu, Demetri Terzopoulos: Artificial Fishes: Physics, Locomotion, Perception, Behavior. in Computer Graphics, USA (1994) 43-50
34. Demetri Terzopoulos, John Platt, Alan Barr, Kurt Fleischer: Elastically Deformable Models. Computer Graphics Vol. 21(4), USA (1987) 205-214
35. Michiel Van de Panne, Eugène Fiume: Sensor-Actuator Networks. in Computer Graphics , USA (1993) 335-342
36. Michiel Van de Panne: Control Techniques for Physically-Based Animation. Theses, Université de Toronto Canada (1994)
37. Jane Wilhelms, Allen Van Gelder: Anatomically Based Modeling. in Computer Graphics, USA (1997) 181-188
38. Keith Waters: A Muscle Model for Animating Three-Dimensionam Facial Expression. Computer Graphics Vol. 21(4), USA (1987) 17-24
39. David Zeltzer: Motor Control Techniques for Figure Animation. in IEEE Computer Graphics and Applications Vol. 2,9, USA (1982) 53-59
40. F.E. Zajac, E. L. Topp, P. J. Stevenson: A Dimensionless Musculotendon Model. in Proceedings IEEE Engineering in Medecine and Biology (1986)
41. F.E. Zajac: Muscle and Tendon: Properties, Models, Scaling, and Application to Biomechanics and Motor Control. in Critical Reviews in Biomedical Engineering, Vol. 17, (1989) 359-411
42. Yuencheng Lee, Demetri Terzopoulos, Keith Waters: Ralistic Modeling for Facial Animation. In Computer Graphics USA (1995) 55-6é

A Sound Propagation Model for Interagents Communication

Jean-Sébastien Monzani and Daniel Thalmann

Computer Graphics Laboratory
Swiss Federal Institute of Technology Lausanne
EPFL, DI-LIG
CH 1015 Lausanne, Switzerland
{jmonzani,thalmann}@lig.di.epfl.ch
http://ligwww.epfl.ch

Abstract. In this paper, we will present a method for generating conversations between human-like agents and this will be done by proposing specific parameters for inter-agents messages with an approximation of virtual sound propagation. We will then be able to simulate appropriate human-like behaviours automatically. For instance, we will demonstrate how to create proper reactions for agents that are not able to understand, but only to hear the sentences. Finally, we will develop the notion of conversation privacy and inter-agents cooperation, as all our agents share the same virtual space.

Keywords:

verbal communication model for human-like agents, agents communication language, cooperation.

1 Introduction

Generating human-like conversation between agents requires a lot of steps in order to produce realistic behaviours, and even if many of the movies and video-games productions today still use motion-capture or keyframe motions designed by hand, a lot of work has been done on trying to automate some parts of this process in order to create *autonomous human-like agents*.

As a first step, a conversation must be leaded by some goal, usually, asking someone for an information. This involves in somehow a way to acquire, store and modify the knowledge of the agent. We will not describe here in details how this can be achieved, since our purpose is to concentrate on the conversation process itself, rather than on the goals of the agent. The reader can refer to well known books and articles on Behaviour-Based Artificial Intelligence, as those from Minsky [8] and Wooldridge [12]. In our examples, we will be using a knowledge database with rules triggered by preconditions, and an inference engine.

J.-C. Heudin (Ed.): VW 2000, LNAI 1834, pp. 135–146, 2000.

Exchanging information also requires the definition of an agent communication language, to carry out the semantic of a conversation. Most popular agent communication languages are, for instance, the FIPA ACL [3] or KQML [5].

The next step is to generate the utterances. Walker, Cahn and Whittaker [11] have presented a method to produce dialogs depending on agents' parameters, such as emotion, power and distance. Loyall and Bates [6] also described how to create natural language text-based dialogs.

Finally, realistic animation of a virtual human is not an easy task. Cassel *et al* [2] studied an automatic generation of movements and facial expressions during conversation, based on the content of the dialog itself.

We will also demonstrate in this paper how to handle the sound propagation in an approximated way, without focusing on accurate 3D rendering of spatial sound. While Tsingos and Gascuel [10] and more recently, Funkhouser, Min and Carlbom [4] introduced interesting algorithms for fast rendering of sound occlusion and diffraction effects, we think that simpler models simulating sound within a room and taking almost no CPU time have many useful applications in social simulations. A good example would be the simulation of a party, with many people speaking at the same time, and background music disturbing them. Our model is able to simulate such situations, without high computational cost.

As spoken dialog exchanges more information than point-to-point communication between two software agents, it is worth to first study in section 2 some major requirements, in terms of messages and messages parameters, and to outline what makes this communication different from others agents communication languages. Once we have defined the messages, we are able to present our model for approximate speech propagation in section 3. Also, in an environment where agents have physical locations and can hear what others say, the problem of cooperation is different, and choosing an ordered list of potential candidates is one of the keypoints, as araised in section 4. Section 5 will finally present our application, before concluding.

2   Messages

2.1   Overview

Simply consider two agents, when Agent 1 (Humphrey) would like to speak to Agent 2 (Lauren). We assume that the message m is divided into two parts: the semantic of the message, which could be implemented as an assertion (see example below), and a sound, corresponding to the utterance. The way this sound is generated is left to the user. The duration of the sound is split into two parts: the *time required to understand* the message, and the remaining time, before the end of the sentence.

Consider for instance the sentence "I need a cigarette, darling.". The *time to understand* there could be the duration of "I need a cigarette.", while the *time to complete the sentence* is "darling". As you will see later on, the semantic of the message is not sent until the *time to understand* is reached, i.e., until the agent is able to understand the sentence. Note that the distinction between these two times should be removed for small sentences like "Yes.", but remains valid for "Yes, I did.".

Given message m, the system automatically adds information to it, before sending it (through the agent's *Communication Interface*). We can also distinguish between *semantic information* (who is speaking, who should receive the message, as stressed in section 2.2) and the *physical data* (where the sound source is located in space, what is the sound volume, an so on...).

Example: Humphrey needs a cigarette. The semantic assertion of m might be: (`Humphrey needs cigarette`), while the produced speech would sounds like: "I need a cigarette, darling."Lauren then tries to match the assertion with her rules data base. If she has a rule like

(`?X needs ?Y`) and (`?Z has ?Y`) $\Rightarrow$ (`?Z give ?Y to ?X`) she will then give him a cigarette.

2.2   Messages Parameters

In addition to the usual messages parameters, **sender** and **receiver** which respectively show which agent is speaking and what is the list of agents who should receive the message, we added a **hearer** list of agents who can *hear* the message. This is determined by the spatial configuration of the agents at the time the message is sent. The **content** parameter contains the semantic of the message. Depending on the message type, the content might be an attribute of the message (for instance, the value **begin** together with the message *conversation-status* to start a conversation), an assertion to match with others rules data bases (*query* message), or any useful information. The last basic parameter for speech simulation is the **sound-volume**: it specifies the volume of the speaker's voice, and ranges from 0 (which is not audible), to 1. This single parameter will be the input for our physical model, as described in section 3.

To control the broadcasting of messages, we introduce two more parameters: **spreading** describes the broadcasting method, either sequentially or in parallel. Thus **spreading** = {**sequential** | **parallel**}. If the broadcasting is done sequentially, this would imply that the sender waits for the first receiver's answer, and then decides (or not) to send the message to the second receiver, and so on. This could be useful for cooperation, as presented in section 4.4. If the spreading is sequential, we can choose the delivering order by setting the **spreading-order** parameter. It could be directly defined by the **receiver** list, or by other criteria, like proximity.

To keep track of the conversation, one can also add **in-reply-to** and **reply-with** to specify if we were replying to a previous message, as in FIPA ACL. We also propose to set up a **time-out** attribute: when this time is over, the message is deleted from the agent's memory. The time-out can be used to re-send a message if no answers have arrived during a certain amount of time.

Finally, people interested in realistic speech generation would include voice parameters, like pitch, emotion, and so on...

2.3   List of All Possible Messages

We will now present all the possible messages: they will be discussed later on and in details, but we can already divide them into three classes:

- **Attention and conversation tracking** The basic messages will be discussed in the example given in section 2.4: **is-speaking** is the first message sent to an agent to warn it that someone is currently speaking to it, but the semantic itself is not yet given to the receiver. It is usually followed by a query message, an answer, or any other message in order to properly exchange the information. Once the spoken message is over, the **end-of-message** will warn the receiver that it is now able to react. Depending on the receiver's state, the speaker might receive back a **not-delivered** message, in order to warn it that the message can not be delivered to the receiver (either the receiver is busy doing something else, or does not want to react, or is perhaps too far to be able to hear the message). This message is sent by the Communication Interface of the receiver, and differs from *sorry*, which is sent by the agent, as explained bellow. Usually, the sender will send the same message again in the near future (for instance, agent moves toward the receiver, and speaks to it again). Together with the *not-delivered* message, if Agent 2 is able to hear but not to understand what Agent 1 says, Agent 2 will receive a **dont-understand** message from its Communication Interface. If the receiver has got the message, but either can't or does not want to answer it, it can send **sorry** back to the sender. This prevents the sender from sending the message again, as with *not-delivered*. Finally, we used a general purpose **conversation-status** message to track the different simultaneous conversations that one agent can handle. The typical way for initiating a conversation is to send this message with the content `begin`. Once the conversation is finished, any of its participants sends this message, but with the content **end**. During the conversation, one agent can momentarily suspend it by sending *conversation-status* with content **suspend**.
- **Information request** Since our purpose is more to focus on speech than on information request, we will not focus in depth on the three messages that we used: **query** is a general message for asking something (it is usually an assertion to match with others' rules). In order to answer, the receiver can send **inform-is-true** or **inform-is-false** back to the initial sender to specify whether it considers something to be true or false.
- **Cooperation** Messages dealing with cooperation between an *employer* and some *candidates* will be discussed in depth in section 4. The first message is **request**, sent by the employer to all potential candidates. Their answers are either **agree** or **disagree**, to accept or reject the proposed job. Finally, the employer sends **cooperate** to the agents it has chosen and which agree to cooperate.

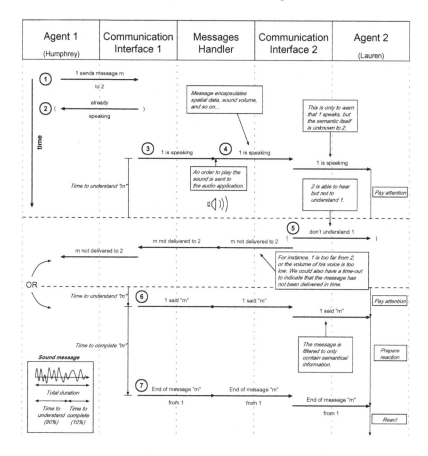

Fig. 1. Agent 1 (Humphrey) speaks to Agent 2 (Lauren). See section 2.4 for details.

2.4   Example

We are now going to demonstrate in practice how a message m is typically sent from agent Humphrey to agent Lauren. Please refer to the corresponding numbers on figure 1:

1. Humphrey sends m to its Communication Interface.
2. He eventually receives a signal that the message can not be sent, since he's already speaking now.
3. If the message can be sent, the Communication Interface adds extra data (who is speaking, where the sound source is located...) and sends this to the Messages Handler. The definition of what we call *Messages Handler* is intentionally vague. The Messages Handler must be able to locate the position

and other data about the agents, and has mechanisms to pass messages. This could be implemented as a client/server architecture, threads, or even one process. The only requirement is that proper messages must be exchanged between the different layers. In our application, we used threads and shared memory (see section 5).

4. The Messages Handler sends the sound file to the proper audio interface, and, assuming that the sound is playing now, it sends an *is-speaking* message to Lauren, to warn her that someone is speaking to her, but without specifying yet what the *meaning* of the message is. This lets Lauren the opportunity to pay attention to Humphrey, by looking at him, for instance.

5. Eventually, if Lauren is busy doing something else, or for any other reason, is not able to listen to the message, a *not-delivered* message is sent back to Humphrey. If Lauren is also able to hear but not to understand what Humphrey says, she will receive a *don't understand* message, to warn her that she might pay attention to this external event.

6. When the *time to understand* is reached, the Communication Interface sends the message *m* to Lauren. This lets her some time to *prepare* her reaction, even if Humphrey is still speaking. At this time, she is really aware of the semantic of the message and able to interrupt Humphrey if she disagrees on something, for instance.

7. Finally, the message *end-of-message* warns Lauren that she can now react to what she has heard.

3   Speech Model

3.1   Motivations

Two common approaches to model the speech are, either to use events triggering the sounds, or simulate the propagation of sound in space, as by Noser *et al* [9].

Whereas the first solution is easy to implement and suitable for real-time applications, we currently lack models to handle parameters like loss of sound amplitude over the distance, or noisy environments. Even if our method is less accurate as the second one, it extends events based communication with a simple model of sound propagation.

Our model relies on two observations: if someone is too far, we won't be able to hear its speech, and it is easier to understand someone who is speaking in our direction (in front of us), especially in noisy environments (a party, for instance).

The variation of speech amplitude for the first case will be called, *radial distribution*, and the second one *angular distribution*. Our idea is to combine these two distributions to compute the sound amplitude at a certain location in the 2D plane (we will consider here a 2D model (actors are both on the ground), but this could be extended to 3D).

3.2   Model for the Speaker

To easily define equations, we will use an axis system attached to the head of the actor: the first axis points toward the "gaze" direction (the direction of the mouth), the second axis points to the left hear[1] and the third, to the top of the head (z axis).

Angular Distribution Let α be an angle around the z axis, with $\alpha = 0$ for the points on the gaze axis. Thus, if α is the angle between the listener and the speaker, when $\alpha = 0$, the listener is standing in front of the speaker, and so, the angular distribution is 100%, whereas, if $\alpha = \pi$, the value falls to A_{behind}. To have smooth transitions, we propose that, for $0 < \alpha < \pi$:

$$D_{angular}(\alpha) = \begin{cases} 100\% & \alpha \leq \alpha_{full} \\ f(\alpha) & \alpha_{full} < \alpha < \alpha_{low} \\ A_{behind} & \alpha_{low} \leq \alpha \end{cases}$$

where $f(\alpha)$ is an interpolation between values at α_{full} and α_{low}. $D_{angular}$ is of course symmetrical for values between 0 and $-\pi$. We used a cubic Hermite interpolation for $f(\alpha)$. Cubic Hermite interpolation for values in $[0, T]$ with range $[x_{min}, x_{max}]$ is defined by $x_{min} + 3\left(\frac{(x_{max}-x_{min})t}{T}\right)^2 - 2\left(\frac{(x_{max}-x_{min})t}{T}\right)^3$, while x_{min} is returned if $t < 0$, and x_{max} corresponds to $t > T$.

Radial Distribution The radial distribution computes the variation of amplitude depending on the distance between the speaker and the listeners. The idea is the same than for the previous distribution. Let x be the distance:

$$D_{radial}(x) = \begin{cases} 100\% & x \leq x_{understand} \\ f(x) & x_{understand} < x < x_{hear} \\ 0\% & x_{hear} \leq x \end{cases}$$

Similarly, we used a cubic Hermite interpolation between 100% and 0% for $f(x)$.

Sound Amplitude The sound amplitude for when agent i is speaking to j is:

$$\text{Amplitude}_i(x, \alpha) = D_{radial}(x).D_{angular}(\alpha)$$

where x and α are the distance and angles between i and j, expressed in the axis system of i. Figure 2 presents the value of the Amplitude in the 2D plane. As one can expect, the value decreases over the distance (radial distribution) and increases for the gaze direction (angular distribution).

3.3 Model for the Listener: Amplitude Thresholds

To evaluate if the listener is able to understand a message, each actor will set two thresholds, $A_{understand}$ and A_{hear}, between 0 and 1. When evaluating the amplitude A of a message, the listener will understand the message if A $\in$ $[A_{understand}, 1]$, hear but not understand when A $\in$ $[A_{hear}, A_{understand}[$ and will not perceive anything if A $\in$ $[0, A_{hear}[$.

---

[1] Since functions are symmetrical, this is not really important.

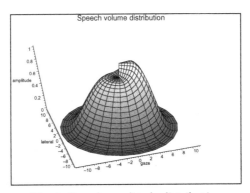

Fig. 2. Speech amplitude distribution

3.4 Summarise of the Parameters

We introduced the following parameters for the speaker:

- α_{full}, α_{low}, A_{behind}: these parameters can be determined based on the sound quality Q of the environment (see next section). We took a linear function of Q for each parameter.
- $x_{understand}$, x_{hear} will depend on the volume of the voice of the speaker (both increase if agent shouts), and are also affected by the sound quality of the environment.
- As one can see, the speaker may simply specify the volume of its voice and still be able to compute the other parameters.

For the audition, parameters $A_{understand}$ and A_{hear} are set for each agent and should not vary over time.

3.5 The Sound Quality of the Environment

The *sound quality of the environment* Q is defined as follow: the higher the noise, the lower the quality will be. The sound quality of the environment is set at the beginning of the simulation. Each time an actor speaks, this value decreases for a certain amount (we call this value the *Environment quality decrease* and use the notation δQ) and will increase again once the sentence is over. Thus, if many actors are speaking at the same time, the quality will be very low, as in real life. For example, if the place is a party or an airport, δQ will certainly be high, whereas it will remain very low for a quiet library.

4 Cooperation

4.1 The Problem

It might occur sometimes that an agent x would like to complete a task (*long term goal*), but that this first requires to achieve three subtasks T_1, T_2, T_3 (*short term goals*). x also knows that it needs some help to perform the second task. So, when the agent has achieved T_1, it will ask other agents to collaborate and help him to perform T_2. Let's consider an environment with four agents: x, y, z and w. If x needs some help, there are many ways to ask for it: x has first to choose the people it would like to work with, it then asks them if they would like to collaborate, and when it has gathered the answers, it chooses the one it will work with.

The choice of agents can rely on theories like Marsh's Trust [7], in which the trust between agents can be modeled and evolve over time.

4.2   With Whom Would I Prefer to Work?

The agent can determine its choice by taking into account what it knows about others.

The first strategy is to set up a *list of priorities*. x establishes a list of all agents it would like to collaborate with, and based upon its beliefs about others, it will assign a priority to each agent. For instance, the list could be $\{z, y\}$, which means that x would prefer to collaborate with z (for instance, because it knows that z can perform the task very efficiently), rather than y, and does not want, or believes, that w will not be able to help him.

If either the agent does not know anything about others, or if it does not have any knowledge about the other's capabilities in the current situation, it can then choose to randomly pick someone to help it, try to gather information about others before making its choice, or use another criteria to make its choice. In the third case, this would lead to a list of priorities (x will tend to favour the ones it likes).

4.3   Who Wants to Help Me?

Assuming that x's priority list is $L = \{y, z\}$, x can send the *request* messages either sequentially or in parallel: in the first case, x asks sequentially each agent $a \in L$, waits for its answer, and chooses the first which wants to cooperate.

In the second case, x asks at the same time for every agent if it wishes to collaborate. It then gathers the answers and picks up one. In the real life, this would look like a meeting, with y and z, where x would say something like "Hello, who would like to help me to do T_2?".

4.4   Messages Passing for a Collaboration

Four messages are required to choose collaborative agents: the agent needing help (*employer*) first sends a *request* to all potential *candidates*, with the job it wishes them to perform. Each candidate agrees or not to do it, the employer chooses one candidate, and sends *cooperate* to ask it to do the job.

5   Checking the Model

5.1   Test-Bed

The Agents' Common Environment (ACE) is an under development system to interactively animate virtual humans. Together with a graphical user interface and a 3D environment, we embedded a scripting language, Python, as it can easily be integrated with existing C++ code, and offers a good solution for prototyping. Our basics Python commands cover animation (walking, looking, motion capture sequences playback...) and visual perception of others (our perception pipeline has been presented by Bordeux *et al* [1]).

In ACE, each agent runs as a separate process (thread), handled by a common *Threads controller*.

This controller is responsible for transporting messages between the threads, as the *Messages handler* we described in section 2.4. It also provides a shared area of memory for the different threads.

5.2   Scenario

We will consider now a complete example: someone has called John to come and fix a broken Cray computer in a company. John enters the hall of the building, but realises that he does not know in which office the computer is. Fortunately, two people are working here: Alice and Peter, and one must know where John has to go. We would like to implement the following behaviours: John stands in the middle of the room, looking around for someone. When he perceives somebody, he asks for help. For instance, if he sees Alice, he will say: "Excuse me, Madam, I'm looking for the Cray, please."[2]. If Alice is able to understand him, she will stop walking, face him and answer, by telling him the office number, if she knows it. If she can hear but not understand what John said, she will raise her shoulders to notify him that she is not able to understand him, and continue to walk (Peter will have the same behaviour). Finally, when John gets the answer, he will go to the correct office.

5.3   Implementation

As explained before, each agent is implemented as a separate thread. We used a simple representation of the audition level for each agent, by creating a 1D scale on top of each agent (see figure 3). This scale has two thresholds: the lowest green one is the limit to hear someone, while the red one is the limit to understand. Sound amplitude at the current location is displayed in blue. On the snapshot, John is speaking and his sound amplitude displayed at Alice's location is between green and red, which means that she is able to hear John, but not to understand him. Consequently, she raises her shoulders, as specified in her behaviour. Peter (who is not displayed in this picture) was not able to hear John and had no specific reaction.

---

[2] Since we used visual perception, it is easy to determine the gender of the receiver and update the sentence accordingly.

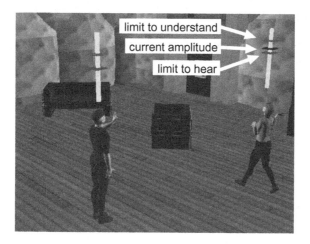

Fig. 3. Snapshot of the application: John is talking to Alice, but she is not able to understand what he said.

An other situation is illustrated on figure 4. John has just seen Alice, so, he starts to talk to her. Unfortunately, she is too far to hear him, and consequently, John gets back a *not-delivered* message. Peter, who is closer to John, is able to understand what he said, and thus, can choose to enter the conversation, or to ignore John's sentence. An agent is said to be *indiscreet* if it reacts to messages which were not intentionally sent to it, but accidentally heard.

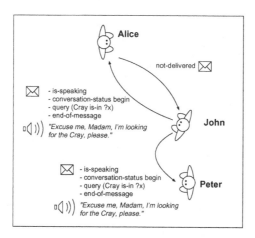

Fig. 4. Top view of Alice, Peter and John

6 Conclusion

We have presented in this paper the necessary requirements for simulating verbal conversation between human-like agents, in terms of messages and parameters, especially we can produce more realistic behaviours using three basic messages (by sending *is-speaking*, a general message and *end-of-message*). An approximate model to simulate the propagation of sound was introduced to help produce automatic reactions depending on the locations and hearing capabilities of the agents. Since the computational cost is very low, this model is well suited for applications such as interactive movies or video games. Further integration of emotional agents is currently being developed, at the same time as agents using Trust theory to analyse incoming messages.

References

1. Christophe Bordeux, Ronan Boulic, and Daniel Thalmann. An efficient and flexible perception pipeline for autonomous agents. *Computer Graphics Forum*, 18(3):23–30, September 1999. ISSN 1067-7055.
2. Justine Cassell, Catherine Pelachaud, Norman Badler, Mark Steedman, Brett Achorn, Tripp Bechet, Brett Douville, Scott Prevost, and Matthew Stone. Animated conversation: Rule-based generation of facial expression gesture and spoken intonation for multiple. In Andrew Glassner, editor, *Proceedings of SIGGRAPH 94*, pages 413–420. ACM Press, 1994.
3. FIPA. Fipa'97 – agent communication language v.2.0. Technical report, Foundation for Intelligent Physical Agents, 1997.
4. Thomas A. Funkhouser, Patrick Min, and Ingrid Carlbom. Real-time acoustic modeling for distributed virtual environments. *Proceedings of SIGGRAPH 99*, pages 365–374, August 1999. ISBN 0-20148-560-5. Held in Los Angeles, California.
5. Yannis Labrou and Tim Finin. A proposal for a new KQML specification. Technical report, Computer Science and Electrical Engineering Department, University of Maryland Baltimore County, Baltimore, 1997.
6. A. Bryan Loyall and Joseph Bates. Personality-rich believable agents that use language. In Katia P. Sycara and Michael Wolldridge, editors, *Autonomous Agents'97 Conference Proceedings*. ACM SIGART, ACM Press, 1997.
7. S. Marsh. *Formalising Trust as a Computational Concept*. PhD thesis, University of Stirling, April 1994.
8. M. Minsky. *The society of mind*. Simon and Schuster, New York, 1988.
9. Hansrudi Noser and Daniel Thalmann. Synthetic vision and audition for digital actors. In *Eurographics '95 Conference Proceedings*, pages 325–336. Eurographics, August 1995.
10. Nicholas Tsingos and Jean-Dominique Gascuel. Sound rendering in dynamic environments with occlusions. *Graphics Interface '97*, pages 9–16, May 1997. ISBN 0-9695338-6-1 ISSN 0713-5424.
11. Marilyn A. Walker, Janet E. Cahn, and Stephen J. Whittaker. Improvising linguistic style: Social and affective bases of agent personality. In Katia P. Sycara and Michael Wolldridge, editors, *Autonomous Agents'97 Conference Proceedings*. ACM SIGART, ACM Press, 1997.
12. M. Wooldridge and N.R. Jennings. Intelligent agents: theory and practice. *Knowledge Engineering Review*, 1995.

Communication and Interaction
with Learning Agents in Virtual Soccer

Cédric Sanza, Cyril Panatier, and Yves Duthen

Image Synthesis and Behavioral Simulation group
IRIT laboratory - University Paul Sabatier
118 route de Narbonne
31062 Toulouse cedex, France
{sanza|panatier|duthen}@irit.fr

Abstract. This paper presents a learning system based on Artificial Life for the animation of virtual entities. The model uses an extension of a classifiers system to build dynamically the behavior of agents by emergence. A behavior is selected into a set of binary rules that evolves continuously to ensure the maximization of predefined goals. The reinforcement allows to reward a rule and then to evaluate its efficiency faced to a given context. We investigate the interaction between virtual agents and a human controlled clone immersed in virtual soccer. In the simulation, each entity evolves in real-time by using the ability of cooperation and communication with teammates. We evaluate the benefits of the communication inside a team and present how it can improve the learning of a group thanks to a rule-sharing and a human intervention.

1 Introduction

Immersion in realistic virtual environments is a growing field of research including user interface, modeling, hardware, network and design [5]. Many distributed platforms allow users to navigate in real-time by using several devices like the mouse, the polhemus or the dataglove [13, 19]. The most impressive examples on the web are ActiveWorlds [21] or SecondWorld [22] where thousands of people meet every day through their avatar. Interactivity with autonomous virtual actors [12] is then a very promising research area. However, the main problem comes from the difficulty to produce complex and adaptive behaviors.

Artificial Life brings a solution with the concept of emergence that generates automatic behaviors. In our approach, we propose to use a classifiers system to give complete autonomy to virtual agents [8, 14]. Such a system is capable of independent actions in unpredictable environment [1], by using reinforcement [20] on binary rules (to update their own strength). The creation and combination of selected rules by Genetic Algorithms [6] ensures diversity and efficiency of these rules. This technique does not require any initial knowledge. The learning stage is made through adaptation to the environment, from a randomly initialized set of rules. Afterwards, the classifiers system enters the evolution stage. Here, the system increases its performances by using modified or new rules (from its own experience) to cope with

J.-C. Heudin (Ed.): VW 2000, LNAI 1834, pp. 147-158, 2000.
© Springer-Verlag Berlin Heidelberg 2000

new situations. This feature is crucial in changing or concurrent environments, where there is a constant evolution of the entities' capability.

Our application "virtual soccer" is an example of such an environment. Indeed, two teams of autonomous players act freely in the game, so as to maximize a set of predefined "fitness" functions [9]. However, two cooperating teams may not be efficient simultaneously because they have exactly the same learning motor and opposite goals. At this stage, it is very interesting to check that there is no possible convergence. Indeed, teams attempt to adapt to each other, behaviors change continuously all along the simulation, according to the rewards computed by the fitness functions.

This endless problem induced us to introduce a new parameter: communication. The principle consists of a dialogue between entities allowing to share knowledge (rules). We will present in the results the influence of the communication on the behavior of the players of a team.

Finally, the simulation enables interactivity with the user. The user can be immersed in the scene to take the control of any agent [18] and play in the virtual world.

2   Learning in Virtual Soccer

Our approach mixes simultaneously human players and autonomous players [11, 16]. The application is a real-time simulation in a 3D virtual environment, built with the WTK toolkit [23]. It runs both on Unix and Windows platforms. During the initialization, the simulation allows to create a variable number of agents but we use the maximum : 11 players per team. Each of the 22 players is either an autonomous agent or a human controlled clone. Its representation is a hierarchy of WTK nodes that strongly simplifies the animation of characters and collision avoidance. To produce coordinated realistic movements, an agent is animated by motion capture. Moreover, it owns characteristics like height, speed or strength to make a differentiation and a personalization of the players.

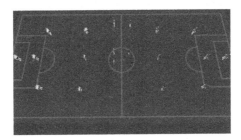

Fig. 1. 22 players in initial positions

The behavior of each agent is generated by a classifiers system [3]. This method has already demonstrated its efficiency in various areas like simulation [2], robotics [4] or medicine [7].

In a classifiers system, an agent perceives the world through its sensorial system and acts by using its effectors. The sensorial system is a set of Boolean sensors that simulates the vision of the agent. In the simulation, an agent can only see in the direction it is facing to get information about a approximate position of the other objects (ball or agents) and the way they move (towards itself or away from it). Thus, if the agent cannot determine whether a sensor is active or not, this latter is considered as false. For each agent, sensors are stored and numbered as follows:

#1: with-ball
#2: without-ball
#3: no-collision
#4: far-from-initial-position
#5: member-of-team-near
#6: in-good-side
#7: in-bad-side

The effectors represent high level behaviors of real soccer players. Contrary to sensors, the numbering of effectors is a very important parameter. Indeed, the probability of appearance of a behavior in the initial rule-base decreases naturally [17] as the number (#X) increases in our system. Effectors are stored and numbered as follows:

#1: go-to-ball
#2: go-to-initial-position
#3: shoot-strong-to-goal
#4: shoot-weak-to-goal
#5: move-forward
#6: pass-strong-to-player
#7: pass-weak-to-player
#8: roam

To use these effectors, we suppose that agents know their initial position and the position of the goal, even if they do not see it. Moreover, an effector only succeeds if the action is possible. For example, the 3rd effector makes the ball move if the agent has the ball when it kicks it. If the agent cannot see the ball when using the 1st effector (go-to-ball) it simply turns around itself until it sees the ball. For the 6th effector, the receiver is the closest teammate facing the agent. Proportionally to the strength given by an agent, the direction and speed of the ball are noisy to add randomness and to be more realistic.

Players are divided into two categories: attacker and defender (including goalkeeper). Each class is initialized with the same sensors and effectors. Thus, there is no specialization for any agent before the simulation starts. Behaviors emerge during the simulation according to the rewards (fitness) coming from the environment. The last ability used by the agents is a communication system which is limited to agents belonging to the same team. As for the sensorial system, communication is restricted by visibility and distance. Indeed, it would be very unlikely for the goalkeeper to learn from an attacker any offensive strategy.

We describe in the next paragraph the general architecture of the classifiers system and the main improvement we have brought.

2.1 The Behavioral System

A classifiers system is a rule-based system. A rule (called classifier) is a binary string composed of a condition part and an action part. Moreover, a rule is endowed with several attributes such as strength, length... As for Genetic Algorithms, the population of classifiers is evaluated from a fitness function to produce efficient solutions. A classifiers system is a powerful method, especially in changing and unpredictable environments, thanks to continuous evaluation of the rules. As shown in figure 2, a complete cycle consists of five main parts.

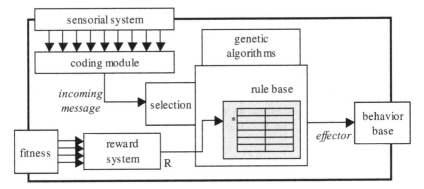

Fig. 2. Architecture of the classifiers system

First, sensors in the virtual world are activated to get information about the external world. They all produce a Boolean value (bit). In the coding module, the concatenation of each bit builds the incoming message. The perception of an agent is then summarized in a single binary string. Now, this message enables the system to select a rule in the base.

The selection starts with a pre-selection and ends with an evaluation. First, the incoming message is compared with the condition part of each rule to determine whether its structure is appropriated. Then, the winner is extracted from the few remaining candidates, by choosing the most powerful classifier. The second criterion evaluates the efficiency of a rule through its strength.

In the third part, the selected classifier triggers a behavior in the virtual environment from the action part of the selected rule. Indeed, the action part obligatorily corresponds to an effector used to initialize the system, whatever its structure.

The strength of the classifier is updated by the reward system according to the effects produced in the virtual world. Considering a multi-task environment, our reward system uses a set of "n" fitness functions [7] as inputs of a neural network [15]. Every function represents a goal to achieve and a goal is defined as a simple function to maximize. For example, we generally use differences of distances for each agent: • difference between previous and new distance to the ball,
  • difference between previous and new distance to the initial position,
  • difference between new and previous distance to the closest adversary and
  • difference between previous and new distance of the ball to the goal.

The neural network is composed of a set of sub-networks [18]. Each sub-network corresponds to a different incoming message. At a given time, the incoming message triggers the sub-network to update its internal weights. With "n" fitness functions as input, there are "n" nodes in the unique hidden layer. Internal weights are dynamically adjusted by back-propagation to give more or less power to rewards when computing the final reward: a weight increases with a very high or low reward, it decreases with an insignificant reward (close to 0).

These fitness functions are separated in Local Fitness Functions (LFF), applied locally to an agent and Global Fitness Functions (GFF). The latter concerns a reward assigned to a group of agents. A global reward is used to favor cooperation. Contrary to LFF, GFF are activated at a selected moment, when a special event happens. For example, such an event may be a goal for a team, too many agents around the ball, or not any agent close to the ball. GFF sometimes imply the destruction of rules that could be efficient in a local context, but inefficient in a global context. Then, the lost of a rule generates a new learning stage and favors the diversity of the behaviors. Thus, the adaptation to all the fitness functions involves the evolution of each agent towards a better behavior.

In the last part, new rules are created by Genetic Algorithms with classic operators like mutation and crossing-over. This mechanism is an essential part of the system. By combining different rules, the system generates more diversity in the binary structure of the rule, in order to cope with any situation (represented by the incoming message). A callback to Genetic Algorithms is triggered every 20 cycles and it slowly decreases as performances increase.

2.2 Communication

An agent uses the dialogue when it is in a bad situation to ask for help, or more precisely to ask for an adapted rule. The principle of communication is then to exchange efficient rules like messages. It strongly contributes to the reduction of the number of classifiers by offering to the agents an extension of their base. Moreover, dataflow engaged in the communication is reduced to a few integer values. All these mechanisms contribute to increase the learning ability of our agents thanks to this knowledge sharing [10].

As for every field, the main obstacle in the communication is the diversity of languages. In our system, a given rule will be valid if the two agents interpret the classifier in the same way. This condition only depends on the list of sensors and effectors (defined by the programmer). The initialization is then very important because it determines the agent's language. Different languages are sorted into different classes, and a message between two entities belonging to different classes needs to be translated before being used.

The user is immersed in the virtual world and he is seen as an agent by the other entities. It is possible that an agent tries to communicate with the user. We have enlarged the communication to a user-agent exchange. The dialogue is made through the graphical interface that enables the user to participate to influence the agents' evolution.

We will now explain the model (figure 3) in the next paragraphs and present its advantages regarding the architecture of the classifiers system.

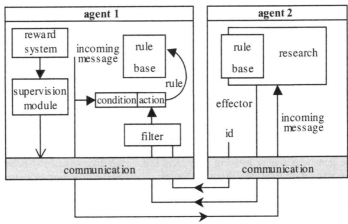

Fig. 3. Communication between two agents

The supervision module controls the final reward of an agent. It computes an average M on the 10 last rewards to evaluate the efficiency of the agent in the virtual worlds. When the average M is negative, the system triggers a message to communicate. The agent (called agent 1) immediately sends its incoming message to close agents. This binary message is translated into an integer value to facilitate its transmission, by compressing the dataflow. The receipt of the message by another agent (called agent 2) implies its translation into the original binary string. This message is then interpreted as a query of agent 1 like "it is my context, what can I do". Agent 2 now tries to reply by using own experience. The search for a solution will be performed in the base. The incoming message of the first agent is compared to the condition part of all the useful classifiers of the second agent. If such a solution is found, the action part of the classifier is translated into an integer value and transmitted to the agent 1 to be tested.

To avoid the same response from the same agent successively, agent 2 sends its identificator which is the key to go through the filter only once.

A message passing through the filter is re-coded into a bit string to form the action part of a new rule. The condition part corresponds to the incoming message. This rule is then injected into the base with a strength equal to 10. The agent finally tests the result of the communication. Indeed, the structure of the rule allows it to be immediately selected and activated in the virtual world. Thus, the agent checks the efficiency of this rule and eventually sends a new request.

Finally, communication between agents belonging to different classes requires an additional stage: translation. The system must convert the incoming message and the action part of the rule, before interpreting them.

The User-Agent communication allows the agents to be guided by human intervention. In this case, the communication is made through the graphical interface and the syntactic generator. As for a communication between virtual entities, the user receives the incoming message from an agent. However, it is impossible for the user to interpret a value. Then, the latter is decoded in quasi natural language and presented in a dialogue box of the graphical interface. The user gets the current state of the agent and just has to select the best-adapted behavior by clicking on the list of available behaviors.

In this case, the agent does not receive an action part of a classifier but the number of the corresponding behavior. Then, the agent generates by itself the correct action part of the rule by establishing the link between the behavior and its behavior base.

In the field of communication, the user is not a simple agent. Indeed, his ability to reply to any question produces a real advantage for his team. His messages do not need to be filtered, they are executed automatically by the agent. Compared to the user, the main limitation of an agent is the fixed number of classifiers that represents its knowledge.

The main drawback of a user-agent communication is the reaction time for the user. Any agent will always answer more quickly than the user. However there are some cases where the user will be able to reply:

- If he is alone with the agent
- If the other agents have already answered unsuccessfully
- If the other agents cannot reply

The first two cases depend on the distribution of the agents in the virtual environment. The second and the third cases are essentially found during the learning stage, but strongly decrease when the agents evolve towards the evolution stage.

3 Results

In this section, we evaluate the effects of the communication on the behaviors of the agents by opposing different configurations. The learning motor of each agent is the extended classifiers system presented in this paper. In the simulation, there is no initial knowledge or training stage. The rule-base is randomly initialized and modified in real-time to make some special rules emerge. The simulation enables to use the same random number seed on several runs. This particularity is very interesting to compare the evolution of a same run with different parameters like using rule-sharing inside a team or not.

The preliminary evaluation of the classifiers system (without using rule-sharing) is very instructive on how learning is performed. Firstly, a majority of players rushes towards the ball, creating many collisions around the ball. Then, some agents move to their initial position to get better rewards (distance to initial position). The others move towards the ball until they cope with a new context: the possession of the ball. In this new situation, they try to find a new behavior when one of them kicks the ball. The movement of the ball produces a sudden event that implies another new context. Now, some of them do not see the ball and they have to move or roam to get information about the environment. Then, new behaviors are used like passing to teammates when other behaviors fail.

In our application, there are very few sensors and effectors. We only use 50 rules for every agent but the number of possible different rules is very wide. Nevertheless, the system rapidly finds out a correct action that brings positive rewards. The most common rules obtained during the simulation are :

- IF without-ball AND far-from-initial-position THEN goto-initial-position
- IF without-ball THEN goto-ball.
- IF with-ball THEN shoot-weak-to-goal.
- IF without-ball AND far-from-initial-position THEN goto-ball

Many rules have the same condition part and a different action part. It shows the diversity of behaviors generated by the system and the emerging specialization of the agents.

3.1 Average Reward of a Team

From now, we conduct two types of simulation. Let teams be called F and B, the first simulation works without any kind of communication, the second one enables team F to communicate. Thus, by running twice the same scenario, we compare the real effects of the communication and conclude on its efficiency. The results are presented in figure 4.

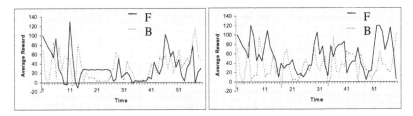

Fig. 4a&b. Evaluation of the communication in two different configurations

In the figure 4, X-axis represents time (1 unit = 5 seconds) and Y-axis is the average reward of a team during 100 time steps of the simulation (for one unit). This average is limited to the rewards of *active* agents (including local and global fitness functions). We define *active* agents as agents playing around the ball. Such limitation does not involve many players and shows a better evaluation of the progression of the game, because the most interesting fitness functions depend on the movement of the ball. This restriction comes from the use of the second effector (going and staying at initial position) by many agents when they are far from the ball. Their behaviors do not reflect the performance of their team, they are then called inactive but they are not really.

The run of 6000 steps of simulation lasts 5 minutes. From the beginning until time 4 (400 iterations), the two simulations produce exactly the same reward. In the curves, we notice a serial of minima-maxima couples (time 6, 13, 45 on figure 4a). These points result in the moving of the ball. Indeed, the fitness computing the distance of the ball to the punctually increases the reward of a team and decreases the other one. Repetitive oscillations show hesitations on behalf of the agents that try to find a better behavior.

At time 4, the difference in the two curves of team F indicates a communication query. From this special ability, several modifications appear. Firstly, rewards of team F remain positive until the end of the simulation. With such a higher reward, communication is there a success. Secondly, rewards of team B are directly influenced by communication. Logically, the benefit for a team becomes a penalization for the other.

At this level, we could think that communication strongly increases the performance of team F. Comparing the two curves shows that in the first simulation, team F reaches the same reward as in the second simulation, with a delayed time. However, communication only enables to speed up the search for a rule in the learning stage. But long simulations are more balanced. Sharing knowledge looses its benefits and attenuates with time.

Indeed, soccer requires various specializations in the game and sharing the same rule could involve a standardization of the behaviors. Moreover, communication generates a loss in the diversity of rules and influences the evolution. For example, if a rule like "IF without-ball THEN go-to-ball" is duplicated for every agent of a same team, all the players will rush towards the ball, involving many collisions and reducing the efficiency of the team.

Nevertheless, in the second simulation, the final score remains in favor of the team F (6-0). Team B learns more slowly but, even if it reaches a high level, it is not sufficient enough to score and to win the game. In contrary, in the first simulation where the two teams have the same ability, the final score is 2-2.

3.2 Communication Queries

Now, we analyze the number of queries intended by two teams able to communicate. In this type of simulation, to evaluate how a team reacts by itself, the user does not take part in the game. As defined above, a query is triggered by a low average reward several times successively. More precisely, it corresponds to a case where an agent cannot find a rule in a limited interval of time. In figure 5, Y-axis is the number of queries and X-axis is the time (20 unit = 1 second).

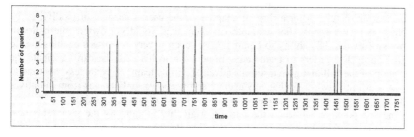

Fig. 5. Number of communications inside two teams in a short simulation

The curve shows interesting results. First, the number of queries slowly decreases during the simulation, though it never stops. It is not a consequence of a bad performance of the classifiers system but the result of the unpredictable events of the environment. As it is a competition, each agent has continuously to cope with new situations. Thus, in such a world, there are no long-term solutions. The constant adaptation of the players generates evolution and then fluctuations that appear in figure 5.

The second remark concerns the distribution of the queries: they are not isolated but concentrated in small groups. This characteristic comes from the interaction between the agents. It happens periodically in the simulation, for example when agents collide, or when they mutually fight for the possession of the ball.

The percentage of answers to any query is close to 100%, although communication between entities is reduced to a fixed distance. Thus, any agent may receive and re-build a maximum of 3 or 4 classifiers to use. Nevertheless, 100% of the rules are not really helpful, but the global result is encouraging. Indeed, in the precedent paragraph, we have evaluated the benefit of the communication and demonstrated that it is not a negligible aspect for the efficiency of a team.

3.3 User Interaction

By using the User Interface (UI), the user can select any player and control it in real-time in the game. During this time, the learning system of the selected agent is totally stopped (sensorial system, reward system and genetic algorithms). The user pilots his avatar thanks to the spacemouse. Such a device allows to move along the 3 axis like a joystick, but we only use movements in 2D. The frame-rate of the simulation is rapid enough to ensure a good level of interaction. We obtain about 20 frames-per-second with an Intergraph Xeon 400.

We have tested our system with many users and deducted several characteristics. Compared to commercial soccer games, the main difference comes from the selection of the active player that continuously changes. In our game, the user implicitly keeps the same player all along the simulation. Indeed, taking the control of another player is not a solution used in the game. The user can play all the roles with the same player because there is no tiredness as for a real game. It give a real advantage with the fact that he rushes on the ball without hesitation and then bothers the adversary.

More generally, although available behaviors for agents are limited, the interaction between all the actors (autonomous and piloted) is satisfying enough to produce a coherent animation. After a time of adaptation, the user is capable of modifying the behaviors of the agents. For example, an agent that would go towards the ball will only go forward. His ability to communicate (even if very few used) enables him to give appropriate orders to teammates. In addition to his skill, he can anticipate the position of the ball and give a serious advantage to its team. Nevertheless, his time to react is infinitively longer than any agents' and his power only comes from initiatives taking the future into account (future position of the ball and the agents).

The last point we notice is the part of originality brought by the user. This new element injected in the game is quite unpredictable. The user creates around him new situations and triggers adaptation stages. Then, by increasing the number of rules used by the system, it generates various behaviors.

4 Conclusion and Further Work

In this paper, we have presented an interactive real-time soccer simulation. Autonomous players use a rule-based system inspired from Artificial Life to evolve into the game. This system is an extension of a classifiers system. The results of an experiment with several configurations give an evaluation of the communication in a multi-agent environment. It shows that rule-sharing allows to speed up the efficiency of a team during the first steps of the simulation. But in the field of competition, taking a preliminary advantage is crucial and makes the team win. The presence of the user is not a negligible parameter as it involves unpredictable modifications on the environment that directly modify the agents' behavior.

The future step is Networked Virtual Soccer (NVS). We will use the WorldToolKit platform that provides a library for distributing an application. In NVS, two or more users will play together or in opposite teams through the network. This kind of simulation will conduct multi-user adaptation and interaction between a mixed population of human controlled clones and autonomous agents.

References

1. B. Blumberg, T. Galyean "Multi-Level Direction of Autonomous Creatures for Real-Time Virtual Environment". Proceedings of Siggraph 95. Computer Graphics Proceedings. Aug 1995.
2. A. Bonarini "Evolutionary Learning of Fuzzy rules: competition and cooperation". In W. Pedrycz (Ed). Fuzzy Modeling: Paradigms and Practise. Kluwer Academic Press. Norwell. MA. 1996.
3. L.B. Booker, D. E. Goldberg, J. H. Holland "Classifier Systems and Genetic Algorithms". Machine Learning, Paradigms and Methods. MIT Press 1990.
4. M. Colombetti, M. Dorigo, G. Borghi "Behavior Analysis and Training: A Methodology for Behavior Engineering". IEEE Transactions on Systems, Man, and Cybernetics-Part B, 26(3):365-380.
5. M. Engeli, D. Kurmann "A Virtual Reality Design Environment with Intelligent Objects and Autonomous Agents". Proceedings Design and Decision Support. Spa, Belgium. 1996.
6. D. E. Goldberg, "Genetic Algorithms in Search, Optimization and Machine Learning". Addison – Wesley. 1989.
7. J.H. Holmes "Discovering risk of disease with a learning classifier system". Proceedings ICGA'97, 7th International Conference on Genetic Algorithms. Morgan Kaufmann, San Francisco. 1997.
8. P. Maes "Modeling Adaptive Autonomous Agents". Artificial Life: An overview. MIT Press 1995.
9. M. J. Mataric, "Reward Functions for Accelerated Learning" in Machine Learning: Proceedings of the Eleventh International Conference, William W. Cohen and Haym Hirsh, eds., Morgan Kaufmann Publishers, San Francisco, CA, 1994.
10. M. J. Mataric, "Using Communication to Reduce Locality in Distributed Multi-Agent Learning". Proceedings, AAAI-97 Providence. Rhode Island. Jul 1997.

11. I. Noda, I. Frank "Investigating the Complex with Virtual Soccer". Proceedings VW'98, 1st International Conference on Virtual Worlds. Paris, France. Jul 1998.
12. S. R. Musse, M. Kallmann, D. Thalmann "Level of Autonomy for Virtual Human Agents". Proceedings ECAL'99, 5th European Conference on Artificial Life. Lausanne, Switzerland. Sep 1999.
13. I. Pandzic, T. Capin, N. Magnenat Thalmann, D. Thalmann "A Versatile Navigation Interface for Virtual Humans in Collaborative Virtual Environments". Proceedings of the Symposium on Virtual Reality Software and Technology 1997. Lausanne. Switzerland. Sep 1997.
14. A. Robert, F. Chantemargue, M. Courant "Grounding Agents in Emud Artificial Worlds". VW'98, 1th International Conference on Virtual Worlds. Paris. France. Jul 1998.
15. A. Rotaru-Varga "Modularity in Evolved Artificial Neural Networks". Proceedings ECAL'99, 5th European Conference on Artificial Life. Lausanne, Switzerland. Sep 1999.
16. R. Salustowicz, M. Wiering, J. Schmidhuber "Learning Team Strategies: Soccer Case Studies". Machine Learning. Kluwer Academic Press. Boston. 1998.
17. C. Sanza, C. Destruel, Y. Duthen "Autonomous Actors in an Interactive Real-Time Environment". ICVC'99, International Conference on Visual Computing. Goa. India. Feb 1999.
18. C. Sanza, C. Panatier, H. Luga, Yves Duthen "Adaptive Behavior for Cooperation: a Virtual Reality Application". RO-MAN'99, 8th IEEE International Workshop on Robot and Human Interaction. Pisa, Italy. Sep 1999.
19. P. Torguet, F. Rubio, V. Gaildrat, R. Caubet "Multi-User Interactions in the Context of Concurrent Virtual World Modeling". 3rd Eurographics Workshop on Virtual Environments. Monaco. Feb 1996.
20. C. Watkins, P Dayan. "Q-learning". Machine Learning, 8(3): pp 279-292, 1992.
21. Active Worlds http://www.activeworlds.com
22. 2nd World http://www.2nd-world.fr
23. WorldToolKit http://www sense8.com

3D Clothes Modeling from Photo Cloned Human Body

Takao Furukawa[1], Jin Gu[2], WonSook Lee[2], and Nadia Magnenat-Thalmann[2]

[1] Department of Kansei Engineering, Shinshu University, Ueda, 386-8567, Japan
furukawa@ke.shinshu-u.ac.jp
[2] MIRALab, CUI, University of Geneva, Geneva, CH-1211, Switzerland
{gu,wslee,thalmann}@cui.unige.ch

Abstract. An important advantage of virtual reality technology is that real 3D objects including humans can be edited in the virtual world. In this paper, we present a technique for 3D clothes modeling based on a photo cloned human body. Photo cloning is an efficient 3D human body modeling method using a generic body model and photographs. A part segmentation technique for 3D color objects is applied for the clothes modeling, which uses multi-dimensional mixture Gaussians fitting. Firstly, we construct a 6D point set representing both the geometric and color information. Next, the mixture Gaussians are fitted to the point set by using the EM algorithm in order to determine the clusters. This approximation gives probabilities for each point. Finally the probabilities determine the segmented part models corresponding to the clothes models. An advantage of this method is that the clustering is unsupervised learning without any prior knowledge as well as integrating geometric and color data in multi-dimensional space.

1 Introduction

An advantage of digitizing information is that record, storage, playback, modification, and editing can be performed without lowering the quality. Virtual, augmented, and mixture reality techniques have recently been popularized, which is based on various technologies as well as computer vision and graphics. For example, past actors and actresses have been reproduced by computer animation[3]. However the cost for accurate human body modeling is still expensive, because it requires special equipment to measure the shape and color, and thus designers have to take long time for the modeling.

Object representation using texture mapping has become a common technique for visualizing complicated color shapes. Reasons for the recent popularity of image-based rendering techniques [15] include the recently increased availability of special hardware architecture for the texture mapping, and its application to both computer vision and graphics. A 3D human body reconstruction method using a generic body model and 2D images has been proposed[10]. This approach is simple and efficient, although it requires a special background when the pictures are taken. Photo cloning is an efficient image-based rendering technique

J.-C. Heudin (Ed.): VW 2000, LNAI 1834, pp. 159–170, 2000.

that generates individualized 3D human body models from photographs of people, without the need of any special equipment. Therefore we can easily immerse the virtual world by using photo cloning. The editing operation is the key area of virtual reality technology. A 3D clothes modeling technique based on the photo cloned human body enables the editing operation in the virtual world. For example, extracted clothes models can be replaced in the virtual world, and can be applied for various fields as well as e-commerce.

Our clothes modeling method is considered as a part segmentation problem in pattern recognition. Part segmentation techniques for range images have been proposed for modeling 3D parts. Proposed range image segmentation techniques can be categorized into shape- or boundary-based methods. In the boundary-based methods, segmentation has generally been performed by surface analysis based on principal curvatures, where the surface is basically assumed to be continuous. However, the principal curvatures calculated by derivatives on the surface are highly sensitive to noises, which is difficult of avoid since range images include measuring and digitizing errors. Thus, a physically-based robust boundary detection technique[21] has recently been proposed. On the other hand, shape-based methods segment the range images by fitting surfaces or volumetric primitives. Bi-quadric surface[8], supuerquadrics[8,14] and deformation of them[17,18,19], and deformable surfaces[5,4], which can be considered as 3D extension of snakes[11] were used as the primitives. Although the primitives can be deformed and combined, there are still limitations on shape representation. Furthermore, these primitive fitting methods depend on optimization techniques in which some tolerances or thresholds and appropriate initial conditions are required. Hence prior knowledge for the target objects is necessary.

Part segmentation can be basically considered as a clustering problem in statistics. In general, mixture density estimation based on function fitting is a popular way to determine clusters. Here, the central limit theorem explains the reasonable choice of Gaussian as the approximate function. The EM algorithm to estimate multi-dimensional Gaussian parameters has been applied texture image segmentation[1], motion tracking from video sequences[20], and so forth. The advantage of object description using the multi-dimensional Gaussians is that such different types of information as position, color, texture, can be integrated in the multi-dimensional space statistically.

In this paper, we present a 3D clothes modeling technique using a photo cloned human body. Here, we focus on the part segmentation technique for 3D color objects using multi-dimensional mixture Gaussians. This method does not require any primitives to describe the target objects except input geometric model. Moreover tolerances and thresholds for the fitting algorithm are not necessary. It can, therefore, be considered as learning unsupervised without prior knowledge. This paper is organized as follows: The photo cloning technique is described in section 2, then we explain mixture Gaussian fitting and its computation in section 3. Experimental results are presented in section 4, and characteristics of this segmentation technique and its limitations are also discussed.

Finally we conclude this 3D clothes modeling method based on the part segmentation in section **5**.

2   Photo Cloning

Human body modeling plays important roles in various fields, for example, industrial and medical applications as well as computer graphics. Currently image-based rendering techniques have been popularized, because texture mapping gives visually real models. We have been developing a photo cloning system[13], which uses front, side, and back view photographs and generates individual 3D human body model based on a generic model. The basic concept of the photo cloning is that the lost 3D information on the photographs can be recovered by the correspondence between the photographs and the generic body model. Here we briefly describe our photo cloning technique for the human body modeling. Processes of the photo cloning are written as follows.

- Fit a generic skeleton to the front, side, and back view photographs.
- Generate an initial skin model using the correspondence between the skeleton and feature points defined on the photographs.
- Skin model modification based on the silhouette extracted from the photographs.

Fig. 1 (a) shows the generic body that consists of the skeleton and the skin surface, where contours surrounding the skeleton define the surface model. This body model is compatible with MPEG-4. The skeleton is compatible with the h-anim 1.1 specification[9], and 94 skeletal joints are used to describe the skeleton. We choose some important joints as key joints shown in fig. 1 (b). These joints give a hierarchy of skeletal parts, and define the origins of each local coordinate system in order to describe the skin parts. The basic skin model is defined by the contours, and the skin surface is deformed accordingly when the skeleton moves. Finally this skin model can be easily converted to polygonal mesh.

First, we define feature points which gives the rough silhouette on the photographs to fit the skeletal model as shown in fig. 2. Positions of these feature points are determined by interactive GUI. Here relation between the key joints and the feature points has been given, so that x-y-z coordinates of the key joints can be estimated from the feature points located in the front, side, and back view pictures. Furthermore, positions of remaining joints defined in the h-anim 1.1 skeleton are calculated by using these key joints, and then the skin contours are modified by this skeletal deformation. Consequently the fitted skeleton and contours can be generated.

Next, we describe how to make an initial skin model. Each part is represented by a polygonal mesh which has some control points. These control points are placed at certain required positions to represent the shape characteristics. Hence the skin model can be deformed by moving these control points. Furthermore, several control points are located at the boundaries between two parts, so that surface continuity is preserved when the posture of the generic body is changed.

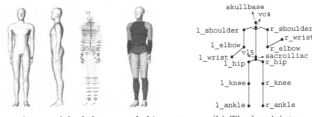

(a) The surface model, skeleton, and skin parts.   (b) The key joints.

Fig. 1. The generic body model and the key joints.

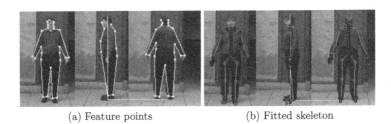

(a) Feature points   (b) Fitted skeleton

Fig. 2. Feature points and fitted skeleton on front, side, and back view photographs.

The accuracy of the initial skin model is insufficient, so we modify it by using the body silhouette extracted from the pictures. Here we detect the silhouette of the human body on the pictures and then fit the skin model to the silhouette. To get the silhouette, we have adopted the following algorithm.

- Apply Canny edge detector[2] for the pictures and fit line segments into edge pixels to form edge segments.
- Evaluate a connection of a pair of edge segments.
  An evaluation function for the connection E_c is defined by parameters such as angles between two segments, edge magnitudes given by Canny edge detector, and the feature points located on the pictures.
- Silhouette extraction.
  This can be considered as a path searching problem. An evaluation function E_p is defined to assess the *goodness* of a path. Here the following procedures are used.
  1. Choose an edge segment.
  2. Find a proper edge segment to connect and move to this edge segment.
  3. Repeat step 2. until the edge segment reaches the feature point, because the path terminals are given by the feature points.
  4. Assess the *goodness* of a path by calculating E_p

5. Repeat step 1 to 4 for each edge segment and finally the best path is determined by finding the maximum of E_p.

An exact silhouette is detected by the proposed method. Finally the contours defining the skin surface are modified by using this silhouette. It can be confirmed that a visually real 3D human body model can be constructed by our method without using special equipment. Fig. 3 shows the extracted silhouette and the modified photo cloned human body.

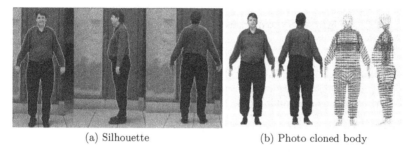

(a) Silhouette   (b) Photo cloned body

Fig. 3. Extracted silhouette and photo cloned human body.

3   Mixture Gaussian Fitting

3.1   Color Coordinates and 6D Vector Normalization

Texture mapping gives projection from pictures to 3D geometric models, so that each pixel has geometric data as well as color data. Therefore a pixel can be represented by a 6D vector that consists of 3D geometric and 3D color components. Although a pixel is described by RGB components, it shows redundancy. Thus conversions from RGB space to YUV space have been used to reduce the redundancy[20]. Here, we use the orthogonal space defined by the principal axes, which are given by solving the eigenvalue problem of the covariance matrix of RGB components. Rotation of the basis vectors in the color space gives a geometric interpretation of this transformation.

A 6D vector is written by $(x, y, z, \xi, \eta, \zeta)$, where (x, y, z) and (ξ, η, ζ) components represent geometric and color information respectively. We determine the ξ axis by the largest eigenvalue that maximizes the variance. The η and ζ axes are determined in the order of the eigenvalues. Furthermore, we normalize geometric and color space on the condition that the maximum lengths of the bounding boxes of (x, y, z) and (ξ, η, ζ) are equal to 1. Fig. 4 shows a 6D point set obtained by the photo cloning technique, where the x, y, z axes correspond to width, height, depth, respectively. This point set is dense in x-y-z space, and

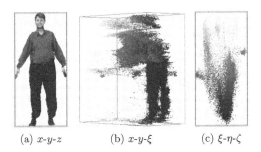

(a) x-y-z (b) x-y-ξ (c) ξ-η-ζ

Fig. 4. Projected pixels from 6D scape into 3D space.

so fig. 4(a) looks like geometric model. Fig. 4(b) replaces the z axis in fig. 4(a) to the ξ axis which corresponds to brightness. Fig. 4(c) plots color space where the vertical axis corresponds to the ξ. Here the number of 6D points is 119,026.

3.2   EM Algorithm

First, we denote i-th sample data in N-D space by a vector $\boldsymbol{x}_i = [\, x_{i1} \; x_{i2} \; \cdots \; x_{iN}\,]$, $(i = 1, 2, \cdots, n)$. Let the probability of $\boldsymbol{x}_i$ be $p(\boldsymbol{x}_i)$. We consider how to approximate the spatial distribution of $\boldsymbol{x}_i$ by using N-D mixture Gaussians, where the number of Gaussians is m. Next we introduce joint probability $p(\boldsymbol{x}_i, c_j)$ which is a product of the probability $p(\boldsymbol{x}_i)$ and the probability $p(c_j)$, where c_j denotes the j-th class $(j = 1, 2, \cdots, m)$. Therefore, the following relation

$$p(\boldsymbol{x}_i) = \sum_{j=1}^{m} p(\boldsymbol{x}_i, c_j) \tag{1}$$

is satisfied in discrete classes. This equation can be rewritten by using Bayes' rule

$$p(\boldsymbol{x}_i) = \sum_{j=1}^{m} p(\boldsymbol{x}_i | c_j) p(c_j), \tag{2}$$

where $p(\boldsymbol{x}_i | c_j)$ means the conditional probability of $\boldsymbol{x}_i$, given c_j. We express $p(\boldsymbol{x}_i | c_j)$ in eq.(2) by N-D Gaussian

$$p(\boldsymbol{x}_i | c_j) = \sqrt{\frac{|C_j^{-1}|}{(2\pi)^N}} \exp\left[-\frac{1}{2}(\boldsymbol{x}_i - \boldsymbol{\mu}_j) C_j^{-1} (\boldsymbol{x}_i - \boldsymbol{\mu}_j)^T\right], \tag{3}$$

where $\boldsymbol{\mu}_j$ and C_j denotes the mean vector and covariance matrix of the j-th class c_j. Moreover the coefficient of the exponential function is required for normalization of the N-D Gaussian. Furthermore, we describe each variable in eqs.(2) and (3). The mean vector of the j-th class $\boldsymbol{\mu}_j$ can be expressed by

$$\boldsymbol{\mu}_j = \sum_{i=1}^{n} \boldsymbol{x}_i p(\boldsymbol{x}_i | c_j) = \sum_{i=1}^{n} \boldsymbol{x}_i \frac{p(c_j | \boldsymbol{x}_i)}{p(c_j)} p(\boldsymbol{x}_i). \tag{4}$$

This can be rewritten by

$$\boldsymbol{\mu}_j = \frac{1}{np(c_j)} \sum_{i=1}^{n} \boldsymbol{x}_i p(c_j|\boldsymbol{x}_i). \tag{5}$$

Similarly, the covariance matrix of the j-th class can be expressed by

$$C_j = \sum_{i=1}^{n} (\boldsymbol{x}_i - \boldsymbol{\mu}_j)^T (\boldsymbol{x}_i - \boldsymbol{\mu}_j) p(\boldsymbol{x}_i|c_j) = \frac{1}{np(c_j)} \sum_{i=1}^{n} (\boldsymbol{x}_i - \boldsymbol{\mu}_j)^T (\boldsymbol{x}_i - \boldsymbol{\mu}_j) p(c_j|\boldsymbol{x}_i) \tag{6}$$

The expansion weights of c_j is also written by

$$p(c_j) = \sum_{i=1}^{n} p(\boldsymbol{x}_i, c_j) = \frac{1}{n} \sum_{i=1}^{n} p(c_j|\boldsymbol{x}_i). \tag{7}$$

By definition of $p(c_j|\boldsymbol{x}_i)$,

$$p(c_j|\boldsymbol{x}_i) = \frac{p(\boldsymbol{x}_i, c_j)}{p(\boldsymbol{x}_i)} = \frac{p(\boldsymbol{x}_i|c_j)p(c_j)}{\sum_{j=0}^{m} p(c_j)} \tag{8}$$

has been given.

An important point of the EM algorithm for mixture Gaussian fitting is that $p(\boldsymbol{x}|c_j)$, $\boldsymbol{\mu}_j$, C_j, $p(c_j)$, and $p(c_j|\boldsymbol{x}_i)$ are related to each other and a loop is formed. By setting initial values of $\boldsymbol{\mu}_j$, C_j, $p(c_j)$ and then iterating the loop, feasible mixture Gaussians can be obtained. Therefore, we can find the probability $p(c_j|\boldsymbol{x}_i)$ at which a given N-D vector $\boldsymbol{x}_i$ belongs to class c_j, and finally $\max_j p(c_j|\boldsymbol{x}_i)$ determines the proper cluster to which $\boldsymbol{x}_i$ should belong.

3.3   Numerical Calculation

The EM algorithm for multi-dimensional mixture Gaussian fitting requires that several techniques in the numerical calculation. Procedures for the numerical calculation that we have used is described as follows.

1. Set initial values.
   We initialize the mean vectors $\boldsymbol{\mu}_j$ by random numbers, and set a constant to each element of the covariance matrix C_j. Moreover, we assign $1/m$ as the initial values of the expansion weights $p(c_j)$.
2. Calculate $p(\boldsymbol{x}_i|c_j)$ by using the Gaussian written in eq.(3).
   Here, C_j^{-1} and its determinant in eq.(3) can be given by a solution of the eigenvalue problem

$$C_j \boldsymbol{s} = \lambda \boldsymbol{s}, \tag{9}$$

where λ and $\boldsymbol{s}$ denote the eigenvalue and the eigenvector. If we determine λ and $\boldsymbol{s}$ on the condition that $\boldsymbol{s}$ gives normalized orthogonal bases, i.e. $\boldsymbol{s}_k \cdot \boldsymbol{s}_l = \delta_{kl}$,

$$C_j S = S \Lambda \tag{10}$$

is given. Here

$$\Lambda = \begin{bmatrix} \lambda_1 & & & 0 \\ & \lambda_2 & & \\ & & \ddots & \\ 0 & & & \lambda_m \end{bmatrix}, \, S = \begin{bmatrix} s_1 & s_2 & \cdots & s_m \end{bmatrix}. \tag{11}$$

By using eq. (10), the inverse matrix of C_j can be expressed by

$$C_j^{-1} = S\Lambda^{-1}S^T. \tag{12}$$

Of course the diagonal elements of Λ^{-1} are $1/\lambda_k$. Furthermore, $|C_j^{-1}|$ in the coefficient of the exponential function can be replaced by the trace

$$|C_j^{-1}| = \prod_{k=1}^{N} 1/\lambda_k. \tag{13}$$

Therefore we can find $p(\boldsymbol{x}_i|c_j)$.

3. Calculate $p(\boldsymbol{x}_i)$ by using eq.(2).

   $p(c_j)$ and $p(\boldsymbol{x}_i|c_j)$ have already been given in step 1 and 2.

4. Assign $p(\boldsymbol{x}_i|c_j)$ and $p(c_j)$ into eq.(8) and get $p(c_j|\boldsymbol{x}_i)$.

5. Rewrite each mean vector $\boldsymbol{\mu}_j$ and covariance matrix C_j by using eqs. (5) and (6), and then return to step 2. and repeat these procedures.

We have used `dspev` in LAPACK[12] to solve eigenvalue problem, since the covariance matrix C_j is a positive symmetry matrix. When a small value is assigned into the initial covariances, $|C_j^{-1}|$ in eq.(3) calculated by eq.(13) may overflows. Thus large covariances are feasible for the initial values.

3.4   Geometric Model for Segmented Object

Although the pixel distribution in x-y-z space represented by 6D vectors are used for clustering, we need to construct a geometric model of segmented objects finally. Geometric objects to be segmented have been represented by triangular faces, and each face contains the corresponding pixels. Furthermore, the probability $p(c_j|\boldsymbol{x}_i)$ for each pixel has been calculated, so we simply define the probability of c_j given triangular face y_k by using the average

$$p(c_j|y_k) = \frac{1}{K} \sum_{\boldsymbol{x}_i \in y_k} p(c_j|\boldsymbol{x}_i), \tag{14}$$

where K is the number of pixels contained in the triangular face y_k.

4   Experimental Results

Fig. 5 shows the result of a 6D mixture Gaussian fitting where four Gaussians are used. Standard deviation of 6D Gaussians are drawn by color ellipses in fig. 5(a)-(d), where longitude and latitude lines of 6D ellipsoids defined by the standard deviation are projected into 3D space. Here, the initial mean vectors are given by random variables as shown in fig. 5 (a) and (b). All initial standard deviations are 0.1. Converged Gaussians are illustrated in fig. 5 (c) and (d), where the number of iterations is 128. Although initial Gaussians do not fit the input data, experiments show the proper convergence can be reached by the EM algorithm. Yellow and red ellipsoids in x-y-z space illustrated fig. 5 (c) show that the blue shirt part and the black trouser form each cluster. On the other hand, fig. 5 (d) shows that blue, black, and mainly skin color clusters are formed, where these clusters are illustrated by red, yellow, and green ellipsoids respectively.

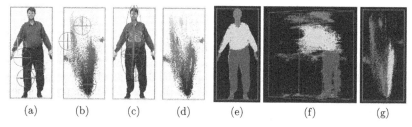

(a)   (b)   (c)   (d)   (e)   (f)   (g)

Fig. 5. A 6D mixture Gaussian fitting by using the EM algorithm where four Gaussian are used. Initial conditions for the EM algorithm in x-y-z and color space are illustrated in (a) and (b), and the converged result is illustrated in (c) and (d). Colored pixels in (e)-(g) show the clustered result where coordinates systems are x-y-z, x-y-ξ, and ξ-η-ζ.

Fig. 5 (e)-(g) show the clustered pixels in x-y-z, z-y-ξ, and ξ-η-ζ spaces. Each pixel has $p(c_j|\boldsymbol{x}_i)$, which is the probability of c_j given $\boldsymbol{x}_i$, so that the $\max_j p(c_j|\boldsymbol{x}_i)$ determines a class to which the pixel $\boldsymbol{x}_i$ should belong. Since the pixels corresponding to the black trouser form the dense cluster in the color space and distribute in the lower part on the y axis, this part is detected exactly. The blue shirt is extracted approximately, however it is not exact at the boundary part. Skin color face and hands are also detected, and this cluster distributes large areas in both the spatial and color space. Thus the accuracy is insufficient.

Fig. 6 shows the convergence process of the EM algorithm, where the color ellipsoids illustrate 6D Gaussinans. Fig. 6(a) and (b) are plots of x-y-z and ξ-η-ζ spaces respectively. Here the iteration steps are 1, 4, 8, and 32, and the initial condition and the convergence have been shown in fig. 5(a)-(d). Although Gaussians are distributed randomly at the beginning, the first EM step brings them close to the mean vector of the entire data. The standard deviations are also similar. Thus, the red, yellow, and green ellipsoids are covered by cyan ellipsoids in fig. 6(a). These Gaussians then start to make clusters in further iterations of the EM, and finally reach convergence. In this case, the result of the 32th iteration shown in fig. 6 gives the convergence approximately.

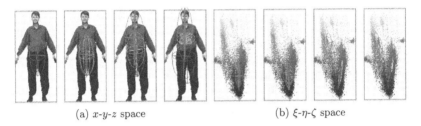

(a) x-y-z space   (b) ξ-η-ζ space

Fig. 6. Convergence process of the EM algorithm, where the numbers of iterations are 1, 4, 8, and 32 respectively.

Probability distributions $p(c_j|y_k)$ defined on the photo cloned human body surfaces are shown in fig. 7, where the probability are shown by the color bar in fig. 7 (e). Fig. 7(a),(b),(d) show that the probabilities at the black trouser, blue shirt, head and hand parts are close to 1. On the other hand, the probabilities at side parts appearing in fig. 7(c) are not very high. Therefore, the reliabilty of the formed cluster c_3 is relatively low.

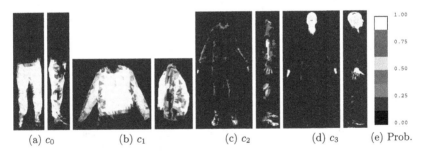

(a) c_0 (b) c_1 (c) c_2 (d) c_3 (e) Prob.

Fig. 7. Probability distributions on the human body model, where the probability interval $[0, 1]$ corresponds to the color sequence shown in (e).

Fig. 8 shows the segmented 3D color parts represented by the triangular faces with textures. The whole human body is segmented to the black trouser, blue shirt, pale blue part and mainly skin color part. These geometric parts are determined by the highest probability of the triangular faces. Side parts shown in fig. 8(c) should be discriminated as the trouser and shirt, though these parts are independent. This is caused by inaccuracy of the input data, so that it will be difficult to correct them without the prior knowledge for the target object.

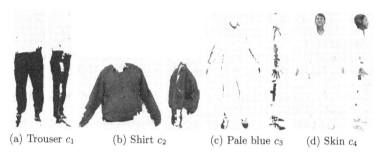

(a) Trouser c_1 (b) Shirt c_2 (c) Pale blue c_3 (d) Skin c_4

Fig. 8. Extracted parts given by the highest probability of each triangular face.

5   Conclusions

We have proposed 3D clothes modeling technique based on a photo cloned human body. The human body model can easily be generated by using the photo cloning technique without any special equipment. In this paper, we focused on a part segmentation technique for 3D color object based on multi-dimensional mixture Gaussians using the EM algorithm. An advantage of the proposed method is that geometric and color data can be integrated in multi-dimensional space, insufficient geometric information to be compensated by color data, which allows the face and hand of the test object are recognized as a single part, even though they are isolated spatially. Furthermore, the clustering can be performed by unsupervised learning without any tolerances or thresholds used for the Gaussian fitting. The convergence process of the EM algorithm is also observed. We could construct the segmented geometric models represented by triangular faces. Consequently 3D clothes models are extracted from the photo cloned human body. However, there are several problems to be solved as well as the accuracy, for example how many Gaussians are required for feasible segmentation and its evaluation still remains. these are problems to be solved.

6   Acknowledgements

This work has been developed at MIRAlab, University of Geneva. The authors would like to thank Prithweesh De and MIRAlab members for intensive discussion about this global topic. We are grateful to people taken photographs including eRENA partners. The first author was supported by the ministry of education, science, sports, and culture of Japan under the fellowship for the academic staff of Japanese national universities.

References

1. Belongie, S., Carson, C., Greenspan, H., and Malik, J." "Color- and Texture-Based Image Segmentation Using EM and Its Application to Content-Based Image Retrieval," Proc. ICCV98 (1998) 675-682
2. Canny, J., A Computational Approach to Edge Detection, IEEE Trans. PAMI, **8** (1986) 679–698
3. Carignan, M., Yang, Y., Thalmann, N. M., and Thalmann, D., Dressing Animated Synthetic Actors with Complex Deefromable Clothes, Proc. SIGGRAPH '92 (1992) 99–104
4. Caselles, V., Kimmel, R., Sapiro, G., Sbert, C, Minimal-Surfaces Based Object Segmentation, IEEE Trans. PAMI, **19** (1997) 394–398
5. Cohen, I., Cohen, L. D., and Ayache, N., Using Deformable Surface to Segment 3-D Images and Infer Differential Structures, CVGIP Image Understanding, **56** (1992) 242–263
6. Gershenfeld N., The Nature of Mathematical Modeling, Cambridge University Press (1999)
7. Gu, J., Chang, T., Gopalsamy, S., and Shen, H., A 3D Reconstruction System for Human Body, Proc. CAPTECH'98, (1998) 229–241
8. Gupta, A., and Bajcsy, R., Volumetric Segmentation of Range Images of 3D Objects Using Superquadric Models, CVGIP Image Understanding, **58** (1993) 302–326
9. VRML Humanoid Animation Working Group: The VRML Humanoid Specification Version 1.1 http://ece.uwaterloo.ca/~h-anim/spec1.1/
10. Hilton, D. B., Gentils T., Smith, R., and Sun, W., Virtual People: Capturing Human Models to Populate Virtual Worlds, Proc. of Computer Animation '99 (1999) 174–185
11. Kass, M., Witkin, A., and Terzopoulos, D., Snakes: Active Contour Models, International Journal of Computer Vision, **1** (1998) 321–331
12. Anderson, E, *et al.*, LAPACK Users' Guide 3rd Ed., Society for Industrial and Applied Mathematics, Philadelphia, PA (1999)
13. Lee, W., Gu, J., Magnenat-Thanlmann, N., Generating Animatable 3D Virtual Human from Photographs, Proc. Eurographics 2000 (to appear)
14. Leonardis, A., Jaklie A., and Solina, F., Superquadrics for Segmenting and Modeling Range Data, IEEE Trans. PAMI, **19** (1997) 1289–1295
15. McMillan, L. and Gortler, S, Image-Based Rendering: A New Interface Between Computer VIsion and Computer Graphics, Computer Graphics, **33**, No. 4, (1999) 61–64
16. Moghaddam, B., Nastar, C., and Pentland, A., A Bayesian Similarity Measure for Direct Image Matching, Proc. ICPR'96 (1996) B7E.5
17. Pentland, A. P., Automatic Extruaction of Deformable Part Models, Internaltinal Jounral of Computer Vision, **4** (1990) 107–126
18. Pentland, A. P., and Schlaroff, S., Closed-Form Solution for Phisycally Based Shape Modeling and Recognition, IEEE Trans. PAMI, **13** (1991) 715–729
19. Terzopoulos, D., and Metaxas, D., Dynamic 3D Models with Local and Global Deformations: Deformable Superquadrics, IEEE Trans. PAMI, **13** (1991) 703–714
20. Wren, C., Azarbayejani, A., Darrell, T., and Pentland, A., Pfinder: Real-Time Tracking of the Human Body, IEEE Trans. PAMI, **19** (1997) 780–785
21. Wu, K., Levine, M. D., 3D Part Segmentation Using Simulated Electrical Charge Distribution, IEEE Trans. PAMI, **19** (1997) 1223–1235

Toward Alive Art

Luigi Pagliarini[1,2], Claudio Locardi[1], Vedran Vucic[1,3]

[1] ARTIFICIALIA
http://www.artificialia.com/
e-mail: {luigi, claudio, vedran }@artificialia.com
[2] LEGO Lab, Computer Science, University of Aarhus
Aabogade 34, DK8200 Aarhus N, Denmark
[3] Project Director for Eastern Europe,
Electronic Music Foundation, USA.

Abstract. Electronics is about to change the idea of art drastically. We know this is going to happen - we can feel it. Much less clear to most of us are the hows, whens and whys of the change. In this paper, we will attempt to analyze the mechanisms and dynamics of the coming cultural revolution, focusing on the «artistic space» where the revolution is taking place, on the interactions between the artistic act and the space in which the act takes place and on the way in which the act modifies the space and the space modifies the act. We briefly discuss the new category of «electronic artists». We then highlight what we see as the logical process connecting the past, the present and our uncertain future. We examine the relationship between art and previous technologies, pointing to the evolutionary, as well as the revolutionary impact of new means of expression. Against this background we propose a definition for what we call «Alive Art», going on to develop a tentative profile of the performers (the «Alivers»). In the last section, we describe two examples of Alive Artworks, pointing out the central role of what we call the "Alive Art Effect" in which we can perceive relative independence of creation from the artist and thus it may seem that unique creative role of artist is not always immediate and directly induced by his/her activity. We actually, emphasized that artist's activities may result in unpredictable processes more or less free of the artist's will.

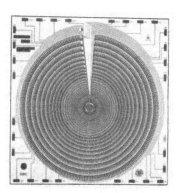

Fig. 1. IMEC and University of Pennsylvania, University of Genova and University of Pisa
Diagram of Neural Net Microchip MOMA, Gift of University of Pennsylvania

J.-C. Heudin (Ed.): VW 2000, LNAI 1834, pp. 171-184, 2000.
© Springer-Verlag Berlin Heidelberg 2000

1   Introduction

In recent decades the so-called western countries have had to face a new fact of life: electronics. No matter whether you prefer virtual or physical reality, regardless of personal likes, dislikes or preferences it is impossible to shut electronics out of our life (or out of the life of society). Moreover, there are so many facets to the electronic cultural revolution that one feels there is no limit to how much we could say about it. If we look more carefully, we will notice that sciences have had always significant impact on arts. There is a lot of evidence for similar cases in ancient Egypt, China and other cultures. Here, however, we will attempt to discuss one particular aspect of the revolution: the impact of the electronic revolution on artistic thought. We will try to do this without moving too far away from art, while at the same time avoiding too detailed an analysis, so as not to get lost. The goal of this paper is to try to depict a new art form which we are going to call «Alive Art». To achieve this objective we will examine the social and human context and the physical space which this new art form inhabits - thereby arriving at a definition of what we mean by electronic art and the «electronic artist». We will try to trace the boundaries of the new art form, the shapes it is likely to take and the way in which it is likely to expand. Finally, we will write a couple of words on the ways in which such an art movement might affect art itself.

2 The Social Context of Electronics

In this section we will discuss the possible relationship between electronics as a technology, and art, in the sense of a specific social context. In order to identify the arts whose roots reach down into electronics we will need to understand the terrain we are discussing. For this reason, we will try to analyze the scene on which electronics plays its role.

2.1 Where Electronics Acts

In our opinion, there are two main spaces where electronics can interact with and perhaps challenge human beings. It is as if electronic machines have two separate identities facing respectively inwards and outwards. There is one side to the machine which exists in the physical world. This is hardware (e.g: a robot). Then there are the machine's «internals», its software (e.g.: a program   interface). Despite this distinction, ordinary people's reaction to the words «electronics» and «computer» is to think of a screen on a PC (or electronic device's interface). It follows that this is one of the places where, socially and psychologically speaking, electronics acts. In some sense, a PC screen (and electronic device's interface) are similar to the human eye; it mirrors the soul of the electronics. Recently, what is more, the PC screen has acquired a new face - people can now perceive electronics in action via the Internet. Materially, there has been no change - the social sense has however completely changed. This previously unknown «virtual space» represented by the Internet is rapidly becoming an essential aspect of arts, business and economics. Socially speaking, this means that it will become a pervasive aspect of our lives. Art will have to cope with this. The Internet is a real if strange kind of space. Just as humans have always done when they have discovered new continents they will attempt to populate it with all kinds of human artifacts. There are many «ordinary» electronic artifacts which people do not consider to be art and which they do not see as being particularly intelligent or autonomous. These are of enormous importance - it is around such devices that some of the toughest battles will be fought in the future. These however lie outside the scope of this paper. Here we will concentrate on two main themes: autonomous robotics, and neuro-informatics - hybridized in the cyborg concept. Society is becoming each day more closely involved with these two areas of electronics. For the first time since humans began to dream about intelligent machines (e.g.: Frankenstein), we have begun to see them every day on the news[1,2,3,4,18]. People now want wearable computers [5,6], emotional computers [7,8], washable and edible computers! The Cyborg concept [9] inevitably follows behind and is getting more and more popular. To summarize: electronics has two main roles in a human social context. Hardware brings electronics into the physical world; software transports the physical world into electronics. Hardware devices are physical objects in the real world, subject to physical rules; software, on the other hand tends to propose itself as a system, governed by its own rules. These are the physical spaces and the social context where electronics acts, but, what kind of relationship can we create with these spaces?

2.2 How Technology Influences Art (the World)

To ask how electronics influences art, and consequentially the world, might sound like a hard question. The history of human ideas and art might help us in understanding it. For example, when photography spread into human societies art, in general, and painting, in particular, it changed abruptly. Painting lost its role as a tool for imitating reality and began to explore new meanings of vision. Then photography began to evolve too - and after initial rejection by conservative critics and artists, it was accepted as a new form of art. This changed the «common sense» view of art and the rituals of perceiving art. Walter Benjamin has explained [10] how photography and, of course, the cinema and music recording, overthrew principles that have been felt indispensable for art: in particular the uniqueness of original works. In the same way, painting was influenced by photography and cinema, investigating and finding new ways of depicting movement as in Cubism and inventing a new vocabulary of the form, as in abstract art. This would suggest that technologies have the power to change the values, even of people who do not use them . Will electronic art influence the world in the some way? What does electronics offer us that photography, cinema and painting cannot? Could it be interactivity? Or «changeability»? We think both factors count; further on in this paper, we will come back to these issues.

2.3 How Technology Gets Feedback (from Art and the World)

Feedback is not a one way process. There are ways in which art gets "revenge" on technologies and science. Technology allows human beings to manipulate their habitat. Art gives human meaning to this process. Pythagoras, for example, discovered the relationship between tone and the length of a string but never thought of playing the instrument he had discovered. Composers on the other hand continually re-discover and "explain" the magic of that same instrument. Thus, when art explores the extreme possibilities of technological products it creates requirements for new technology. Will electronics and digital arts follow this same path? Will they be influenced by art movements? We believe this has already happened. We strongly argue that electronic works of art [9,10,11,13,14] would never have been accepted or recognized without the influence of forerunners using traditional techniques as in so-called Contemporary Classical Music (e.g.: Berio or Stockhausen) or in movements such as Futurism. Later on, in this paper we will present evidence of this tendency. First however let us retrace out steps and try to figure out what we mean when we talk about an «electronic artist».

3 What Artist?

Western societies usually segregate/divide artists and scientists into two different mental spaces. Today, however new electronics-based technologies are giving birth to a new kind of artist who is closer to technological and scientific knowledge - artists who share the approach of a Leonardo Da Vinci, who recognized that there is no clear cut between art and science. We have to look closer at what artists actually do to understand the need for this kind of science-oriented artist.

3.1 Two Different Concepts or Aspects of the Artist

There are many possible definitions of what it means to be an artist. Among these we can identify two main conceptions: the concept of the "immaterial" artist and that of the "material" artist. This makes it possible to distinguish, if not two different kinds of artist, at least two different categories of «artistic act». The former is based on the abstract idea, the concept, which lies behind a work of art; the latter is centered on the phenomenon: the material translation of the concept into the physical world (in a wider sense). To become real art an artifact requires both. Better, the first category of act, artist conception, refers to a mental process, state or, attitude that leads to the production of ideas. It has to do with language and the sense of a work of art. This is what we call "immaterial" art: the way in which it is produced (in this case via linguistic revolution or evolution) is the same for any kind of art. The second kind of art action, on the other hand, is much more closely related to the workings of mind, in the modern sense of a body and brain functioning as a whole. The idea of a "material" artist, in our sense, has much to do with body action (e.g. the movements of dancer using the peripheral part of the nervous system) and with the technology the artist might use. In this context the search for new «tools» is a key part of the artistic process in which a number of artists play a pioneering role. As the object relationships develop it is expected that scientists and artists develop more complex tools and processes which will result in artifacts. This work is very similar to the work performed by scientists. Let us clarify with two examples.

Fig. 2. Sergio Lombardo. Disegno stocastico 1983 [15]

3.2 Art and Human Language: The "Immaterial" Artist

Art critics identify conceptual arts as these arts in which there is no transformation of matter. This corresponds to an idea of society where the relationship between the things is more important than the things themselves. The aim is to invent expressive codes, processes and systems which will, in turn, produce aesthetic matter. We are talking of artists like Marcel Duchamp's son/daughter. Another example might be Sergio Lombardo [15] with his emphasis on the ways and means of artistic creation. Lombardo's methodology involves sciences like stochastic mathematics and psychology. Moreover, it is important to stress that artists like John Cage have developed theories and concepts behind the idea of stochastic processes and developments by chance. For example John Cage while working with Merce Cunningham a choreographer, said: "I am not interested in expression or relationships as I am supposed to be, I am interested in things which I cannot analyze, which I do not understand". The resulting aesthetic, while a product of these disciplines, is nonetheless unpredictable. Artists like Duchamp and Lombardo can be called artists because of the way they changed the use of symbols, language and ideas respectively in sculpture or painting. It would not matter at all if their works had no aesthetic content - (although we would miss it); the revolution in language is enough. Joel Chadabe composed several pieces using Intelligent Muisic's software called "M" which are the real peices of art published on CD "After Some Songs", a group of improvisational pieces based on well known jazz compositions. Joel Chadabe described how he composed that music with percussionist Jan Williams: " The electronic sounds also function as a kind of interactive accompaniment. In performance, I'm sitting at a computer, manipulating screen controls, while the computer is generating variations on the basic material and controlling a synthesizer. Jan plays along witt what he hears. At the same time, I'm following what he does. It's as if I'm conducting improvising orchestra which is accompanying an improvising soloist. We're following each other in performance, matching sounds and gestures, letting the music unfold as the result of that mutually influential processes"[27].

3.3 Art and Human Technique, the "Material" Artist

As we said before, part of the artistic approach to the world, besides being related to the physical skill of the artist, is a very scientific one - being closely related to the techniques or technologies the artist uses. In a way, this aspect of the art can be easily abstracted from the language and the meanings art usually brings with it. One example might be Simone Martini, a renaissance artist. His famous "blue" color was the fruit of a deep chemical knowledge of pigments. That blue was at the time a unique aesthetic result which many of his contemporaries tried to reach in vain (and which brought him celebrity). No doubt, it had something to do with painting and the aesthetics of painting. However, it was at the same time a purely scientific discovery. The same can be said of Bach that, whose musical work, the Well-Tempered Clavier solved the old problem of instrument tuning with respect to the physical constraints of harmonic scale tonality. Accordingly, Trewor Wishart, who is a contemporary programmer and composer, said: "Our principal metaphor for musical composition must change from one of architecture to one of chemistry. We may imagine a new personality combing the beach of sonic possibilities, not someone who select, rejects, classifies and measures the accepptable, but a chemist who can take any pebble and, by numerical sorcery, separate its constituens, merge the constituens from two quite different pebbles and, in fact, transform black pebbles into gold pebbles". [28]Thus, specific sound which may be characteristic for one musical composition may be made from various sounds in the process of computer sound transformation.

4 Electronic Art

So far we have highlighted two kind of art action: one related to ideas, language and meaning (i.e.: "immaterial" art) and one related to physical action by the artist and to art technologies (i.e.: "material" art). We then depicted two specific social spaces where electronics plays a role, the machine (hardware) and the inner workings of the machine (software). So, given all this, what are the implications of electronics and how are artists going to use it? Many of us have the feeling that we are at the beginning of a new techno-cultural revolution which will bring us to new frontiers of knowledge and will change our lives significantly. Electronics is leading the revolution which, it seems, is going to involve every possible category of human artifact, right up to human thoughts, in short, the whole of society. Art will not be external to this process; rather the contrary, it might even have the hard task of somehow, at least partially, guiding it. As the first section argued, when discussing Pythagoras' discoveries, artistic movements, philosophically speaking, «fight» the abnormalities of science and technology by modeling, shaping and finally bending them to the real human needs. Art acts together with religion (when the two can be separated) as a guardian of the conscience of the human race - as demonstrated by George Orwell. So let us return to art and try to understand the nature of the new frontiers introduced by technology, how art might influence them and how art itself might be influenced by them. Let us try and describe the essential techno-artistic scenario.

4.1 A New Electronic Space

Besides the social space occupied by electronic software and hardware, electronics also occupies a physical space of its own that we will introduce in this paragraph. As suggested above we can distinguish between «material» and «immaterial» art. Where do we find this distinction in electronic art? Although the categories today seem outmoded, the history of ideas and philosophy has identified five main artistic disciplines. These are: painting (we include here all the visual arts such as photography and cinema), dancing, sculpture, music and poetry. As a consequence, you can call yourself an artist if you deal with and excel in at least one of these disciplines. What does this mean? A closer examination shows that in order to be considered an artist you should be able to move in a smart, aesthetic and emotional way in one or more of five different spaces. The painter has always been the one who smoothly steps out across a canvas surface; the sculptor sharply slides into rock, wood and marble while the musician flies in among sound waves, the dancer moves tenderly in body space; finally, the writer jumps surprisingly between words. Each has a well defined, and recognizable role; for each there exists a well defined physical place where skills can be demonstrated and compared - allowing the identification of true artists - expert «walkers» in their own specific space. These are what we called "material" artists. But what has this to do this with electronics? This is a difficult question. It seems to us that electronics and what we call software and hardware have defined a new kind of space where the "old artists", actions would find it hard to fit. The boundaries of this new space are, of course, rather loosely drawn. But the deeper you step into electronic space, the closer you get to identifying what we mean by an electronic artist.

4.2 The "Material" Electronic Artist

The space in which electronic art takes place is new space, and even though we usually identify it with a PC screen it is, in reality much more than that. It is not a print-out or a «wave file». We can play the violin or a synthesizer and still remain traditional musicians: the space we are moving in is the traditional one for musicians. In the same way, we will soon be able to design an amazing three dimensional file format and print it out on a 3D printer or design a new robot. In both cases we can still consider ourselves sculptors. In the same way, we can work out a poem on a word editor, (perhaps a hypertext editor), without this having anything to do with real electronic art. What we are trying to say is that, electronic art works in a different space. Electronic art (as opposed to the traditional arts, mediated by electronics) can be identified by the physical space it occupies, by the kind of matter it shapes. This is closer to the underlying electronic logic (if not to the CPU and to specific hardware circuitry). The space defines the way we can move in it, the ways in which we can exert or loose our control. Yes, of course, we act in the space and like any other action in our universe what we do may be in some way audible, touchable, visible and so on. Still, this might not be the focus of the artistic action or the most important thing for the artist - the walker in this new kind of space. Let us take an example. We sit in front of a PC and start writing a code, let say, a Java code. We are going to write a genetic algorithm [16,17,19]. Our algorithm takes shape and we write nice functions which give us back amazing results and, maybe, some errors which we don't care about since we are not scientists. (Scientists cannot neglect uncertainty in the same way as artists might and usually do). OK, now we have got billions of nice numbers coming out of our debug console, what shall we do with them? Say that we plot them on a graphical display. What will does that make us? Will we be painters? And what if we plot them onto a sound file? Does that make us musicians? What if we do both? What if we do both simultaneously? Well, we think that it does not matter at all. Insofar as we have a broader sense of art we seek the best possible representation for our numbers - the one which best shakes people's hearts. If, on the contrary, we lack this sense of «material art», we will end up like Pythagoras. In both cases we might presume to call ourselves artists (or scientists). What we would not do is call ourselves musicians or painters. In addition, it is important to emphasize that various genres or media converge and that for example movement trigger sound or visual presentations, that digitized photograph may be transformed into sound etc. Thus, convergence put artists in a position to transcend, transform or sublime not only the basic content but the ways of expression too. By using electronic devices including computers artists have chance to become meta-artists.If you agree with this, you will also agree that we still need a definition of what we mean by an «electronic artist». Before reaching such a definition, let us make one further consideration.

4.3 The "Immaterial" Artist and the Uses of Electronics

The sort of process we have just described is not of course the only possible use for electronics. We can bend electronics to our aesthetic and our will without physical contact - without programming or assembling a circuit. We could, for example, hang a computer from the ceiling. This might still be considered art. It is a kind of art that has quite a lot to do with electronics but, is not electronic art and has nothing to do with it. This is a kind of art which does not focus on the object but relates only to the meanings objects, and facts, carry with them. It has nothing to do with science, not directly. This is what we called here "immaterial" art.

5 Alive Art

Electronics and arts have already developed a significant dialog. As a result, the number of artistic movements which make use of electronics, grows day by day, rather like biological species during the Cambrian period in geology. One of the most evident effects of this "Cambrian explosion" is confusion. This is fair enough. The growth of electronics affects other arts and produces art itself. This in turns modifies the use of electronics in art and is influenced by it, in a sort of endless loop. Nevertheless, before introducing the concept and definition of «Alive Art», let us first refer to a number of electronic art movements and make a few general considerations.

5.1 Other Artistic Movements Based on Electronics

The most famous and widespread electronic art movements are Electronic Art, Digital Art and Computer Art. These "old" definitions, despite their popularity and historical importance, have, in our opinion, lost much of their theoretical significance. This kind of approach to electronic art is too vague for the current situation. What they express is the concept that art has something to do with electronic, digital or computer based materials. It is self evident that we need clearer analytical distinctions. The first thing to be noticed is that, most of the time, there is a quite brutal distinction between artists who use software and those who work with hardware. Considering our analysis of electronics' social context this is not surprising. On the software side, we have artists who use various kind of Artificial Life [20] algorithms to paint a PC screen (or its equivalent) or (more rarely) to generate sound. Hardware artists on the other hands create (primarily) cybernetics-based works of art with a minority basing their efforts on pseudo (i.e. non-autonomous) robotics. Among these artists the most productive have been (for solid economic reasons) those engaged in the design of algorithms for sounds and images. There are dozens of proposals of this kind: Artificial Life Art, Genetic Art, Generative Art, Evolving Art, Evolutionary Art, Organic Art, Fractal Art and so on [11,12,13].

Fig. 3. Vedran Vucic. Green-s, 1999. Produced with the Artificial Painter [13,14].

The common feature of all these movements, is that they are based on algorithms which in some way produce their own rules and which generate their own behavior. In our opinion, the most appropriate descriptions of this work might be Genetic Art (because of the connection to Darwin), Artificial Life Art (because of the connection to Langton and like thinkers) and Generative Art because of the link to the Chomsky. It should be observed that, as far as the authors know, none of these artistic movements have concretely applied their basic concepts to hardware and modeled hardware and software as a unified whole. In other words, most of the time it is the software which operates the artistic transformation while the hardware is "hand crafted" with at most the ability to reiterate some limited "movements". This is crucial. While technically possible there has, in practice, been no revolution in the material structure underlying this kind of art. In hardware-based electronic art things are quite different. There is not room here to go into a detailed analysis. It is nonetheless necessary to make a distinction between early Cybernetics, and later Cybernetics or movements like that of the Kinetic Sculptors. Earlier Cybernetics artists, were from all points of view, the precursors of computer science and life like algorithms. Indeed, Cybernetics, originating prior to the transistor, was successful, right from the beginning, in creating electromechanical analogies to living systems. These artists made direct use of electromagnetic fields in art. Today Cybernetics artists [9], Kinetic Sculptors for example, are quite different. Not only do they give a bigger role to computer based technologies and a lesser one to electromagnetic fields; they also make heavy use of technicians, computer scientists and engineers in their artistic production. In other words, they are moving far away from the original type, and philosophy, of the artist and opening to a conception of artwork as work by a team. Philosophically speaking, this drastically changes the artist's attitude; the use of human material becomes, of necessity, part of the act itself - a fine challenge. Politically speaking this might be a constraint. Materials, which include other humans, are very expensive. For this reason many of these works of art are financed by companies. Inevitably, it turns out that the artist looses his or her freedom. A good example of a similar tendency is the cinema where the artistic component is weakened by the need to generate profit. This is a danger which we should keep clear in our mind and which leads us to additional considerations. As we said earlier the situation is a little confused and the overall scenario is so dynamic that more time is needed before the relationship between art and electronics becomes fully clear. We can nonetheless attempt to outline this relationship.

5.2 Alive Art

Art history tell us we are following a path which leads towards immateriality. As a consequence, visual artists for example have moved from painting to photography to cinema to computer graphics and from figurative painting, to impressionism to futurism to generative art. It appears as if there is a need for an artistic discipline which underlines the restless aspect of representation (in this case visual representation). We are searching for a meaning of dynamics which is not only moving and changeable but which can go further. For these reasons it seems to us that we now have the possibility of shaping a new art movement or approach, whose medium is mostly but, not necessarily, electronics. This is Alive Art. Alive Art should be a discipline where the dynamical aspect of the work of art is crucial if not essential. The use of the term «Alive» stresses that works of «Alive Art» should be ever changing as well as ever moving. Things which are Alive can die - and they can also react. As a consequence, the characteristic of Alive Artworks, would be perpetual change (which can also lead to extinction or death) and interactivity. There is in this definition a strong drive to define an artwork which is, conceptually speaking, immaterial, abstract, difficult to seize in words. This should be an art movement which has a strong relation with the deepest aspect of life which is not, or not only, change but perpetual change, which is not only action but constant action and reaction which leads not only to changes in life but also, at times to the end of life (i.e.: to vulnerability). If we were asked: "what kind of changes are we talking about?" the obvious answer would be: "In Alive Art, as in life, there should be unpredictable, as well as, predictable changes". That is, in our opinion, the way to go. It is the course of art. We want to emphasize two factors which created common sense in this century. The first one is that we are influenced in a great deal by the mechanistic industrial perception of the world around us and that consequently, we tend to interpret things by using mechanistic approach. Secondly, our perception of ourselves is determined by the mechanisms created in our early childhood. For that matter, one changed attitude would bear in mind that Alive Art assume that evolutionary transformational processes are natural phenomena in material world around us. Though many psychologists paid a lot of attention to the early childhood developments we think that Cristopher Bollas is closest to our perception of the development of generative developmental processes. In his book The Shadow of the Object [29] he stressed that:" A transformational object is experientially identified by the infant with processes that alter self experience. With the infant's creation of the transitional object, the transformational process is displaced from the mother-environment (where it originated) into countless subjective-objects, so that the transitional phase is heir to the transformational period, as the infant evolves from experience of the process to articulation of the experience. With the transitional object, the infant can play with the illusion of his own omnipotence (lessening the loss of the environment-mother with generative and phasic delusions of self-and-other creation); he can entertain the idea of the object being got rid of, yet surviving his ruthlessness; and he can find in this transitional experience the freedom of metaphor." Such transitional experience may be helped by Alive Art processes and for that opurpose developed devices and various hardware and software. As said above Alive Art would be recognizable by perpetual change, interactivity and by the vulnerability of the works of art it produces. But how should we identify the performer of Alive Art, the Aliver? In section one we introduced the social context where electronics moves, while, in section three, we suggested that electronics has introduced a "new" space where the artist can «walk». We went on to emphasize the risks the artist is taking (i.e.: loss in artistic freedom). These two elements are relevant to understanding the Aliver. The Aliver should move easily in the social contexts and spaces of relevance to electronics. Although we agree that in some recent artworks human material is, more or less necessary, we also believe that the new electronic artist, in this case the Aliver, should, like a sculptor, be as close as possible to the materials he is working with - relying as little as possible on other human beings. This is crucial, not only for the "political" reasons we discussed above but, also because of the relationship the artist builds with the "life" of the object. In brief, the Aliver should be as close to the software as he/she is to the hardware (or whatever material he/she uses. If the Aliver concept is taken to its extreme consequences it is the Aliver who kick starts the life of the work of art (i.e.: an object which changes constantly), to the things, allowing it to reach a point where it (e.g.: a robot) can produce art on its own. At least from an electronic point of view, this is not just a vision. It is something which is, at least partially, already happening in robotics (LEGO has already produced the first Robot Musician and Robot Painter [24]). It is what was done by the inventor of Internet. So, the nearer you get to the electronics the closer you are to being a pure Aliver. The techniques one of today's Alivers might use are very different ranging from Artificial Life techniques, such as Genetic Algorithms [16], Neural Networks [21,22] and Cellular Automata, to techniques from electronic engineering such as sensors, motors, chips and lasers, or even biological techniques, such as genetic engineering, microsurgery and neurosurgery. The Aliver might design both the outer and inner body of the work of art itself and of those who interact with it. He/she should be no more outside the technological process than the artist is outside the artistic process. Indeed, to use and deeply know new techniques and technologies is one way, maybe the best way, to give the right emphasis to what society is, to what it is becoming and to the meanings it is carrying along to the third millennium.

5.3 The "Alive Art Effect"

In line with the above definition and with the categories previously discussed (i.e.: the internal and the external aspect of the machine), we can try to imagine two kinds of Alive Artwork. An example of what we called "outward-looking" electronics, that acts in the real world and obeys real world physics, might be a Robot Artist with the ability to evolve and print or modify, time after time, its own body or, at least, its electronic circuitry. This might consist, for example, of a Neural Network controller, which adapts to past interactive experiences with objects, animals and humans. An example of "inward-turned" electronics, could be an Alive Artwork suggested by some expressive phenomena which spontaneously emerged from the Internet. Imagine an interactive Genetic Programming program with the ability to modify itself every time a user uses (or downloads) the software. Both these two artworks would be life-like objects whose creator, the artist, having designed and set in motion their generative principles would control over his/her own work. That would be what we call the "Alive Art Effect".

Conclusion

In a human social context electronics has an inner and an outer aspect - respectively, the software and the hardware. Moving from this background we have investigated the relationship between art and technology. Technology, or science produces deep changes in art. We have cited, as an example of this, the influence of photography on painting. We then highlighted the current relationship between art and electronics with respect to what we called "immaterial" and "material" art. We emphasized that while the exponential growth of electronics requires science oriented artists, the explosion of technical knowledge also calls for team work. We pointed out the dangers to which this can lead. We summarized the current state of electronic and outlined the characteristics of a new art form -«Alive Art» -characterized by perpetual change, interactivity and vulnerability. We presented examples showing what an Alive Artwork might look like and the way in which the performer of Alive Art might loose his/her artistic authority. While Benjamin, in his time, saw a loss of spatio-temporal unity in art (i.e.: pointing to the problem of the reproducibility of the work of art), electronics seems to undermine the very identity of the artist.

Acknowledgements

We would like to thank Richard Walker (Department of Psychology, University of Naples) and Teresa Numerico (ARTIFICIALIA, Turner Broadcasting System Italia) for revising this manuscript and for precious suggestions. A big thank you goes to Floriana Orazi for all kinds of help she gave us. Special thanks to the poet Alfredo Baldinetti, the musician Helena Hong and to the painters Federico Pietrella and Emanuele Costanzo for the endless inspiration they give us.

References

1. Lund, H. H., and Pagliarini, L. RoboCup Jr. with LEGO Mindstorms To appear in *Proceedings of Int. Conf. Robotics and Automation 2000* (ICRA2000), IEEE Press, NJ. 1999

2. Lund, H. H., and Pagliarini, L. Robot Soccer with LEGO Mindstorms In *Asada and Kitano (eds.) RoboCup'98*, LNAI 1604, Springer-Verlag, Heidelberg. 1999

3. Lund, H. H., Arendt, J. A., Fredslund, J., and Pagliarini, L.Ola: What Goes Up, Must Fall Down. In *Proceedings of Artificial Life and Robotics* (AROB'99), ISAROB, Oita. 1999

4. Lund, H. H., Miglino, O., Pagliarini, L., Billard, A. , Ijspeert, A. Evolutionary Robotics - A Children's Game. In Proceedings of *IEEE 5th International Conference on Evolutionary Computation*. IEEE Press. 1998

5. http://lcs.www.media.mit.edu/projects/wearables

6. http://www.wearcomp.org

7. Pagliarini L., Lund H.H., Miglino O., and Parisi D. Artificial Life: A New Way to Build Educational and Therapeutic Games. In *Proceedings of Artificial Life V*. MIT Press/Bradford Books, 1996.

8. http://gracco.irmkant.rm.cnr.it/luigi/ lupa_face.html

9. http://www.stelarc.va.com.au

10. Walter Benjamin. Das Kunstwerk im Zeitalter seiner techniscen Reproduzierbarkeit. In *Schriften*. By Suhrkamp Verlag, Frankfurt am Main. 1995

11. http://gracco.irmkant.rm.cnr.it/luigi/ alg_art.htm

12. Sims, K. Artificial Evolution for Computer Graphics. *Computer Graphics* 25, 4, 319-328. 1991

13. Lund, H. H., Pagliarini, L., and Miglino, O. Artistic Design with Genetic Algorithms and Neural Networks. In J. T. Alander (Ed.) *Proceedings of 1NWGA*, Vaasa University, Vaasa. 1995

14. Lund, H. H., Pagliarini, L., and Miglino, O. The Artificial Painter. In *Abstract Book of Proceedings of Third European Conference on Artificial Life*, Granada. 1995

15. Lombardo Sergio. Percezione di figure grottesche in alcune strutture casuali. In *Rivista di Psicologia dell'Arte*, Anno V, nn.8/9 giugno e dicembre. 1983

16. Holland, J.J. Adaptation in natural and artificial systems. Ann Arbor, Michigan, University of Michigan Press, 1975 (or MIT Press, 1992)

17. Mitchell. M. *An introduction to genetic algorithms*. MIT Press. 1997

18. Miglino, O., and Lund, H. H. (1995) Robotics as an Educational Tool. Technical Report. C.N.R., Rome. 1995.

19. Goldberg D.E. *Genetic Algoritm in search, optimization and machine learning*. New York, Addison-Wesley. 1998

20. Langton C.G. Artificial Life. In L. Nadel e D. Stein (ed.) *Lectures in Complex System*, SFI Studies in the Sciences of Complexity, Lect. Vol. IV, Reading MA, 1992.

21. Rumelahart, D.E. , McClelland, J.L. *Parallel Distributed Processing. Explorations in the Microstructure of Cognition*. MIT Press, Cambridge, MA. 1986

22. Parisi, D., Cecconi, F. and Nolfi, S. 1990 Econets: Neural networks that learn in an environment. Network, 1(2), 149-168. 1990
23. L. Pagliarini, A. Dolan, F. Menczer, and H. H. Lund ALife Meets Web: Lessons Learned. In *Proceedings of Virtual Worlds*, First International Conference, J.C. Heudin (Ed.) Springer-Verlag Press. 1998
24. http://legolab.daimi.au.dk
25. http://gracco.irmkant.rm.cnr.it/luigi/wica/vedran
26. http://gracco.irmkant.rm.cnr.it/luigi/wica/luigi.html
27. Joel Chadabe, Electric Sound - The Past and Promise of Electronic Music, Published by Prentice Hall, Inc. USA, 1997
28. Trevor Wishart, Audible Design, Published by Orpheus the Pantomime Ltd. 1994
29. Christopher Bollas, The Shadow of the Object, Free Associations Books.lTd. 1993

In Search of Vital Presence - Evolving Virtual Musics

Rodney Berry

ATR Media Integration & Communications Research Laboratories
2-2 Hikari-dai, Seika-cho, Soraku-gun, Kyoto, 619-0288 Japan
rodney@mic.atr.co.jp
www.mic.atr.co.jp/~rodney

Abstract. A long-standing interest in the boundaries and relationships between art and science, animate and inanimate, technology and biology all serve to drive my work as an artist and composer. Technological changes that exploit biological paradigms will change our way of seeing nature, technology and culture. Virtual worlds provide an ideal arena in which to explore these ideas. The interactive virtual environment, Feeping Creatures generates music and graphics in real time based on the evolution and behavior of a population of artificial organisms. The Vital Presence project attempts to take this idea further and provide more scope for evolution of all aspects of the music. Along the way, I find opportunities to share my opinions on various issues surrounding this kind of work, and speculate on the implications and future directions of my own work.

1 Introduction

I am a composer, musician and sound-artist and currently a visiting researcher at ATR Media Integration and Communications Laboratories near Kyoto, Japan. My artwork mostly concerns itself with exploring the boundaries and relationships between the worlds of the animate and inanimate, technology and biology as well as art and science. For quite a long time, I have been fascinated with the idea of making artifacts that seem to be alive in some sense. I often use the term vital presence to describe the feeling one has when in the presence of a living thing. This fascination has led me to build a number of automated instruments and sound installations each inspired by living systems in one way or another. In recent years however, I have become very interested in computer based artificial life in the context of virtual worlds for making music.

As our mechanical technology becomes more sophisticated and autonomous, it is not surprising that we tend to personify it and treat it as if it is alive (For example, I would not print the things I have said to my computer over the 24 hours before this publishing deadline!). Now that we have software that actually evolves and adapts, it is not hard to think of such things as being alive at least to some extent. It has been said that the mechanical view of nature and the organic way of seeing technology are rapidly merging into a *bionic* [1] or *neo-biological* [2] worldview. Also, our culture

J.-C. Heudin (Ed.): VW 2000, LNAI 1834, pp. 185-191, 2000.
© Springer-Verlag Berlin Heidelberg 2000

exhibits some of the qualities we associate with living things. Culture is passed from one person to another. It changes to adapt to changing circumstances. It seems to have a life of its own. Biologist, Richard Dawkins [3] talks about the idea of the meme, a metaphorical basic transmissible unit of culture or thought. Memes live inside our heads and travel from host to host using our language and media as vectors of infection. This is all rich territory for an artist to explore. My early compositions and soundworks used space as a major structural element so, once I began using the computer as a tool, it was a logical step to start experimenting with virtual worlds and populating them with artificial life. The book Artificial Life by Steven Levy, especially his description of Larry Yaeger's Polyworld simulation [4], inspired me to really focus on making a musical virtual environment.

2 Feeping Creatures

Feeping Creatures is an interactive virtual world. It was developed over the last three years in collaboration with programmers Tom Mander, Brian Murray and Ben Ross of Proximity Pty.Ltd. a Sydney-based software company. The development was assisted financially by the Australia Council, the Australian Government's arts funding body. The title is a spoonerism or word play on Creeping Features, the tendency among software developers to cram so many features into a program that it becomes overweight and clumsy. The name was chosen to remind the programming team and myself to keep this piece as simple as possible. The ideal is to see how much variety and complexity can be generated with a bare minimum of complication. For my purposes, complexity is what emerges in nature as a result of interactions between essentially simple interdependent elements. Complication on the other hand, comes from human attempts to create the outer appearance of natural complexity. The latter approach tries to carve a tree out of a blank block of wood while the former simply plants a seed and waits. My own ultimate goal in this area is to create a perpetual novelty engine. Left to its own devices, such a machine would go on forever producing new and unique output independent of the hand of its creator. In nature, the process of evolution is such an engine of variation, perpetually churning out diverse forms and behaviors. This is why I chose to explore artificial life and evolutionary computing for their potential to bring life-like qualities into my own artworks.

The world of Feeping Creatures is a flat green grid across which the inhabitants (feeps) and the observer move. Feeps are represented by simple cubes covered with moving textures. Food is represented by green triangular pyramids (trees) that grow up through the floor of the grid. The user of the program moves a mouse to steer a virtual camera and its attached virtual microphone across the grid. A projected video screen shows the view from the camera while loudspeakers play the sounds collected by the microphone. Each feep has a sequence of musical pitches that form its chromosome. These are mapped to MIDI note numbers that are sent to an external synthesizer (in this case, a Kurzweil K2000). When two feeps mate, portions of each parent's note list are passed on to their offspring to form a new chromosome or pitch series. At birth, a feep is randomly assigned a numerical value to determine its preference for mating. If this value is high, the new feep will seek out partners that are, on average, musically consonant to its own note series. If the value is low, its preference will be for those more dissonant to itself.

Parent 1

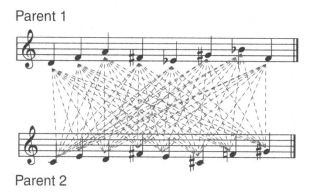

Parent 2

Fig. 1. Mating occurs by comparing all the notes of one creature with all the notes of another to determine their compatibility

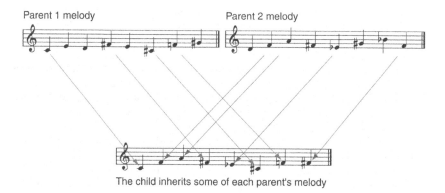

The child inherits some of each parent's melody

Fig. 2. A baby feep has a sequence of musical pitches in its chromosome. A portion of this sequence comes from each of its parents

The degree of consonance or dissonance is found by first finding the difference between the first MIDI note numbers of each series. The result is then divided by 12 while keeping the remainder (modulo 12). This returns a value of less than 12 that is then compared with a hierarchical table of intervals. The unison or octave would have a value of 0 (most consonant), and the semitone a value of 11 (most dissonant). The remaining intervals fall between these extremes in an arbitrary order. The hierarchy could easily be changed and would also apply to microtonal (using intervals less than a semitone) even-tempered tuning systems. The process is then repeated between every note in both lists before averaging out the results. By tabling these results, the program can keep track of who will mate with whom in the world of the feeps.

In musical terms, we are only dealing with average vertical harmonic relationships. A similar process could be used to find average horizontal relationships as well. For the moment, voice-leading and octave displacements are ignored (except for the fact that young feeps transpose down a few octaves when they reach puberty) in favor of a quick and dirty calculation of general trends in the population. I am looking for a similar method of dealing with rhythmic information. Different ways of ordering and evaluating proportions of durations and articulations are currently being explored. The challenge is always to find simple formulae, which, although imprecise, give the system (and its internal components), some general ideas about its own internal states.

In Feeping Creatures, rhythm is analogous to energy flow through the system. Each item of food (tree) contains a duration value (how much time passes before the next note is played) and an articulation value (how long the note sustains once initiated). When a feep finds a tree and eats it, the tree's duration and articulation values are added to the feep's rhythm list. Unlike the pitch list, which is fixed at birth, the rhythm list increases when the feep eats a tree and decreases as it ages or fails to find food. When a feep's rhythm list falls below a given length, meaning its energy level is low, the feep dies and vanishes from the world. Because rhythm is dealt with separately to pitch, repeated cells of melodic material cycle with rhythmic figures of a different length. Different parts of the melody return with other parts of the rhythm in each subsequent cycle. These note/duration isorhythms manifest as short repeated patterns somewhat like bird songs.

The main program oversees all the interactions between the feeps, their positions and the position of the user. When a feep is within an arbitrary hearing range, the program assigns it a new MIDI channel and a timbre that corresponds to its visual texture. The texture is one of 8 animated texture movies that are mapped onto the cubic shapes. As a feep comes nearer to the microphone, its MIDI volume increases causing it to become louder. The program also uses MIDI to adjust each feep's location between left and right, front and back of the four loudspeakers. This is achieved by making a synthesizer voice consisting of two layers. One layer is assigned to the front left and right speaker pair and the other to the rear pair. Another MIDI controller is used to cross-fade between the front and rear output layers. Although cheap and crude, this method allows for up to 12 independently moving sound entities in the four-speaker field with no noticeable delay.

A great deal of care was taken to integrate sound, visual and kinesthetic information in this work. Much of our kinesthetic sense involves a convergence of cues from our senses of hearing, sight and touch. More broadly, this cross-modal cueing between different modes of perception is probably the most crucial factor influencing one's degree of immersion in a virtual world. The surround sound, coupled with the projected video and simple mouse interface, creates a sense of being drawn into the imaginary world of the feeps. The sound and visual outputs change to provide instant feedback to the user as he or she moves the mouse. I believe that it is this integration of stimuli that makes it easier for the user to be absorbed into the work. This kind of absorption or engagement is not necessarily brought about by interactivity. In my opinion, many multimedia presentations quickly lose engagement through gratuitous interactivity. A microwave oven is interactive. It has buttons, even a bell that rings. A good painting can be deeply engaging without a mouse and buttons to press. Engagement comes from addressing the user at many levels simultaneously. It is my hope that multimedia will move away from its current fixation with pointing and clicking through a fixed database toward something more fluid and organic.

It has become apparent to me that Feeping Creatures will never be finished. I guess that no world ever really is. The ecology badly needs a predator, a feep-lion to prowl the landscape devouring feeps and incorporating their rhythms. The feep-lion would be a kind of virtual music critic. This would influence the evolution of pitch series along more diverse lines than the simple sexual selection currently in operation. The environment itself will become more of a shaping force for evolution including terrain and weather as selective pressures on the evolving feeps. The goal is to create a complex system of deeply interdependent variables, which continually modify each other in an endless game of Rock, Scissors, Paper, the elusive perpetual novelty engine.

3   The Vital Presence Project at ATR's M.I.C.Lab

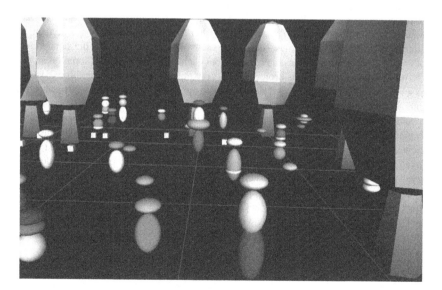

Fig. 3. Screenshot of the 'spinners' world from the MICLabs Vital Presence project

Currently, I am working with programmers at ATR to build another biologically inspired virtual environment. Similar in concept to Feeping Creatures, this project also uses an onscreen rendering of a 3D world and uses MIDI for sound. The creatures of this world are nicknamed Spinners because of their resemblance to children's spinning top toys. They have three sexes and all three must contribute genetic material for a successful conception to occur. Over the course of a spinner's lifetime, it changes sex several times. It begins life as a soprano with only one body segment and a relatively high-pitched voice range. At puberty, it becomes an alto with two body segments and a slightly lower pitch range. Altos initiate mating and bear the children with both a bass and a tenor. Later, an alto metamorphoses into a tenor with three body segments before finally becoming a bass with four segments.

Each spinner has a chromosome consisting of a long string of binary digits. Parts are taken from those of each parent to form a new and unique string. Segments of this string can then be mapped to different visual and musical traits. For example, the width and height of each body segment, is determined by the same parts of the chromosome as the durations and articulations of the creature's rhythmic elements. These musical traits provide values that are then used to trigger individual MIDI events. These MIDI events are fed to the outboard synthesizer, which turns them into sound. As rhythm is determined by genetic factors, we would expect rhythm to remain fairly consistent throughout a creature's lifespan (unlike in Feeping Creatures where the rhythm is continually changing). Melody is more dynamic, being governed by the way the creature responds to environmental changes in the form of neighboring creatures' activities. Timbre (the color or texture of the sound) is also controlled by the changes in the creatures' behavior and genetics. In practice, this means that parts of the chromosome are used to generate continuous MIDI controller messages. These messages control such timbral parameters as filter frequency and resonance, dynamic attack and decay rates and times. In this way, new individuals will have the same kind of overall instrument sound as their parents but each will have a distinct tonal quality.

At the time of writing, this project is still very much a work in progress. I expect it to go through many changes as it develops. We are trying a number of approaches to interactivity so the user develops a closer relationship with the work. One approach is to allow a live musician to create new creatures from what is played on an instrument. A kind of slow dialog would develop between the user and the system as new musical elements are added or culled by the player. Beginner musicians would have to be given a slightly easier way of doing this. Ideally I would like to be able to scale the level of difficulty and detail to the abilities of the user. Different styles of music will be possible although I think styles that favour repetition (such as trance techno) will work best. The important thing is that the user or participant should feel that they are now a part of this artificial world and have a strong sense of being somewhere different.

4 Future Directions

In the future, I would like to make at least one environment in which graphics are virtually non-existent. I would like the sound to provide all the cues necessary for the user to have a meaningful experience with the work. Some of the digital convolution-based spatial sound systems appearing on the market will probably facilitate this kind of work. However, I find such systems have trouble when handling many moving sound sources and still prefer to use MIDI with four-way panning. I would also like to explore some models which are even less like the 'real world'. Such models could perhaps even evolve their own physics and biology. We invest so much of our resources in making jerky versions of normal reality. I am not convinced that simply throwing faster computers and more polygons at the problem will make it go away. Given different constraints, I think that current technology could give us a quite a fluid sense of something truly alien.

Finding ways to sonify existing artificial life environments is another avenue I wish to explore, where the mappings of state, location, actions etc. need not be so literal as in a typical 3D visualization. Another direction would be to treat sets of musical rules as the physics of an artificial environment. Such rules could be determined by a particular style of music that evolves creatures adapted to stylistic constraints. One could model a whole music industry in such a manner.

5 Conclusion

There is so much potential in the combination of artificial life and virtual worlds. It is my conviction that organic paradigms can offer some startling new territory for an artist to explore. More than anything, such an approach allows the artist to step back from his or her traditional role as God/Creator to become instead a farmer or maybe even a hunter of aesthetic experience. Finally, I hope that artificial biologies somehow allow us to better understand and appreciate the complexity and fragility of the natural world. Such an appreciation would go hand in hand with an aesthetic based on *systems and processes* rather than simply *objects and images.* It is my belief that, when exposed to the artistic products of this kind of aesthetic, people may be led to value more the things they now exploit and discard.

References

1. Channell, D.F.: The Vital Machine – a study of technology and organic life, Oxford University Press, New York, Oxford, 1991, p112
2. Kelly, K.: Out of Control – the new biology of machines, Fourth Estate, London, 1994, p236
3. Dawkins, R.: The Selfish Gene, Oxford University Press, Oxford, 1976, p206-215
4. Levy, S.: Artificial Life – A Report From The Frontier Where Computers Meet Biology 1992 Vintage Books New York Paperback edition (pp3-4, 6, 7, 168)

Birth of a New World Order: IceBorg

Andy Best

MEET Factory OY, Tallberginkatu 1 Box 45, 00180 HELSINKI, Finland
Best@meetfactory.com

Abstract. This paper describes the creation and development of the new multiuser virtual community *IceBorg* and *Rallying Cry,* the community game platform that will form the basis of a new breed of collaborative online virtual communities.

1 Introduction

IceBorg is a multimedia pop-cultural project under development by MEET Factory to be launched in June 2000.

IceBorg combines narrative and performance together with strategy and adventure game structure into an immersive and fully interactive 3D environment on the Internet. The work functions as a socially interactive stimulating multiuser space, bringing geographically distant people together in an online world. The overall aim of IceBorg is to create a self-sustaining virtual community within a media art work combining the Internet, TV broadcast, and live performance as the basis for research and development of a future entertainment creation and delivery platform for the converged Web, TV, and mobile communication markets.

2 Background

IceBorg's content references political and social satire including the zany humour of Monty Python, 2D animations and their anarchistic humour such as Southpark, Beavis and Butthead, and Ren and Stimpy, while the navigation and level design are familiar from 3D games such as the Tomb Raider series and Super Mario 64. MEET Factory's production IceBorg will represent the reality of fictions thought up by science fiction writers like William Gibson[1] and Neal Stephenson[2] with 3D inhabited virtual worlds allowing users around the world to "jack in" and interact in social online communities. According to Allucquere Rosanne Stone[3], Gibson's book "Neuromancer" was of critical importance in the development of the "Cyberspace"

---

[1] "Neuromancer" William Gibson, Ace Books 1984

[2] "Snowcrash" Neal Stephenson, Bantam Books 1992

[3] "Will the Real Body Please Stand Up?" Allucquere Rosanne Stone, Chapter 6, "Cyberspace First Steps" MIT Press 1991

J.-C. Heudin (Ed.): VW 2000, LNAI 1834, pp. 192-204, 2000.

community – until then a dispersed group of VR researchers, suddenly with a common vision and cause – to make the fiction reality. In IceBorg we attempt to get closer to that ambition.

Fig. 1. Examples of avatars created for IceBorg

Online social interaction, developed as virtual communities, can be found in many "traditional" 2D web sites today. "Virtual Community" has become a buzz word within the Internet industry, and many sites such as eBay.com (auctions) and Amazon.com (books) use effective community building strategies to develop their customer loyalties. Happy customers return time and again, developing into a thriving (and profitable) community. Other examples can be found within the gaming world, especially now that online multiplayer games have become so important. Quake 3 Arena is designed for pure multiplayer use. New 3D role playing games such as Everquest have emerged, along with 3D virtual communities such as Cybertown and Active Worlds. Many of the role playing principals in IceBorg are also derived from real world role playing games, and the early text based MUDs. Previous projects combining television broadcast and 3D virtual worlds include Heaven 'n Hell (Illuminations, British Telecom, Channel 4, UK) , Deuxieme Monde (Canal+, France), and Terranet Café (3DSAT, Germany).

None of the examples listed above represent media art, nor are they visually or thematically comparable to IceBorg. This work is one of the very first serious attempts to combine dramaturgical and narrative elements familiar from audio visual productions into the interactive situation of virtual reality and the architecture of 3D worlds in the Net. IceBorg intends to learn from these earlier projects, exploring the possibilities for online-real world interaction, but keeping firmly the target of delivering exciting and interesting content to the ordinary Internet user and TV viewer.

3 A Virtual Community

Fig. 2. Example of a plant growing near to an iceblock house on the surface of the IceBorg asteroid

Audience or Participant?

IceBorg is designed to appeal to a target audience between 15 and 40 – young, media literate, looking for provocative and stimulating entertainment. IceBorg's background story creates a futuristic scenario with which to deal with contemporary environmental and social issues such as global warming, ecological destruction, nationalism, displaced peoples and economic refugees, while the aesthetic style is a blend of retro-scifi and classic animation.

Community building is extremely important and a key element – many activities are provided to encourage repeat visits, such as allowing users to build virtual homes, grow plants that need to be tended, and create sub-groups or clans in order to build real social hierarchies within the virtual world. Chat and message boards allow users to quickly meet and make new friends, so increasing IceBorg's social value to each individual user and encouraging them to bring more and more of their real world friends into the virtual world as well. User interaction is designed to be straightforward but exciting, encouraging participation in the community, rather than just a purely one way feed-me viewer experience. The more a user participates, the more rewarding they will find the whole activity.

IceBorg is an online 3D virtual world and community accessible to ordinary Internet users. No special hardware is required, only an up to date multimedia home computer, Internet connection, and 3D VRML plugin for a web browser. No fee is charged to end users for participation, although value added products may be offered for purchase. The familiar 2D graphical interface of the World Wide Web is replaced with a three dimensional multiuser world, where visitors can wander around freely, move and create objects, experience live performances, and actually see and chat with other real people online by using a 3D figure as their virtual standin – their so-called avatar. As the IceBorg environment is totally artificial we are not governed by physical constraints, so neither are the avatars, which can walk, fly, teleport (move instataneously between points) and take on various forms all the way from realistic human to organic blobs!

Fig. 3. Avatars in the club space, DJ in background

Users are required to register as members for added benefits and full participation in the community. Visitors (or Aliens as they are known!) only have access to the main public worlds. All live events such as clubs, concerts and performances take part in these public areas. Video and audio media is streamed into the virtual world from live venues or pre-recorded material, creating a rich mediascape for users experiences. Live performances will be created by invited artists, DJs and musicians from around the world. Live guides will inhabit the online world, helping newbie users and also acting as provacateurs. By taking certain key roles in the world, the guides will ensure the world does not become *just another chat space*. Regular events and competitions will be arranged for members, keeping their interest and hopefully fueling the development of a thriving virtual community from the seeds planted at the launch. It is also planned to experiment with Interactive Digital TV, combining happenings in the virtual world with a real live TV show, creating a mixture of fully interactive online and broadcast media.

4 Once Apon a Time…..

"The transport cruiseship "Princess Gabriella", a Boeing 949-s hyperspace passenger liner, en route from Earth to the pleasure spacestation "New Eden™ 23" suffers a mysterious power failure. Unable to control the spacecraft the captain is forced to make an emergency landing on the abandoned mining asteroid Z851X, a cold and inhospitable lump of rock and ice, made worse by the illegal dumping of industrial waste over the centuries……." And so the story starts. Users are guided to create their own character and role within the developing community. We pay particular attention to providing tools for community building. In our opinion, deep user interaction *and* satisfaction are keys to the successful development of the community.

Fig. 4. IceBorg surface – early morning

5 Social Engineering

We have a story and we have a desire to create a community, but how to achieve that? Humans are notoriously fickle, and especially the new breed of web-savvy surfers are hard to impress. How to get them to login and stay in (on?) IceBorg? We utilise social engineering skills, and good old fashioned carrot and stick techniques!

According to Amy Jo Kim[4] it is important to create the right social conditions for a virtual community to evolve. It is not just a matter of cool technology, but a believable social space. Some of the key points for community development are:

- Background story – creates a common focus for community members
- Personal member profiles – develops a sense of history
- Community rituals – regular events to be involved with
- Organised events such as hosted chat with guests
- Initiation rites of passage – gives a sense of achievement
- Social hierarchy within the community – satisfaction to reach a certain level
- Gain extra interactive privilages with user experience
- Expandable gathering spaces – if it's successful, the community will grow
- True interactivity – give the members the tools to build their world how they want it

Message

The main issue behind IceBorg as a community experience is to deal with the environmental destruction and hostile climate found on the asteroid. Users have to find clothes for their avatar and other special items in order to access all the worlds. Pollution has to be cleared in order to gain experience points and also to exchange for money (borgos). The relationships between the different sub-groups defined in the backstory draw parallels with human conflicts on Earth – the mis-treatment of minorities, power grabbing and control by the rich and powerful over the poor. We hope that users will identify these issues, presented as they are intertwined within an entertaining experience. In order to succeed in the IceBorg community a member has to interact socially with many other members, and especially with those from other clans, and so the idea of collaboration and community building should be reinforced.

We also hope that the environmental message will be clear enough, so that users will start to think about their own actions in the real world. There will also be links available direct to organisations and websites highlighting and working with the real serious environmental issues facing the World today.

Narrative

Iceborg is divided into a number of distinct themed areas or worlds. Each virtual world is a visual entity of its own, although loosely linked to one another on the meta

---

[4] "Community Building on the Web" Amy Jo Kim, presentation at VirComm99, 1999

level of the main narrative running through the whole work. Each world contains not only an autonomous sub-story but also distinctive social rules of behaviour, spatial architecture, visual aesthetic, and method of navigation. In some worlds you navigate by walking, in others by swimming, flying, etc. The narrative unfolds to the user by becomming familiar with the environments, by discussing with the live (human driven) characters or AI bots, interacting with other users in the multiuser virtual world, and by additional graphical 2D information pages provided outside the 3D environment.

New users are guided first through an *entry tunnel* or prologue, introducing them to the backstory scenario. The first registration login is short and simple, but on entering the 3D world they find themselves naked (well, almost!) with just their underpants! They have just woken from cyrogenic freezing and inter-galactic space travel, so what do you expect?

Action=Reward

The first task is to visit the four main clans or sub-groups in the world – the Grannies (Over 101's), the La Coochis, the Soulband, and the Kidz. Each clan will give a special object to the user, which can be exchanged to gain entry to the avatar builder – a special place to create a visual online identity in 3D. Your avatar is the virtual you, your representation in the 3D world, created from a wide range of body parts, and is animated with a choice of gestures. In order to steer users into their IceBorg character they are encouraged to fill out a *character profile* questionaire form which guides and gives hints to what type of person they might be. This is stored in the database for other members to access, and can be updated at any time by the user.

IceBorg is set on a highly polluted asteroid deep in space. In order to survive users have to collect the pollution, build shelter, and create a community. The worlds all contain objects that users can pick up and later exchange for either money or other more useful objects. Basic materials such as wood, steel, and ice, and pollution objects can be recycled in special areas. New objects like chairs and tables are created in exchange. Users can also find objects with special properties like alcohol or knowledge (a map or book) to be used at a later time.

Habitats

Apart from the main world, which is an icey asteroid surface, IceBorg contains three other types of world – Pollution world, Lava world, and Ice World, each of which have smaller building worlds attached to them. Users can colonise the building worlds by first reserving a piece of land, and then once they've gained enough points and experience, are able to create their own 3D home from a number of choices provided. These include cardboard box, igloo, teepee, waste barrel, and crashed spaceship! Just as in real life, your home reflects your life experience, wealth, and identity. Once they

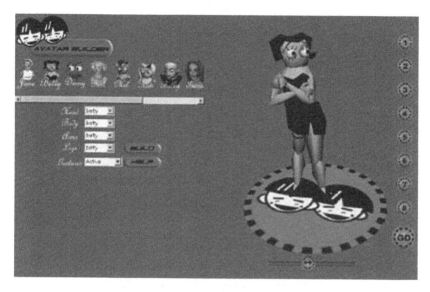

Fig. 5. Example of avatar gesture being tested in Avatar Builder. Left side of page contains user interface for choosing body parts, right side is 3D VRML interface. Example shown is complete *Betty* character

have a home users are able to install the objects they've found or created in the worlds into the house interior, creating their own personal space. They are able to set access rights, giving them a unique 3D cyber space for their own use. With special texture packages available in the worlds, a user can create a totally original space. More experienced users will be able to upload their own textures and even objects, which can later be traded to further increase the diversity within the virtual community.

Plants

Of course, we humans need plants to survive, especially in a cold and inhospitable place like IceBorg! Members can buy (or find if they're lucky) seeds which will grow into virtual plants with care and attention. With skill, an owner will be lucky enough to even grow a fruit on their plant, but bad and unattentive gardeners will find a dying withered plant on their next visit! No two plants will be the same, as their growth is dependent on seed, soil, and food types, plus a little bit of randomness thrown in to make things interesting. As an owner feeds her plant with different types of food the growth will be affected in different ways, so a skilled and experienced gardener will be able to create particular personal varieties with their own combinations. Plants will send reminder emails to their owners if they haven't come to feed them regularly, and each plant will have a lifespan of about two weeks to full growth, to encourage re-planting! Each member will be able to grow a maximum of three plants on their plot of land. Prizes will be awarded for the best plants grown each month.

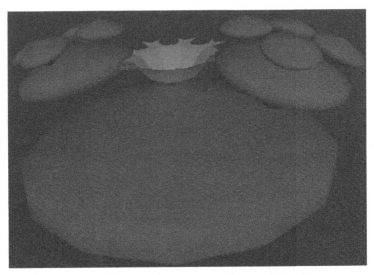

Fig. 6. Example of plant grown from seed (Roman Dolgov)

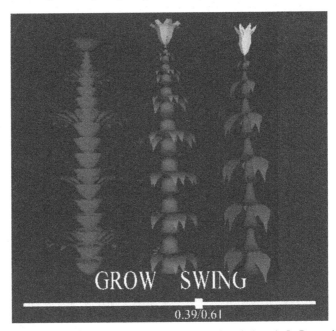

Fig. 7. Example showing plant type mixing. The actual seeds and plants in IceBorg mix three different plant types rather than two illustrated here, and include other hidden features not apparent to the user (Roman Dolgov)

Trade

Rare and useful objects in the world will form the focus of trade and exchange between members. Particularly fruits grown by successful gardeners will be very valuable, giving special rare objects or powers in exchange. Users can barter objects with the easy to use drag and drop interface provided. Prices can be quickly updated. It's also possible to buy and sell at official shops provided by the community – the price might not be the best, but they are always available. Price speculation between the different worlds is also possible with built in fluctuations in the global market rates.

Fig. 8. IceBorg surface - daytime

6 Technical Realisation

IceBorg uses a number of standard technologies, plus proprietory software where needed. All the 3D graphics are rendered using VRML97 with the ParallelGraphics Cortona browser for viewing. The multiuser server is also provided by ParallelGraphics, but as it is purely used for communicating information between clients (users) it has no need of knowledge of VRML. The IceBorg database server uses mySQL and PHP, allowing full customisation of the database functions. The open nature of all these technologies creates a very powerful combination with great flexibility. The avatars are built around a skeleton derived from the Humanoid Animation Standard allowing interchangability of body parts and animations. This allows the use of third party animations for example for the live performances.

For the live performances IceBorg will stream live media data directly into the 3D virtual world, as well as use live actors puppeteering special avatars inside the world. It is also intended to experiment bringing together two different media: traditional broadcast television and the Internet. Data from the real world such as music, video, and motion capture from live dancers/performers can be simultaneously streamed into the virtual world, while virtual cameras can relay images to broadcast TV live, with both locations mixed in time and space! A live real audience can participate in a real location, watching and interacting with a live virtual audience, while the performers and presenters move between different realities.

Rallying Cry

The technical development behind IceBorg is the basis for the virtual community creation platform *Rallying Cry*. Rallying Cry will be an easy to use interface for both community developer, administrator, and users. Using the generic worlds, objects, and functions developed for use with IceBorg, other communities with very differing aesthetics can quickly be created. Within the structure of Rallying Cry are the social engineering tools developed by MEET Factory, enabling new communities to quickly grow due to the high user satisfaction gained by participating in the virtual society.

Fig. 9. IceBorg surface - evening

7 Development Team

People

The idea and concept for IceBorg was developed by Andy Best and Merja Puustinen of MEET Factory. Best and Puustinen have worked together as artists since 1994, and have achieved world wide recognition for their groundbreaking Internet art projects such as DAD@ (1996) and Conversations with Angels (1997-98). Their work has been presented at major media art and graphics festivals such as SIGGRAPH99, the European Media Art Festival, Osnabrück (1999) and ISEA 98 (Revolution), Liverpool. IceBorg brings together themes and ideas from these earlier works, together with "bleeding-edge" virtual world technology to create a totally new type of art, entertainment and community experience to be launched as part of the programme for Helsinki European City of Culture 2000.

Other key members of the development team include Frank Amos from Feuersee Software AG., Stuttgart, Germany developing the database, and VRML expert Roman Dolgov from ParallelGraphics, Moscow, Russia. ParallelGraphics provide the multiuser server used for IceBorg, and also develop the VRML browser Cortona used for viewing the 3D worlds. Josquin Bernard from France and Hu Jia from China provide additional programming and modelling assistance. Bernie Roehl from the University of Waterloo, Canada, is also involved as development consultant.

Finance

Funding is provided by the Finnish Centre for the Development of Audiovisual Culture (AVEK) and the Finnish Centre for the Promotion of Technological Development (TEKES), a section of the Ministry of Trade and Industry. Co-production support is provided by the Banff Centre for the Arts, Alberta, Canada and from Kiasma, the Museum of Contemporary Art, Helsinki, Finland. Technological support is provided by ParallelGraphics Software, Moscow, Russia.

Fig. 10. IceBorg surface - night

8 Conclusion

IceBorg represents a very ambitious and challenging production within the realm of media art and online virtual communities. In this multimedia art work different distribution channels from the truely interactive Internet to TV broadcast are being combined and tested. IceBorg is a serious attempt to create functional dramaturgical models for the forthcoming era of the digital interactive and inhabited entertainment world.

In our opinion it is very important that designers and artists are able to experiment and investigate the possibilities for using these new technologies. Despite Marshall

McLuhan's well known thesis "The content of any medium is the other (old) medium" it is clear that this new medium demands from both the content producer and the end user a radical re-thinking of their approach to narrative and the dramaturgical construction of a story within the work. The new online multiuser space demands a totally new narrative approach, one that cannot be simply transfered from print or broadcast media. New methodologies have to be created and defined, experiments made, while experience has to be gained in inhabited cyberspace! As we move into the new millenium, the new online generation will metamorphose into true cyborgs – or cyburghers – citizens living large parts of their lives immersed in cyberspace communities. The lessons we learn in these early virtual communities will lay the foundations for the future, so it's vital that real social and environmental issues are not abandoned in the search for a cyber utopia, rather we use the virtual world to make the whole Earth a better, cleaner, and more peaceful place for all living creatures to co-exist.

References

1. "Cyberspace: first steps", edited by Michael Benedikt, MIT Press 1991
2. "Cyberspace/Cyberbodies/Cyberpunk", edited by Mike Featherstone & Roger Burrows, Sage Publcations 1995
3. "Data Trash", Arthur Kroker, New World Perspectives 1994
4. "CyberSociety: Computer-mediated communication and community", edited by Steven G. Jones, Sage Publications 1995
5. "Cultures of Internet", edited by Rob Shields, Sage Publications 1996
6. "Neuromancer", William Gibson, Ace Books 1984
7. "Snowcrash", Neal Stephenson, Bantam Books 1992

A 'Virtual Worlds' Theatre of Memory (Scheme for a Contemporary Museum)

Bernardo Uribe Mendoza

Rodolfo Ramirez, Neslson Cruz, Manuel Guillermo Forero, Patricia Cervantes

Instituto de Investigaciones Estéticas, Edificio de Arquitectura Of 405, Facultad de Artes, Universidad Nacional de Colombia,Ciudad Universitaria , Calle 45 Carrera 30, Bogotá, Telefax: 91- 3165473
buribeme@bacata.usc.unal.edu.co

PUI de Comunicaciones, División de Investigaciones, Sede de Bogotá, Edificio Uriel Gutierrez, Of 212, Universidad Nacional de Colombia,Ciudad Universitaria , Calle 45 Carrera 30, Bogotá, Colombia, Tel-Fax 91-3615078
dibdir@bacata.usc.unal.edu.co

Abstract. Architecture experience of order and hierarchies in spatial event plays an important role in virtual environments notion of 'presence'. Architecture monument urbane definition is currently shifting due the new body and mind interfaces in 'virtual worlds'.The artistic example of a museum design extended to 'virtual worlds' adresses this bifurcation of Architecture order or the building of a new one more complex. The paper unfolds the design of a 'wunderkammer' (chamber of treasures) as a new museum design idea for virtual worlds.

1 Introduction

In a broad sense, Architecture experience deals with the constructiveness of spatial events ,forms, material, figures. Human collective memory of ordered events in spatiality is associated to the building of dwelling , cities and territory . Repetitively during the recent years, Architecture critical essays state the blurring of the traditional physically bounded experience of spatial construction due the rapidly changing practice in new body/machine interfaces. The notion of an architectonic order or constructiveness of spatial events expanded into virtual worlds. [1]

The paper unfolds the idea for a project of a ' Theater of Memory' (a museum) extended into ´virtual worlds'.

The 'Theatre of Memory' or 'Theatre of the World' was an historic renaissance period rationally illustrated and cultured approach to the traditional architectonic myth of many peoples in history, of the ´chamber of treasures' or 'wonders' , where

J.-C. Heudin (Ed.): VW 2000, LNAI 1834, pp. 205-213, 2000.
© Springer-Verlag Berlin Heidelberg 2000

power or lineage of rulers , their temple, and for the case of the classical hellenic tradition , the *museion* or the temple of the muses or inspiration was embodied.

The modern idea of Museum buildings devoted to preserving collectively the material expressions of a cultural, historical or sociologically defined 'wealth' , 'power', knowledge or 'wonder' can be traced back to renaissance artists like Claudio Camillo Delmino's ' Theatre of memory' project.[2].

'Virtual Worlds' open a new chapter in contemporary museum experiences of sensorial and intellectual realms with image and text indexing, object simulation and scenography , data visualization, all experiences related to curator shows in museums exhibitions today.

As a demonstration of the new Museum Architecture event 'order', a 'Virtual Worlds' Theatre of Memory project was drafted for extension planned for the Museo Nacional de Colombia, at Bogotá's International Centre.

The paper presents the results of the artistic / architecture design idea and includes a substantial redefinition of the public role of the museums body (the collection) and the building monument due new possible accessibility   and information communication. Random actual access to a complete material body of the collection and extended sensorial and intellectual experience to the networked terminal of the collection are explored in the design of a new museum cellular addible vault building where the exhibits are stored in intelligent environment transparent capsules plugged to virtual environment display and interaction..

2 A Theater of Memory

In urbane memory history human constructed space in architectural monuments have been a source for human body operation/behaviour (edilia) and of social hierarchy representation information (iconology). Imagined and physical territory operation are mixed symbiotically in architectures' material presence, thus permeating every day's experience of human spatiality.

Changing current media society life towards digital and computational artificial/ intelligent worlds of image and space experience thus substantially affect the 'pnemonic' traditional role of architectural monuments: the pnemonic architectonics of human space are projected beyond its' basic physiological extensions construct into new body/machine interfaces, where a crucial separation of 'optic'(imaging) and 'haptic' (topology) experience of spatial order occurs. [3]

A thorough redesign of a museum's *'wunderkammer'* (wonder chamber or a chamber of the treasures of a collection) edilian typology is possible upon multimedia experiences of the new complexities of space, information and memory relation, thus introducing ' museal' functions into new fields of expansion .

A museum's task now focused on scenographic (curator) shows in exhibition wings , shift to a new set of forms of objective memory by the means of interactive Architecture and monument designs in such fields as 'virtual worlds'.

The project for a 'Virtual Worlds' extension for a museums 'wunderkammer' is an artistic Architecture representation based on 'virtual worlds' relative information/ image world indexing and objective space   simulation and modelling in VRML technology

'Virtual worlds' techniques on object/ image relative indexing and scanning/ tracking simulation representation and modelling of object events in VRML are graphic computing fields linked to new body and space constructiveness experiences , and thus with edilia and iconology Architecture order and hierarchies in a cultural and 'media' expanded museums' new body.

In that a museum's Architecture monument is doubly pnemonic ,as a usual edilia and iconolgy or an urbane information source and as a collection's exhibits display a cultural or civilization memory information within a 'public' body, a museums 'wunderkammer' project expanded into 'virtual worlds' unfolds such double realm of architectonic experiences.

The museum's 'wunderkammer' artistic design was drafted unfolding new complexities of architecture:

- Random placed in cellular addible vaults, the collection exhibits are preserved within intelligent environment capsules containing built-in scanning and tracking devices and plugging to interactive communication. The cellular vaults and the encapsulated display of the collection work as a 'material memory terminal'.
- The vaults or cells with the collection exhibits are designed to be actually visited, but   a global architectonic pnemonic experience of the collection is to be achieved only by interacting with it at an opposite end, at the display chamber terminals where information (curatorial texts) is indexed and processed in animated   haptic experience   worlds in constructed multimedia or virtualized environments .
- Both end terminals build the new museum   'wunderkammer' design as the complex of the body/mind extension's of information, memory and experience architecture.

A museums public body is today restricted to   exhibition wings, where curators display only privileged parts of the collections exhibits. Figure 1 shows the 'wunderkammer' design proposed expands the museums public body interiorly, by allowing full display of the collections exhibits and presence visit to them within the cells, and exteriorly by expanding the sensorial and intellectual experience panorama of the exhibit with new   curator open displays   and communication modes in objective experience networked interactive environments.

In the text "Suchmaschinen" published in the web german magazine 'Telepolis' [4] the editorial board pointed the outstanding resemblance of Giullio Camillo Delmino's (1480-1544) Memory Theater , a display of the world of preserved classical

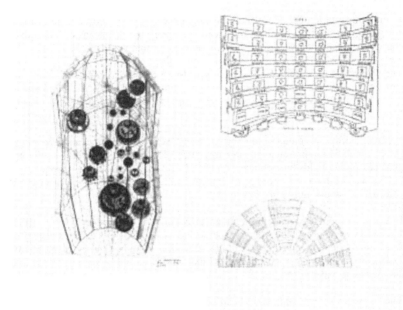

Fig. 1. . 'Wunderkammer' cellular building with exhibit capsules and the Camillo's Memory theatre drawing showing a curvilinear arrangement of the storing cases.

knowledge following an organized array of the Seven Arts and the Seven Elements, with the 'ontological' display of life , leisure, science, technology etc. in web memory machines today.

While in Camillo Delmino's theatre circular aligned memory display of stored texts and image representations build an *optic* space world experience definition, current animated relative human centered interaction image worlds and new physiological sources of information and memory experiences in a 'virtual worlds' design build a non- systemic fashion of information display and acces paths, thus an 'haptic' memory experience of complex Architectures construct of body/mind extensions in Riegl's definition.[5]

'Haptic' pnemonic architectonics related to a 'virtual worlds' theatre of memory work as the sensorial bifurcation of open- ended complex body extensions or a 'wonders' sensorial exploration architecture. In it the 'wunderkammer' design body and mind, edilia and iconolgy always redefine its links and interconnections, this endless pursuing operation being an '*Architecture*'.

Contemporary museums curator 'object aligned' display shows unfold the Camillo's Memory Theatre circular aligned display in muesum wings. The 'Virtual

Worlds' 'wunderkammer' design is an alternative 'haptic' display version to these museum's pnemonic architectonics.

According to Telepolis editorial, Camillo Delmino´s Memory theatre is a metaphor to web current intelligent memory machines. The 'wunderkammer' artistic design is a metaphor to the 'haptic' architectonics of space/ information / memory complex in 'virtual worlds'.

3 The 'Wunderkammer' Architecture.

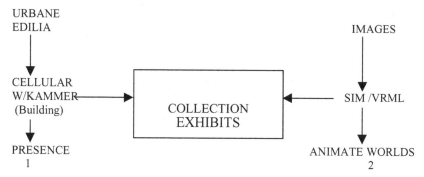

Fig. 2. A Contemorary Musum's Pnemonic 'haptic'Architectures bifurcation diagram.

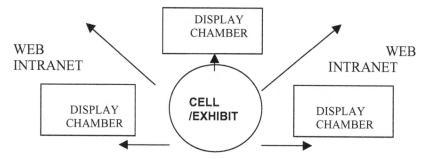

Fig. 3. . A Museum's 'Wunderkammer' installation . Building core and virtual environment .

Figure 2 displays the bifuracation and relations of the new building architecture for the collection deposit and visit with extended ubiquitous exhibition virtual environment . Figure 3 represents an installation diagram for the virtual environment in 'display chambers' located within an intranet area , and internet plugging from the museums core.

The Capsules containing the collection are disposed in the cellules according to mechanical and material properties of the exhibit objects.
- Size
- Weight
- Preservation conditions

Thus, when visited, the cell vault appears to be randomly disposed when compared to normal storage-indexing and display in museum wings. The heterogeneity in form, figure, color (image) inflicting a strong and flattening sensorial experience upon visitors, compared to present linear display scenarios in current exhibition wings.

Tracking and scanning models of objective properties (sim/vrml) would comprehend 2 main categories.
- Bio-physicals. Body mechanics, chemics, Models (Haptic/ body-sensorial)
- Stereoptics, Video ,Studio, Multimedia constructs.(optic/ imaging-representational)

Interactive mechanics link the exhibit´s capsule for smooth communication to exterior display chambers (cave architecture).

3.1 The Animated Gallery-Wing

A basic idea for an animated gallery wing or a museum' s 'display chamber' Architecture was drafted conforming to recent research development on graphic computing science in virtual environment interaction and multimedia production. [6]

- Within a studio-like environment in the cellular vaults , multiple view video camera images of the exhibit are a real image/ real time source for interactive output. .[7]

Studio image source is introduced and merged into a multimedia virtual or virtualized environment formed by : [8]
-Display interactive background arrangements for color, lighting, texture/material ,depth maps.
-Arrays or array-series of related exhibits object's virtual images.

The animated gallery wing work as an environment for interaction with the studio image of an exhibit selection. Interactive environment is to include arbitrary view selection, data visualization, moving indexing of images and text. (Curator moving or visitors relative arrangements)

3.2 Intallation Project (The 'Museo Nacional de Colombia' New Exhibition Wing.)

Fig. 4. . The *Museo Nacional de Colombia* location at the 'Centro Internacional' with proposed building additions and a instalation diagram of the terminals display chambers within intranet networked area. The graphic includes a collage of the new building facilities and the existent facilities.

The Museo Nacional de Colombia is the countries' main information sources on pre-columbian, colonial, republican life history incluiding Etnology, Antropology and Arts collections. Existent facilities are located at the heart of the 60-70s built International Centre district of Bogotá's central area. The existing buildings was refurbished from a turn of the century panopticon into its present museal function.

Besides   addition of the new cellular vaults serial construction, where the collections are preserved, the installation project includes:
* 3 'Display chambers' (interactive virtual environment ´terminal ') installed at 3 surrounding parks: Parque de la Independencia, Parque Bavaria and Parque Nacional.
* Web network information outside the 'Centro Internacional' district area (intranet networked area).

- A further developement step would include more intranet communication from other buildings complexes and public plazas with the museum core. (Studio based image output)

The collection's expanded public display cultural and social impact would be a main source of study.

3.3 The 'Wunderkammer' Architecture

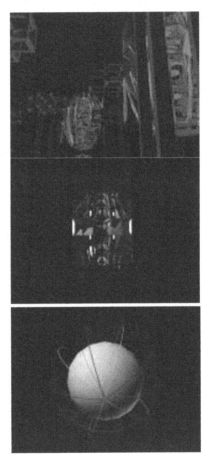

Fig. 5. A contemporary museum building architecture's drawing renderings. In the upper-drawing render represents the serial construction of the new museums 'wing. The addible cell vaults are suspended from a steel frame and they are reached by vertical elevators and folding decks. A cell vault is displayed in the middle- drawing render. The lower- drawing render represents an exhibit's preserving capsule environment.

In the new ´museum's chambers building the addible cellular isolation vaults are suspended from a steel frame and left freely in the air, access is possible by vertical and horizontal elevator and decks running along the steel frame. The capsules with the exhibits are also freely hanged inside the vaults void interior space as showed in the figure 1 drawing. A studio-like lighting , video and interactive environment infrastructure is to be disposed flexibly around the exhibits in the cell vault void space. Small observation and working pads and decks unfold from the inner structure and peripheral walls .

4 Conclusion

The work presented in the paper, was focused mainly on the architectonic substance of a 'Theater of memory' extended to 'virtual Worlds', a contemporary redefinition of a museum building.

Following development of the work will be centered in the 'Display Chamber' s architecture drafting, which depends on graphic computing and hardware implementation and experiments.
* Studio viewing of exhibit object experiment.
* Studio input and multimedia interactive environment.
* Image and text information ontological processing.

A collaborative work will be sought with a Graphic Computing Laboratory institution and with the Museo Nacional de Colombia for the experiment development proposed at this stage of the work.

References

1. Mitchell, W.City of Bits, The MIT Press, Cambridge-London, 1996
2. Yates, Francis A.The Art of Memory, The University of Chicago Press, Chicago, 1966.
3. Rajchman, J, Constructions, The MIT Press, Cambridge-London, 1998.
4. Editorial Board, Telepolis, aktuelles Magazin, http://www. Telepolis.de
5. Yates, Francis A., Theatre of the World, The University of Chicago Press, Chicago 1969.
6. Heudin, Jean Claude, ed, Virtual Worlds 98, Proceedings of the International Conference, Springer Verlag, Lecture Notes on Computer Science, Berlin-Heidelberg-New York, 1998
7. Park, J and Inoue, I, "Real Image Based Virtual Studio", Virtual Worlds 98, Proceedings of the International Conference, Springer Verlag, Lecture Notes in Computer Science, Berlin-Heidelberg- New York, 1998 , 117-122.
8. Kimoto, H.,"Human Centered Virtual Interactiv World for Image Retrieval", In Virtual Worlds 98, ibidem, 311-322.

The World of Framsticks:
Simulation, Evolution, Interaction

Maciej Komosinski

Institute of Computing Science,
Poznan University of Technology
Piotrowo 3A, 60-965 Poznan, Poland

Maciej.Komosinski@cs.put.poznan.pl

http://www.frams.poznan.pl/

Abstract. A three-dimensional virtual world simulation is described, where evolution takes place and it is possible to investigate behaviors of creatures in real-time. Bodies of these creatures are made of sticks, and their brains are built from artificial neurons. There are no constraints on topology and complexity of neural networks, as well as on the size of morphology. The model is inspired by biology, so energetic issues such as energy gains and losses are also considered. The evolutionary process can be guided by some pre-defined criteria, however, it is possible to mimic spontaneous evolution when the fitness is defined as the life span of the organisms. Interactions in the virtual world are discussed (including the possibility of worldwide-distributed simulation), and the results of so-far experiments are presented.

1 Introduction

Systems qualifying as virtual worlds have been built for a long time, but it is only recently that such systems achieved a superior level of realism, opening up the way for new applications. This is mainly due to the rapid development of computing machines, which now allow for fast simulation of complex systems. Such systems could earlier be investigated only theoretically. Another feature of present virtual world simulations is the existence of possible areas of their application, which range from medicine and economy to entertainment.

Creating artificial worlds usually involves simulation of an environment and its habitants, interacting with each other and with the world they live in. Whereas such simulations of complex worlds are popular, it is not so easy to find the property of nature-like evolution included in the model [8, 14, 18]. Yet the evolution is an important source of complexity (emergence), because the amount of complexity explicitly designed in a system via its rules is limited. In particular, evolution is a force that can produce complexity going beyond the reach of the initial design. There are many studies that focus on evolution of living forms within the field of Artificial Life [12]. However, these simulations are usually kept simple to focus on underlying mechanisms and allow for their efficient analysis and study [4, 5, 6].

J.-C. Heudin (Ed.): VW 2000, LNAI 1834, pp. 214-224, 2000.
© Springer-Verlag Berlin Heidelberg 2000

The system described here tries to comprise the typical features of virtual world, together with its attractiveness for the human user, and to allow for evolution of the creatures which are simulated within the world. Although the simulation captures currently only a subset of properties of the natural world, its assumptions are inspired by natural laws [2, 17]. Moreover, the properties included are rich enough to allow a host of interactions to develop. Such a setup guarantees that the whole system is attractive for its observer/participant, and the evolutionary adaptation property together with the realistic three-dimensional simulation seem to be its most important features.

While there have been experiments with the guided evolutionary processes in sophisticated systems [20], there was no attempt at *spontaneous* evolution using environments and creatures as complex as Framsticks. We hope that the presented model is suitable to give rise to sophisticated, real-like dependencies and behaviors. If they appear as the result of the spontaneous evolution, they will most probably astonish the beholder of Framsticks' virtual world, thus displaying the emergence property [19].

In Framsticks, the three-dimensional world and creatures (their "bodies" and "brains") are simulated. The creatures are capable of interacting with themselves (locating, pushing, hurting, killing, eating, etc.) and the environment (walking, swimming, ingesting, etc.). Framsticks are made of "sticks", which allows for fast simulation, thus letting the evolution occur in a reasonable time. The virtual world itself can be composed of any combination of flat land, hills, and water. Despite simple simulation, this setup allows for realistic behaviors.

Evolutionary process may be directed by some pre-defined criteria. One of them is life span, which can be used to mimic spontaneous evolution: the life span of a creature depends directly on energetic issues, and longer life span results in greater reproduction abilities. Various genetic representations are proposed, each of which is based on different qualitative ways of creature development.

The paper is organized as follows: section 2 describes Framsticks system, its architecture, and models of simulation and evolution. Section 3 is devoted to the evolutionary properties of the system, describing various genotype representations, genetic operators, etc. Section 4 presents abilities of interaction within and with Framsticks simulator, and sections 5 and 6 discuss results of experiments, summarize the work and present future goals of the project.

2 Simulation

2.1 System Architecture

In general, our main goal is to design the model so that it allows for spontaneous (with natural selection), open-ended evolution. The creatures live in a three-dimensional world, and are controlled by neural networks. Currently, the system is more appropriate for guided evolutionary processes: the rules of selection and reproduction are pre-defined in the system architecture. That differs Framsticks from some other artificial life simulators (like Tierra [16] and Avida [1]), however, attempts have been made to avoid explicit reproduction rules [10].

In Framsticks system, the basic evolutionary framework is defined in a similar way, as in evolutionary models designed for optimization, such as genetic algorithms [7, 15] and most of artificial life simulations [3, 20, 21]. Therefore, evolution means optimization of creatures according to some predefined criteria. However, it is possible to mimic spontaneous evolution with the 'directed' model of evolution, when the fitness criterion is directly connected with the survival and reproduction abilities.

The life span criterion is suitable for such a purpose. Using life span as fitness value affects selection phase: the longer a creature lives, the better it reproduces. One could simulate breeding of offspring or laying eggs, the amount of which would be proportional to the life span of the parent individuals, and would depend on their energy. However, there is no need to simulate those specific mechanisms as long as life span directly affects the reproductive success. Such an imitation of spontaneous evolution is reasonable.

Simulating creatures in the virtual world is needed to estimate their fitness. In our model, it is possible to adjust the number n of individuals which are simulated at the same time. Thus, the virtual world does not contain the whole set of individuals, but a user-defined part: the artificial world is a reduced model of the whole ecosystem. The advantage of such an architecture is that a few individuals can be simulated much faster than a few thousand, so one can see the simulation in real-time, study the behavior of creatures, and affect them. Also, there is no need to save the detailed state of all the habitants of the world when the simulation is to be finished (that would mean a large amount of data). Only the genotypes and their multi-criteria performances are saved.

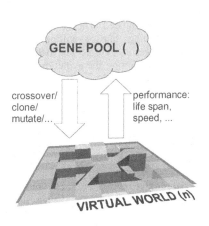

Fig. 1. Architecture of the system.

In order to construct such an architecture (see fig. 1), two parameters are needed: the maximum total number of genotypes, N, and the maximum number of individuals simultaneously simulated, n. Individuals are selected to be simulated and evaluated when there is a free place in the virtual world (when the number of simulated creatures is less than n). When an individual dies, the performance of its genotype is updated.

Usually, n is significantly smaller than N. When the interaction between simulated creatures is not important, n may be set to 1 (only one organism simulated at a time). Larger values of n mean that a larger part of the whole set of individuals is simulated, and more interactions between creatures may happen. Thus, when setting the value for n, the size of the virtual world and the goal of evolution should also be considered.

These rules can also be employed when the simulation is distributed. In such a case, it is assumed that the virtual world is not divided into areas or individuals, which would be then simulated in parallel. What is divided is the main gene pool, which is sent in parts to computing sites for evolution, and after some time these sites send their gene pools back to the main process.

2.2 Physical Simulation

Framsticks simulates a three-dimensional world and creatures (finite element method is used for step-by-step simulation). We decided to use such a sophisticated environment for evolution hoping that a range of complex, various stimuli affecting organisms will be the origin of dynamic development and interesting behaviors will emerge. The environment is used to evaluate individuals (genotypes), and the first behaviors tested were the mechanisms of locomotion and orientation. We considered all the kinds of interaction between physical objects: static and dynamic friction, damping, action and reaction forces, energy losses after deformations, gravitation, and uplift pressure – buoyancy (in water environment). The most important forces are shown on figure 2.

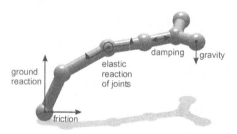

Fig. 2. Forces involved in the simulation.

One should note that there is always a tradeoff between simulation accuracy and simulation time. We need fast simulation to perform evolution, on the other hand, the system should be as realistic as possible to produce realistic behaviors.

Currently, in order to make the simulation faster and due to the computational complexity, some aspects were discarded: collisions between parts of an organism itself and the movement of a water medium were both ignored. Including these in the simulation would make it more realistic, but would not introduce any qualitatively new (important from the viewpoint of the simulated creatures) phenomena. From the viewpoint of evolution and the investigator of the evolved behaviors, meaningful interactions are more important than very realistic, but too slow simulation [13].

The current model implies some constraints concerning structure of organisms. The basic element is a stick made of two flexibly joined particles (finite element method is used for simulation). Sticks have specific properties: biological (muscle strength, stamina, energetic: assimilation, ingestion, and initial energy level), physical (length, weight, friction), and concerning stick joints (rotation, twist, curvedness).

Neurons (connected in any way) and receptors can also be placed on sticks. Rather than evolving neural networks exclusively [3], morphology – "body" is evolved together with "brain" in Framsticks.

Muscles are placed on stick joints. There are two kinds of muscles: bending and rotating. When a muscle is sent a zero signal, it becomes neutral (as if it was absent). Positive and negative changes make the sticks move in either direction – it is analogous to natural systems of muscles, with flexors and extensors. The strength of a muscle determines its effective ability of movement and speed (acceleration). However, stronger muscle consumes more energy during its work. Additionally, an increase in the "strength" property of a muscle results in a decrease of the other properties of a stick.

Framsticks have currently three kinds of *receptors* (*senses*): those for orientation in space (equilibrium sense, gyroscope), detection of energy/food (non-directional smell) and detection of physical contact (directional touch). Receptors and effectors are shown on figure 3. Details are illustrated at [11].

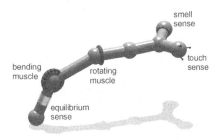

Fig. 3. Senses and effectors of Framsticks.

2.3 Neural Network

In order to enrich capabilities of creatures' brains, the typical artificial neurons were equipped with three additional parameters which can alter the behavior of each neuron independently. As Nature was our inspiration, we did not introduce sophisticated and unnatural processing units (as in [20]); it is possible to construct complex modules (integrating, differentiating, summing, subtracting, and generators with different shapes) from simple neurons.

The additional neuron parameters (*force*, *inertia* and *sigmoid*) are under control of evolution. They affect the way neurons work: *Force* and *inertia* influence changes of the inner neuron state (speed and tendency of changes, respectively). *Sigmoid* coefficient modifies the output function. Details and sample neuronal runs can be found at [11].

The neural network can have any topology and complexity. Neurons can be connected with each other in any way (some may be unconnected). Inputs can be connected to outputs of another neurons, constant values, or senses, while outputs can be connected to inputs of another neurons or effectors (muscles).

3   Evolution

3.1   Genotype Representations

In order to test the properties and abilities of evolutionary processes, various genotype encodings have been designed. All of them are expressed with symbols, so they can be relatively easily investigated, modified and understood. All of them combine "body" and "brain" in the same genotype, so that both morphology (body made of sticks) and control (brain made of neurons) evolve at the same time.

The common basic layer for describing a phenotype is the *basic direct encoding*. It is least restrictive and allows for building of any creatures which can be simulated within the virtual world. Such a genotype simply lists all the parts of an organism.

The *recurrent direct encoding* was designed to allow human users to build their own creatures in a possibly simple way, nevertheless some important properties of the encoding were also maintained to make the evolution efficient. Generally, users can write recurrent genotype expressions, which are interpreted as phenotypes. Due to the recurrent nature of the language, the morphology has a tree-like structure. Special signs can be used to modify (increase or decrease) properties of parts of the body (see 2.2). "Brain" is made of neurons with their connections described *relatively*. Two genetic operators are used: crossover and mutation. It often happens that genotypes are invalid after crossover and mutation because of small errors. That is why a simple repair procedure is used. This procedure can fix little mistakes (like references to non-existing neurons) and validate an invalid genotype.

In nature, the genetic code of complex organisms does not encode their body layout directly, but rather their process of development. That is why a *developmental encoding* was designed. An interesting merit of developmental encoding is that it can incorporate symmetry and modularity, features commonly found in natural systems. The developmental encoding is similar to the recurrent direct one, but codes are interpreted as commands by cells (sticks, neurons, etc.). Cells can change their parameters, and divide.

Another encodings (like *direct similarity development* and *implicit embryogeny development*) are also proposed in order to test various representations of creatures (morphologies and brains), and the influence of the representations on the evolutionary process. Trying various approaches to describe creatures is also important from the viewpoint of a human user: some representations may be better than others to use in a graphical, user-friendly editor of phenotypes. It should be as easy as possible to build a creature for non-experts, on the other hand, they should be able to control details of such design if needed. It is relatively easy to add support for more encodings suggested by developers.

3.2   Selection and Speciation

When a new individual has to be created, the simulator selects an existing genotype using the standard roulette wheel rule [7], proportionally to its fitness. The genetic operators are then applied.

In nature, groups of similar individuals share the same ecological niche and constitute one species. In Framsticks, similarity to other coexisting species may lower the given species' fitness [7]. This introduces a pressure for populations of species to diversify. The second mechanism which allows speciation is the specific crossover operation: if possible, corresponding parts of genotypes of similar species are exchanged.

The described mechanism of aiding speciation by lowering fitness of similar genotypes is somehow artificial. However, such a phenomenon happens spontaneously in Framsticks when a large number of individuals are simulated at the same time in the virtual world. Then, depending on the behavior, if many individuals exhibit the same method of achieving energy, their situation will become more difficult, and competition within species will arise.

3.3 Creatures' Evaluation

During the life span of simulated organisms some features are measured, like distance (center of gravity movements), age, average velocity (equal to distance/age) etc. In practice, movements are not measured from the moment of birth, but from the moment when a creature becomes stable. This is because some oscillations take place immediately after creation, causing shifts of the center of gravity. Measuring those movements would be unfair, as they are not caused by the creature itself, and do not depend on a creature's ability to move on its own.

After a creature dies, all the values of various performance criteria are weighted to produce the final fitness value for the given genotype.

4 Interaction

Interaction happens on many levels of the Framsticks system architecture. There is interaction between creatures and their world, where senses are the sources of information for organisms, and muscles are their way to influence their own state and their environment.

Potentially, as there is no limitation concerning the complexity of neural network, creatures can become intelligent, and it is unknown to what degree. Framsticks can learn about their orientation, and sense their world (and, potentially, remember it). From the set of three senses, the smell receptor is the most important. It allows to find food, but also to tell food from other creatures. With the proper use of many smell sensors, creatures can virtually discriminate between various morphologies of other habitants, sense their movement, their number, etc. The great help of complex brain allows for the unlimited use and exploitation of smell, even for diversification of species, group and social behaviors, and mutual preferences. If the simulator is very complex, it may resemble The Matrix [22] from the viewpoint of the creatures, and they can learn its imperfections in order to utilize them (as it was already observed, but it was evolution what explored simulator faults).

In Framsticks, there is a lot of the interaction with the human role. It is the human who can affect living creatures, revive them (put into artificial world), kill (remove from the world), move in the world with the "robotic arm", feed them (put energy into the world), cause crashes etc. As Framsticks interface may show simulation in real-time, responses to user actions are instantaneous and highly visual. This facilitates the exploration of many aspects of evolutionary process, like fitness criteria, creation of offspring (mutation, crossover, cloning, etc.), population mixing, partial evolution, etc. Through the process of interactive experimentation, users can develop an understanding of some of the fundamentals of evolutionary dynamics. Users can also affect the gene pool by designing their own creatures, editing genotypes, and modifying and improving them with an instant preview of phenotypes.

It is possible to define the virtual world: its size, hills, slopes, water level, and boundaries (like walls, teleport, or no boundaries). Humans can adjust the architecture for the evolutionary process (maximum numbers for genotypes and simulated individuals), turn on or off destructive collisions (whether collisions break creatures), adjust the rate of auto-feeding, adjust energy usage rates for brain and body work, etc.

As the evolutionary process is the source of development in the Framsticks world, the most powerful ability is to understand and adjust the parameters of evolution, like weights for fitness criteria, origin of offspring (mutation, crossover, cloning, etc.), mutation rates, speciation, the ability to exclude some creatures' elements from evolution, etc.

Finally, the virtual world itself affects a human user, who is influenced by what they can see, the way creatures behave: move, seek energy, swim, walk, fight, etc. This kind of interaction is the subtlest one, as it does not concern the apparent action, but it certainly happens. When the simulation is distributed over Internet [11], the collective, worldwide experiments will connect their participants, and enable sharing of ideas, knowledge and experience of the system, analysis of results, and discussions. Distributing evolution of realistic 3D creatures in large scale may change the way people think about evolution, making it more (or less) unusual and ambiguous. Eventually, experiments with open-ended setups may bring unexpected results.

5 Results

The majority of our experiments concerned directed evolution, with fitness defined as speed (on the ground or in water). Many walking and swimming species evolved during these runs [11], and we were able to see the evolution of ideas of "how to move" [9]. In one evolutionary run, a limb was doubled while crossing over, and after some further evolution the organism was able to move with two limbs – one for pushing back and one for pulling [11]. We also noticed a case when a limb is simultaneously bent and rotated, which was a more effective method of pushing against the ground. In one case a neuron used its saturation to produce delayed signals, which is a kind of a simple "short-term memory". More sophisticated creatures which were evolved could not be easily examined because of their high complexity.

Generally, as long as there is no really good way of locomotion in a population, there is a tendency to try a lot of ideas. The creatures with stronger muscles, better control and many limbs (to achieve stability) survive. Evolution tends to promote strength, and make the pushing/pulling limbs longer and rougher. The really great innovations seem to be discovered once and then sustained throughout the run, until they are replaced by better ideas. We noticed that it was hard to evolve a low-frequency signal generator, perhaps because it cannot be created by little, step-by-step improvements. Movement in water was easier to achieve than on land, see figure 4 for example of swimming movement (evolutionary redundancy and random character can be observed).

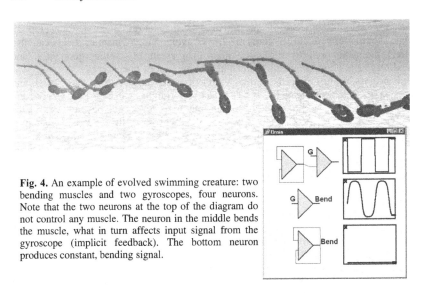

Fig. 4. An example of evolved swimming creature: two bending muscles and two gyroscopes, four neurons. Note that the two neurons at the top of the diagram do not control any muscle. The neuron in the middle bends the muscle, what in turn affects input signal from the gyroscope (implicit feedback). The bottom neuron produces constant, bending signal.

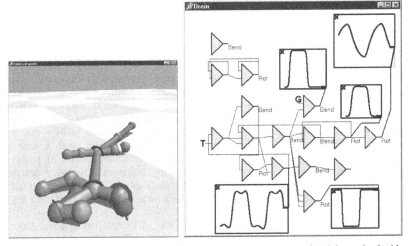

Fig. 5. Pre-designed creature ("lizard"). Neural network connections and weighs evolved with fitness defined as speed. One touch and one equilibrium receptors. Walks in a realistic way.

The experiments concerning evolutionary improvement of human pre-designed structures have also been conducted. An example is the evolution of control (neural network) for a pre-designed morphology in order to obtain a creature that lives long. In order to live long, it is required to find energy sources and ingest them. The user can design a genotype, and then turn off crossover and structure mutations, allowing only mutations of neural network (connections, topology and weights). Thus a food-seeking creatures are evolved on the basis of pre-designed morphology. See figure 5 for an example of pre-designed body and brain, with further directed evolution of movement.

6   Discussion and Future Work

During our evolutionary experiments, we had to modify simulation rules and fix bugs several times. Evolution turned out to be a very good method of searching the space of solutions (organisms), and was capable of finding good individuals, regardless of their sensibility and validity. Faults in the simulator were sooner or later discovered by evolution and exploited to the highest possible extent in simulated organisms.

There are a few limitations of the current model. The genotypic representations need to be investigated and tuned to allow efficient evolution of creatures, not restricting various, complex body and brain plans. Our future work will thus concern various genotype representations (see 3.1), implementation of specific genetic operators, experiments and their study. We hope that it will make the search of the organism space even more effective. The preliminary results show that it will lead to creation of more diverse constructions and their easier modification. A suitable representation for user-friendly design of creatures will also be investigated.

Our future work will also concern defining a similarity function on the phenotype space, improvements of simulation rules and their parameters, and spontaneous, open-ended simulations. More receptors and more complex criteria for directed evolutions may be introduced. If the increase in computing power permits, we will use more realistic (but slower) physical simulator, so that the evolved creatures will behave more like if they would be built in the real world. Generally, realism and open-endedness are properties that require much more computation and effort than simple and/or directed evolutionary models, but we hope to employ Internet worldwide distribution to fully exploit capabilities of the system.

The results we have achieved are promising, and it is really interesting to look forward to the behaviors and phenomena that will emerge with the new genotype encodings, and after collective, distributed experiments are performed.

Acknowledgement

This work has been supported by the research grant from KBN, Polish State Committee for Scientific Research.

References

1. Adami, C., Brown, C. T., Evolutionary learning in the 2D artificial life system "Avida". In: Rodney A. Brooks and Pattie Maes (eds.), *Artificial Life IV*. MIT Press/Bradford Books, 1994.
2. Balkenius, Ch., *Natural Intelligence in Artificial Creatures*, Ph. D. Thesis, Lund University Cognitive Studies, 1995.

3. Cruse, H., Kindermann, T., Schumm, M., Dean, J., Schmitz, J., Walknet – a biologically inspired network to control six-legged walking. In: *Neural Networks* **11** (1998) 1435-1447, Elsevier Science Ltd.
4. Dawkins, R., *Climbing mount improbable*, W.W. Norton & Company, 1997.
5. Ficici, S. G., Pollack, J. B., Coevolving communicative behavior in a linear pursuer-evader game. In: *Proc. Fifth International Conference of the Society for Adaptive Behavior*, Pfeifer, Blumberg, Kobayashi (eds.), Cambridge: MIT Press, 1998.
6. Ficici, S. G., Pollack, J. B., Challenges in coevolutionary learning: arms-race dynamics, open-endedness, and mediocre stable states. In: *Proc. Sixth International Conference on Artificial Life*, Adami, Belew, Kitano, Talor (eds.), Cambridge: MIT Press, 1998.
7. Goldberg, D. E.: *Genetic Algorithms in Search, Optimization, and Machine Learning*, Addison-Wesley Publishing Co., 1989.
8. Heudin, J.-C., *Virtual Worlds – Synthetic Universes, Digital Life, and Complexity*. Perseus Books, Reading (MA), 1998.
9. Komosinski, M., Ulatowski, Sz., Framsticks: towards a simulation of a nature-like world, creatures and evolution. In: *Proceedings of 5th European Conference on Artificial Life (ECAL99)*, September 13-17, 1999, Lausanne, Switzerland, Springer-Verlag, 261-265.
10. Komosinski, M., Rotaru-Varga, A., From Directed to Open-Ended Evolution in a Complex Simulation Model. In: *Proceedings of 7th International Conference on Artificial Life*, Portland, USA, August 2000, MIT Press.
11. Komosinski, M., Ulatowski, Sz., Framsticks Internet site, http://www.frams.poznan.pl/
12. Langton, Ch., *Journal of Artificial Life*, Volume 1, Number 1/2, MIT Press, Fall 1993/Winter 1994.
13. Maes, P., Darrel, T., Blumberg, B., Pentland, A., The ALIVE system: full-body interaction with autonomous agents. In: *Proc. of the Computer Animation '95 Conference*, Geneva, Switzerland, IEEE-Press, 1995.
14. Maes, P., Artificial Life meets Entertainment: Interacting with Lifelike Autonomous Agents. In: *Special Issue on New Horizons of Commercial and Industrial AI* **38**, 11 (1995) 108-114, Communications of the ACM, ACM Press.
15. Michalewicz, Z.: *Genetic Algorithms + Data Structures = Evolution Programs*, Springer-Verlag, 1996.
16. Ray, T. S., An approach to the synthesis of life, *Artificial Life II*, Langton C. G. et al. (eds.), Addison-Wesley, 1992, 371-401.
17. Ray, T. S., An evolutionary approach to synthetic biology: Zen and the art of creating life. In: *Artificial Life 1*, 1994, 195-226.
18. Reynolds, C., Flocks, herds and schools: a distributed behavioral model. In: *Computer Graphics: Proceedings of SIGGRAPH '87*, 21 (4), ACM Press, 1987.
19. Ronald, E. M. A., Sipper, M., Capcarrère, M. S., Testing for Emergence in Artificial Life. In: *Proceedings of 5th European Conference on Artificial Life (ECAL99)*, September 13-17, 1999, Lausanne, Switzerland, Springer-Verlag, 13-20.
20. Sims, K., Evolving 3D Morphology and Behaviour by Competition. In: R. Brooks, P. Maes (eds.), *Artificial Life IV Proceedings*, MIT Press, 1994, 28-39.
21. Terzopoulos, D. et al., Artificial fishes with autonomous locomotion, perception, behavior and learning, in a physical world. In: *Proc. of the Artificial Life IV Workshop*, Pattie Maes and Rod Brooks (eds.), MIT Press, 1994.
22. Wachowski, A., Wachowski, L., *The Matrix*, USA, 1999, Warner Bros, 135 min.

A 3-D Biomechanical Model of the Salamander

Auke Jan Ijspeert

Brain Simulation Laboratory & Computational Learning and Motor Control
Laboratory, Hedco Neuroscience Building, University of Southern California,
Los Angeles CA90089, USA
ijspeert@rana.usc.edu,
http://rana.usc.edu:8376/~ijspeert/

Abstract. This article describes a 3D biomechanical simulation of a
salamander to be used in experiments in computational neuroethology.
The physically-based simulation represents the salamander as an articulated body, actuated by muscles simulated as springs and dampers,
in interaction with a simple environment. The aim of the simulation is
to investigate the neural circuits underlying the aquatic and terrestrial
locomotion of the real salamander, as well as to serve as test bed for
investigating vertebrate sensorimotor coordination *in silico*.

1 Computational Neuroethology

This article describes the design of a 3D biomechanical model for experiments
in *computational neuroethology* [1, 2], a field which studies how behaviors of an
autonomous agent (a simulated animal or a robot) arise from neural circuits. A
central aspect of computational neuroethology is that it integrates the simulated
central nervous system into a body and an environment, and that it investigates
behavior as the result of a *sensing-acting loop* within an environment.

Several experiments in computational neuroethology inspired by simpler animals have recently been carried out. Insect locomotion [1, 3, 4], cricket phonotaxis [5], and visual systems of fly [6, 7] have, for instance, been investigated
using simulation and/or robots. Vertebrates have also inspired computational
models such as Rana computatrix [8, 9, 10], lamprey swimming [11], Artificial
Fishes [12], and models of classical conditioning [13].

The interesting features of such computational models are that: 1) they allow hypotheses on central nervous systems to be tested *in silico* within a complete sensing-acting loop, leading to a better understanding of the dynamics and
functioning of nervous systems embedded into a body in interaction with the
environment, 2) they can potentially give new ideas for neurobiological experiments and measurements, and 3) they provide inspiration for control algorithms
which could be useful to other domains such as robotics. In addition, these
neuroethological experiments in silico possess all the positive aspects of a computational approach: experiments are reproducible, all parameters of the model
are controlled, neural activities can be accurately measured at all levels and simultaneously in all places, and the effect on behavior of altering parameters can

J.-C. Heudin (Ed.): VW 2000, LNAI 1834, pp. 225–234, 2000.
© Springer-Verlag Berlin Heidelberg 2000

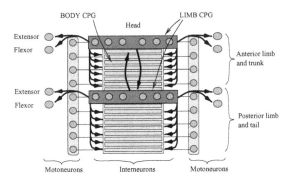

Fig. 1. Structure of the hypothesized salamander locomotor central pattern generator (see [14, 15, 16]). The circuit is based on a lamprey-like body CPG, extended by a limb CPG which unilaterally projects to the body CPG.

readily be investigated (e.g. lesion studies on the real animal can be reproduced). Computational neuroethology has therefore the potential to bring a significant contribution to neurobiology and neuroethology.

Following these experiments, the aim of our work is to develop a comprehensive computational model of a salamander, with a special emphasis on the physical realism of its body. We are, in particular, interested in the locomotor circuitry underlying the typical locomotion gaits of the salamander. This article describes a 3D biomechanical simulation of the salamander in which potential neural controllers for locomotion will be embedded. This work follows initial experiments in which biologically plausible neural circuits were developed using evolutionary algorithms for controlling the locomotion of a 2D salamander [14, 15, 16]. Although a brief summary of that work is given, this paper focuses on the design of the new 3D biomechanical simulation and presents results of locomotion control using algorithmic (rather than neural) controllers.

2   Salamander Locomotion

The salamander, an amphibian, is capable of both aquatic and terrestrial locomotion. It swims using an anguiliform swimming gait in which a traveling undulation of the body is propagated from head to tail. On ground, it switches to a trotting gait in which the body makes an S-shaped standing wave coordinated with the movements of the limbs. EMG recordings have shown that two different motor programs correspond to these different gaits, with a traveling wave of neural activity for swimming and a standing wave for trotting [17, 18, 19, 20]. The locomotor circuitry underlying these gaits has, however, not yet been decoded.

In [14, 15, 16], we developed, using evolutionary algorithms, a potential neural controller for salamander locomotion which was based on a lamprey-like swimming central pattern generator (similarly to what has been hypothesized by neurobiologists [21, 20], Figure 1). That work used the same staged-evolution approach used to evolve swimming controllers for a lamprey model [22, 23]. When connected to a 2D biomechanical simulation of the salamander, the locomotor circuit simulated as a leaky-integrator neural network was capable of exhibiting the typical swimming and trotting gaits observed in the real animal. It produced, in particular, a motoneuronal activity very similar to the EMG recordings reported in [17, 20]. Interestingly, by simply varying the level of tonic input applied to different parts of the locomotor circuitry, the speed and the direction of motion, as well as the type of gait (swimming or trotting), could be modulated.

3   Three-Dimensional Biomechanical Simulation

The new simulated salamander is composed of 18 rigid links, 10 for the body (the trunk and the tail) and 2 for each limb (Figure 2). The links of the trunk and tail are connected by one degree-of-freedom (DOF) hinge-joints, limbs are attached to the pelvis by two DOFs double-hinge joints, and knee-joints have one DOF. Each DOF is actuated by a pair of opposed muscles simulated as springs and dampers (see below). The aim is not to reproduce accurately one specific species of salamander and all its biomechanical properties, but to make an "average" model of salamander which satisfies general characteristics of salamanders such as the range of speeds at which they can locomote. The limb geometry is based on [19].

The acceleration $\ddot{\boldsymbol{X}}_i$ and angular acceleration $\ddot{\boldsymbol{\theta}}_i$ of each link i depends on $\boldsymbol{E}_i$, the forces exerted by the environment, on $\boldsymbol{T}_i^j$, the torques due to the paired muscles of joint(s) j, and on $\boldsymbol{C}_i^j$, the inner forces due to the constraints of joint(s) j:

$$m_i \ddot{\boldsymbol{X}}_i = \boldsymbol{E}_i + \sum_j \boldsymbol{C}_i^j \tag{1}$$

$$[\mathbf{I}]_i \ddot{\boldsymbol{\theta}}_i = \sum_j \boldsymbol{T}_i^j + \sum_j \boldsymbol{C}_i^j \times \boldsymbol{r}_i^j \tag{2}$$

where m_i and $[\mathbf{I}]_i$ are the mass and the moment of inertia of link i. $\boldsymbol{r}_i^j$ is the position vector of joint j compared to the center of mass of link i. The number of joints attached to one link vary from link to link (see Figure 2). Table 1 gives the masses and moments of inertia of the different links.

These dynamics equations are solved using MathEngine's Fastdynamics which computes the internal forces keeping the links connected, as well as the forces due to contacts, while the external forces such as the muscles torques and the forces due to the water are given by the user.

Muscle torques A muscle is simulated as a combination of spring and damper. The torques exterted on each joint is determined by a pair of opposed flexor

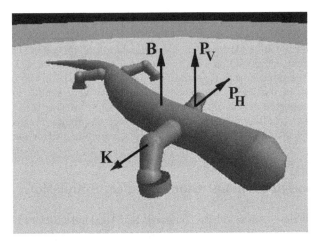

Fig. 2. Biomechanical simulation. The body is composed of 18 rigid links. Body (trunk and tail) links are connected by one-DOF hinge-joints, with vector **B** as axis of rotation. Limbs are attached to the body by two-DOF joints with one vertical axis of rotation **P_V** and one horizontal **P_H**. Finally, knee joints have one DOF and they rotate around axis **K**.

and extensor muscles. These muscles can be contracted by input signals from motoneurons, which increase their spring constant, and therefore reduce their resting length. The torque acting at a particular joint is therefore determined by the motoneuron activities (M_f and M_e) of the opposed flexor and extensor muscles:

$$T = \alpha(M_f - M_e) + \beta(M_f + M_e + \gamma)\Delta\varphi + \delta\Delta\dot{\varphi} \qquad (3)$$

where $\Delta\varphi$ is the difference between the actual angle of the joint and the default angle. The different coefficients α, β, γ, and δ determine, respectively, the gain, the stiffness gain, the tonic stiffness, and the damping coefficient of the muscles. These values vary slightly depending on the type of joints (Table 2).

Forces due to the environment The forces linked with terrestrial locomotion are contact and friction forces. These forces are handled by the Fastdynamics software and are applied to links of the tail and the trunk, as well as to the feet, as soon as these links enter in contact with the (flat) ground. Friction coefficients of 0.8 and 0.1 are used, respectively, for the feet contacts and the body (tail and trunk) contacts. Note that during trotting, the body of the salamander is not supported by the limbs but slides on the ground.

In water, similarly to [11], it is assumed that the speed of the water relative to the body is sufficiently high for the forces exerted by the water to be mainly inertial forces (high Reynolds number). It is also assumed that the water is

Table 1. Parameters for the mechanical simulation. B_i stands for the body links with B1 being the head link, and L1 and L2 stand for the upper and lower part of a limb, respectively. Fore- and hindlimbs are identical.

Link	l_i [mm]	w_i [mm]	m_i [g]	$I_\perp$ [g mm^2]	$I_\parallel$ [g mm^2]	$\lambda_\perp$ [Ns^2/m^2]	$\lambda_\parallel$ [Ns^2/m^2]
B1	30	30	17.7	2319	1988	0.38	0.3
B2	30	25	14.7	1679	1150	0.38	0.2
B3	30	30	17.7	2319	1988	0.38	0.1
B4	30	30	17.7	2319	1988	0.38	0.0
B5	30	30	17.7	2319	1988	0.38	0.0
B6	30	22	13.0	1364	784	0.38	0.0
B7	30	20	11.8	1178	589	0.38	0.0
B8	30	16	9.4	857	301	0.38	0.0
B9	30	10	5.9	478	74	0.38	0.0
B10	30	5	2.9	225	9	0.38	0.0
L1	25	10	2.0	62	20	0.30	0.1
L2	15	10	1.2	29	15	0.30	0.1

Table 2. Muscle parameters.

	α [N m]	β [N m]	γ	δ [N m s]
Body joint	0.01	0.0015	10.0	0.00010
Pelvis joints	0.01	0.0020	5.0	0.00010
Knee joint	0.01	0.0020	5.0	0.00002

stationary and that the parallel and perpendicular components of that force on each link can be calculated separately. The components of the force can therefore be calculated as: $F_{env\parallel} = \lambda_\parallel v_\parallel^2$ and $F_{env\perp} = \lambda_\perp v_\perp^2$ where $v_\parallel$ and $v_\perp$ are the components of the speed of the link relative to the water and $\lambda_\parallel = \frac{1}{2}C_\parallel S\rho$ and $\lambda_\perp = \frac{1}{2}C_\perp S\rho$ are coefficients which depend on the density of the fluid ρ, the area perpendicular to the movement S and the drag coefficient C dependent on the shape of the link (here $C_\perp =1$, and $C_\parallel =0$ for all links except those close to the head. See Table 1).

The equations for the mechanical simulation are solved with the fourth order Runge-Kutta method with a fixed time step of 1 ms. The simulation is written in C, within the Fastdynamics framework. The OpenGL library is used for graphics.

4   Control of Locomotion

In this article, locomotion of the simulated salamander is investigated using simple algorithmic controllers rather than the neural networks developed in [15, 16] which have yet to be extended to control the new DOFs of the articulated limbs.

The outputs of the motoneurons connected to the muscles are computed as simple sinusoidal functions. For the body (trunk and tail) muscles:

$$M_l(t,j) = \text{Max}\{\ \alpha\sin(\omega t - \lambda_j),\quad 0.0\ \} \tag{4}$$

$$M_r(t,j) = \text{Max}\{\ \alpha\sin(\pi + \omega t - \lambda_j),\quad 0.0\ \} \tag{5}$$

where $M_l(t,j)$ and $M_r(t,j)$ are, respectively, the outputs of left and right mo-toneurons for joint j at time t ($j \in [1,9]$, with $j = 1$ being the head joint). The maximal amplitude of the signal is given by α. ω and λ_j correspond to the frequency of oscillation and the phase of joint j, respectively.

Similarly for the limb joints:

$$M_e(t,d) = \text{Max}\{\ \beta_d\sin(\omega t - \phi_d),\quad 0.0\ \} \tag{6}$$

$$M_f(t,d) = \text{Max}\{\ \beta_d\sin(\pi + \omega t - \phi_d),\quad 0.0\ \} \tag{7}$$

where $M_e(t,d)$ and $M_f(t,d)$ are, respectively, the outputs of flexor and extensor motoneurons for the DOF d at time t. As mentioned earlier, each limb has three DOFs, two at the pelvis and one at the knee, with $d{=}1$ being the DOF around the vertical axis in the pelvis, $d{=}2$ the DOF around the horizontal axis in the pelvis, and $d{=}3$ the DOF of the knee. Note that, by definition, all joints oscillate at the same frequency ω and that the signals sent to opposed muscles (either the left-right muscles in the body or the flexor-extensor muscles in the limbs) are out of phase.

5 Results

Swimming gait The swimming gait is produced by a wave of neural activity traveling from head to tail along the body. Similarly to what has been observed in the real salamander [17, 20], we define the phase between consecutive links such that the body makes a complete wave, with a constant phase lag along the spinal cord: $\lambda_j = j \cdot 2\pi/9$ (i.e. the first and last body joints are in phase). During swimming the limbs are kept against the body through the contraction of the horizontal flexor at the pelvis and the flexor of the knee ($M_e(t,1){=}0.0$, $M_f(t,1){=}0.9$, $M_e(t,2){=}0.0$, $M_f(t,1){=}0.0$, and $M_e(t,3){=}0.0$, $M_f(t,3){=}0.6$).

Figure 3 (top) illustrates a swimming gait with 4Hz oscillations. The neural wave is transformed into a mechanical wave which propels the salamander forward. By keeping the limbs against the body, drag is reduced. The resulting movements are particularly realistic and life-like. The speed of swimming can be varied, and increased, for instance, by increasing either the amplitude of the signals sent to the muscles (α) or the frequency of the oscillations (ω). By simply giving some asymmetry of signal amplitude between left and right sides, turning can also be induced.

Trotting gait On ground the salamander uses a trotting gait in which all joints in the trunk are in synchrony, $\lambda_j{=}0$ for j=2,3,4,5, while being out of phase compared to the joints in the tail, $\lambda_j{=}\pi$ for j=6,7,8,9. The joint of the head (the neck) also oscillates out of phase compared to the trunk such as to limit head movements, $\lambda_1{=}\pi$. Crossed limbs oscillate in phase and are out of phase

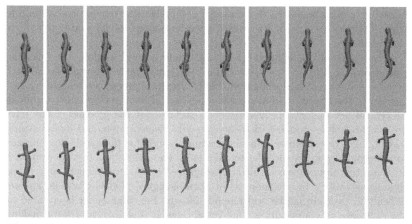

Fig. 3. Top: swimming, Bottom: trotting. Note the traveling wave along the body while swimming, and the standing wave while trotting. Animated gifs of the different simulations can be found at: http://rana.usc.edu:8376/~ijspeert/salamander.html

compared to adjacent limbs. Limbs are coordinated with the body movements as follows: muscles in joints $d=1$ and $d=3$ oscillate in phase and are also in synchrony with the body muscles on the same side. This means that when, for instance, the left trunk (i.e the upper part of the body) is in contraction, the left forelimb flexors in the knee and in the pelvis around the vertical axis contract such as to pull the limb backwards. Approximate circular movements of the limbs are obtained by having the muscles which create torques around the horizontal axis in the pelvis (i.e. which determine the elevation of the limb) to be ahead by a $\pi/2$ phase compared to the other pelvis muscles.

Figure 3 (top) illustrates a trotting gait with 2Hz oscillations. The biomechanical simulation produces the typical trotting gait of the salamander, with movements of limbs coordinated with those of the body such as to increase their reach during the swing phase. Similarly to swimming, the speed of trotting can be modulated by varying the frequency of oscillations and/or the amplitudes of the signals sent to the muscles. Turning can also be induced, primarily by giving different amplitudes to left and right signals sent to the trunk muscles.

Animated gifs of the different simulations can be found at:
http://rana.usc.edu:8376/~ijspeert/salamander.html

6   Discussion

This article presented a 3D biomechanical simulation of a salamander which extended the 2D model that we had developed in previous work [14, 15, 16]. Our aim is to gain a better understanding of the neural mechanisms underlying behavior in vertebrates by developing a comprehensive model of a vertebrate which includes models of its central nervous system, of its body, and of its environment.

The choice of the salamander as case study is motivated by the following considerations. Firstly, the salamander —an amphibian— is capable of both aquatic and terrestrial locomotion, and represents, among vertebrates, a key element in the evolution from aquatic to terrestrial habitats. Secondly, although its central nervous system has not been decoded for the moment, many data are available characterizing its locomotion, its visual system and its behaviors, which makes the salamander an interesting testbed for the synthetic approach to neurobiology we would like to take [15]. The basic idea of that approach is to use techniques from artificial intelligence such as evolutionary algorithms to automatically generate subparts of neurobiological models whose details are difficult to measure in the real animal. Finally, the salamander is situated at the right level of complexity among vertebrates: it is simple enough for making a comprehensive model of the animal possible (it has, for instance, orders of magnitudes fewer neurons than primates), while the similarities of its central nervous system with more complex vertebrates offers the possibility of general insights into the functioning of vertebrates.

Having a physically-based representation of the body is crucial to understand the dynamics of locomotion and motor control in general. A body has indeed its own dynamics and intrinsic frequencies with complex non-linear properties, to which the frequencies, phases and shapes of motoneuron signals must be adapted for efficient locomotion and motor control. Only a dynamical simulation (rather than just kinematic, as used in most experiments in computational neuroethology) can realistically represents the inertial, elastic, damping, etc. properties of the body. This is not only important for studies of locomotion, but also for investigations of sensori-motor control in general as body dynamics strongly influences sensory inputs (e.g. movements of the head influence visual perception).

The experiments reported in this article illustrated how the simulation could realistically reproduce the swimming and trotting gaits observed in the real salamander. The motoneuron activity was here produced by a simple sinusoidal function which allowed modulation of the speed, direction and type of gait. We are currently extending the biologically plausible 2D neural networks developed in [15, 16] to control the new DOFs of the articulated limbs (see [24]).[1] Finally, we are working on the addition of a model of the salamander's visual system to the simulated body and locomotor circuitry in order to investigate the neural mechanisms underlying visually-guided behavior (see [25] for a preliminary experiment).

While our main interest is to gain a better understanding of the functioning of biological central nervous systems, this type of work may also bring a contribution to graphic animation on one hand —for the generation of like-like animations—, and to biologically inspired robotics on the other. Robots which

---

[1] In the previous biomechanical simulation, a limb was represented by a single rigid link attached to the body with only one DOF.

use animal-like types of gaits are indeed confronted to the same type of control problems as animals, that is, how to transform simple commands concerning the speed and direction of motion into the complex rhythmic signals sent to multiple actuators. Understanding biological control may prove to be very useful for the construction of a salamander-like amphibian robot, for instance.

7 Conclusion

This article described the design of a 3D biomechanical simulation of a salamander. The physically-based simulation represents the salamander as an articulated body actuated by spring and damper muscles. A simple algorithmic controller was developed to illustrate how the simulation could reproduce and modulate the typical aquatic and terrestrial locomotion of the salamander. This model is currently used for the investigation of potential neural mechanisms underlying the locomotion of the real salamander, and extended with a model of the salamander's visual system for sensori-motor experiments in silico.

Acknowledgements: Facilities were provided by the University of Southern California. Many thanks to Michael Arbib for his insightful comments on this project. This work was supported by a grant for young researcher from the Swiss National Science Foundation.

References

[1] R.D. Beer. *Intelligence as Adaptive Behavior, an Experiment in Computational Neuroethology.* Academic Press, 1990.

[2] D. Cliff. Computational neuroethology. In M.A. Arbib, editor, *The handbook of brain theory and neural networks*, pages 626–630. MIT Press, 1995.

[3] R.D. Quinn and K.S. Espenschied. Control of a hexapod robot using a biologically inspired neural network. In R.D. Beer, R.E. Ritzmann, and T.M. McKenna, editors, *Biological neural networks in invertebrate neuroethology and robotics.* Academic Press, 1993.

[4] H. Cruse, D.E. Brunn, Ch. Bartling, J. Dean, M. Dreifert, T. Kindermann, and J. Schmitz. Walking: A complex behavior controlled by simple networks. *Adaptive Behavior*, 3(4):385–418, 1995.

[5] B. Webb. Robotics experiments in cricket phonotaxis. In D. Ciff, P. Husbands, J.M. Meyer, and S.W. Wilson, editors, *Proceedings, From Animals to Animats III.* MIT Press, 1994.

[6] N. Franceschini, J.M. Pichon, and C. Blanes. From insect vision to robot vision. *Phil. Trans. R. Soc. Lond. B*, 337:283–294, 1992.

[7] D. Cliff. Neural networks for visual tracking in an artificial fly. In F.J. Varela and P. Bourgine, editors, *Proceedings of the first European Conference on Artificial Life (ECAL91).* MIT Press, 1992.

[8] M.A. Arbib. Levels of modeling of visually guided behavior. *Behavioral and Brain Sciences*, 10:407–465, 1987.

[9] A. Cobas and M. Arbib. Prey-catching and predator-avoidance in frog and toad: defining the schemas. *Journal of Theoretical Biology*, 157:271–304, 1992.

234   Auke Jan Ijspeert

[10] M.A. Arbib and J.S. Liaw. Sensorimotor transformations in the world of frogs and robots. *Artificial Intelligence*, 72:53–79, 1995.

[11] Ö. Ekeberg. A combined neuronal and mechanical model of fish swimming. *Biological Cybernetics*, 69:363–374, 1993.

[12] D. Terzopoulos, X. Tu, and R. Grzeszczuk. Artificial fishes: autonomous locomotion, perception, behavior, and learning in a simulated physical world. *Artificial Life*, 1(4):327–351, 1994.

[13] P.F.M.J. Vershure, J. Wray, O. Sporns, G. Tononi, and G.M. Edelmann. Multilevel analysis of classical conditioning in a behaving real world artifact. *Robotics and Autonomous Systems*, 16:247–265, 1995.

[14] A.J. Ijspeert, J. Hallam, and D. Willshaw. From lampreys to salamanders: evolving neural controllers for swimming and walking. In R. Pfeifer, B. Blumberg, J.-A. Meyer, and S.W. Wilson, editors, *From Animals to Animats, Proceedings of the Fifth International Conference of The Society for Adaptive Behavior (SAB98)*, pages 390–399. MIT Press, 1998.

[15] A.J. Ijspeert. Synthetic approaches to neurobiology: review and case study in the control of anguiliform locomotion. In D. Floreano, F. Mondada, and J.-D. Nicoud, editors, *Proceedings of the Fifth European Conference on Artificial Life, ECAL99*, pages 195–204. Springer Verlag, 1999.

[16] A.J. Ijspeert. Evolution of neural controllers for salamander-like locomotion. In G.T. McKee and P.S. Schenker, editors, *Proceedings of Sensor Fusion and Decentralised Control in Robotics Systems II*, pages 168–179. SPIE Proceeding Vol. 3839, 1999.

[17] L.M. Frolich and A.A. Biewener. Kinematic and electromyographic analysis of the functional role of the body axis during terrestrial and aquatic locomotion in the salamander *ambystoma tigrinum*. *Journal of Experimental Biology*, 62:107–130, 1992.

[18] M.A. Ashley-Ross. Hindlimb kinematics during terrestrial locomotion in a salamander (dicampton tenebrosus). *Journal of Experimental Biology*, 193:255–283, 1994.

[19] M.A. Ashley-Ross. Metamorphic and speed effects on hindlimb kinematics during terrestrial locomotion in the salamander (dicampton tenebrosus). *Journal of Experimental Biology*, 193:285–305, 1994.

[20] I. Delvolvé, T. Bem, and J.-M. Cabelguen. Epaxial and limb muscle activity during swimming and terrestrial stepping in the adult newt, *pleurodeles waltl*. *Journal of Neurophysiology*, 78:638–650, 1997.

[21] A.H. Cohen. Evolution of the vertebrate central pattern generator for locomotion. In A. H. Cohen, S. Rossignol, and S. Grillner, editors, *Neural control of rhythmic movements in vertebrates*. Jon Wiley & Sons, 1988.

[22] A.J. Ijspeert, J. Hallam, and D. Willshaw. Evolving swimming controllers for a simulated lamprey with inspiration from neurobiology. *Adaptive Behavior*, 7(2):151–172, 1999.

[23] A.J. Ijspeert and J. Kodjabachian. Evolution and development of a central pattern generator for the swimming of a lamprey. *Artificial Life*, 5(3):247–269, 1999.

[24] A.J. Ijspeert. A neuromechanical investigation of salamander locomotion. In *Proceedings of the International Symposium on Adaptive Motion of Animals and Machines, Montreal, Canada, 8-12 August 2000*. 2000. To appear.

[25] A.J. Ijspeert and M. Arbib. Visual tracking in simulated salamander locomotion. In *Proceedings of the Sixth International Conference of The Society for Adaptive Behavior (SAB2000), Paris, France, 11-15 September 2000*. MIT Press, 2000. To appear.

Virtual COTONS®, the Firstborn of the Next Generation of Simulation Model

Eric Jallas[1], Pierre Martin[1], Ronaldo Sequeira[3], Sammy Turner[2], Michel Cretenet[1] and Edward Gérardeaux[1]

[1] Programme Coton, CIRAD-CA, BP 5035, 34032 Montpellier Cedex 1, France.
[2] USDA-ARS-CSRU, P.O. Box 5367, Mississippi State, MS 39762, USA.
[3] USDA-APHIS-CPHST, 1509 Varsity Drive, Raleigh, NC 27606, U.S.A.

Abstract. Traditional plant architectural models or 'visualization models' propose to visually create realistic three-dimensional plants. The visualization is based on field sampling and the application of an algorithm to standardize the three-dimensional description of a plant. "L-systems" and the "Reference Axis" are two such approaches. Mechanistic or physiologically based models describe how a plant functions. They simulate physiologically realistic plants based on estimates of physiological development and growth. Their equations are derived from field experiments. In this study we integrated both modeling paradigms. We used functions and concepts obtained from mechanistic and architectural modeling theories and developed an integrated system. The resulting model allows vastly improved model output interpretation, use of the model as a surrogate experimental environment and to better integrate our knowledge about how plants grow into a unique system. The new model, named COTONS, produces "life-like" plants, it symbolizes crop models for the next century.

1 Introduction

Worldwide cotton represents about 50% of the fiber used in the world, it is the fifth row-crop and in some countries it is the first agricultural resource [11]. Cotton is also a complex plant. It is a perennial plant with an indeterminate growth habit, but it is cultivated as an annual crop. It develops monopodial structures at the same time as sympodial structures, and it regulates its carrying capacity through fruit abscission [9]. The main stem and the vegetative branches are monopodial structures, which means that the terminal apex produces all internodes. Fruiting branches are sympodial structures. This implies that each internode is produced by an axillary bud, which will be transformed into a fruiting site. Each internode bears a leaf and two axillary buds; thus a cotton 'tree' increases its photosynthesis potential by increasing the size of its light captors and by increasing their number through morphogenesis by adding nodes. Fruiting sites can be abscised in response to nutritional stresses. These characteristics are important because there is competition between vegetative development and reproduction within a cotton plant. The number of bolls per plant at harvest will depend on events, which occurred long before boll setting. Square and boll abscission determine this number, but they are dependent on crop development and growth which is under the control of the dynamic states of their environment.

J.-C. Heudin (Ed.): VW 2000, LNAI 1834, pp. 235-244, 2000.
© Springer-Verlag Berlin Heidelberg 2000

Thus the period where there is interaction and competition between growth and development is relatively important.

2   The COTONS Model

COTONS is a physiologically detailed simulation model of the growth and the development of the cotton plant. It is based on the GOSSYM model [1], [9], [18], developed at the Crop Simulation Research Unit. Like GOSSYM it includes a plant model and a soil model. Weather information, some cultural practices and genetic characteristics drive the plant model. Plant development is limited by water and nitrogen supply and also by soil water potential status. When the plant grows its shade limits soil water evaporation, but at the same time the plant uptakes water and nitrogen. From GOSSYM, the plant sub-model of COTONS includes two important concepts: "materials balance" and the use of different stresses (N, H2O, C) to regulate plant growth. The model runs on a daily basis. Each day, the model first calculates carbohydrate supply based on external factors (light, temperature, water supply, etc), plant water status and leaf area. Second, the system calculates the carbohydrate demand for Growth, Respiration and plant Maintenance based again on external factors and plant status. Third, the system partitions the carbohydrate supply to the different organs based on their demand and priority levels. Fruit having the highest priority and storage the lowest.

2.1   Production of Carbohydrates

COTONS uses canopy characteristics to estimate the proportion of light going through the canopy. Two parts of incident light are identified: the light transmitted directly to the ground which is a function of plant height, plant width and row spacing and the light transmitted to the ground through the canopy which is a function of genetic plant characteristics and of the Leaf Area Index. This light interception model incorporates Beer-Lamber's law [6], [19], to estimate the light intercepted by the canopy. Equation 1 is an example of carbohydrates production modeling. It describes the gross photosynthesis (Pg) model. This sub-model is a function of incident radiation (Tg), potential gross photosynthesis per unit area of canopy intercepting light ($pstand$), area of soil per plant ($popfac$), plant width ($pwidth$), row spacing ($rowsp$), plant spacing ($pltsp$) within the row, leaf area ($leafarea$), plant water status ($ptsred$), and [CO_2] concentration ($pnetcor$). There are two variety-dependent parameters (a and b) and k is the light extinction coefficient.

$$Pg = pstand \times popfac \times \left(1 - \left(Tg \times \left(1 - e^{-k \times leafarea}\right) + e^{-k \times leafarea}\right)\right) \tag{1}$$

$$\times (1 + ae^{-b(pltsp \times pwidth)}) \times ptsred \times pnetcor \times 0.001$$

This photosynthesis model takes into account the size of the canopy and its age. The sub-model of carbohydrate production allows the simulation of light competition for plants growing in parallel.

2.2   Demand in Carbohydrates

The modeling of carbohydrate demand in COTONS is based on the idea [5] that "crops have a growth potential when there are no limiting factors such as availability of carbon, nitrogen or water". The generic equation 2 is an example of this concept.

$$Potential\_Growth_{Organ(i)} = Biomass_{Organ(i)} \times (a + b\overline{T} + c\overline{T^2}) \times \left(\prod R(f)\right) \times Dt \times C \qquad (2)$$

where:

$Biomass_{Organ(i)}$ = the actual biomass of the organ *(i)*, expressed in weight or area,

$\overline{T}$ = the average temperatu re "experience d" by the organ,

$R(f)$ = a reduction coeficient linked to the factor f,

Dt = the interval of time,

C = a varietal calibratio n factor,

a, b and c = three parameters.

In a first stage, the model estimates potential growth for the different parts of the plant. This is done organ by organ (except for the root) according to the weight and/or area of each organ, its age, and the temperature. These potentials for growth are reduced according to the water status of the plant and the use of growth regulators. In a second step, COTONS uses the adjusted growth potentials to calculate the demand (the sum of the potentials) for carbohydrate and compares it with supply, the sum of net photosynthesis per day, and the available pool of carbohydrate. The demand/supply ratio [0, 1], 'representing carbon stress', is then used for adjustment of growth potentials by plant organ type.

2.3   Partitioning of Carbohydrate Supply

The partitioning process links the carbohydrate supply sub-model and the carbohydrate demand sub-model. During each daily time step the partitioning process that drives the yield components and storage, balances the whole system. This process needs information on the plant structure, which is dependent on the morphogenesis sub-model. The plant morphogenesis routine simulates the emergence of organs and the development of these organs according to the temperature "experienced" by the plant part being considered in the daily time step interval. Stresses experienced by the plant modify that growth and development. The morphogenetic events are estimated from the calculated age of each organ in relation to an age threshold. The temperature "experienced" is used in (usually) quadratic polynomial equations to determine the age thresholds at which the various organs should emerge or change [1], [9]. Nitrogen stress and vegetative stress combined are also used in the calculation of age thresholds. There are two pathways (both are supported and can be invoked from the interface) in the morphogenesis model: the "plant average" path and the "plant population" path. In the plant average it is assumed that one "plant average" represents the crop [8]. In this case the simulation process is deterministic and fruit production per position is the proportion of fruit present at this position in the field. In the "plant population" path, the model simulates 'n' plants growing in parallel with the same environmental condition. The population of plants represents the actual variability [17] observed in commercial fields. This variability is the interaction of a plant phenotypic variability and a competition between plants linked to the phenotypic variability and differences in stand establishment. Plant variability is modeled by adding stochasticity into the node initiation and abscission processes, and by modeling these two main processes as a queuing system. For example, the probability density function of the node appearance can be fitted with the reciprocal of the normal function. Morphogenesis is modeled as a queuing system with three queues, the first one is the internode elongation, the second is square abscission and the third is for boll abscission. Queue disciplines are different: for internode elongation the discipline is "First In First Out", for abscission processes it is "Last In First Out" [10]. The variability linked to plant competition is modeled by adding an emergence sub-model and by growing plants in parallel on an area basis. The emergence model is currently only a function of temperature. It partially takes into account soil humidity, planting depth and other characteristics because the model uses the emergence date indicated by the farmer as the median for emergence distribution.

2.4   Morphology, Geometry, and Visualization

The use of a crop model by producers and even scientist is difficult. The main reason for this problem is the interface of this kind of system. In crop models both data input and interpretation of the output of the system may seem too abstract or too cumbersome for users. Graphical tools now exists and are available on desktop computers. Thus, it is possible to visualize output as "Virtual Plants" resulting from the simulation and making the simulation more understandable to farmer and scientists [13]. The level of detail simulated by the model facilitated the integration of a visualization tool to COTONS. This visualization is done using an Architectural engine which simulates the sizes of each organ (length, diameter and width), their spatial position, the shape of each organ, and displays all these information. Each day the plant model of COTONS simulates plant growth and development, it then it calls a "Plant Morphology" sub-model which simulates sizes of all organs. This morphology sub-model calculates volume and area variables (length and diameter) from dry weights simulated by the plant model and ages. For example equation 3 shows the relationship between boll dry weight (*Weight_Boll*) and boll diameter (*Size_Boll*), and open boll shape (*Angle_Boll*) and boll age (*Age_Open_Boll*):

$$Size\_Boll = a + b \log Weight\_Boll, \text{ with } Weight\_Boll \le c \tag{3}$$

$$Angle\_Boll = dAge\_Open\_Boll$$

where *a, b, c* and *d* are three variety-dependent parameters

After calling the morphology sub-model the architectural engine calls another routine to build the 3D-plant architecture. This routine constructs the 3-dimensional plant geometry from organ lengths and diameters, phyllotaxy angles, insertion angles and deviation angles (see figure 1). All angles are fixed and they are assumed to be variety dependent. The arrangement of the organs verifies the following rules: the normal of a fruiting organ is vertical, the insertion angle of two subsequent vegetative leaves corresponds to the phyllotaxy angle, the inter-nodes on mainstem and vegetative branches are lined up and the inter-nodes on fruiting branches (with its axillary leaf) are alternatively shifted of by 30°. These angles are startup references and they are modified by the organs weight carried by each organ.

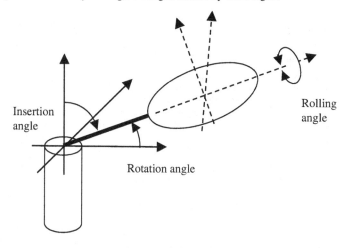

Figure 1: organ positioning.

An iterative process places each organ, relatively to its bearer, in the 3D space. Then a shape made from polygons (see figure 2) is associated to each organ and it size is derived from the morphology sub-model.

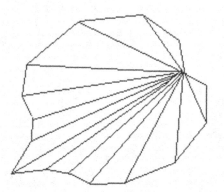

Figure 2: Leaf symbol use by the visualization system.

Finally, a routine displays the results. The visual displays were developed with OpenGL™ functions. The output of the architectural sub-model is a 3D matrix that

OpenGL functions project on the 2D space of the screen. There is more than 150 functions in OpenGL [7] and these functions allow the user to manage scene lighting, shading, object texture, color, 3D depth, perspective effects, and so on.

3   Simulating the Cotton Crop with COTONS, Key Results

3.1   Some Simulation Results

To initialize and run COTONS the user needs three kinds of inputs: single point descriptors as soil hydrology characteristics, plant density, date of emergence and so on, the driving variables (temperature, solar radiation, rainfall and wind speed) and the cultural (agronomic practices or technical itineraries) practices.   With this information the system is able to simulate the growth of the crop during the crop season.   At the end of the simulation the system provides the following outputs: organs mass and number, plant topology, plant status indicators and the variables used.   During the simulation the user can visualize the plant growth as shown in figures 3 and 4.

Figure 3 shows the visualization at three different days for an average plant corresponding to a crop with high nitrogen fertilization and good water supply.   The plant is well developed and the production is localized at the bottom.   It is obvious that this kind of output is more accessible for users than a simple listing of tables (which are also available).

Figure 3: Visualization at three different days of a plant average for a crop with high nitrogen fertilization and good water supply.

Figure 4 shows 8 plants growing in parallel as they are simulated by the new system. All the plants are different, plant height, number of bolls, boll position, etc., are different.   They did not emerge necessary the same day and they had to compete for light interception.

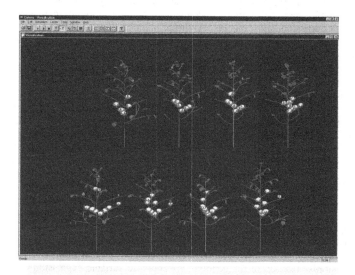

Figure 4: Visualization of 8 plants growing in parallel

3.2   Discussion

Whereas crop architectural models [2], [14], insisted on topology and architecture and mechanistic modeling [1], [9], [12], [16], insisted on physiological functionality, Virtual Crop Models integrate both approaches [10].   Virtual crops are life-like computer representations based on individual plants. Because virtual plants can be manipulated and examined from any angle, features observable in the field can be also analyzed on the virtual plants [13]. Applications being implemented in the area of plant topology and visualization include the use of virtual crops for the study of population dynamics, optimal plant architectural forms, radiative phenomena, evapo-transpiration, and the study of the implications of field variability.

A key feature of biological systems is the fact that they are variable (due to genetic and phenotypic expression). This variability is important for management because very dis-uniform fields will behave differently than more homogenous fields. With virtual representations we can assess, compare, and understand the nature of this variability to better manage the system. Room *et al.,* [15], in Australia have developed a simple, L-system-based approach to the virtual representation of cotton plants. Earlier de Reffye [3], [4], in France developed probability-based virtual representations of cotton, coffee, and other plants. The applications being implemented by these researchers include the use of virtual crops for the study of population dynamics, optimal plant architectural forms and the study of the implications of field variability to productivity.   Despite the existence and exploitation of these techniques in several countries, they are not yet available to a large public including farmers, students, and researchers.

Research applications of virtual cotton may become very important. For example virtual cotton decision support systems will be an important extension of the possibilities for simulation models. A virtual plant can be tagged with light sensors and different plant architectures. Different models of photosynthesis can be tested to determine optimal plant forms. A researcher can initiate a simulation, apply stresses and then measure intercepted light, growth characteristics, and other aspects before ever planting an actual seed. Different leaf shapes, plant spacing, weed competition, etc. can be similarly studied with a virtual tool. Another advantage is the direct correspondence between computer and real world observations which make the translation of observed to modeled phenomena-and associated variability-more straightforward. In addition to providing a direct surrogate for field experiments, the *a priori* knowledge gained from virtual experiments will make it easier for researchers to interact by examining the expected behavior before setting out research in the field [15]. The potential savings to funding and research institutions of these kinds of tools would be enormous. Another application is in the area of sampling research. The availability of a virtual cotton field with virtual insects distributed in user-defined patterns will enable researchers to test many sampling schemes and pre-filter algorithms prior to their field validation.

Virtual cotton can also be a decision-aid tool for producers. Virtual cotton fields will permit the modeling of heterogeneous areas analogous to real fields and will permit the inclusion/simulation of the genotypic/phenotypic variable expression of the crop. Plant maps, a key tool for model correction and record keeping are more easily constructed using virtual representations than with two-dimensional abstractions. The visualization of the effects of different management practices on fruit distribution, for example, will be useful in selecting practices that minimize the adverse effects of sub-optimal fruit set and demonstrating clearly and convincingly the results of alternative practices.

Another important use of Virtual Plants resides in its use as training tools. One of the hurdles to overcome in introducing computer-based techniques to farmers is the learning curve associated with complex, management-oriented software. The use of virtual plants, of being able to traverse a virtual cotton field all the while making observations and recording data, will be an unparalleled tool for teaching optimal cultural practices, and sampling and monitoring techniques.   For example in agricultural colleges, students will interactively see field effects of different management practices.

4   Conclusion

The new COTONS model integrates many features available only individually in other models. For the first time, a mechanistic model associates an architectural engine, a visualization tool and is able to simulate field variability using parallel population processes. COTONS' light interception and photosynthesis sub-models take into account plant and crop structures giving the foundation for a "plant population" model as an alternative to the common "average plant" model approach. With the inclusion of stochasticity and emergence process, COTONS is able to simulate field variability. It will allow management based on more indicators than other cotton models (weights, number of fruiting and vegetative branches, number of bolls by position, distribution of yield, etc.). The visualization tool is really a Producer-Level Decision-Aid system. For example, the visualization of the effects of different management practices will demonstrate the results of alternative practices. COTONS, produces "life-like" plants and the farmer deal with simulation results analogous to the ones he dealt with in a 3-dimensional world. Now dry weights, nitrogen stress, water stress, etc correspond to the daily reality of the farmer so he/she is able to understand and accept recommendations provided by the system. Finally Virtual Plants are an ideal training tool. COTONS can be used to teach farmers and students optimal cultural practices, sampling and monitoring techniques, and the overall complexity, interactions and feedback associated with agricultural production.

References

1. Baker, D., McKinion, J. M., and Lambert, J. R. (1983). "GOSSYM: a Simulator of Cotton Crop Growth and Yield.,". S.C. Agric. Exp. Stn.
2. de Reffye, P. (1979). Modélisation de l'architecture des arbres par des processus stochastistiques. Simulation spatiale des modèles tropicaux sous l'effet de la pesanteur. Application au *coffea robusta*, Paris-Sud, Orsay, France.
3. de Reffye, P., Edelin, C., Françon, J., Jaeger, M., and Puech, C. (1988). Plant Models Faithful to Botanical Structure and Development. *Comput. Graphics* **22**, 151-158.
4. de Reffye, P., Blaise, F., and Guédon, Y. (1993). Modélisation et simulation de l'architecture et de la croissance des plantes. *Revue du Palais de la Découverte* **209**, 23-48.
5. de Witt, C. T., and Brouwer, R. (1968). A Dynamic Model of the Vegetative Growth of Crops. *Das Zietschrift Fur Angewandte Botanik*.
6. Duncan, W. G., Loomis, R. S., Williams, W. A., and Hanau, R. (1967). A model for Simulating Photosynthesis in Plant Communities. *Hilgardia, Journal of agriculture and Science* **38**, 181-205.
7. Fosner, R. (1997). "OpenGL. Programming for Windows 95 and Windows NT," 1/Ed. Addison-Wesley Developers Press.
8. Gutierrez, A. P., Falcon, L. A., Loew, W., Leipzig, P. A., and Van Der Bosch, R. (1975). An Analysis of Cotton Production in California: A Model for Acal Cotton and the Effects of Defoliators on Its Yields. *Environmental Entomology* **4**, 125-136.
9. Jallas, E. (1991). Modélisation de Développement et de la Croissance du Cotonnier. Mémoire de DEA, INA-PG, Paris.
10. Jallas, E. (1998). Improved Model-Based Decision Support by Modeling Cotton Variability and Using Evolutionary Algorithms. PhD Dissertation, M.S.U., Mississippi.
11. Jallas, E., Sequeira R. A., Martin P., Turner S. and Cretenet M. (1998). COTONS, a Cotton Simulation Model for the Next Century. Second World Cotton Research Conference, Athens, September 1998.
12. Mutsaers, H. J. W. (1984). KUTUN: a Morphogenetic Model for Cotton. *Agricultural Systems* **14**, 229-257.
13. Prusinkiewicz, P., and Hammel, M. (1994). Visual models of morphogenesis. . WWW URL http://www.cpsc.ucalgary.ca/projects/bmv/vmm/animations.html.
14. Room, P. M., Maillette, L., and Hanan, J. S. (1994). Module and metamer dynamics and virtual plants,. *Adv. Ecol. Res.*, 105-157.

15. Room, P. M., Hanan, J. S., and Prusinkiewicz, P. (1996). Virtuals plants: New Perspectives for Ecologists, Pathologists and Agricultural Scientists. *Trends in Plant Science* **1**, 33-38.
16. Sequeira, R. A., Sharpe, P. J. H., Stone, N. D., El-Zik, K. M., and Makela, M. E. (1991). Object-oriented Simulation: Plant Growth and Discrete Organ to Organ Interactions. *Ecological Modelling* **58**, 55-89.
17. Sequeira, R. A., Stone, N. D., Makela, M. E., El-Zik, K. M., and Sharpe, P. J. H. (1993). Generation of Mechanistic Variability in a Process-based Object-oriented Plant Model. *Ecological Modelling* **67**, 285-306.
18. Sequeira, R. A., and Jallas, E. (1995). The Simulation Model GOSSYM and its Decision Support System, COMAX: its Applications in American Agriculture. *Agriculture et Developpement* **8**, 25-34.
19. Thanisawanyangkura, S., Sinoquet, H., Rivet, P., Crétenet, M., and Jallas, E. (1997). Leaf Orientation and Sunlit Leaf Area Distribution in Cotton. *Agricultural and Forest Meteorology* **86**, 1-15.

Basins of Attraction and the Density Classification Problem for Cellular Automata

Terry Bossomaier, Llewylyn Sibley-Punnett, and Tim Cranny

Charles Sturt University
tbossomaier@csu.edu.au

Abstract. The density classification problem has long been recognized as a benchmark for exploring cellular automata rules with global properties. One of the major difficulties in evaluating rules is the enormous number of configurations which have to be tested, particularly important in any search process. We consider an approach to rule evaluation, which is in some ways the reverse of the standard methods, and discuss problems and opportunities raised by the approach.

1 Reformulation of the Density Classification Problem

Cellular automata (CA) have excited interest over a long period as minimal computational systems. The most popular example is a two-dimensional grid world, the Game of Life, invented by John Conway [4], in which binary counters live and die on a grid. Life or death is determined by a *rule* which specifies, for every possible pattern of nearest neighbours, whether the grid point in the next generation will be occupied or not. The interesting thing about this very simple system was the enormous range of diverse patterns and behaviour it generated. This is just one example: CAs may be of arbitrary dimension from one dimensional strings and upwards and have all sorts of different rule structures.

But in their canonical form they are minimal in two respects: they have no memory and they operate locally. Despite this CAs can achieve certain forms of global computation. One well-known form is the ability of some CA rules to partially solve the density classification problem, in which a one-dimensional, two-state CA (with circular boundary conditions) is required to relax to a state of all 1s if the density of 1s in the initial configuration (ie. at time-step zero) is greater than some previously specified critical density ρ_c, and, conversely, to relax to a state of all 0s if the initial density of 1s is below ρ_c. This task is intrinsically global in nature and is therefore difficult for a CA to solve, since it has neither the 'memory' to keep a cumulative count nor the spatial range of perception to make a correct assessment.

The density classification problem has therefore attracted a great deal of interest from those studying the emergence of global behaviour. All the work to date on this problem has used the natural approach of determining a rule's performance for a given CA configuration by taking the configuration and moving forward the specified number of time-steps in order to see if it has relaxed to the required state.

J.-C. Heudin (Ed.): VW 2000, LNAI 1834, pp. 245–255, 2000.

An alternative, however, is the use the algorithm developed by Andy Wuensche [12] for running a CA rule *backwards*. In other words, given a CA configuration it is possible to determine *all* the precursor states. This opens up the possibility of using a dynamical-systems approach to CA problems.

Such an approach is seemingly very well suited to the density classification problem, since it can be cleanly reformulated as follows: find a CA rule such that the whole of configuration-space is divided into precisely two basins of attraction; one of which consists of all rules with density greater than the critical density and has as its attractor the state of all 1s, and the other consisting of all other configurations and having as its attractor the state of all 0s.

This then raises the possibility that one can now avoid some of the difficulties, both conceptual and computational, of the standard 'forwards' approach. For example, one might be able to more efficiently estimate the performance of a rule not by picking CA configurations at random and following each of them forward to their attractor, but by starting with a *single* configuration, following it forward to its attractor (so as to determine which basin of attraction we are in), and then working backwards from that configuration, secure in the knowledge that *all* precursors also belong to that same attractor. The percentage of these precursors which are in the right density range would then give some sort of measure of the rule's performance.

2   Characteristics of Rule Evaluation by the Forwards Method

In the forwards method of rule evaluation one takes a CA configuration and uses the CA rule to move forward a prescribed number of time-steps, then checks to see if the CA has reached the desired final state.

For the benchmark CA size of 149 cells, there are a total of $2^{149} \approx 10^{45}$ different CA configurations against which a rule could be tested to determine its performance in density classification. Obviously some form of sampling is needed. The standard for majority classification has become to generate a sample group of CA configurations in which we randomly and independently assign a 1 or 0 to each cell giving rise to an equal probability for the two outcomes.

The density of 1s thus created obviously follows a binomial distribution about 0.5. Some authors have used CA configurations with densities uniformly distributed in $[0, 1]$, but this is an inferior choice for a number of reasons. The above binomial distribution is closely approximated by a normal distribution with mean 0.5 and variance $(4n)^{-1}$ where n is the number of cells in the CA. For 149-cell CAs this gives a standard deviation of 0.04, equivalent to 6 cells.

The rule in question is assessed on that sample group of configurations, and the percentage correct taken as an approximate measure of the 'true percentage'. Such a measure obviously has a sampling error problem, an issue that is frequently underplayed, both in the design and the reporting of experimental work.

If we approximate the success of a given rule over such configurations as being given by a Bernoulli distribution with probability p (typically p is known to be in the range $[0.8, 0.9]$), and if we take N samples, then by the DeMoivre-Laplace theorem the success rate determined by sampling has a distribution which is approximately normal, with mean p and variance $p(1 - p)/N$. The approximation is traditionally considered valid if $Np > 5$ and $N(1 - p) > 5$, which is always the case for this problem.

So, if we wish to assign a fitness value to a rule based on sampling which will have three significant figures to 95% confidence, we require that .0005 be at least two standard deviations. This means that $2\sigma = 2\sqrt{p(1 - p)/N} \leq 0.0005$, or

$$N \geq 4p(1 - p)/(0.0005)^2 \approx 2.5 \times 10^6$$

since the above figure is not particularly sensitive to p.

Since most success measures are given in terms of percentage-correct we will also express the uncertainty in those terms.

The above shows that, to find a fitness score with an uncertainty of $\pm 10\%$ one needs approximately one thousand tests (this gives a 95% confidence interval). To reduce the uncertainty to $\pm 1\%$ one needs 10^4 tests, to $\pm 0.1\%$ one needs 10^6 tests, and to $\pm 0.01\%$ one needs 10^8 tests.

For the 149-cell CAs the best rules over a decade's research all concentrate in the low-to-mid 80% range as measured in the above way [7, 6, 8, 1, 9]. At present we do not know – and have no way other than empirical search of knowing – just what performance the best rules possible are capable of. Work by Land and Belew [10] shows that for any rule there are some starting conditions which will be misclassified, so perfect performance is impossible. However, the argument in [10] shows failure on a statistically insignificant set of rules, and does not impose a practical upper limit on performance. While there are undoubtedly other types of configurations, for which similar arguments can be made, it remains likely that there are rules still to be found which will perform far better than any yet known. There may be rules whose performance is essentially indistinguishable from 100%.

There are several known problems intrinsic to the forwards method. One is that, with the exception of Cranny's work on structured density classification rule [5], all good rules identified in the last decade have been found by evolutionary search methods. Such methods (as with hill-climbing techniques) require one to distinguish (at least in some probabilistic sense) between closely related rules that have minor differences in peformance. However, as shown above, rules close in performance require a vast number of tests to discriminate between them, making it all the harder for the evolutionary process to make progress once the early dramatic improvements have been made. This tends to frustrate the evolutionary search just when the results were becoming interesting.

For some while the best available rule was the GKL rule [8], essentially designed for stability in the presence of noise rather than the density problem *per se*. Subsequent progress on the density classification problem came through the use of evolutionary methods, and in such techniques noise plays a complicating role which is not yet understand properly. For example, the numerical, if not conceptual, progress on the density classification problem in the last decade has often been hailed as a sign of increasing sophistication in the evolutionary tools used (moving from simple GAs (Mitchell and others [7, 6]) to genetic programming (ABK rule from André, Bennett and Koza [1]). Bossomaier and Cranny [2] switched back to a simple evolutionary procedure, but using a restricted, structured search space where Cranny had discovered most of the good rules to lie. Cranny also introduced a whole range of superior rules by enumeration based on this approach [5]. The most recent significant step was the introduction of coevolution with resource sharing (the JP rule from Jordan and Pollack [9]).

A possible contributing factor to progress (which is less likely to be true and which does not seem to have been properly addressed) is that evolutionary methods of little increasing intrinsic merit have become more successful over time because sampling noise has diminished over time through the use of larger samples, as made feasible by increasing computational power.

Another problem specific to the forwards method is that many CA configurations saturate long before the prescribed number of time-steps have elapsed. The massive number of calculations needed for the forwards method means that most researchers find themselves using high-performance computers with vector- or parallel-processing, but the constraints of such approaches make it almost impossible to exploit these 'early saturators'.

3   Evaluating Attractor Basins

The above problems make it worthwhile to ask if a fundamentally different approach to density classification can be found. One alternative is the dynamical systems approach mentioned in the Introduction, using the backwards algorithm of Andy Wuensche [12]. Such an approach may have some qualitative advantages as well as possibly offering greater efficiency than the forwards approach. For example, it is reasonable to hope for computational savings since we are not following each configuration all the way to the attractor, but merely moving between configurations directly linked by the system dynamics.

The language of dynamical systems needs a little latitude of interpretation in this context, since we are dealing with intrinsically finite and discrete systems, but we will use words like 'attractor', 'basin of attraction' etc. in the appropriate sense.

To measure a rule's performance in this context one can start with a single configuration, map out the 'backwards' part of the basin of attraction, and take as a measure of the rule's performance the fraction of that following that back-basin. We need to emphasise this 'back-basin' idea, since we cannot map the entire basin: it is likely to have of the order of 10^{45} members. We therefore are not free of sampling and sampling-error, but it reasonable to check to see if these problems are reduced.

We implemented the Wuensche algorithm and ran it on some of the most significant rules for the density problem (GKL, ABK, Cranny and JP1). As is typically the case, any configuration generated at random is highly likely to be a *Garden of Eden state,* i.e. a state which has no predecessor states. Wuensche's approach to developing the attractor is then to run the CA forward a few iterations and work back from the resultant state. Since we are typically using fairly large CAs even three or four steps forward will produce a back-basin with thousands or tens-of-thousands of precursor states. There is no way of being more precise as to what will happen, but some results of Wuensche (for example the Z parameter [11]) does give some indication of how expansive the attractor will be.

One might reasonably expect the density of Garden of Eden states to diminish as one moves from critical-density to the extremes, but this was found not to be the case: even when we generated populations of configurations with 120 of 14 cells set to 1, over 9.9% of configurations were Garden of Eden. We explain below why such a result might be expected for good density-classification rules.

The computational efficiency of the above process is hard to measure. In practice the running time is strongly affected by the efficiency of memory allocation/deallocation, cache and main memory size and the effectiveness with which the compiler/system libraries implement recursion. We have therefore adopted a simple estimate. We count every lookup table access made in developing the attractor, a total of N_l. Many of these will not lead to a precursor state at all. Now if we imagine running the CA forwards, then each time-step requires L, the length of the CA, lookups. So if the attractor has N_a states, then we can define the effective number of iterations of the CA, I_{eff} as

$$I_{eff} = \frac{N_l}{N_a L}$$

Ideally I_{eff} should be smaller than the number of iterations one would run a CA for to determine if it saturates. A typical value would be 300.

Table 1 shows results for the GKL rule on 37-cell CAs . To generate the above table the following process was used: to avoid a Garden of Eden starting configuration a random configuration with 19 out of 37 cells set at 1 was generated, and followed forward three time-steps to a non-Garden of Eden state. (In fact it was followed to its attractor, to ensure that it was in the appropriate basin of attraction). From there the Wuensche backwards algorithm was used to find all precursor states. These precursor states can be labelled 'correct' or 'incorrect' based on whether or not they are on the right half of the density divide. The 'starting density' column shows the number of 1s out of 37 after the three time-steps forward (i.e. at the state from which the back-basin was calculated).

Several things are readily apparent from Table 1. One is that I_{eff} is noticeably lower than 300, suggesting a computational gain. The other, and more problematic, point is that the values in the 'Percentage Correct' column fluctuate quite noticeably. This is to some extent unavoidable, since we are still resorting to sampling; it is just that here we are sampling regions of the attractor basin.

There is some correlation in the above table between the starting density (i.e. the density of 1s in the CA after the 3 time-steps) and the percentage correct. As

Number of Steps Back	Number of Correct Precursors	Total Number of Precursors	Percentage Correct	I_{eff}	Starting Density
5	1242	1314	94	102	22
5	827	1192	69	144	20
9	46907	79439	59	91	19
14	395905	740364	53	94	19
8	36092	39111	92	68	24
10	25067	31633	79	148	22
7	1150	1290	89	181	21
16	2545243	2763887	92	38	24
24	4526149	6875618	65	13	20
8	3759	4692	80	129	20
10	1472	1692	86	117	21
8	10728	12415	86	109	19
8	11426	13012	87	94	23
7	20620	20712	99	126	25
8	3661	3805	96	83	25
4	3070	3295	93	129	22
6	495	1493	33	105	19
11	63592	84649	75	79	22
9	3015	4107	73	121	23
6	935	1512	61	114	19

Table 1. 37-cell CA results for the GKL rule.

would be expected, the higher the density, the higher the percentage of correct precursors the state has.

Since all good rules perform almost-perfectly on configurations sufficiently away from the critical density, it was thought that perhaps a better measure of rule performance would come from only considering those configurations where the density after the 3 time-steps remained at the critical level. The data collected is given in Table 2.

This and other data showed that, as expected, the success percentage recorded went down. Little other improvement was noted, and this avenue was abandoned.

Data comparable to the above were collected for several other rules (the ABK, JP1 and Cranny rules), and show the same phenomena. (The data is available in [3].)

This raises another potential problem with the backwards scheme: by its very nature it does not detect or measure any basins of attraction other than the one it is actively studying. But this is less of a problem for *good* rules than poor, since those rules typically have only the two major basins of attraction (as desired) and a few minor limit cycles which do not contribute much to the failure rate of the rule. The vast majority of failures by good rules come from configurations

Number of Steps Back	Number of Correct Precursors	Total Number of Precursors	Percentage Correct	I_{eff}
9	9542	12218	78	78
8	683	2983	22	83
7	46543	135368	34	91
29	4347652	7906988	54	12
18	989078	1674155	59	21

Table 2. 37-cell CA results for the GKL rule with starting density constrained to 19.

being drawn into the wrong one of the two main attractors, a failure-mode which is easily detected by the above process.

At this point it is worth-while to introduce an image as to what we believe is happening. Those rules which perform well at density classification all seem to do so by forming 'domains', whereby regions which are locally 1-heavy form a solid block of 1s, and similarly for 0s. This can be seen in Figure 1, as can the subsequent blending of the two regions when the white (or 0) domain is on the left of the black (or 1) domain.

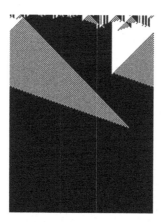

Fig. 1. Spacetime diagram for the GKL rule on a 149-cell CA.

In terms of what is happening in CA configuration-space, this corresponds to the movement from an arbitrary point in configuration-space to a quite small subspace (corresponding to the 'domain' configurations). The rule then processes these domains in ways that are now well-understood (It is largely in the first few time-steps that our understanding is uncertain). The domain-configurations therefore act as some sort of 'royal road' forward to the attractor: states typically do not move independently towards the attractor, they first converge on one of these special configurations. This goes some way to explaining why almost all configurations are Garden of Eden, even for extreme densities. The many precursor states do not pass through these configurations on their way to the attractor, but have already joined one of the royal roads.

We claim that in the above algorithm used to generate Table 1, the three time-steps moved forward usually corresponding to the movement from the arbitrary state to a domain state. This is in fact relatively easy to see from spacetime diagrams such as in Figure 2. This means that we are in fact investigating the back basin generated not from a 'random' configuration, but from precisely those configurations most important to the configuration's movement to the attractor.

Fig. 2. Two examples of substantial domain formation within three time-steps for a density classification rule (here, the GKL rule).

One useful side-effect of this phenomenon is that it is reasonably easy to generate the precursor states for domain configurations for a good density classification rule. If one has a local block of 1s, say, then any good rule will immediately extinguish an isolated 0 in that block. One can therefore 'seed' the existing domain structure with random 1s in the blocks of 0s, and/or random 0s in the blocks of 1s. This will generate a large number of precursors (for larger CAs, a vast number). One testable consequence of this argument is that from elementary combinatorial arguments we would expect that one will get far more precursors with approximately the same density as the 'seed' state than precursors with significantly different densities. This is because while we can seed the 1s with 0s, lowering the density, or the 0s with 1s, raising it, there are far more combinations where we do *both*, keeping the density approximately stable. This would suggest a roughly binomial distribution of densities around the existing density. This is precisely what can be observed, as in Figures 3 and 4.

4   Conclusions and Future Work

The backwards algorithm approach for the density classification problem provides an alternative formulation which avoids many of the problems intrinsic to

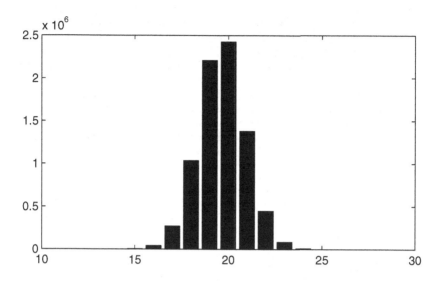

Fig. 3. Histogram of precursor densities for a configuration giving a high percentage correct (19 and above is super-critical density).

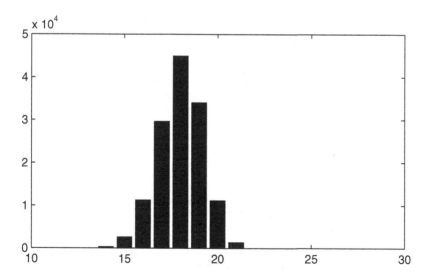

Fig. 4. Histogram of precursor densities for a configuration giving a low percentage correct (19 and above is super-critical density).

the standard forwards approach. At this early stage there remain several problems with the use of the backwards algorithm, but it has already provided a number of valuable insights into good density classification rules and the flows they create through configuration space. It is a sign of the value of the approach that the results obtained proved meaningful and consistent across different rules and CA sizes.

The main problem at this point is the wide variation in quantitative results obtained when sampling different parts of the attractor basin. This problem may be amenable to more detailed statistical analysis in future work, and to a deeper conceptual understanding of the 'royal road' paths through trajectory space created through domain formation.

5   Acknowledgements

The authors would like to thank Andy Wuensche for a number of useful discussions regarding his CA precursor algorithm.

References

[1] D. Andre, F. H. Bennett III, and J. R. Koza. Evolution of intricate long-distance communication signals in cellular automata using genetic programming. In *Artificial Life V: Proceedings of the Fifth International Workshop on the Synthesis and Simulation of Living Systems*. The MIT Press, 1996.

[2] T. R. J. Bossomaier, T. R. Cranny, and D. Schneider. A new paradigm for evolving cellular automata rules. In *Proc. Congress on Evolutionary Computation, Washington DC*, pages 169–176, 1999.

[3] T.R.J. Bossomaier, L. Sibley-Punnet, and T.R. Cranny. Basins of attraction and the density classification problem for cellular automata. Technical Report RRAI-01-00, Research Reports in Adaptive Informatics, Charles Sturt University, 2000.

[4] J. Conway. What is life? In E. Berlekamp, J. H. Conway, and R. Guy, editors, *Winning Ways for your Mathematical Plays*, volume 2. Academic Press, New York, 1982.

[5] T.R. Cranny. On the role of symmetry, structure and simplicity in emergent computation. Technical Report RRAI-99-02, Research Reports in Adaptive Informatics, Charles Sturt University, 1999.

[6] R. Das, J.P. Crutchfield, M. Mitchell, and J.E. Hanson. Evolving globally syncronized cellular automata. In L.J. Eshelamn, editor, *Proceedings of the Sixth International Conference on Genetic Algorithms*. Morgan-Kaufmann, 1995.

[7] R. Das, M. Mitchell, and J.P. Crutchfield. A genetic algorithm discovers particle-based computation in cellular automata. In Y. Davidor, H-P. Schwefel, and R. Maenner, editors, *Parallel Problem Solving from Nature - PPSN III*, volume 866 of *Lecture Notes in Computer Science*, pages 344–353. Springer-Verlag, 1994.

[8] P. Gacs, G.L. Kurdymunov, and L. Levin. One dimensional uniform arrays that wash out finite islands. *Problemy Peredachi Informatsii*, 12:92–98, 1978.

[9] H. Juillé and J. Pollack. Co-evolving the "ideal" trainer: application to the discovery of cellular automata rules. In *Proceedings of the Third Annual Genetic Programming Conference, GP-98*, 1998.

[10] M. Land and R.K. Belew. No two-state ca for density classification exists. *Physical Review Letters*, 74(25):5148–5150, 1995.

[11] A. Wuensche. Classifying cellular automata automatically. Technical Report 98-02-018, Santa Fe Institute Working Paper, 1998.

[12] A. Wuensche and M. Lesser. *The Global Dynamics of Cellular Automata*. Addison-Wesley, 1992.

Text-to-Audiovisual Speech Synthesizer

Udit Kumar Goyal, Ashish Kapoor and Prem Kalra

Department of Computer Science and Engineering,
Indian Institute of Technology, Delhi
pkalra@cse.iitd.ernet.in

Abstract. This paper describes a text-to-audiovisual speech synthesizer system incorporating the head and eye movements. The face is modeled using a set of images of a human subject. Visemes, that are a set of lip images of the phonemes, are extracted from a recorded video. A smooth transition between visemes is achieved by morphing along the correspondence between the visemes obtained by optical flows. This paper also describes methods for introducing nonverbal mechanisms in visual speech communication such as eye blinks and head nods. For eye movements, a simple mask based approach is used. View morphing is used to generate the head movement. A complete audiovisual sequence is constructed by concatenating the viseme transitions and synchronizing the visual stream with the audio stream. An effort has been made to integrate all these features into a single system, which takes text, head and eye movement parameters and produces the audiovisual stream.

1. Introduction

The visual channel in speech communication is of great importance, a view of a face can improve intelligibility of both natural and synthetic speech. Due to the bimodality in speech perception, audiovisual interaction becomes an important design factor for multimodal communication systems, such as video telephony and video conferencing. There has been much research that shows the importance of combined audiovisual testing for bimodal perceptional quality of video conferencing systems [1]. In addition to the bimodal characteristics of speech perception, speech production is also bimodal in nature. Moreover, visual signals can express emotions, add emphasis to the speech and support the interaction in a dialogue situation. This makes the use of a face to create audiovisual speech synthesis an exciting possibility, with applications such as multimodal user-interfaces. Text-to-visual speech synthesis (TTVS) systems have conventional applications in computer animation, its use in communication is becoming important as it offers a solution to human 'face to face' communication and human communication with a computer. These TTVS systems also find applications in graphical user interfaces and virtual reality where instead of being interested in face-to-face communication, we are interested in using a human-like or 'personable' talking head as an interface. These systems can be deployed as visual desktop agents, digital actors, and virtual avatars. This system can also be used as a tool to interpret lip and facial movements to help hearing-impaired to understand speech.

   This paper describes a text-to-audiovisual speech synthesizer system, which takes text as input and constructs an audiovisual sequence enunciating the text. This system introduces both eye and head movements to make the sequence more videorealistic.

J.-C. Heudin (Ed.): VW 2000, LNAI 1834, pp. 256-269, 2000.

The 3D model based facial animation techniques though may be flexible, lack video realism. In this paper, an image based approach has been used in which the facial model is constructed using a collection of images captured of the human subject. This results in a great improvement in the levels of video realism. Bregler, et al. [3] described an image based approach in which talking facial model was composed of a set of audiovisual sequences extracted from a large audiovisual corpus. Each short sequence corresponds to a triphone segment and a large database is built containing all the triphones. A new audiovisual sequence was constructed by concatenating the appropriate triphone sequences from the database. The problem with this approach was that it requires a very large number of images to cover all possible triphones context, which seems to be an overly redundant sampling of human lip configurations.

Cosatto and Graf [4] have described an approach, which attempts to reduce this redundancy by parameterizing the space of lip positions, mainly the lip width, position of the upper lip, and the position of the lower lip. This lip space was then populated using images from the recorded corpus. Synthesis was performed by traversing trajectories in that imposed lip space. The trajectories were created using Cohen-Massaro's coarticulation rules [5]. The problem with this approach was that if the lip space was not densely populated, the animations might produce jerks.

Another approach was used by Scott, et al. [6] in which facial model was composed of a set of 40-50 visemes, which were the visual manifestation of phonemes. They have used a morphing algorithm that is capable of transitioning smoothly between the various mouth shapes. However, morphing required a lot of user intervention, making the process tedious and complicated. This work was further explored by Tonny Ezzat and Tomaso Poggio [7]. They use a method for morphing developed by Beymer, et al. [8], which did not require user intervention and was capable of modeling rigid facial transformations such as pose changes and non-rigid transformations such as smiles.

This paper explores further the use of viseme morphing representation for synthesis of human visual speech by introducing nonverbal mechanisms in visual speech communication such as eye blinks, eye gaze changes, eye brow movements and head nods due to which the talking facial model has became more lifelike. One approach was proposed by Tony Ezzat and Poggio [9] using a learning network, but that was found to be computationally inefficient. For eye movements, a simple cut-and-paste approach has been used. Head movements are generated using view morphing [10] in which valid intermediate views are generated by extending the existing morphing techniques.

2. Overview

An overview of the system is shown in figure 1. For converting text to speech (TTS), Festival speech synthesis system is used which was developed by Alan Black, Paul Taylor, and colleagues at the University of Edinburgh [14]. Festival system contains Natural Language Processing (NLP) unit which takes text as an input and produces the timing and phonetic parameters. It also contains an audio speech-processing module that converts the input text into an audio stream enunciating the text

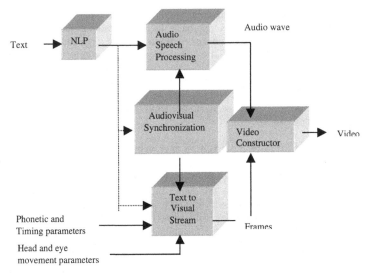

Fig. 1. Overview of the TTVS System.

One primary concern is synthesis of the visual speech streams. The entire task of visual speech processing can be divided into three sub-tasks: firstly, to develop a *text to visual stream* module that will convert the phonetic and timing output streams generated by Festival system into a visual stream of a face enunciating that text. Secondly, to develop an *audiovisual synchronization* module that will synchronize the audio and visual streams so as to produce the final audiovisual stream. Thirdly, to extend visual speech processing module to take head and eye movement parameters as input, and reflect the corresponding changes in the visual streams so as to make the facial animation more lifelike.

3. Text-to-Audiovisual Stream Conversion

The entire process of text-to-audiovisual stream conversion can be divided into four sub-tasks: viseme extraction, morphing, morph concatenation, and finally audiovisual synchronization. These sub-tasks are discussed in detail in the ensuing sections.

3.1 Viseme Extraction

The basic assumption of facial synthesis used in this approach is that the complete set of mouth shapes associated with human speech is spanned by a finite set of *visemes*. The term *viseme* is used to denote lip image extracted for the phoneme. Due to this assumption, a particular visual corpus has to be recorded which elicitates one instantiation for each viseme.

Since the Festival TTS system produces a stream of phonemes corresponding to an input text, there is a need to *map* from the set of phonemes used by the TTS to a set of visemes so as to produce the visual stream. If all the American English phonemes are covered, the one-to-one mapping between the phonemes and visemes will result in a total of 52 images, out of which 24 represent the consonants, 12 represents the monophthong, and 16 represent the diphthongs. Since current viseme literature indicates that mapping between phonemes and visemes are many-to-one, the viseme set is reduced by grouping the visemes together that are visually alike. This results in the reduction of total number of visemes, six represent the 24 consonants, seven represent the 12 monophthong phonemes and one for silence viseme.

For diphthongs, that are vocalic phonemes involving a quick transition between two underlying vowel nuclei, we use two images to model them visually, one to represent the first vowel nucleus and the other to represent the second. All these vowel nuclei are represented by the corresponding monophthong visemes. The only exception occurs in case of two nuclei: second nucleus of \au\ diphthong and first nucleus of the \ou\ diphthong. For them, two separate visemes are extracted. Hence, the final reduced set contains a *total of 16 visemes* that are to be extracted.

monophthongs		consonants	
/ i, ii /	sh**ee**p	/ p, b, m /	a**b**out
/ a, e /	b**e**d	/ f, v /	**f**ather
/ aa, o /	f**a**ther	/t, d, s, z, th, dh/	**th**ank
/ uh, @ /	b**u**d	/ w, r /	**w**as
/ ir /	b**ir**d	/ch, jh, sh, jh /	**sh**eep
/ oo /	b**au**d	/ k, g, n, l, ng, h, y/	**k**ey
/ uu, u /	b**oo**t		
diphthongs			
/ w-au /	ab**ou**t		
/ o-ou /	b**oa**t		

Fig. 2. Phonemes recorded for extracting visemes. The underlined portion of each word corresponds to the target phoneme being recorded.

Initially, a video of a human subject enunciating a set of keywords is recorded. A set of keywords is chosen in such a way that it covers all the required phonemes. The recorded corpus is shown in the figure 2. After the recording of whole corpus, it is digitized and one viseme is extracted for each phoneme.

The final reduced set of extracted visemes is shown in figure 3. As the figure shows, a single viseme is extracted for many phonemes as they look alike visually.

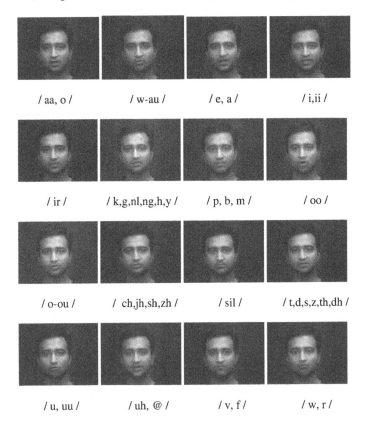

Fig. 3. Reduced set of extracted visemes

3.2 Morphing

After extracting all the visemes, a correspondence between two visemes is computed using optical flow as given by Horn and Schnuck [11]. Optical flow technique has been used since visemes belong to one single object that is undergoing motion. An advantage of using optical flow technique is that it allows automatic determination of correspondence vectors between the source and destination images. A smooth transition between viseme images is achieved using morphing along the correspondence between the visemes. In the morphing process, first forward and reverse warping is carried out to produce intermediate warps, which are then cross-dissolved to produce the intermediate morphs.

3.3 Morph Concatenation

To construct a visual stream of the input text, we simply concatenate the appropriate viseme morphs together. For example, the word **"man"**, which has a phonetic transcription of \m-a-n\, is composed of two visemes morphs transitions \m-a\ and \a-n\, that are then put together and played seamlessly one right after the another. It also includes the transition from silence viseme in the start and at the end of the word.

3.4 Audiovisual Synchronization

After constructing the visual stream, next step is to synchronize the visual stream with the audio stream. To synchronize the audio speech stream and the visual stream, the total duration T of the audio stream is computed as follows.

$$T = \Sigma_i \, l(D_i) \tag{1}$$

where, $l(D_i)$ denotes the duration (in sec) of each diphone D_i as computed by Festival system.

Viseme transition streams are then created consisting of two endpoint visemes and the optical flow correspondence vectors between them. The duration of each viseme transition $l(V_i)$ is set to be equal to the duration of corresponding diphone $l(D_i)$. The start index in time of each viseme transition $s(V_i)$ is computed as

$$s(V_i) = \begin{cases} 0 & \text{if } i=0 \\ s(V_{i-1})+l(V_{i-1}) & \text{otherwise} \end{cases} \tag{2}$$

Finally, the *video stream* is constructed by a sequence of frames that sample the chosen viseme transitions. For a frame rate F, we need to create TF frames. This implies that start index in time of kth frame is

$$s(F_k) = \frac{k}{F} \tag{3}$$

The frames are then synthesized by setting the morph parameter for each frame to be

$$s_k = \frac{s(F_k) - s(V_i)}{l(V_i)} \qquad \text{if } s(F_k) - s(V_i) < l(V_i) \qquad \textbf{(4)}$$

The morph parameter is simply the ratio of the time elapsed from the start of a viseme transition to the frame, and the entire duration of the viseme transition. The condition on right hand side of the above equation ensures that correct viseme is chosen to synchronize a particular frame. Considering figure 4, it implies that frames 0,1,2,3, and 4 are synthesized from the \m-a\ viseme transition, while frames 5,6,7,8 and 9 are synthesized from the \a-n\ viseme transition.

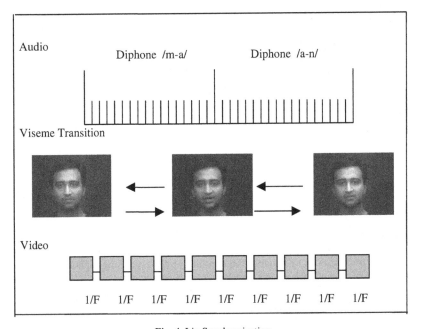

Fig. 4. Lip Synchronization

The variation of the morph parameter α for each viseme transition is shown in figure 5. This indicates that for each viseme transition, the morph parameter α varies linearly from 0 to 1 resulting in the saw-tooth type variation.

Finally, each frame is synthesized using the morph algorithm discussed earlier and hence, the final visual sequence is constructed by concatenating the viseme transitions, played in synchrony with the audio speech signal generated by the TTS system. It has been found that lip-sync module produces very good quality synchronization between the audio and the video.

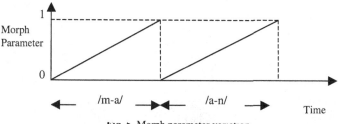

Fig. 5. Morph parameter variation

4. Eye Movement

Although conversion of text to audiovisual speech stream gives good animation results, yet the video does not look much video realistic since only the lips of the face are moving. As a step towards making it more video realistic, eye movement has been incorporated in the facial model.

A simple *mask-based* approach has been used to incorporate eye movement in the facial model. Since eyes affect only upper portion of the face and do not overlap with the lip movement, mask-based approach can be used. First, images are extracted for the various eye movements like opening and closing of eyes, raised eyebrows, eyeball movement, etc. While taking the sample images, it has been assumed that head remains still in all the sample images. A *base* image of the face is taken which in our case is taken to be the same as /sil/ viseme. The next step is to define a mask that consists of all the pixels contained in the portion covered by left and the right eye.

After defining the mask, depending on the parameters that control the position of the eye, morphing is carried out between the source and destination images. Source image is taken to be the base image and destination image can be closed eye image, raised eyebrow image, or left eyeball movement image, etc. The intermediate image is determined using the morph eye parameter, the mask is then applied to the intermediate image to find the intermediate eye position, which is then pasted on an image of the face giving the resulting intermediate image. Since, the eye movement is performed in parallel with the text-to-audiovisual conversion, the image on which the eye mask is pasted, is taken to be the intermediate image generated during the text-to-audiovisual stream conversion process. In this way, the effect of eye movements is achieved in parallel with the text-to-audiovisual conversion, thus resulting in an increase in video-realism. This is shown in figure 6.

We have associated separate parameters with the eye movement. These parameters will be the start time and the duration of eye movement. The start time can also be specified as a percentage of the entire duration of the audiovisual stream. From the start time and the duration of the eye movement, end time of the eye movement can be determined.

Base image with closed eyes

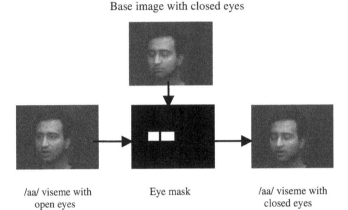

/aa/ viseme with   Eye mask   /aa/ viseme with
open eyes   closed eyes

Fig. 6. Eye Masking

During this duration, the eye movement is carried out such that eyes will first make transition from open eyes to closed eyes for half of the duration, and closed to open eyes for the remaining half of duration of eye movement.

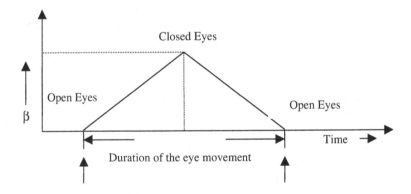

Fig. 7. Transitions for eye movement

This transition from open to closed eyes and vice versa is controlled by a separate morph parameter β. This parameter will control the extent of morph that is to be done to determine the intermediate position of eyes in the image. As figure 7 indicates, the morph parameter β varies linearly from 0 to 1 to produce intermediate eye images for open to close eyes transition for half of the duration and then varies linearly from 1 to 0 for close to open eyes transition for the rest of the duration.

5. Head Movement

The head being stable for a long time makes an impression of a dummy. The head movement is introduced to make the animation more realistic. We use view morphing approach as proposed by Seitz and Dyer [10] to interpolate human face in different poses. View morphing is a simple extension of the normal morphing technique that allows current morphing techniques to synthesize changes in viewpoint and other 3D effects. This technique is *shape-preserving* i.e., from two images of a particular object, it produces a new image representing a view of the same object.

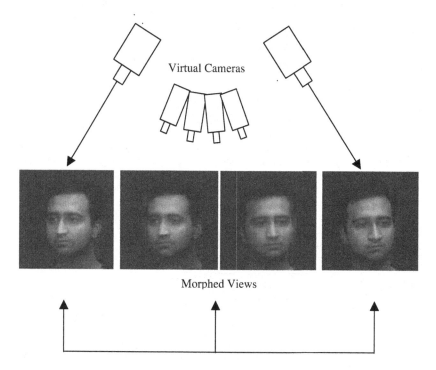

Virtual Cameras

Morphed Views

Fig. 8. View morphing of an object taken from the different viewpoints produces intermediate images that preserve the shape.

If the different views of the same object are parallel, then normal morphing techniques produce valid intermediate views. The term *valid* means that they preserves the shape. However, for non-parallel views, the intermediate views are not valid, i.e. they do not preserve the shape. To generate the valid intermediate views I_α between two images I_0 and I_1, where α lies between 0 and 1, Seitz [10] described an approach which requires following steps:

a) Prewarping the images I_0 and I_1.
b) Generate intermediate image $I_\alpha\tilde{}$ from the prewarped images using morphing techniques.
c) Postwarp image $I_\alpha\tilde{}$ to produce final intermediate view I_α

The reader is referred to [10] for details of this approach. As shown in figure 8, it appears that the intermediate images are the head image at the intermediate positions (α=0.7, α=0.3) while moving from left to right. In our case, during the construction of visual stream, a pause is inserted in the visual stream. During the pause interval, head is moved from left to right or vice-versa to give a feel of realistic animation with head turning. Similarly, effects such as head nod and head roll can be produced using this approach.

6. Integration

This system conceives speech – affecting a part of the mouth, expressions – consisting of eye movements, and head movements as three channels or streams. The integration of these channels involves superposition or overlaying of associated actions to each channel. This requires temporal specification of each action constituting a particular channel. This contains the start and the duration of the action. A scripting language may be designed to incorporate the action schedule of actions in all three channels. Figure 9 depicts temporal integration of channels in a form of action chart.

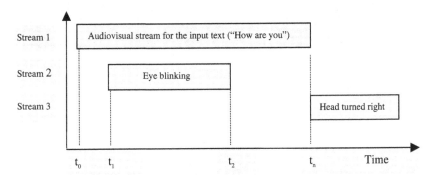

Fig. 9. Integration of the system

7. Results

We have developed a text-to-audiovisual speech synthesizer system. Several audiovisual sentences are synthesized to test the process of visual speech synthesis, audio synchronization, eye and head movements. Some of the generated audiovisual sequences can be accessed at http://www.cse.iitd.ernet.in/~pkalra/VW2000/results.

These include sequences where the actor speaks sentences like 'Let me tell where you have gone' and 'Good Morning Sir, thank you for coming here'. Some sentences with simultaneous non-verbal clues like eye blinks have also been generated. Finally, an example is included where all three channels --speech, eye movements and head movement -- have been integrated. Figure 10 shows a sequence where the model speaks a sentence while blinking its eyes and then turns its head from left to right.

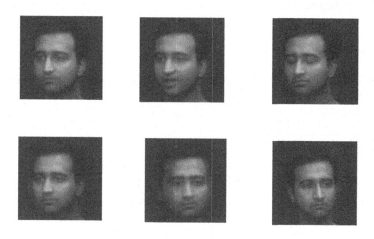

Fig. 10. A generated audiovisual sequence where the model first speaks, blinks its eye and then turns its head.

There are some constraints imposed in the process of sequence generation. While recording the video sequence, the subject should refrain from moving the head. If there is a relative head movement among the images, it may cause discontinuity or jerkiness in the animation. Similarly, artifacts may be observed while masking for eye movements, when images get miss-aligned due to the head movement. Methods for stablizing are being explored to account for small head movements.

8. Conclusion

In this paper we present, a text-to-audiovisual speech synthesis system capable of carrying out text to audiovisual conversion. The efforts have been mainly focused on making the system more video-realistic. This system also takes care of nonverbal mechanisms for visual speech communication like eye blinking, eye ball movement, eyebrow raising, etc. In addition, the system includes head movement, which has been incorporated during the pause or at the end of the sentence.

The work is being extended to introduce co-articulation in the facial model [15]. The lack of parameterization in the image-based model makes it difficult to use the techniques used in 3D facial animation models for introducing co-articulation. The introduction of co-articulation in the synthesis would further improve the audiovisual realism of the system. Introducing composition of speech with facial expressions that affect the mouth region can further enhance the system. The Festival system supports intonation parameters, we plan to incorporate them to change the emotion accordingly. Further there is a need to incorporate the head movement while enunciating the text.

Acknowledgments

Authors would like to extend their thanks to Vineet Rajosi Sharma, who helped in getting the samples made.

References

1. Tsuhan Chen and Ram R. Rao, *Audio-Visual Integration in Multimodal Communication,* Proc. IEEE, Vol 86, No. 5, pages 837-852.

2. G. Wolberg. Digital Image Warping, IEEE Computer Society Press, Los Alamitos, *C.A., 1990.*

3. C.Bergler, M.Covell and M.Slaney. *Video Rewrite. Driving visual speech with audio.* In SIGGRAPH'97 Proceedings, Los Angeles, CA, August 1997.

4. E.Cosatto   and   H.Graf. *Sample based synthesis of photorealistic talking heads.* In Proceedings of Computer Animation'98, pages 103-110, Philadelphia, Pennsylvania, 1998.

5. M.M.Cohen and D.W.Massaro, *Modeling coarticulation in synthetic visual speech.* In N.M.Thalmann and D.Thalmann, editors, Models and Techniques in Computer Animation, pages 138-156, Springer-Verley, Tokyo, 1993.

6. S.H.Watson, J.P.Wright, K.C.Scott, D.S.Kagels, D.Freda and K.J.Hussey. *An advanced morphing algorithm for interpolating phoneme images to simulate* speech. Jet Propulsion Laboratory, California Institute of Technology, 1997.

7. Tony Ezzat and Tomaso Poggio. *Visual Speech Synthesis by Morphing Visemes (MikeTalk).* A.I Memo No: 1658, MIT AI Lab, May 1999.

8. D.Beymer, A. Shashua and   T. Poggio. *Example based image analysis and synthesis.* Technical Report 1431, MIT AI Lab, 1993.

9. Tony Ezzat and Tomaso Poggio. *Facial Analysis and Synthesis using Image-Based Models.* In Proceedings of the Workshop on the Algorithmic Foundations of Robotics, Toulouse, France, August 1996.

10. Steven M. Seitz and Charles R. Dyer. *View Morphing.* In Proceedings of SIGGRAPH'96, pages 21-30, 1996.

11. B.K.P Horn and B.G.Schnuck. *Determining Optical flow.* Artificial Intelligence, 17:185-203, 1981.

12. F. Parke and K. Waters. *Computer Facial Animation.* A. K. Peters, Wellesley, Massachusetts, 1996.

13. Alan Watt and Fabio Policarpo. *The Computer Image.* ACM Press, New York, SIGGRAPH Series, New York.

14. Black and P.Taylor. *The Festival Speech Synthesis System.* University of Edinburgh, 1997.

15. Catherine Pelachaud. Communication and Coarticulation in Facial Animation. Ph.D. Thesis, Department of Computer and Information Science, Univ. of Pennsylvania, Philadelphia, 1991.

Virtual Environments for Visually Impaired

Sudhanshu Kumar Semwal and Debra Lee Evans-Kamp

Department of Computer Science, University of Colorado at Colorado Springs,
Colorado Springs, CO, 80933-7150, USA
semwal@redcloud.uccs.edu

Abstract. We provide a systematic study for generating interactive,
virtual environments for the blind. We present our system as a tool
for shape recognition and mobility training for the blind. In our system, head movement can be detected to indicate horizontal and vertical
movements. Audio feedback is used for reinforcement. Our experiment
for shape learning can guide the user in tracing the surface of a sphere
by using the audio feedback. We also present a compelling case for using
force feedback devices for visually impaired, and our experience with the
PHANToM(TM) force feedback device is summarized. A detailed survey
of present research is also presented.

1 Introduction

The number of visually disabled people in the world is expected to double in the
next fifteen years, mostly in poorer countries and among the aged. Currently,
fifty-five percent of the blind population live alone [34]. A visual impairment can
be since birth (congenitally blind), or can also occur later in life (late blind).
Blind children typically have difficulty with tasks requiring mental spatial organization, such as rotations and orientations [7]. The fundamental question is:
What is really involved in spatial thinking? What is missing and needed to help
a blind child capture spatial knowledge? [7]. In the past, the dominant mode
for producing visual information was by printing it on paper. For the blind it
meant learning Braille or having someone read and describe the material to
them. Today, electronic coded information is displayed on computer terminals
using refreshable Braille displays, and speech synthesizers [9].

Graphical information can be displayed by using tactile displays. For example, aluminum sheets have been used to provide variable height tactile pictures.
Uniform height pictures are used for two dimensional information or line drawings. Bar graphs can be displayed using swell paper where a thermo pen is used
on special paper that swells underneath it, or a photocopy of the picture is run
through a swell paper machine. The above approaches are *manually* done. Today, however, graphical pictures also can have new meaning (icons) associated
with them. These "icons" are used to represent a concept, such as a computer
program being represented by a square with a name attached inside it. These
GUIs require direct manipulation of graphic objects which is difficult for visually impaired persons. With electronic information being transmitted over phone

J.-C. Heudin (Ed.): VW 2000, LNAI 1834, pp. 270–285, 2000.

lines at fast speeds, the Internet has become a source and a viable option for unlimited information. Real-time graphics and sound are exciting, but they leave the visually impaired "out in the cold". The exploration of these worlds are difficult for them. Once it was thought that new technology would help the visually impaired, but now it seems to have caused severe problems for them.

Computer image recognition is promising but image recognition and analysis of images to obtain precise meaning is difficult because images can have arbitrary complexity in comparison to characters. Once again, human intervention may be necessary [9]. In Kurze's, a moderator describes graphical information by using software that a blind user would explore and use later [41]. Auditory displays use speech or non-speech sound to convey the different components of the graphical user interface to the blind [9]. This work has been done by Mynatt on the Mercator system [10], and by many others on the European TIDE project for the development of Graphical User Interface for Blind People, GUIB [41].

Graphs, maps and histograms may represent complex information. More complex forms are photos, videos and animated graphics that represent real world scenes. How are these to be presented to the blind? To present useful and meaningful descriptions to the blind, spatio-temporal relationships between objects or images need to be modeled. Work has been done by many educators and psychologists in trying to understand the blind's concept of space. Their work has been primarily concerned with mobility training for the blind, such as orientation and mobility training (O and M) methods, using a cane, a tactile map or sound locator [39]. How the blind "see" 3D-space and how this is converted into 2D-space has been the study of cognitive maps. These studies are pertinent to the field of virtual reality and graphics where we consider the aspect of modeling the visual world for the blind.

We begin with some psychological and perception issues in Sections 2-4. Difference in sighted and visually impaired persons are highlighted in Sections 5-8. Existing software systems are summarized in Sections 9 and 10. Our experiments in providing directional mobility and shape learning using sound are in Sections 11 and 12. Sections 13 and 14 contain description of our sense of touch experiments. Conclusions are in Section 15.

2 Psychological Background

"How we understand and represent the space around us is part of how we think and act (p.8 in [1])." The question then is: *How do we develop this perception of space for a blind person?* Our spatial world is not just 3D objects and textures which we see, it also includes the ability to perceive and discriminate locations in spatial environments [20]. Spatial perception described by Millar is shape and spatial coding. Shape recognition is identifying an object's shape by distinctive features via contours. Spatial coding, that is locating an object in space, requires some frame of reference to know where that object is, such as the box is by the door. Spatial tasks examples are: defining shapes, locating an object, moving in 3D space, pointing to an object, performing actions, such as measuring, or changing direction [1]. The array of visual stimuli bestows a mental model of our 3D world. But, this visual perception is fostered by the interplay of information coming from many different sources.

3   Senses and Our Perception

In [9], sensory inputs are described from a mechanical view. Electronic transducers transform different types of energy found in the physical universe, such as mechanical pressure, chemical bonding, thermal gradation, etc., into electrical impulses that can be interpreted by the brain. Vision is the most obvious source of spatial information [1,20,3]. Yet, Heller [20] showed that when vision was obscured through stained glass, shape recognition was not as precise as touch alone. But, when touch and obscured vision were combined, shape recognition was better than either touch or obscured vision. Heller also showed that texture recognized visually or tactilely was perceived usually equivalently. When touch was combined with vision, texture recognition improved [20]. Millar in 1971 [1] showed how three and four-year-olds could match 3D arbitrary shapes using vision or touch alone, or with both. Auditory input can be dominant over vision when dealing with the perception of time-related events; if discrepancies arise involving temporal rates, auditory information dominates vision [20]. When infants hear a sound, they move their heads and eyes in the sound's direction [1]. Dobb in 1983 [4] showed that seeing mouth gestures as well as hearing a word pronounced helps with word clarity.

We must note that there is a difference in perception between a person blind since birth, blind some years after birth, and a person with proper eyesight. Millar [1] states that vision, hearing, touch, taste, and smell are senses that give specific information about our world. Yet, they provide interrelated information that come together and partly overlap in our brain, thus affecting our perception. This overlapping provides a redundancy that is needed, especially in development of infants and young children. One example is the explanation about depth perception. Multiple inputs help when conditions of uncertainty impair the dominant sense, such as vision. This is seen in night vision with the use of touch and sound as aids. Millar states that convergence of simultaneous inputs from different senses is the norm rather than the exception in our world. Yet, they may not convey the same information. For example, two eyes are better than one because two eyes give two different views of the same scene creating depth perception [1].

4   Inter-relationship of Senses

Touch and movement give spatial references in relationship to our body [5]. Millar's studies have shown that the movement-based and body-centered strategies create correct solutions to spatial problems [1,5]. The important point is that another sense can provide information about a concept when a sense is not present. This sensory information may be different, causing the concept to be encoded differently and causing the problem-solving approach to be different, but not less accurate. The empiricist's view that senses are separate, and their information cannot be replaced, is therefore not complete. If this was so, a blind child could never play chess, but they do. Ungar, Blades and Spencer [6] point out studies where adults use self-reference or body-centered coding strategies when external cues are unreliable as at night. Millar points out that congenitally blind children also use body-centered references because they are the most appropriate means to solve spatial tasks [1,5,6].

The unitarian idea accounts for other senses providing similar information about the world, such as the way in which human vision, touch and movement convey spatial information. Dealing with spatial information, Stein in 1991 [12] discovered that the brain also converges the stimulation from proprioceptive, auditory, vestibular and limb movement which is necessary for motor control. The proprioceptive senses are the nerve terminals in the muscles, tendons, and joints, which relay information about the position of body parts relative to each other [1]. Vestibular sense, controlled by the body's inner ear [11], balances one's body. Having sensory information that is convergent and complementary is not enough if a sense is removed. Redundancy and convergence does not completely replace information that is lost from a sense that is missing [7]. For example, visual deprivation from birth leads to changes in the visual cortex of the brain which is not reversible [1]. Information from a deprived sense must still be supplied somehow through the complementary senses to ensure the needed redundancy and specialization for a particular concept. This is done by giving the complementary senses more opportunity to supply information to an individual. An example of providing information about external surfaces and planes usually supplied by vision would be to extend a person's experiences with their proprioceptive and kinesthetic senses [7]. The kinesthetic sense provides information about the movements of the body and its interaction with the environment [1]. Thus, Virtual Worlds, which encourage constant 3D-interaction can be natural choices for visually impaired persons.

A blind child's perception of a square is different than a sighted child's perception, though both understand that the object is a square. The blind child perceives a cube as six flat surfaces with straight equal length edges that are connected at corners in a special way. All this is "felt" with the hands and arm movements. In visual perception, one would not see all the sides of a cube, because some would be occluded, yet one would know it was a cube. Both modes of information lead to the same symbolism of a cube, but the perception of a cube is obtained in completely different ways. Perception is not just influenced by how we encode our sensory information, but also by a person's prior knowledge. Sensory information can be perceived differently based on a person's prior learning [1]. An example is when a congenitally blind and a late blind person were asked by Kurze [27,28] to draw a table on swell paper. The late blind said they had a "visual image" of the shape and drew the table from this image. The images looked like pictures drawn by sighted people. The congenitally blind drew the table using tactile contours, surfaces to edges. Shapes were defined by their surrounding edges. The table had folded out legs extended from the top surface. This is how the congenitally blind perceived a table based on prior knowledge [27,28].

5   Sensory Deprivation and Sensory Training Issues

Three different ideas dealing with the sensory deprivation are discussed by Fletcher [8]. The first is based on the empiricist view. It is called the Deficiency Theory. If one is blind, then spatial concepts are impossible to develop without vision. This theory is mainly dismissed as incorrect. The second theory is the Inefficiency Theory. If one is blind, then spatial concepts and representations are developed but are inferior to the sighted. This is based on Piaget's view and also the views of some of Gibson's followers. The third is the Difference Theory. The visually impaired build a set of spatial relations, which are functionally equivalent to the sighted. This stage takes longer to achieve and is acquired by the blind person by alternate means. Millar also holds this point of view [6]. Millar points out that infants and young children lack knowledge and maturity which produces conditions of uncertainty. With redundant information from their environment, i.e., sensory information, greater familiarity occurs.

This suggests that by adding more experience at a younger age through haptic and movement inputs for the blind child, along with hearing, more synaptic neuron connections between the posterior parietal cortex, auditory and movement control systems can develop. Senses converge to bimodal neurons in certain areas of the brain and the brain's neural connections are more malleable at a younger age. By providing experiences that would provide redundant information, such as spatial coding information, for a blind child, tasks, i.e., spatial tasks, would become familiar. The child would increase the probability of making inferences and solving problems. An example is emphasizing and providing opportunities using more body-centered reference cues as external frames. Mental spatial reorganization should then improve [1,7]. By providing additional and complementary information to a sense-deprived child through the remaining sensory routes, and believing that the brain's makeup includes converging interrelated sensory-networks, the necessary redundancy and balance of information can be restored. This would provide a mature knowledge base for the child. Ambiguities and disparities in the environment would diminish. The child's activities and responses to his environment would be efficient. The child would organize information in appropriate mental representation and symbolic thought.

The problem is to decide what substitutional information is needed to overlap and converge with existing coding schemas for a blind child. This implies figuring out what complementary sense needs to be used. The haptic-proprioceptive senses provide precise spatial data within the scope of the body [1,5,6,7].

An example of substituting sensory information by using a complementary sense such as hearing is Bower's study. In 1977, Bower [13] showed that an ultrasonic device developed by Leslie Kay attached to a head band could be used by a blind baby to locate objects. Ultrasonic devices did have a detrimental effect when natural occurring sounds cannot be heard. It is important to understand what information needs to be supplied and by what means. This is no small task.

Warren [14] discusses studies that examine the differences between perceptions of shape, texture and spatial location using touch and vision. He states there is no general rule of perception for shape and spatial location though touch and vision as sensory information is closely related.

6 Shape Recognition and Small Scale Spatial Skills in the Blind

In Millar's work, body movements are used in small shape recognition and small spatial coding. Spatial coding is the coding which uses a reference to establish a distance or direction of an object with respect to oneself or external reference frames [1]. Small scale spatial coding is locating objects within arm's length of your body. Mental imagery does not have to only relate to human vision, but can relate to body movements. An object can be recognized by its contours. For the blind, recognizing small 3D shapes, active touch and movement by the hands are important. But, this exploration has to be systematic, using knowledge about where to start and stop. Also, the person needs to have prior knowledge of the forms not just its contours. Shape recognition methods change with the size of an object. To shape code larger 3D objects larger body-hand movements are needed. In identifying large objects, active movements are used. Joints and stretching muscles get into the act. These movements need to be coordinated to explore and recognize a large shape. Identifying objects requires a frame of reference. For the blind this reference frame or anchor is usually the body [1]. Mental imagery can be derived from all senses. The blind can derive mental images from the senses they have, especially audition and touch [6].

7 Orientations and the Blind

Some orientations are easier to code than others for all humans. Surprisingly, the vertical upright and straight ahead projection are easier than the horizontal orientations. The hardest is the oblique, which requires three reference planes to establish the angle the object is tilted at. Vertical direction for spatial coding is related to gravity. We have a mid-body axis that is kept in line with gravity. Vertical directions are the most accurate with vision or without, because many proprioceptive sources are involved, such as the spinal cord alignment. With vision, straight-ahead directions are easy to assess. Horizontal directions are easier to detect in the light than dark, because there are less proprioceptive sources involved than in vertical directions and external references are needed for proper alignment, thus vision is needed [1].

It has been shown that vertical directions are easier to remember than horizontal, because the body is upright and coincides with vertical directions [15]. The difficulty in coding vertical, horizontal and oblique directions depends on the amount of consistent and unambiguous information that is available. Thus, oblique directions have the least sensory information available versus the other directions, and requires more mental work with the three reference planes [1].

8 Large Scale Spatial Coding and Blind Mobility

Mobility of the blind requires large scale spatial coding which uses more than one form of coding. This coding can be in terms of external cues, frames, configurations, body-centered frames, and memory of movement information. When a person moves, it is not appropriate to use only body-centered cues, instead it is possible to code movements in terms of kinesthetic sequences which can be remembered. These mental configurations are called cognitive maps. Ungar et. al. has suggested using tactile maps to assist in creating cognitive maps for the child [6].

9 Existing Software Systems

The usual input and output devices for the blind are based on audio and tactile representations, e.g., desktop with folders [16]. A data glove with simple gesturing can also be used for selecting a folder by counting the fingers held up. Color can be described by verbal description and by varying sound pitch frequencies to emphasize its intensity [16]. Body tracking can be used to convey 3D spatial information, e.g., moving one's arm from the shoulder in circular movements to communicate a conical shape. Vanderheiden, et. al., suggests using many technologies for input and output channels to present information. This will encourage the disabled to use as many senses as possible which will provide redundant experiences [16], which follows Millar's ideas.

Examples of a www-based system are ACCESS and V-Lynx. ACCESS Project [29] presents hypermedia information in Braille, synthetic speech and sound with navigation facilities. ACCESS is another project funded by TIDE. V-Lynx is a WWW client that uses audio output for documents obtained from a WWW server. Lynx is a full text-mode browser from the University of Kansas [41].

Conveying pictorial images or 3D objects to the blind use various aural devices. The first system is developed by Meijer [30], called vOICe. It takes a picture from an attached video camera which is converted into a digitized image of 64 X 64 pixels. A sound is associated with each pixel. If the pixel is on a high row, the sound has a high tone; if low, then a low tone. The brighter the pixel the louder the sound. Shading is reduced to sixteen levels. The image-to- sound mapping has been implemented in Java and can be browsed on the WWW [30]. Agranovski, Evreinov and Yashkin [31] developed a graphic audio display that used special acoustic cursors moving in space. Hollander [32] investigates auditory shape perception. He develops a system which uses HRTF functions loaded into a Crystal River Convolvotron. At the Vision Systems Group at Dublin City University a system is being developed that converts visual information, such as shape, color and motion, using auditory outputs, and auditory visualization techniques [33].

10   Systems Using Sound Feedback for the Blind

The human hearing system's acoustic channel has a large, effective bandwidth, up to 10 kHz, to convey information. The ear is capable of processing and interpreting complicated, and rapidly changing sound patterns [41]. Auditory modality is ideal for alerting and conveying changes in an environment. However, one can only handle a limited number of sounds simultaneously [10].

Humans can recognize up to 120 taped spoken words per minute [33]. This is one reason speech synthesizers are used so abundantly, besides being commercially available and cost effective. Non-speech sounds are used to compensate lengthy verbal descriptions. Non-speech sounds have the potential of communicating complex messages to the listener [35] without interfering with other modalities. The non-speech sounds come in an assortment, e.g., tones and musical sounds [40]. However, there is a variation from listener to listener in the interpretation of sound [31]. It was shown in [36] that visually impaired users preferred using tonal sounds when trying to locate a target in 3D space, while the sighted preferred musical environments [36]. With Mercator [10, users compared 8kHz tones as being harsh and low frequency sounds being "industrial."

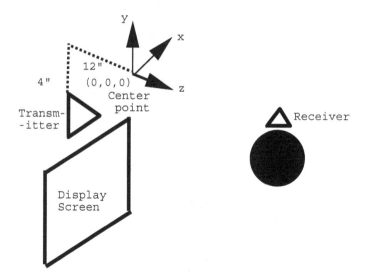

Fig. 1. The Logitech Headtracker using transmitter and receiver.

Virtual environments can help, as Braille-literacy rate can differ and be very low in some societies. For example, in Europe only 20 percent of the blind can read Braille. Tactile displays, such as pin matrix arrays, and Braille keyboards are expensive and only a few are capable of using them [1,28,34]. The Haptic feedback devices like the PHANToM or Pantograph offer high resolution at one point on a virtual surface, but two-handed exploration is not possible [28]. Haptic sense has a low bandwidth communication channel. Haptic exploration interprets information sequentially, though it has been shown that shapes of letters are recognized when a small shape impression is applied to the skin [1]. The movement over a pattern improves perception [1]. The Optacon is a vibrotactile stimulator that dynamically displays shapes of letters that have been scanned by a camera. The vibrating pattern can be felt by passive finger-tips [26]. Its success is varied [1.37]. Reading rates are 30 to 60 words per minute. Normal braille reading speeds are 50 to 80 wpm. Another example of recent passive devices are single-cell braille displays, which display one braille character at a time. With passive single-cell displays, the finger has trouble feeling the transition from one character to the next . This also results in a slower reading rate than normal braille reading [26]. Millar's research, as discussed before, shows active hand and body movement are needed in small and large scale spatial and shape recognition using 3D objects or 2D tactile maps [1].

Visual to haptic representation implies a drastic reduction in the amount of information. Getting an overview of the visual representation is not possible in haptic experiences. The "picture" needs to be presented in smaller sections. Exploration over time and integration of information give rise to clearer perception. Although the fingers have good discriminative abilities, too much detail presented to the haptic senses leads to coding confusion [1]. Although visual properties, shape and size can be translated into haptic coding, haptic and visual mapping is not one to one. Color is one of those properties that cannot be translated into an haptic form [9].

Karshmer puts forth the need to conduct experiments to establish a better understanding of the physical and mental needs of the blind, so better tools

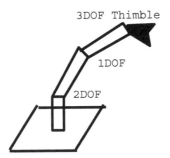

Fig. 2. The PHANToM force feedback device. The user can insert one finger in the thimble at the end of robotic arm and feel 3D-surfaces.

can be developed [18]. As Millar has pointed out, visual persons perceive the world visually, while the blind have completely different experiences and perceptions based on the hearing and haptic senses [1]. The need for more research to establish a good knowledge base of what will work or will not work is necessary.

11 Our Experiments in Exploring Sound

Shape perception using sound has been studied for many years. Mainly auditory vector displays arranged in a matrix of speakers are used. In these studies, shapes were drawn on the matrices by sequentially pulsating a speaker to trace a pattern or shape [32].

Body-centered referencing and planned body movement are used in our implementation. It promotes shape perceptions by encouraging body movement by the user using non-speech sound feedback. It helps promote body-centered referencing by developing exercises that track body positions in X, Y, Z directions using audio cues. It develops a method to represent three dimensional objects as "tangible images" by tracing an object surface using body movement, thus expanding shape perception for the visually impaired.

Sound has been used in developing an electronic travel aid (ETA). One such system is called MoBIC supported by the TIDE Program. Another system for physically disabled persons that uses magnetic position trackers is a CAVE project that would aid in wheelchair mobility training [38].

In our experiments, we were concerned with: how to produce sound from an SGI Indigo workstation, how to coordinate multi-processes, i.e., the graphical and headtracking process, and the sound processes; tracking a user's head movement by an ultrasonic headtracker; relating a virtual object's shape to head movement and audio feedback; developing a graphical interface that could be manipulated by both a blind individual and a designated visual trainer. For all the programs we used the World Tool Kit (WTK) library available from Sense8, CA. The WTK provides library functions to interact with the 3DCrystalEyes harware which includes stereoscopic-glasses and an ultrasound tracker.

We developed three programs: (a) A program used for training relating the user's head movements with the directions left, right, up and down accompanied by four different musical tracks. Change in z directions are ignored so that it is easier to get used to the system. (b) A program relating the user's head movements with the directions left, right, up, down, forward and backward, accompanied by six different musical tracks. Same as (a) with added forward and backward motion added. 3D movements are detected and the music track for the dominant axis is played. (c) A program conveying a sphere's shape by tracing the surface shell using head movements accompanied by three different musical tracks designating the surface, inside or outside of the sphere.

The first program is a training program. It creates one virtual object that moves up, down, right or left depending on the direction the user's head is moving in. It is used to acclimatize the blind user and the trainer to the general system, the headtracker and the audio feedback. Based on the amount and the direction the user's head movement, the object translates along X and Y axis at right angles on the screen with a certain musical track being heard. When the head abruptly moves in another direction, another musical track will play which relates to the new direction. This program allows the user to become familiar with the audio feedback related to the direction of the head movement. It orients the blind user with his body-centered axis, vertical and horizontal in reference to his upright head position.

The second program extends the training program by adding forward and backward movement. The head and virtual object can now move in six directions. The object moves on the screen along the X, Y, and Z axis and not at right angles. The object movement is of a floating nature corresponding to the natural movements of the head. Once again a particular musical track is played based on the direction the head is moving in.

The third program guides the user in tracing the surface of a sphere by using audio feedback. The virtual object that is modeled is a sphere whose size and surface thickness can be changed. As the user traces the spherical surface with his head movements, audio feedback tells the user if he is on the surface, inside the sphere or off the surface. The user can explore the sphere's surface in all directions. The user traces a 3D virtual object completely without being hindered. The shape and size of the 3D object is discovered by the user.

The project uses musical track recordings for non-speech sound, and voice recordings for verbal instructions. It adjusts the intensity or loudness of the track to coincide with a particular user interaction. A particular musical track gives feedback to the user according to his head movements. Active audio feedback confirms the user's actions, such as moving his head to the right. The sound feedback is artificial, not natural, because there is no natural sound associated with moving to the right. The sounds are dynamic, changing as the user's head movements change. Sound provide cues to how far a user is from a particular point in 3D space. By mimicking a Doppler effect which increases or decreases the loudness of a musical track, the user can predict how close he is to the center of the screen. Also, sound cues are used by the user to direct his movement in tracing a spherical surface. We have simulated this effect in our experiments. Silicon Graphics Indigo is the hardware platform. Since we did not have support for MIDI hardware, the audio libraries used to manipulate sampled sounds are Audio Library, libaudio, Audio File Library, libaudiofile, and Audio Utility Library, libaudioutil.

We used the CrystalEyes(TM) ultrasound 3D sensor which we use for our implementation. The transmitter is a set of ultrasonic speakers mounted on a triangular frame. The receiver is three microphones mounted in a small triangular area on a pair of stereographic glasses or frame. A 3D auditory hierarchical navigation system developed for the blind by Savidis, Stephanidis, Cripien and Fellbaum [22] used a magnetic sensor.

12   Evaluation of Our System

The evaluation procedure for the project consisted of testing four sighted individuals, two adults and two children. The visual aspects of the project, such as menus, were tested extensively. The visual and audio feedback characteristics where persuasively real time. The audio changed as quickly as the head did. The children seem to enjoy these VR effects immensely. The main characteristics of a VR application, to provide real-time interaction, were obtained.

Some testing was performed by using the two sighted children when they were blindfolded. These tests basically revealed that the audio cues were helpful in directing the child in tracing the sphere in Program 3. Yet, tracing the sphere blindfolded or with eyes closed was difficult. It was hard to keep the head and upper torso aligned correctly to stay on the surface without having the sphere surface thickness quite large. With much practice the children were able to trace a sphere clumsily. It tested, successfully, the interaction with the mouse command for toggling the audio and motion detection on or off with no visual input. But, as Millar has concluded in her studies, trying to collect testing information about blind children's spatial skills using blindfolded, sighted children is not a correct approach.

13   Existing Tactile and Force Feedback Based Systems

The Mercator Project from the Georgia Institute of Technology explores access to X Windows [17]. It uses a force feedback device called Pantograph, that allows a user to perceive interface objects, such as 2D-windows, and actions, such as moving 2D-windows [19]. It was combined with a small, braille, pin-array display that had two standard braille cells. The force feedback device gives the user a sense of the position of the mouse relative to the screen and he can locate objects on the desktop easily.

Interactive Haptic Displays are important as it can include both, touch and kinesthetic information [1]. Tactile sense is the awareness of a sensation on the skin by receptors under the skin. Kinesthetic sense provides information about the position of limbs and joints, such as a sense of motion, position or force [25]. Some devices that are tactile and provide some 3D sensation and force feedback are actuated by pin arrays, and some by electrorheological fluid pads [23].

An interactive tactile display system was developed by Kawai and Tomita [26] to recognize three dimensional objects. The system has three parts. The stereo vision component is made up of two cameras. The colored camera image is grabbed every 1/15 second. The 3D computer data is matched to a database to recognize the object. The tactile display is an actuated pin array with varying heights in the vertical dimension. The pins in the position mode or the selection keys will activate the voice synthesizer to say something about the object, such as "this is a cup with a grip". This system is dynamic and interactive, allowing the blind to recognize 2D objects and environments by themselves [26].

Besides his work with the GUIB project team, Kurze has developed many tactile systems for the blind. Two of his most recent works are discussed [27,18].

The first system is a tactile drawing tool for the blind, called TDraw [27]. Kurze raises many questions when developing a drawing device for the blind. He maintains that the blind perceive the 3D world differently than the sighted, objects are surfaces and edges, such as a table is a flattened square with long rectangles, legs, folded out. Kurze's [28] second haptic interface system is a haptic renderer. It creates a two dimensional representation of an n-dimension object. Haptic devices have problems: small workspace, inadequate force feedback, too expensive, too fragile, low resolution, especially for pin arrays, little data displayed at once, and slow interactive speed. Haptic devices alone cannot reveal a visual 3D object. Touch, movement and sound need to be also included [27].

14 Evaluation of Our Force Feedback and Tactile Experiments

We used the Haptic force feedback device called PHANToM by SenSeable Inc. The device applies a force to a user's fingertip or tip of a pen stylus [23-15] as shown in Figure 2. Our motivation to explore shape-issues with both sighted and blind persons were to explore the importance of the force-feedback devices. The experimental set-up consisted of the PHANToM force feedback device connected to the SGI Octane machine. We used the GHOST library provided to us by the SensAble Inc for our experiments. The 3D-Touch experiment consisted of simple spherical and planer surfaces to be displayed on the screen as well as the 3D-space. The 3D-space was explorable by inserting a finger in the thimble of the robotic-arm of the force feedback device (see Figure 2). There was a one-to-one correspondence with what was displayed on the screen and what was felt by using the force feedback devices. With sighted persons, it was observed that the vision cues are always more powerful as everyone looked at the screen *while feeling* the object. With blind subjects, it was observed that the concentration of focus was (as expected) in the area where the object was to be felt. In particular, great success was achieved when the late-blind person was asked to explore the scene. Both the sphere and a planer surface was correctly identified. This proves our contention that 3D-exploratory virtual environments can successfully provide shape information.

15 Conclusions

The need to develop aids that expand a blind child's spatial experiences using existing sensory information was the purpose for our research. This research concentrates on using body movements based on body-centered coordinates. A software system was developed that enhances the spatial perceptions in a visually impaired person using sound, 3D tracking, and haptic interface. This exploits the capabilities of a virtual reality environment by combining sound, head movements, and sense of touch in a real-time interactive environment. The software system uses sound feedback to provide information about body planes, and directions related to the body. The body movement exercises help to define horizontal directions more clearly. The research promotes systematic body movements to develop shape perceptions, i.e., non-verbal spatial imagery.

The validation of the success of the research just discussed is still in question without a thorough evaluation involving congenital (since birth) blind subjects. However, we have shown that late-blind benefit from haptic-interaction and can recognize planer and spherical surfaces. Creating cognitive maps of new surfaces remains an open, and challenging area of future research. We hope to address these issues in future.

16   Acknowledgments

We would like to thank Bonnie Snyder of the Colorado Springs Deaf and Blind School for all her help. She was the catalyst for this research.

References

1. S. Millar, Understanding and Representing Space, The Claredon Press, Oxford (1994).
2. M. A. Heller and W. Schiff (Eds.). Psychology of Touch. Lawrence Erlbaum Associates, Hillsdale, New Jersey (1991).
3. M. Kurze and E. Holmes. 3 D Concepts by the Sighted, the Blind, and from the Computer. In Proceedings of the 5th ICCHP '96; Linz, Austria 1996. R. Oldenbourg, Munich (1996).
4. B. Dobb. The Visual and Auditory Modalities in Phonological Acquisition. In A. E. Mills (Ed.), Language Acquisition in the Blind Child. Croom Helm, London (1983).
5. S. Millar. Models of Sensory Deprivation: The Nature/Nurture Dichotomy and Spatial Representation in the Blind. International Journal of Behavioral Development, 11:1, p. 69-87 (1988).
6. S. Ungar, M. Blades and C. Spencer. The Construction of Cognitive Maps by Children with Visual Impairments. In J. Portugali (Ed.), The Construction of Cognitive Maps. Kluwer Academic Publishers, Netherlands (1996).
7. S. Millar. Understanding and Representing Spatial Information. British Journal of Visual Impairment, 13:1, p. 8-11 (1995).
8. J. Fletcher. Spatial Representation in Blind Children : Development Compared to Sighted Children. Journal of Visual Impairment and Blindness, 74, p. 18-385 (1980).
9. P. Emiliani, C. Stephanidis, J. Lindstorm, G. Jansson, H. Hamailainen, C. Cavonius, J. Engelen, J. Ekberg. Access to Pictorial Information by Blind People. In S. von Tetzchner (Ed.), Issues in Telecommunications and Disability, Commission of the European Communities, Luxembourg (1991).
10. E. Mynatt. Auditory Presentation of Graphical User Interfaces. In G. Kramer (Ed.), Auditory Display: Sonification, Audification and Auditory Interfaces. Addison-Wesley, Reading, MA (1994).
11. Compton's NewMedia. Compton's Interactive Encyclopedia (1994).
12. J. Stein. Space and the Parietal Association Areas. In J. Paillard (Ed.), Brain and Space. Oxford University Press, Oxford (1991).

13. T. Bower. Blind Babies See with Their Ears. New Scientist, 3, p. 255-257 (Feb. 1977).
14. D. Warren and M. Rossano. Intermodality Relations: Vision and Touch. In M. A. Heller and W. Schiff (Eds.), Psychology of Touch. Lawrence Erlbaum Associates, Hillsdale, New Jersey (1991).
15. S. Millar. Movement Cues and Body Orientation in Recall of Locations of Blind and Sighted Children. Quarterly Journal of Experimental Psychology, 37:A, p. 257-279 (1985).
16. G. Vanderheiden and H. Mendenhall. Presence, 3:3, p. 193-200 (Sum.1994).
17. E. Mynatt and G. Weber. Nonvisual Presentation of Graphical User Interfaces: Contrasting Two Approaches. In Proceedings of the CHI'94, Boston 1994. ACM (1994).
18. A. Karshmer. Navigating the Graphical User Interface: A Case for Interdisciplinary Research to Support People with Special Needs. In Proceedings of the 5th ICCHP '96; Linz, Austria 1996. R. Oldenbourg, Munich (1996).
19. C. Ramstein, O. Martial, A. Dufresne, A. Carignan, P. Chasse and P.Mabilleau. Touching and Hearing GUI's: Design Issues for PC-Access System. In Assets' 96, Vancouver, BC Canada 1996. ACM (1996).
20. D. H. Warren and M. J. Rossano. Intermodality Relations: Vision and Touch. In M. A. Heller and W. Schiff (Eds.), Psychology of Touch. Lawrence Erlbaum Associates, Hillsdale, New Jersey (1991).
21. M. Lumbreras and G. Rossi. A Metaphor for Visually Impaired: Browsing Information in a 3D Auditory Environment. In Proceedings of the CHI '95. ACM (1995).
22. K. Crispien, K. Fellbaum, A. Savidis and C. Stephanidus. A 3D-Auditory Environment for Hierarchical Navigation in Non-visual Interaction. In Proceedings of the ICAD 96, Santa Fe Institute, Santa Fe. Addison-Wesley (1996).
23. J. Fritz, T. Way and K. Barner. Haptic Representation of Scientific Data for Visually Impaired or Blind Persons. Applied Science and Engineering Laboratories, A.I. duPont Institute, University of Delaware. WWW site, The Haptics Community Web Page (1996, 1997).
24. K. Salisbury, D. Brock, T. Massie, N. Swarup and C. Zilles. Haptic Rendering: Programming Touch Interaction with Virtual Objects. ACM Symposium on Interactive 3D Graphics, Monterey CA, 1995. ACM (1995).
25. T. Massie and K. Salisbury. The PHANToM Haptic Interface: A Device for Probing Virtual Objects. ASME Winter Annual Meeting, Symposium on Haptic Interfaces for Virtual Environment and Teleoperator System, Chicago, Nov. 1994.
26. C. Ramstein. Combining Haptic and Braille Technologies: Design Issues and Pilot Study. In Assets' 96, Vancouver, BC Canada 1996. ACM (1996).
27. M. Kurze. TDraw: A Computer-based Tactile Drawing Tool for Blind People. In Assets' 96, Vancouver, BC Canada 1996. ACM (1996).
28. M. Kurze. Rendering Drawings for Interactive Haptic Perception. In Proceedings of the CHI '97. ACM (1997).
29. H. Petrie, S. Morley, P. McNally, P. Graziana and P. Emiliani, Access to Hypermedia Systems for Blind Students. Sensory Disabilities Research Unit, University of Hertfordshire, Hatfield UK. WWW site, SDRU Home Page (1996).
30. P. Meijer. The vOICe Home Page. WWW site, voice.htm (June 1997).
31. A. Agranovski, G. Evreinov and A.Yashkin. Graphic Audio Display for the Blind. In Proceedings of the 5th ICCHP '96; Linz, Austria 1996. R. Oldenbourg, Munich (1996).

32. A. Hollander and T. Furness III. Perception of Virtual Auditory Shapes. In G. Kramer and S. Smith (Eds.), Proceedings of ICAD'94, Santa Fe Institute, Santa Fe. Addison-Wesley (1994).

33. D. Molloy, T. McGowan, K. Clarker, C. McCorkell and P. Whelan. Application of Machine Vision Technology to the Development of Aids for the Visually Impaired. Vision Systems Group, School of Electronic Engineering, Dublin City University. WWW site School of Electronic Engineering at Dublin City University (June 1997).

34. J. Gill. A Vision of Technological Research for Visually Disabled People. The Engineering Council for the Royal National Institute for the Blind, UK (1993).

35. S. Brewster, P. Wright, A. Edwards. A Detailed Investigation into the Effectiveness of Earcons. In G. Kramer (Ed.), Auditory Display: Sonification, Audification and Auditory Interfaces. Addison-Wesley, Reading, MA (1994).

36. S. Mereu and R. Kazman. Audio Enhanced 3D Interfaces for Visually Impaired Users. In Proceedings of the CHI'96, Vancouver BC, Canada 1996. ACM (1996).

37. C. Sherrick. Vibrotactile Pattern Perception: Some Findings and Applications. In M. A. Heller and W. Schiff (Eds.), Psychology of Touch. Lawrence Erlbaum Associates, Publishers, Hillsdale, New Jersey (1991).

38. D. Browning, J. Edel, C. Cruz-Neira, D. Sandin and T. Defanti. Input Interfacing to the Cave by Persons with Disabilities. California State University Center on Disabilities (1994).

39. L. Kay. Electronic Aids for the Blind Persons: An Interdisciplinary Subject, IEEE Proceedings, 131: A-7, pp. 559-576 (1984).

40. J. Ballas. Delivery of Information Through Sound. In G. Kramer (Ed.), Auditory Display: Sonification, Audification and Auditory Interfaces. Addison- Wesley, Reading, MA (1994).

41. Debral Lee Evans-Kamp. Spatial Enhancement in Virtual Environments. MS Thesis at the Department of Computer Science, University of Colorado, Colorado Springs, CO (1997).

VR American Football Simulator with Cylindrical Screen

Motonori Doi, Takeshi Takai, and Kunihiro Chihara

Graduate School of Information Science, Nara Institute of Science and Technology,
8916-5, Takayama, Ikoma, Nara, 630-0101 JAPAN
{doi,takesi-t,chihara}@is.aist-nara.ac.jp

Abstract. American football players are required quick judgment in the game. For the training of the quick judgment, American football teams analyze games of the opponent team with video and reproduce the same situations in the games according to the analysis. The training needs many players and consumes much time. In this paper, we propose a VR American football simulator with a large cylindrical screen. The large cylindrical screen gives the user immersion in a VR space. In this system, the user can watch reproduced plays from any positions. The contents of the simulation are produced simply with a video analysis tool. This system gives American football players an indoor field for training of the quick judgment in the game.

1 Introduction

American football is a very exiting sport. Football players strike their strong bodies against the enemy. However, it is difficult to defeat the enemy only by the physical power. The quick judgment of the situation in the game is required. For instance, the quarter back (QB)[1] must find quickly a player who can receive his ball, or secondary[2] must find quickly his target.

For the training of the quick judgment, football teams simulate the situations in the game. First, they analyze the tactics of the opponent team in the game with the video. Secondly, they have meeting to decide the role of each player. Then, they reproduce the same situations in the games. This simulation needs many players and consumes much time. It is not easy for each player to train sufficiently.

We propose an American football simulation system by Virtual Reality (VR). This system can reproduce the view of each player into a cylindrical screen. The contents of the American football simulation are produced with a video analysis tool. The virtual players run in the VR field projected onto the cylindrical display. Each player can train alone in this system without complicated procedures.

---

[1] The center player of offense. He will hand the ball off to the running back or throw (pass) the ball to a receiver.

[2] The personnel of the defensive backfield

J.-C. Heudin (Ed.): VW 2000, LNAI 1834, pp. 286–293, 2000.

2   Video Analysis for American Football Game

2.1   Video Analysis Tool

We developed a video analysis tool for American football. The user can make contents of the simulation with this tool. There are many reports on sports image analysis [1,2,3] and on tracking of the person based on image processing [4]. Our video analysis tool uses simple methods on image processing for quick computation. The procedures for making of contents are as follows.

1. Video sequence for each play[3] is digitized as a MPEG file.
2. The first frame in the file is browsed on the tool.
3. The user points an area of a player.
4. The tracking of the player in each frame is carried out automatically (Fig.1).
5. If the tracking is failed, the user can correct the track manually.
6. The tracking procedures are done for all players.
7. The user marks 4 points crossing of the side line and inbounds line.
8. The tracks of the players in the video image are transformed into the tracks in the top view of the field by coordinate transformation according to the four points (Fig.2).

Fig. 1. Tracking of a player

---

[3] The period from snapping of the ball to ball dead.

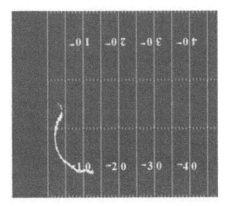

Fig. 2. Player's track in the top view of the field

2.2   Image Processing for Video Analysis

The main processes of the tool are tracking of players and coordinate transformation of the field. The tracking uses template matching on inter-frame subtraction images. The pointed area in the first frame of the play is subtracted from the same area in the next frame. The subtracted image is transformed into a binary image. This binary image is used as a template. Each frame is subtracted from the prior frame and transformed into a binary image. The template matching is done on the neighbor pixels of the prior player's position in the binary images. It is difficult to track the player crossing other players. In this case, the user detects player's position manually in key frames.

The players' positions in a video image are transformed to the positions in the top view of the field by coordinate transformation. The coordinate transformation is done by the following equation.

$$O = A_1 F P^{-1} A_2 I \tag{1}$$

$I(u, v, 0, 1)$ is a point in the video image. $O(u^*, 0, v^*, w^*)$ is a point corresponding to I in the top view. A_1 and A_2 are affine matrices. P is a matrix for perspective transformation. F is a matrix for parallel viewing transformation. The 4 cross points marked by the user are used for the decision of the elements of these matrices. Fig.3 shows this transformation. $V(x, y, z, 1)$ in Fig.3 is a point corresponding to I in 3 dimensional (3-D) space.

3   American Football in VR Space

3.1   Reproduction of Game Scenes

The game scenes are reproduced in a VR space with a graphics library (IRIS Performer). We constructed a replica of a real stadium in the VR space. The

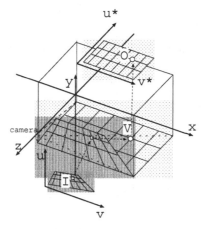

Fig. 3. Coordinate transformation

virtual players run on the field in the VR stadium according to tracks extracted by video analysis. The speed of each virtual player is corresponding to the speed of the real player in the video. The virtual players consist of simple columns. The colors of them show their team. The shapes of them mean the pose of players. This system can reproduce the view of each player or the view from any position in the stadium. The view can be change with the progress of the play. Fig.4 shows the reproduced image sequence according to the tracks in Fig.2.

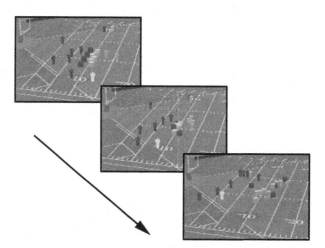

Fig. 4. Reproduced image sequence

3.2   Display on CYLINDRA

Our simulation system projects the reproduced scene onto a VR system named as CYLINDRA. CYLINDRA consists of a cylindrical screen and 6 projectors. The screen has an arc of 330 degrees, a diameter of 6.0 meters and a height of 2.7 meters. The screen covers the lateral visual field of the person who stays at the center of the cylindrical screen. In the case of CAVE, the user sees the joints of the screen. In CYLINDRA, there are no joints on the screen. Therefore, the person can be immersed in the VR space. The total system for the VR American football simulator consists of CYLINDRA, a workstation (SGI Onyx2), a scan converter and a video player (Fig.5).

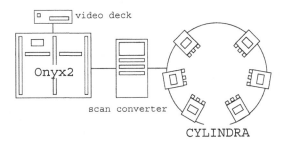

Fig. 5. VR American football simulator

In the case of the head mounted display, the field of vision is very narrow and the vision has delay for head movement. The merit of CYLINDRA is the wide field of vision. The user can look around quickly without the restriction by equipment. It is very important for football players to catch the movement of players in the corner of the field of vision and move only eyeballs for looking around to hide his target from the enemy. Therefore, CYLINDRA is very suitable for the football simulation. Fig.6 shows the view of QB in CYLINDRA. This system can display the reproduced scene with 3-D scenography. In this system, the football player can train for quick judgment in the game.

4   Evaluations

4.1   Displayed Field

In corroborate of the effects of displaying reproduced game scene on CYLINDRA, the sense of compatibility for the scale of the VR field was investigated. We compared the sense for the VR field displayed on CYLINDRA with that on flat screens. VR field (replica of a real stadium) was presented to the 6 subjects on the 94 inches screen first, then on CYLINDRA with both 2-D and 3-D mode view in turn. The subjects were the members of a Japanese collegiate American

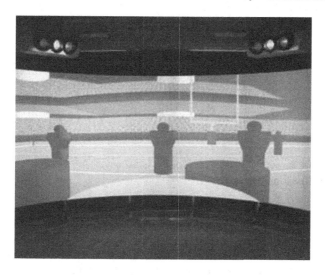

Fig. 6. The view of QB in CYLINDRA

football team. Each subject was to select his sense from 5 choices (larger, a little larger, exact, a little smaller, smaller), comparing his sense for the real stadium. The results are shown in Table 1.

Table 1. Sense of compatibility for scale of VR field

Display	Sense for scale of VR field				
	larger	a little larger	exact	a little smaller	smaller
94 inches plane screen	1	1	2	0	2
CYLINDRA with 2-D view	0	3	1	2	0
CYLINDRA with 3-D view	0	0	4	2	0

4.2 Simulation of Plays

In order to investigate the effects of the simulation by the system, we tested judgment of players for simulated scenes. The plays of different types were shown to the 6 subjects in CYLINDRA. The plays are 3 different pass plays and a running play. The ball was not appeared in these examinations. The subjects recognized the type of play by movement of virtual players. The results are shown in Table 2. SE(Split End), FB(Full Back), SB(Slot Back) and TB(Tail Back) mean the positions of players.

Table 2. Simulation of plays

Type of play	Correct recognition	False recognition
Short pass play to SE	5	1
Middle pass play to FB	5	1
Middle pass play to SB	5	1
Running play by TB	5	1

4.3 Discussions

The results in Table 1 showed that CYLINDRA with 3-D view can give us almost the same sense of scale on the real field. The results of simulation showed that the user was able to judge the situation in the system. The correct judgment of the play depended on the experience of the subjects. The subjects who played for 5 years or over recognized the type of play perfectly. The subjects who played for 3 years or under made miss judgment.

We collected the impressions and suggestions for the system from some persons who have experience of playing the football game. Their remarkable impressions and suggestions are as follows.

- This system gives the user deep immersion.
- This system is very available for the training of beginners who have few chances to take part in the actual game.
- The experience of other players' positions in this system will improve the teamwork.
- Reproduction of sounds are desired.
- It is difficult to recognize the virtual player who runs near the user.
- The virtual players are too simple.

5 Conclusions

This paper presented a VR American football simulator for training of quick judgment. The contents of the simulation are produced simply with a video analysis tool. The main processes of the tool are tracking of a player and coordinate transformation of the field. We constructed VR stadium by a cylindrical display -CYLINDRA-. In CYLINDRA, the user can look around quickly in VR space without the restriction by equipment. We evaluated the system and showed the feasibility of the system. This system will contribute to the improvement of the skill of foot ball players.

Acknowledgment

The authors would like to thank National Football Association (Japan) for their cooperation in the shooting of the football games and Doshisha University American football team (Wild Rover) for their cooperation in evaluations of the system.

References

1. S. S. Intille and A. F. Bobic : "Visual Tracking Using Closed-Worlds", M.I.T Media Lab. Tech report, No.294,1995.
2. A. F. Bobic : "Video Annotation: Computers watching video", Proceedings of 2nd Asian Conference on Computer Vision,Vol.1,pp.19-23,1995
3. S. S. Intille, W.Davis and A. F. Bobic : "Real-Time Closed-World Tracking", M.I.T Media Lab. Tech report, No.403,1996.
4. I. Haritaoglu, D. Harwood and L. S. Davis : "W^4: Who? When? Where? What? A Real Time System for Detecting and Tracking People", Proceedings of the 3rd International Conference on Automatic Face and Gesture Recognition,pp.222-227,1998

Augmented Reality Based Input Interface
for Wearable Computers

Hiroshi Sasaki, Tomohiro Kuroda, Yoshitsugu Manabe, and Kunihiro Chihara

Graduate School of Information Science, Nara Institute of Science and Technology,
8916-5 Takayama Ikoma Nara, 630-0101, JAPAN
{hirosi-s, tomo, manabe, chihara}@is.aist-nara.ac.jp

Abstract. The recent developments of computer hardware have stimulated the study of Wearable Computers [1]. However, there are few research works on the interface system, which determines the usability of wearable computers. Therefore, the authors proposed "Hand-Menu System" [2], an innovative input interface for wearable computers, utilizing Augmented Reality techniques. This system gives the user a truly intuitive non-contact input interface with visual feedback and physical senses. When the wide opened hand in the users sight calls up this hand-menu system, the menu appears on the fingertips of a hand through the head mounted display. The user selects a certain item from the menu by touching a certain fingertip with the index finger of the other hand. As the user touches on a menu item with his/her own finger physically, the user can be certain that he/she selects the menu item. Therefore, this hand-menu interface enables the user to select a menu intuitively without any additional devices.

1 Introduction

The recent developments of computer hardware have stimulated the study of the Wearable Computers. Many research works focus on various applications and hardware configurations of wearable computers. However, there are few research works on the interface system, which determines the usability of wearable computers.

Section 2 presents "Hand-Menu System", an innovative input interface for wearable computers, utilizing visual feedback and physical senses with Augmented Reality technology. The proposed system gives users a truly intuitive non-contact input interface. As this interface requires only one camera mounted on a see-through head mounted display without any devices, this interface enables the user to operate the wearable computer with empty hands.

Section 3 introduces the real-time fingertips detection and presents the implementation of the hand-menu system.

J.-C. Heudin (Ed.): VW 2000, LNAI 1834, pp. 294-302, 2000.

2 Hand-Menu System

2.1 Input Interface of Wearables

The input interfaces for wearable computers proposed till now can be divided into two types, contact devices and non-contact devices, such as:

1. Contact devices

    - Keyboard, Mouse [3], [4]
    - Pen interface with touch panel [5]
    - Wearable sensor [6], [7]

2. Non-contact devices

    - Speech recognition [8], [9]
    - Image recognition[10]

The input interface system should enable users to use wearable computers easily, anytime and anywhere. However, users may feel troublesome and restricted to wear these contact devices when using and carrying these devices with themselves.

On the other hand, foregoing non-contact devices require user's efforts; the speech recognition system makes users to teach their voice to the system by reading many sentences beforehand, and the motion recognition system makes users to learn enormous gestures beforehand.

The above discussion gives the insight about the conditions of the favorable input interface for wearable computers. The interface needs to be...

- Non-contact
  To require users to wear no special device for input interface

- Instant
  To require users no special preparation

- Intuitive
  To require users no preceding knowledge

This paper introduces an innovative concept of input interface, which satisfies above conditions utilizing image recognition technique.

2.2 Conceptual Design

The conceptual design of "Hand-Menu System" is shown in Fig.1.

In the following part, we call the weak hand as "Menu-Hand" because menu is projected on the weak hand in this system. In the same manner, we call the strong hand as "Selection-Hand".

When the wide opened menu-hand in the user's sight calls up this hand-menu system, the menu appears on the fingertips of the menu-hand through the see-through HMD. The user selects a certain item from the menu by touching a certain fingertip of the menu-hand with the index finger of the selection-hand. As the user touches on a menu item with his/her own finger physically, the user can be certain that he/she selects the menu item.

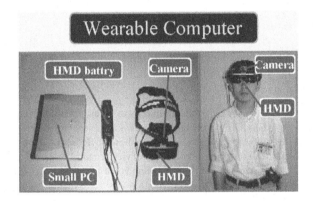

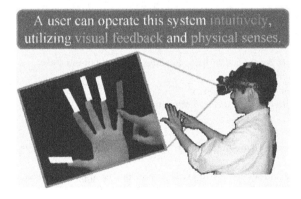

Fig. 1. Conceptual design of hand menu system

2.3 System Procedure

In order to realize the hand-menu system as a non-contact interface system, the system needs to acquire all selecting motion through image recognition techniques. Additionally, the image processing must not exhaust whole computational resources of the wearable computer as the system is just a part of the wearable computer system. Therefore, this paper utilizes some simple image recognition techniques for the hand-menu system.

The hand-menu system recognizes the user's input in the following manner:

1. Hand-area extraction
2. Fingertips detection
3. Fingertips tracking
4. Distinguishing the menu-hand and the selection-hand
5. Displaying menu
6. Menu selection

The flowchart of the hand-menu system is shown in Fig.2. In order to make the hand-menu system practical, all of these processes should be done in real-time. The following sections explain detailed techniques.

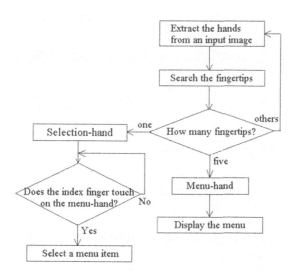

Fig. 2. Flowchart of hand menu system

3 Implementation Manner

3.1 Hand-Area Extraction

At first, the system requires to detect the menu-hand and the selection-hand. To make the system simple, these areas are detected through color matching technique. The obtained RGB color image is projected into HSV color space. The look-up table developed in advance speeds up this process. Using H and S value, skin color regions are extracted from the image. The biggest connected region and the second biggest connected region are selected as the menu-hand or the selection-hand.

As shown in Fig.3, when both hands overlap each other, the system divides the menu-hand and the selection-hand using the edge detection.

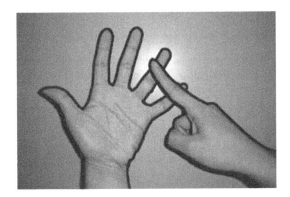

Fig. 3. Overlapped hand

3.2 Fingertips Detection

Consequently, the system needs to detect the fingertips of the hands in order to know the place to show menu items and to know the pointer. Fingertips are extracted through the outline tracking.

Fig.4 shows the tracking algorithm. The point O is the tracking point. The points A and B are the points on the outline in a certain distance from O. The triangle AOB becomes the fingertip tracker. When the exterior angle θ becomes bigger than a certain threshold λ, the point O is marked as a candidate point of a certain fingertip. Through this process, the candidate section $\alpha\beta$ is extracted.

In order to avoid selecting the bottom of a ravine as a fingertip, the direction of the angle θ is decided as the anti-clockwise direction. Thus, the angle θ becomes negative and the ravine cannot be a candidate.

At last, the system regards the middle point M of the candidate section as a fingertip.

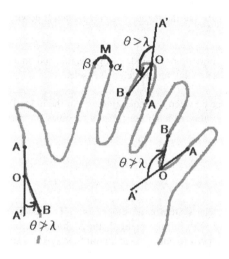

Fig. 4. Tacking algorithm of fingertips

3.3 Fingertips Tracking

Fingertips obtained by above process are tracked with template matching. For better performance, the searching areas of pattern matching are limited around the position of detected fingertips in the preceding frame.

3.4 Distinguishing the Menu-Hand and the Selection-Hand

The method to distinguish the menu-hand and the selection-hand is quite simple. The system recognizes the region with five fingertips as the menu-hand, and the region with one fingertip as the selection-hand.

3.5 Displaying Menu

As soon as the system recognizes that the menu-hand is exposed, the system superimposes the menu on the menu-hand in the user's sight through the see-through HMD.

A menu-box is a rectangle of 25x125pixels. The bottom line of a menu-box sits inside of hand area, 15pixels apart from the fingertip of the finger displaying a menu item. The height direction is parallel to the finger displaying a menu item.

3.6 Menu Selection

The system recognizes that the menu is selected when following conditions are satisfied in 3 continuous frames:

1. The index fingertip of the index-finger is touched on a fingertip of the menu-hand, that is a menu item which a user selects.

2. The distance between the index fingertip of the index-finger and the fingertip of the menu item which a user selects becomes shorter than a certain threshold.

4 Prototyping

The prototype interface system is developed on a Toshiba DynabookSS 3300, SGI O2, and SGI Onyx2 with infinite reality2. Fig.5 shows the output of the prototype. The features and the performances of each prototype systems are as follows:

Toshiba DynabookSS 3300
 CPU: Intel Mobile PentiumII 266PE MHz
 Video Capture Card: RATOC REX9590, 320x240pixels, 16bit-colors
 Video Output: NeoMagic MagicMedia256AV
 Performance: 3.57fps

SGI O2
 CPU: MIPS R5000 180MHz
 Video Input: 640x480pixels, 32bit-colors
 Performance: 2.17fps

SGI Onyx2 InfiniteReality2
 CPU: MIPS R10000 195MHz 16processers
 Video Input: 640x480pixels, 32bit-colors
 Performance: 4.76fps

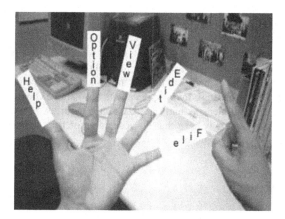

Fig. 5. Displaying result

5 Discussion

The performance of the prototype system on notebook PC(Toshiba DynabookSS 3300) was 3.57fps. For smooth communication, the system should perform more than 10fps. The system wasted most of the time in the hand-area extraction. The other processes went well.

The skin-color area extraction is quite time consuming. Therefore, the active image sensing technique projecting infrared light to eliminate the view volume of the camera may help much for the better performance.

In other respect, the hand-menu system is much good, and enables the user to operate this system much easily and intuitively. As the hand-menu system doesn't require any additional devices to wear, the users are free from restrictions comparing to foregoing system [3-10]. Moreover, this system, essentially, can be realized by one-unit, eyeglass type wearable computer with future improvement of compact hardware.

Therefore the hand-menu system is much suitable as the menu type interface for wearable computers.

6 Future Work

The main factor which makes the hand-menu system unpractical is the robustness for the lighting conditions. Therefore, the authors will introduce a certain active image sensing technique for the prototype.

7 Conclusion

This paper presented the hand-menu system, which is truly intuitive non-contact input interface for wearable computers, and experimented the prototype.

For better performance, the active image sensor should be introduced to the system.

Many researches propose so many applications of wearable computers to make our lives convenient. Hand-menu system can increase the usability of wearable computers dramatically. The authors believe that the realization of hand-menu system accelerates the realization of wearable computers.

Acknowledgement

This research is partly funded by International Communications Foundation.

References

1. Thad Starner, Steve Mann, Bradley Rhodes, Jeffrey Levine, Jennifer Healey, Dana Kirsch, Rosalind W.Picard, and Alex Pentland: Augmented Reality Through Wearable Computing. M.I.T. Media Laboratory Perceptual Computing Section Technical Report No.397. Presence, Special Issue on Augmented Reality, 1997
2. Hiroshi Sasaki, Tomohiro Kuroda, Kosuke Sato and Kunihiro Chihara: HIT-Wear: A Menu System Superimposing on a Human Hand for Wearable Computers. In Proceedings of the 43nd Annual Conference of the Institute of Systems, Control and Information Engineers, 1999 (In Japanese)
3. Bruce Thomas, Susan Tyerman, Karen Grimmer: Evaluation of Three Input Mechanisms for Wearable Computers. Presented at the IEEE International Symposium on Wearable Computer, 1997.
4. Handykey Corporation. Twiddler™: http://www.handykey.com/
5. Sharp Corporation. ZAURUS™: http://www.sharp.co.jp/
6. Akihiko Sugikawa and Kaoru Suzuki: FMRID: Finger Motion Recognition Input Device, In Proceedings of the Interaction 2000, IPSJ Symposium Series Vol.2000, No.4, 2000.
7. Masaaki Fukumoto, Yoshinobu Tonomura. "Body Coupled FingeRing": Wireless Wearable Keyboard.
   http://www.acm.org/sigchi/chi97/proceedings/paper/fkm.htm
8. Nitin Sawhney, Chris Schmandt. Speaking and Listening on the Run: Design for Wearable Audio Computing. In Proceedings of the International Symposium on Wearable Computing, 1998.
9. IBM Corporation. ViaVioce™: http://www.ibm.co.jp/voiceland/
10. James Davis, Mubarak Shah. Recognizing Hand Gestures. In Proceedings of Conference on Computer Vision, 1994.

Multi Screen Environment with a Motion Base

Haruo Takeda[1,2], Satoshi Kiyohara[2], Kunihiro Chihara[2,3], Hiroshi Kawase[1],
Yuji Matsuda[1], and Masami Yamasaki[1]

[1] Hitachi, Ltd., Systems Development Laboratory,
1099 Ohzenji, Asao-ku, Kawasaki, Kanagawa 215-0013, Japan
[2] Telecommunications Advancement Organization of Japan
Nara Research Center, 8916-19 Takayama, Ikoma City, Nara 630-0101, Japan
[3] Nara Institute of Science and Technology
8916-5 Takayama-cho, Ikoma City, Nara 630-0101, Japan
{takeda,h-kawase,yamasaki}@sdl.hitachi.co.jp,kiyohara@nara.tao.go.jp,
chihara@is.aist-nara.ac.jp,ymatsuda@head.hitachi.co.jp

Abstract. We put a motion base in a cubicle where three walls and the
floor are video screens. The motion base works in two ways to enhance
immersive feeling of the player. Firstly, it adds physical acceleration as
most simulation rides do. Secondly, it reduces the discontinuity of an
image on the multi screen system. Two planar screens placed at an angle
generally have a problem that the image over the two screens does not
look continuous at the seam of the screens unless the image is seen at
one particular point where the perspective transformation was made. In
the conventional systems, the position of the player's head is tracked by
sensors, then the image is rendered using the senced head position as the
image viewpoint. Because of the inherent delay from the head motion
to the appearance of the rendered image, the player is often distracted
by the above discontinuity as well as by motion sickness. We introduce a
method to anticipate the forecoming head motion which will be caused by
the acceleration of the motion base. Then each image frame is rendered
at the corresponding ideal viewpoint and displayed in a synchronized way
with the base motion. This new control method substantially reduces the
above problem when the player can change his/her head position only
through driving operations for a vehicle.

1 Introduction

A cubicle where three walls and the floor are video screens was developed in
early 1990's[1]. This was the pioneering work for an immersive and interactive
environment using multi planar screens. One more screen has been added for
the ceiling[2]. All six faces is covered today[5]. Numbers of such environments
are being connected over the network[3].

Unlike VR environments based on a head mounted display, this kind of environments does not have to update the image when the player looks aside or
around, because it covers much wider scope than the human vision (i.e. robust against rotation). Unlike VR environments based on a dome or a shperical

J.-C. Heudin (Ed.): VW 2000, LNAI 1834, pp. 303–312, 2000.
© Springer-Verlag Berlin Heidelberg 2000

screen[4], transparent screen materials for rear projection are easily of use. If projecting from rear, it does not cast any shadows of human players onto the screen.

However in a multi planar screen environment, the seams between adjacent screens produce conspicuous discontinuity of an image unless the eye position of the player is exactly where the CG is rendered (i.e. fragile against translateion). For example, a straight line in the virtual world bends as soon as the player's eye leaves the camera position of the image. In the conventional systems, the position of the player's head is tracked by sensors. Then the image is rendered using the senced head position as the image viewpoint. Because of the inherent delay from the head motion to the appearance of the rendered image, the player is often distracted by the above discontinuity at the screen seams as well as by motion sickness. The state of the art technology for head tracking and CG rendering is not fast enough to avoid this kind of distraction, thus a damage to immersive feeling.

We put a motion base in a multi screen environment. The motion base works in two ways to enhance immersive experience of an interactive walk-through. Firstly, it adds physical acceleration as most simulation rides do. Secondly, it reduces the image discontinuity over the screen seams. We introduce a method to anticipate the forecoming head motion which will be caused by the acceleration of the motion base. Then each image frame is rendered at the corresponding ideal viewpoint and displayed in a synchronized way with the base motion. This new control method substantially reduces the above problem and enhances immersive feeling when the player can change his/her head position only through driving operations for a vehicle.

In Section 2, we overview the whole system. It includes image processing units to connect adjacent images pixel by pixel in real-time. In Section 3, examples of typical image distortion are shown. In Section 4, we present our control method for the motion base and the video display. They are synchronized without delay by estimating the head motion against the base motion. In Section 5, we introduce a dynamic model of a human body seated on the motion base. It models the movement of the eye position after the base is accelerated. A method to render an image at a given viewpoint is briefly described in Section 6. The model is evaluated through an experiment in Section 7.

2   System Overview

Fig. 1 is an overview of the environment. Three walls are video screens to which images are projected from outside (rear projection). The floor, which is opaque, is the other screen. The floor image is projected from the upper front mirror (front projection). In this environment, we use off-the-shelf LCD (liquid crystal device) projectors. The shape of an image from a LCD panel cannot be transformed easily in its nature, especially in a non-linear way. In order to precisely connect adjacent images between two walls or between three walls and the floor, we use *skew filter*[4].

Fig. 1. Overview of the environment. A motion base is put in a cubicle where three walls and the floor are video screens. The base is driven interactively by a player sitting on it.

The skew filter was developed to show a high-resolution image on a hemispherical screen using many LCD projectors. One filter unit corresponds to one projector. Each filter unit performs a digital image transformation of geometry and color in real time. The transformation function can be defined for all the pixels to connect images on any curved screen. In our environment with multiplanar screens, it works to correct image distortion caused in the optical process from a LCD panel through prisms, lens, and/or mirrors to a screen. As a result, every pixel on the seam from two different screens comes to exactly the same spot with the same color. The error of the shape is within one pixel all over the image. Note that it does not say at this moment that the derivative function of a smooth 3D curve or a line does not look continuous when it crosses the seam.

A motion base is placed at the center of the floor. The one seen in Fig. 1 is an electro-magnetic base having four degrees of freedom. It can move forward or backward, heave, pitch, and/or roll. The maximum stroke is defined in the 4-D motion space. The interior region of the maximum stroke is called *motion envelope*. The maximum speed is designed at each position of the motion space not to hit the boundary of the motion envelope hard. Given the current stroke and speed, the control sequence for acceleration is planned in the motion envelope not to hit the maximum stroke or speed hard. At the neutral position, the eye position of the player comes close to the center of the cubicle.

Each LCD projector is connected to an off-the-shelf graphics accelerator through a skew filter. The n graphics accelerators for n projectors render an image synchronously. Three speakers in upper front, one speaker in upper rear, one on the floor, and a woofer make surrounding sound. The whole system is connected to another system via IDSN allowing a simultaneous virtual experience at a remote site.

3   Image Distortion

In this section, we show some examples of the distortion of an image when the eye is displaced off the ideal viewpoint.

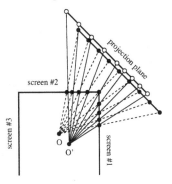

Fig. 2. Image distortion caused by a displacement of the viewpoint. Point O is the ideal eye position, and O' is the actual eye position. Ideal image shown as black dots is distorted to the image shown as white dots.

Fig. 2 shows an example of image distortion. O is the eye position where the image is rendered. Through the screen #1 and #2, along the dotted rays, it should look at the image (represented as black dots on the screens) as the one shown as black dots on the virtual projection plane. In this case, a smooth curve or a line in the virtual world looks smooth in the image. It is at least geometrically correct. However, if the eye is displaced at O' off O, then the image is changed to the one shown as white dots on the virtual projection plane. Note that a white dot is the intersection between the projection plane and the ray from O' going through one of the black dots on the screen. Because the scope of vision itself changes, there is not a very reasonable method to compare two images. In this figure we use a common projection plane in the same direction in the screen space. We observe a sudden change of dot density in the middle of the mapped image in this case, though the distribution should stay uniform as in the original image.

Fig. 3 shows some examples of distortion of a test image. (a) is the original test image. It consists of a regular grid and regular circles with different radii and the same center. This is the image from the ideal viewpoint O in Fig. 2. If the actual viewpoint moves off the corner of the screen #1 and #2, the image is distorted like (b). The view angle decreases. The image is squashed toward its center from both sides. In the center, the upper side is raised while the lower side sinks. On the contrary, if the viewpoint comes closer to the corner, the image is distorted as if it gets a tension from both sides (c). The upper side of the center sinks while the lower side rises. When the eye point goes parallel to the screen #2 and off the screen #1, the image is distorted like (d). This is the opposite case of the previous figure. The dot density increases when traveling on the image from right to left. (e) is the case when the eye is above the ideal point. The center of the image is raised, while the right and left sides are lowered. Note that the coordinate center of the view plane corresponds to the center of the seam in these figures.

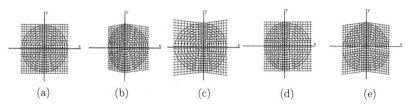

(a)   (b)   (c)   (d)   (e)

Fig. 3. Examples of image distortion. (a) the view point is at the center in Fig. 2, (b) apart from the upper right corner, (c) closer to the upper right corner, (d) translate to right, (e) translate downward.

In the case of (b), (c), and (e), a horizontal line bends at the seam of the screen, if it is not the line just at the height of the eye. In the case of (d), the image density changes between two screens. Through all the cases, the distance between the ideal eye position and the actual one is about one tenth of the screen width, which is about the maximum error in the experiments. The ideal eye position happens to be at the center of the environment.

4   Video and Motion Control

The main idea of this paper is given in this section. A method is described to control the video and motion synchronously. The content can be fully interactive, fully passive, or a combination of interactive and passive[4].

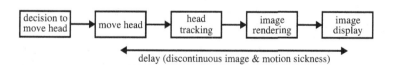

Fig. 4. Prior method without a motion base. Upon the head movement of the player, the computer recognizes the new head position by sensing, renders the image using the new viewpoint, and displays the image. Because of the delay from the head motion to the image display, discontinuous image and motion sickness are often observed.

Fig. 4 shows a typical method to display an image in the conventional virtual environments. The computer traces the position of the head of the player. Upon the movement of the head, the computer recognizes the new head position by sensors. Sensors attached to eye glasses for stereopsis are often used for head tracking in such an environment. When the new head position is recognized, the computer renders an image using the head position as the rendering viewpoint. Because of the delay from the head motion to the image display, discontinuous image and motion sickness are often observed.

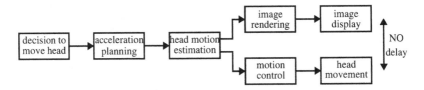

Fig. 5. New method with a motion base. Based on the desire to move head, acceleration of the motion base is planned. The head motion is then estimated. Image display and the head motion is controlled synchronously, thus no delay between head movement and image display.

Fig. 5 shows a new method with a motion base. When the player desires to move the head translationally, the computer plans the acceleration of the motion base. Then the head motion after the base is accelerated is estimated by the computer before the actual acceleration. A sequence of images is rendered using the sequence of the image viewpoints derived from the estimated head motion. Those images are displayed on the screen. At the same time the motion base is controlled to synchronize the head motion with the images.

This control method substantially reduces the delay in Fig. 4 when the player can change his/her head position only through a driving operation for a vehicle.

We show the procedure in detail for different types of contents.

(1) Path planning and acceleration planning: A path is planned in the 3D world. Then a sequence for adding acceleration is planned within the limited stroke and axis. If it is an interactive content, a short term plan is continually made at an execution time. If it is a passive content, all of them are planned prior to the execution. For a combination of interactive and passive, acceleration is basically planned at an execution time, though the path is planned before execution.

(2) Image rendering: Based on the planned path in (1), images of the 3D world are rendered. CG rendering is done in every direction. Real images shot by a real camera can also be used. The background of the content can be shot by a camera for 35mm film with a fisheye lens. An omni directional camera is another choice.

(3) Eye position estimation: From the planned acceleration in (1), an expected trajectory of the eye position is estimated. The dynamic model is introduced

in the next section. The model should be well calibrated before execution. It may even reflect the difference of individuals.

(4) Image transformation: Given an estimated eye position, the rendered images in (2) are geometrically transformed and mapped to the screen. The procedure in Section 6 ((b) of Fig. 7) is used. Passive contents are transformed off-line.

(5) Synchronization of video and motion: In order to synchronize viewpoints of CG and the eye in an interactive content, we control the motion base in such a way that it waits for the corresponding images to be prepared. In the case of a passive-interactive combination, both the motion base and the background video wait for the foreground CG to be rendered. This of course can be a drawback. But in the situation where the player is driving a vehicle, there are not many cases when it is inferior to the method to overlook the image distortion, which is certainly distractive.

5   Motion Model

We introduce a dynamic model of the motion of the player's eye position after the motion base is accelerated. As in Fig. 6, the eye position and the eye direction are expressed as X and n, where X is the position vector of the player's eye, and n is the normal to the seat plane of the motion base. The vector e_1 is the forward direction of the seat, e_2 is the unit vector perpendicular to n and e_1. The vector C is the eye position when the human body being fixed to the seat is assumed to be rigid. We further assume that X relative to C is contained in the plane perpendicular to n. In the plane with the origine C, we define the vector x as $X - C$.

Fig. 6. A motion model. The eye position has weight m at height L from the seat.

As in Fig. 6, we assume that the eye position has a weight m at the height L from the seat. If we introduce damping forces against the distance and the speed, we get the equation

$$m\ddot{x} + \alpha\dot{x} + kx = F, \tag{1}$$

where α is the damping ratio against the speed, and k is the the one against the position.

The force $\boldsymbol{F}$ is a composite of gravity and the acceleration of the motion base. It is written as

$$\boldsymbol{F} = (F_1, F_2) + (g_1, g_2),\tag{2}$$

$$m\ddot{\boldsymbol{C}} = F_1 \boldsymbol{e}_1 + F_2 \boldsymbol{e}_2 + F_3 \boldsymbol{n},\tag{3}$$

$$\boldsymbol{g} = g_1 \boldsymbol{e}_1 + g_2 \boldsymbol{e}_2 + g_3 \boldsymbol{n},\tag{4}$$

where $\boldsymbol{g}$ is the gravity. If we write

$$\boldsymbol{x} = (x_1, x_2),\tag{5}$$

the relation between $\boldsymbol{X}$ and $\boldsymbol{C}$ is

$$\boldsymbol{X} = \boldsymbol{C} + x_1 \boldsymbol{e}_1 + x_2 \boldsymbol{e}_2.\tag{6}$$

This model is verified through an experiment in Section 7.

6   Rendering for Multi Screens

Fig. 7 shows an example for the process to render an image of a virtual world at a given eye point in the cubicle. For a moment, the floor image is ignored. Only three images on the walls are considered.

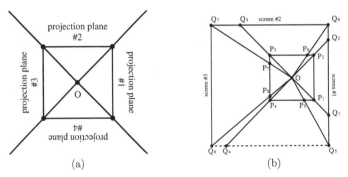

Fig. 7. CG rendering process. Images rendered at O are P_1-P_2, P_2-P_3, P_3-P_4, and P_4-P_1. To compensate for the displacement of O in the cubicle, post-processes of 2D division, concatenation, and geometrical transformation is executed. Points $P_1, \cdots, P_8$ are mapped to $Q_1, \cdots, Q_8$ respectively.

In the first step, CG images are rendered in the virtual world at the player's eye position O on four projection planes. The square in the Fig. 7(a) is the top view of the projection planes. A region between two diagonal lines is the scope of vision. The view direction of the player is the center of the projection plane #2.

In the case when the player's eye is at O in the cubicle as shown in (b), we map the projection planes of (a) into the multi screen environment. Fig. 7(b) is the top view of the environment. The points $P_1, \cdots, P_4$ are the four corners of the square made by four projection planes. Let the vertical edges of the screens be $Q_5, \cdots, Q_8$. On the projection lines, we define $P_5, \cdots, P_8$ on the line between O and $Q_5, \cdots, Q_8$ respectively. On the screens, we define $Q_1, \cdots, Q_4$ on the line from O toward $P_1, \cdots, P_4$.

We have four rendered images: P_1–P_2, P_2–P_3, P_3–P_4, and P_4–P_1. In this configuration, the image to be shown on the screen #1 (Q_5–Q_6) should be the composite of the P_5–P_1 portion of the image on the projection plane #4, the full P_1–P_2 image on the plane #1, and the P_2–P_6 portion on #2. Similarly the image on the screen #2 (Q_6–Q_7) is the composite of P_6–P_3 and P_3–P_7. The screen #3 is projected with the image P_7–P_8. For each portion, an appropriate linear geometrical transformation is made. We have a similar strategy for the floor image.

The above procedure generates an image which is geometrically correct when viewed from O. A smooth curve or a line in the virtual world looks smooth from the ideal viewpoint O.

7   Experiments

The model we defined in Section 5 is obviously too simple to express dynamics of a human body. It lacks the joints of a body. The damping force is assumed linear to the speed or the position. It does not consider the dependency of the forces on the situation of the content. A substantial difference between individuals exists. However it is of some effect over the simple assumption that the body is rigid and afixed to the seat (i.e. the eye position moves as X), if the parameters are carefully chosen.

We've made some experiments to determine the parameters. We used a larger motion base to get more stable parameters. The larger the acceleration is, the more physically and the less voluntarily a human reacts. In our case, the player was covered by a cabin. It may remove the content dependent factors, because all the world in the cabin is just relative to the gravity and to the motion base. The head position was traced by a video camera. Through the experiments, the same seat with the same seat belt as in our environment is used.

Fig. 8 is a result of a simulation. A set of parameters determined through the above experiments is used. The solid curve represents the motion of the seat (i.e. the trace of C). The dotted curve is the motion of the eye position (i.e. the trace of X) under our model. These traces are drawn in a horizontal plane. Because of the damping factors in the above equation, some delays and overshoots are observed. In this case, the maximum error between C and X in the horizontal distance is about 30cm, which is about a tenth of the screen width. This is a non-negligible error in terms of image distortion.

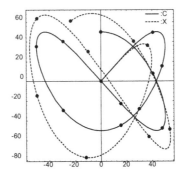

Fig. 8. Example of trajectory of the eye position. Solid curve represents the motion of the seat. Dotted curve does that of the eye position. Delays and overshoots are observed.

8   Conclusion

We have proposed a method to control a motion base in a multi screen environment. It reduces the distortion of an image at the seam of two planar screens. We have made a physical model of a human body to estimate the position of the player's eye when the motion base is accelerated. Because the image is rendered at the eye position, the image geometry is closer to the real one. Because the estimation of the viewpoint is done before acceleration, the image and the motion can be controlled synchronously with no delay at all. Applications include interactive contents, passive contents, and the intermediate ones which we call V_2R [4].

References

[1] C. Cruz-Neira, D. Sandin, and T. DeFanti, "Surround- screen projection-based virtual reality: The design and implementation of the CAVE," *ACM SIGGRAPH '93*, pp. 135-142, 1993.

[2] M. Hirose, T. Ogi, S. Ishiwata, and T. Yamada, "Development and evaluation of immersive multiscreen display CABIN," *Trans. of the Institute of Electronics, Information and Communication Engineers*, J81-D-II(5), pp. 888-896, 1998. (in Japanese)

[3] A. Johnson, J. Leigh, T. Defanti, M. Brown, and D. Sandin, "CAVERN: the CAVE Research Network," *Proc. of International Symposium on Multimedia Virtual Laboratory*, pp. 15-27, 1998.

[4] H. Takeda, M. Yamasaki, T. Moriya, T. Minakawa, F. Beniyama, and T. Koike, "A video-based virtual reality system," *ACM VRST '99*, pp.19-25, 1999.

[5] T. Yamada and M. Hirose, "Development of full immersive display," *Fourth International Conference on Virtual Systems and Multimedia*, 1998.

Author Index

Lecture Notes in Artificial Intelligence (LNAI)

Lecture Notes in Computer Science